COLUMBIA COLLEGE

W9-CNG-085

m71-53

Text—Sound Texts

OTHER BOOKS BY RICHARD KOSTELANETZ

Columbia College Library
600 South Michigan
Chicago, IL 60605

Text–Sound Texts

Edited by
Richard Kostelanetz

William Morrow and Company, Inc.
New York 1980

memory
ly-Nagy

Copyright © 1980 by Richard Kostelanetz

Every effort has been made to trace the ownership of all copyrighted material and to make full acknowledgment of its use. If any error or omission has occurred, it will be corrected in any future editions, provided that appropriate notification is submitted in writing to the Publisher.

All rights reserved. No part of this book may be reproduced or utilized in any form or by any means, electronic or mechanical, including photocopying, recording or by any information storage and retrieval system, without permission in writing from the Publisher. Inquiries should be addressed to William Morrow and Company, Inc., 105 Madison Ave., New York, N. Y. 10016.

Library of Congress Catalog Card Number 79-93246

ISBN 0-688-03616-3
ISBN 0-688-08616-0 pbk.

Book Design by Bliem Kern

Printed in the United States of America

First Morrow Quill Paperback Edition
1   2   3   4   5   6   7   8   9   10

811.5408 T355k 1980

Text--sound texts

Credits and Acknowledgments

ABISH, WALTER: "Auctioning Australia," reprinted by permission of the author. Copyright©1979 by Walter Abish.

ALBERT, JONATHAN: Excerpt from "Long Songs II : The Schuman Dreams," reprinted by permission of the author. Copyright©1979 by Jonathan Albert.

AMIRKHANIAN, CHARLES: "Sniro," "Spoffy Nine," "Ablaze Obeys," "Another Norther," reprinted by permission of the author.

ANDERSON, BETH: "If I Were A Poet," "Crackers and Checkers," reprinted by permission of the author. Copyright©1979 by Beth Anderson.

BARBOUR, DOUGLAS & STEPHEN SCOBIE: "Particularize the Particulars," "Shore Lines," reprinted by permission of the authors. Copyright©1978 by Douglas Barbour.

BIRNEY, EARLE: "To Swindon from London by Britrail aloud/Bagatelle," reprinted by permission of the author. Copyright©1973 by Earle Birney.

BISSETT, BILL: Three poems reprinted by permission of the author.

BURT, WARREN: Excerpts from *Nighthawk* (Lingua Press, 1978), by permission of the author and the publisher. Copyright©1977 by Warren Burt.

CAGE, JOHN: "Empty Words, part III," reprinted from *Big Deal*, 3, by permission of the author. Copyright©1975 by *Big Deal*; copyright©1978 by John Cage.

CALDIERO, ALISSANDRU: "Form & Sand," and other pieces, reprinted by permission of the author.

CASTORO, ROSEMARIE: "Title," reprinted by permission of the author. Copyright©1975 by Rosemarie Castoro.

COINTET, GUY DE: "Axtherastral," reprinted from *Espahor ledet ko uluner!* (Privately published 1973). Copyright©1973 by Guy de Cointet.

COOK, GEOFFREY: "Jabberwocky," reprinted from *Intermedia* by permission of the author.

COOPER, MICHAEL: "Bob Is Able To Bend the Back of the Book," reprinted by permission of the author. Copyright©1978 by Michael Cooper.

CORNER, PHILIP: "Word Music," reprinted by permission of the author. Copyright©by Philip Corner.

CORY, JEAN-JACQUES: "Form" from *Lists* (Assembling Press, 1974); "Rhymed Couplets," from *Poetry Australia*, 59 (1976); "Purling," from *La-Bas* (1979); reprinted by permission of the author. Copyright©1974, 1976, 1979 by Jean-Jacques Cory.

CURLEY, BRUCE: Reprinted by permission of the author. Copyright © 1978.

DODGE, CHARLES: *"Speech Songs,"* plus notes, reprinted by permission of the author.

DORIA, CHARLES: "The Secret Book of Moses on the Great Name," reprinted by permission of the author. Copyright©1979 by Charles Doria.

ERICKSON, JON: "Frequency Modulation," published by permission of the author. Copyright©1979 by Jon Erickson.

FEDERMAN, RAYMOND: "Voices Within Voices," reprinted from *Performance in Post-Modern Culture* (Coda Press, 1977), by permission of the author. Copyright©1977 by Raymond Federman.

FOSS, CAMILLE: "One-Half Two," reprinted by permission of the author.

FOUR HORSEMEN: "Extracts from Eight Part Suite," "Particular Music," reprinted by permission of Paul Dutton.

FRANK, SHELDON: "As I Was Saying," published by permission of author. Copyright© 1978 by Sheldon Frank. All rights reserved.

GABURO, KENNETH: "Dante's Joynte," "Dwell," reprinted by permission of the author. Copyright©1979 by Kenneth Gaburo; published by Lingua Press, P.O. Box 1192, La Jolla, CA 92038.

GIBSON, JON: "Who Are You," published by permission of the author. Copyright© 1966 by Jon Gibson.

GILLESPIE, ABRAHAM LINCOLN: "A Purplexicon of Dissynthegrations," "Voks,"

reprinted from *The Syntactic Revolution* (Out of London, 1980), by permission of the publisher.

GINSBERG, ALLEN, with Jack Kerouac: "Snicker Snoop," reprinted from *Journals* (Grove, 1977) by permission of the author and the publisher. Copyright©1977 by Allen Ginsberg.

GIORNO, JOHN: Reprinted by permission of the author.

GLASS, PHILIP: "1 + 1," reprinted from *Aspen*, 8, with emendations, by permission of the author. Copyright©1964, 1979 by Philip Glass.

GNAZZO, TONY: "Escapade," "Gloryette Gockheck 55," "Pasadena 8:10," reprinted by permission of the author. Copyright© 1972, 1974, 1979 by Anthony J. Gnazzo.

GOLDSTEIN, MALCOLM: "Illuminations from Fantastic Gardens," reprinted by permission of the author. Excerpts from Louise Varese's translation of Rimbaud, reprinted by permission of New Directions Publishing Corporation. Copyright©1946, 1957 by New Directions Publishing Corp.

GOODMAN, MARK: "Shades: Emergence," published by permission of the author.

GOULD, GLENN: Excerpts from "Radio as Music," *The Canada Music Book* (Spring-Summer 1971) and audio texts, reprinted by permission of the author. Copyright©1971, 1979 by Glenn Gould.

GRAHAM-GAZAWAY, COURTENAY P.: "Sound Poems, I, II, III," reprinted from *ime* (Pym-Randall, 1969); "Sound Poem IV," reprinted from *Poemstills from Movie-earth* (1974); by permission of the author.

GYSIN, BRION: "I AM THAT I AM," reprinted from *Let the Mice In* (Something Else, 1973) by permission of the author.

HANLON, TERRI, & FERN FRIEDMAN: "E (1) (ff) usive," reprinted by permission of the authors. Copyright©1978 by Fern Friedman and Terri Hanlon.

HELLERMAN, WILLIAM: "What(?)," reprinted by permission of the author.

HELMS, SCOTT: "A Sound Poem," published by permission of the author.

HIGGINS, DICK: "Glasslass," reprinted by permission of the author.

JOHNSON, TOM: "Three from Secret Songs," published by permission of the author. Copyright©1979 by Tom Johnson.

JOLAS, EUGENE: Reprinted by permission of Maria McDonald Jolas, Paris, France.

LIBRARY OF COLUMBIA COLLEGE CHICAGO, ILL.

JONES, KEVIN: Excerpt from "Dialogue IV," reprinted by permission of the author. Copyright©1979 by Kevin Jones.

KEARNS, LIONEL: "Omen," "The Woman Who," reprinted by permission of the author.

KERN, W. BLIEM: "Crickets," "Nuclear Prayer," "Sound Poetry," reprinted respectively from *Meditations* (New Rivers, 1973), *Nuclear Prayer* (1978) and *Poetry Australia*, 59 (1976) by permission of the author. Copyright©1973, 1976, 1978 by W. Bliem Kern. All rights reserved.

KEROUAC, JACK: "Old Angel Midnight," reprinted from *Evergreen Review*, 64 (Aug.-Sept., 1964) by permission of Diane Root, Grove Press; Excerpt from *Desolation Angels* (1965) reprinted by permission of Coward, McCann & Geoghegan, Inc. Copyright©1960, 1963, 1965 by Jack Kerouac. "The Sea," from *Big Sur* (1962), reprinted by permission of the Sterling Lord Agency, Inc. Copyright©1962 by Jack Kerouac.

KING, KENNETH: "Word Raid," reprinted from *Paris Review* (1979) by permission of the author. Copyright©1979 by Kenneth King.

KNOWLES, CHRISTOPHER: "Get Wreck," "Rhyming," reprinted by permission of the author. Copyright©1979 by Christopher Knowles.

KOSTELANETZ, RICHARD: excerpts from *Recyclings* (Assembling, 1974); "Audio Art," "Self-Interview on Recyclings," from *Wordsand* (RK Editions, 1978); "Text-Sound Art: A Survey," from *Performing Arts Journal*, II/2 (1977); reprinted by permission of the author. Copyright©1974, 1977, 1978 by Richard Kostelanetz.

KUCHARZ, LAWRENCE: "City Scenes II," reprinted by permission of the author. Copyright©1978 by Lawrence Kucharz.

LEON, S.J.: "Epilogue: Blind," "Le Dernier Cri," from *Between Silences* (Philadelphia, 1974); "Threnody for A.L. Gillespie," reprinted by permission of the author.

LEVENDOSKY, CHARLES: "Microphone Poet," reprinted from *Interstate*, 6-7, by permission of the author. Copyright©1976 by Charles Levendosky.

LOCKWOOD, ANNEA: "Malaman," reprinted by permission of the author. Copyright©1974 by Annea Lockwood.

LUBAR, CINDY: Untitled text reprinted by permission of the author.

LUCIER, ALVIN: "I Am Sitting in a Room," reprinted from *Source*, 7, by permission of the author. Copyright©1970 by Alvin Lucier.

LURIE, TOBY: "Innocence," "Color Improvisation," "Chart of Musical Values," reprinted from *New Forms, New Spaces* (1971) by permission of the author.

MAC LOW, JACKSON: "A Word Event for George Brecht" (1961), "Word Event(s) for Bibi Forbes" (1971); "The 5 Young Turtle Asymmetries" (1967) & newly revised introduction (1978) reprinted by permission of the author. Copyright©1979 by Jackson Mac Low. All rights reserved.

MAHLER, DAVID: "The Canonization of All Saints," reprinted by permission of the author. Copyright©by David Mahler.

McCAFFERY, STEVE: "Some Reflections on the Current Work of the Four Horsemen," from *Sound Poetry: A Catalogue* (Underwhich 1978); "For a Poetry of Blood," from *Stereoheadphones*, 4; "Capuccino," reprinted by permission of the author.

MILLER, AARON: "Krishna Crossing Atomland," published by permission of the author. Copyright©1979 by Aaron Miller.

MORROW, CHARLES: "1976 Buddhist Wedding of Dan & Bonnie," "Recipe for Sounding," "Counting to Nine in Three Locations," reprinted by permission of the author.

NICHOL, BP: "From Sound to Sense," "Poem #1," reprinted from *Stereoheadphones*, 4, by permission of the author. Copyright©1979 by bp Nichol.

OLDENBURG, CLAES: "Panodramra" and "On the Bus," reprinted by permission of the author.

OSWALD, JOHN: "Catalog for Animal Voices Human," reprinted by permission of the author. Copyright©1979 by John Oswald.

PANTOS, SPIROS: "notornis," published by permission of the author.

PHILLIPS, MICHAEL JOSEPH: "Sound Sonnet of Samantha & Michael," published by permission of the author.

PIETRI, PEDRO: "Breaking/Making Up with the One You Love," from *CAPStan* (1976); "Prologue" (1978); reprinted by permission of the author.

PRITCHARD, NORMAN HENRY, II: "Gyre's Galax," "The Visitary," reprinted from *The Matrix* (Doubleday, 1970) by permission of the author. Copyright©1970 by Norman Henry Pritchard, II.

RAN, FAYE: "Mis one ism," published by permission of the author.

RASOF, HENRY: "Wichita," reprinted by permission of the author; copyright©by Henry Rasof.

ROBSON, ERNEST: "Prosodynes" and selected texts, reprinted from *Transwhichics* (Dufour, 1969) by permission of the author. Copyright©1969 by Ernest & Marion Robson.

ROTHENBERG, JEROME: "Total Translation" (1969), with an addendum, reprinted by permission of the author.

SAARI, PATRICK: "A Litany," "Ghandi," with notes, published by permission of the author.

SCHAFER, R. MURRAY: Dedication pages to *Smoke* (A Novel), reprinted by permission of the author. Copyright©1976 by R. Murray Schafer.

SCHLOSS, ARLEEN: "#11 Instant Double EE," "#16 Instant B," "#45 Instant Double OO," "#55 Instant 3-Letter Words," "#130 3-Letter Double," published by permission of the author.

SCHWERNER, ARMAND: Excerpts from *The Tablets* (Grossman, 1971), reprinted by permission of the author. Copyright© 1971 by Armand Schwerner.

SHERWIN, JUDITH JOHNSON: "Shake," reprinted from *Connections* and *The Town scold* (Countryman, 1977) by permission of the author. Copyright©1971 by Judith Johnson Sherwin.

SOLT, MARY ELLEN: "Zig-Zag," published by permission of the author.

STEIN, CHARLES: Three verbal poems and three visual poems, reprinted by permission of the author. Copyright©1979 by Charles Stein.

SUBLETTE, NED: "Sonnets," published by permission of the author.

VILLA, JOSE GARCIA: Poems 98, 99, reprinted from *Selected Poems and New* (McDowell, 1958) by permission of the author. Copyright©1949, 1977 by Jose Garcia Villa.

WEINER, LAWRENCE: "Nothing To Lose/Niets Aan Verloren," reprinted by permission of the author. Copyright©1975 by Moved Pictures, NYC.

WENDT, LARRY, & STEVE RUPPENTHAL: "Vocable Gestures," reprinted from *Art Contemporary*, 9, (1977) by permission of Larry Wendt & Steve Ruppenthal.

WHYTE, JON: "Urge-Emerge," reprinted from *Open Spaces* (Banff, 1977); "Wavering," published here for the first time, by permission of the author. Copyright©1977, 1979 by Jon Whyte. All rights reserved.

WILLIAMS, EMMETT: "Duet," reprinted from *Selected Shorter Poems 1950-1970.*

WILLIAMS, REESE: "8x: Mode for Audiotape," published by permission of the author. Copyright©1977 by Reese Williams.

WILSON, ROBERT: "Dyna Sore," reprinted by permission of the author.

WRIGHT, A.J.: Reprinted by permission of the author.

YANKOWITZ, NINA: Reprinted by permission of the author.

YOUNG, KARL: "Canon: Duet of Spines," reprinted by permission of the author.

ZINNES, HARRIET: "Space-Time," published by permission of the author. Copyright©1979 by Harriet Zinnes.

ZWEIG, ELLEN: "III Movement Toward," reprinted by permission of the author.

REFACE

> Notation is an attempt to render aural facts by visual signs. The value of notation for both the preservation and analysis of sound is therefore considerable.
> —R. Murray Schafer, *The Tuning of the World* (1977).

There has not been a book like this in the past—a comprehensive collection of texts of and about text-sound art in North America. European practitioners have had a more mature sense of what they were doing. They sponsored performance festivals, organized conferences, issued records and anthologies. In America, the art has been practiced in relative isolation, text-sound artists rarely cooperating or coming together, either in person or in print.

Text-sound I use to define language unspecific in pitch, which coheres in terms of sound, rather than syntax or semantics. The contents of this book are *texts*, which can be broadly defined as anything reproducible in a book. In the following pages are scores, manifestoes, self-interviews, scripts, performance instructions, critical essays, theoretical remarks, all done by text-sound practitioners.

Some anthologies are edited to "keep people out." This one, to be frank, was edited to put everybody in. Critical discriminations were made, to be sure, within certain kinds of work, or within an individual's work; but I have consciously endeavored to include everyone in North America doing text-sound works. Conspicuous omissions can be attributed to the reluctance of certain text-sound artists to allow their work to be reprinted or to respond to letters and phone calls; one first-rank figure tried in vain to break my bank. There are simply limits to a lone editor's generosity or persistence.

The sequel to this project should be an anthology of the works themselves, a *Text-Sound Tapes*, which a sound organization ought to produce in the next few years, if only so we can *hear* what here can be read.

The book's introduction, the first part of my own essay on "Text-Sound Art in North America," originally appeared in *Performing Arts Journal,* 11/2-3 (Autumn, 1977-Winter 1978). The second part, the most comprehensive critical survey published so far on North American text-sound work, will be reprinted in a book collecting my essays on poetry, *The Old Poetries and the New* (Univ. of Michigan, 1980). I considered reprinting it here, but finally decided that discriminations there might prejudice a reader's appreciation of the following pages. This book is not necessarily about that essay, or vice versa.

For support in both the publication of this book and the research informing it, I am particularly grateful to the Visual Arts Program of the National Endowment for the Arts, directed successively by Brian O'Doherty and James Melchert. The contributors to this book have earned my debt for letting me reproduce their work. Bliem Kern collaborated with me on the design and production of the book, and Edward J. Hogan did most of the new typesetting. James Landis accepted the book for William Morrow & Co.; Meredith Davis expedited it conscientiously. Thanks to them both. The book's dedication acknowledges a long-standing debt in my understanding of artistic intermedia—the new arts between the old arts—in our time.

Richard Kostelanetz
New York, New York
14 November, 1979

CONTENTS

CONTENTS (Continued)

Text—Sound Texts

These poets hope to liberate the word from syntax. They aim at an intuitively comprehended interrelation of words, and at times they achieve a coherent totality, determined by a peculiarly autonomous "syntax."
—Stefan Morawski, "What Is a Work of Art?" (1967).

Abstract or concrete poets do w/ language—spoken & written—& w/ its elements & subelements—sounds syllables phonemes letters phrases words— what painters & sculptors do w/ shapes & colors—what electronic/concrete musicians do w/ sinusoidaltone/foundsounds—all art is abstract but the more it abstracts from its models the less it becomes mimetic descriptive or deceptive & the more it becomes concrete truthful & human.
—Dom Sylvester Houédard, preface (1965).

In these phonetic poems we totally renounce the language that journalism has abused and corrupted. We must return to the innermost alchemy of the word, we must even give up the word too, to keep for poetry its last and holiest refuge.
—Hugh Ball, *Flight Out of Time* (1927).

We have three graphic notational systems available: 1.) that of acoustics, by which the mechanical properties of sounds may be exactly described on paper or a cathode-ray screen; 2.) that of phonetics, by which human speech may be projected and analyzed; 3.) musical notation, which permits the representation of certain sounds possessing "musical" features.
—R. Murray Schafer, *The Tuning of the World* (1977).

TEXT-SOUND ART:

A Survey

I

The art is text-sound, as distinct from text-print and text-seen, which is to say that texts must be sounded and thus heard to be "read," in contrast to those that must be printed and thus be seen. The art is text-sound, rather than sound-text, to acknowledge the initial presence of a text, which is subject to aural enhancements more typical of music. To be precise, it is by non-melodic auditory structures that language or verbal sounds are poetically charged with meanings or resonances they would not otherwise have. The most appropriate generic term for the initial materials would be "vocables," which my dictionary defines as "a word regarded as a unit of sounds or letters rather than as a unit of meaning." As text-sound is an intermedium located between language arts and musical arts, its creators include artists who initially establish- ed themselves as "writers," "poets," "composers," and "painters"; in their text-sound works, they are, of course, functioning as text-sound ar- tists. Many do word-image art (or "visual poetry") as well, out of a commitment to exploring possibilities in literary intermedia.

The term "text-sound" characterizes language whose principal means of coherence is sound, rather than syntax or semantics—where the sounds made by comprehensible words create their own coherence apart from denotative meanings. A simple example would be this "tongue-twister" familiar from childhood:

If a Hottentot taught a Hottentot tot to talk 'ere the tot could totter, ought the Hottentot to be taught to say ought or naught or what ought to be taught 'er?

The subject of this ditty is clearly neither Hottentots nor pedagogy but the related sounds of "ot" and "ought," and what holds this series of words together is not the thought or the syntax but those two repeated sounds. It is those sounds that one primarily remembers after hearing this sentence read aloud. As in other text-sound art, this language is customarily recited in a voice that speaks, rather than sings. Thus, the vocal pitches are non-specific.

The first exclusionary distinction then is that words that have intentional pitches, or melodies, are not text-sound art but *song*. To put it differently, text-sound art may include recognizable words or phonetic fragments; but once musical pitches are introduced, or musical instruments are added (and once words are tailored to a pre-existing melody or rhythm), the results are music and are experienced as such. Secondly, text-sound art differs from "oral poetry," which is syntactically standard language written to be read aloud. These exclusions give the art a purist definition, I admit; but without these distinctions, there is no sure way of separating text-sound art, the true intermedium, from music on the one side and poetry on the other.

The firmest straddles I know are the records made by a changing group of New York blacks calling themselves "The Last Poets," whose lead voice chants incendiary lyrics to the accompaniment of pitched background voices and a rapid hand drum, which seems to influence verbal rhythm (rather than vice versa, to repeat a crucial distinction); and *Philomel* (1963), by Milton Babbitt and John Hollander, where the text is syntactically fragmented and aurally multiplied in ways typical of sound poetry, but the sounds in most of the work are specifically pitched, rather than unpitched.

"Text-sound" is preferable to "sound poetry," another term for this art, because I can think of work whose form and texture is closer to *fiction* or even *essays*, as traditionally defined, than poetry.

One issue separating work within the art would be whether the sounds are primarily recognizable words or phonetic units. Pieces with audible words usually have something to do with those words, which are meant to be perceived as certain words, rather than as other words. Poems without recognizable words are really closer to our experience of an unfamiliar (i.e., "foreign") language. An example is this passage from Armand Shwerner's *The Tablets* (1971):

min-na-ne-ne Dingir En-lil-ra mun-na-nib-gi-gi
uzu-mu-a-ki dur-an-ki-ge

Such words need not be "translated," because the acoustic experience of them is ideally as comprehensible to one culture as to another.

"Morse Code" is not text-sound art, even though it communicates comprehensible words to those who know its language; it is a code whose rhythm cannot be varied if communication is to be secure.

In my opinion, the better work in text-sound art emphasizes identifiable words, rather than phonemes; but it would be foolish, at this point, to establish blanket rules about the viability of this or that material.

One could also distinguish pieces which are performed live from those which can exist only on electronic recording tape; those which are multi-voiced (and thus usually canonical in form) from those which are uni-voiced; those which are texts composed exclusively of words from those which add scoring instructions; those which involve improvisation from those which can be repeated with perceptible precision.

Though superficially playful, text-sound art embodies serious thinking about the possibilities of vocal expression and communication; it represents not a substitute for language but an expansion of our verbal powers.

One major factor separating present work from past is the text-sound artist's increasing consciousness of the art's singularity and its particular traditions.

II

Though text-sound art is, in its consciousness of its singular self, a distinctly new phenomenon, it has roots in the various arts it encompasses. On one hand, it extends back to primitive chanting which, one suspects, was probably developed for worship ceremonies. One extension of this tradition is non-melodic religious declamation in which the same words are repeated over and over again, such as Hebrew prayers which are spoken so rapidly that an observer hears not distinct words but repeated sounds. (Harris Lenowitz calls them "speed mantras.") Modern text-sound art also reflects such folk arts as the U.S. tobacco auctioneer's spiel, the evangelical practice of "speaking in tongues," and *Ketjak: The Ramayana Monkey Chant*, in which several score Indonesian men rapidly chant in and out of the syllable "tjak." (This last, which is available on a Nonesuch record, is a masterpiece of the art.) To Charles Morrow, a contemporary practitioner, these folk text-sound arts exemplify "special languages for special communication." However, one critical difference between these precursors and contemporary practitioners is that the former do not consider themselves "artists."

In the history of modern music, text-sound art draws upon an eccentric vocal tradition, epitomized by Arnold Schoenberg's *Sprechgesang*, in which the singing voice touches a note but does not sustain the pitch in the course of enunciating the word. In practice, this technique minimizes the importance of musical tone (and, thus, of melody) and, by contrast, emphasizes the word. One measure of this shift in emphasis is the sense that language in *Sprechstimme* is usually easier to understand than that in music. This technique also appears in Chinese and Korean opera, which may have influenced Schoenberg, and in German cabaret singing, which probably did. Survivors of the latter include Ernst Toch's *Geographical Fugue* (1930), which is composed of place names spoken in overlapping rhythms; and the patter-song, in which words are spoken while instruments play melody in the background (e.g., in *My Fair Lady*, "I've grown accustomed to her face . . .").

In visual arts, text-sound work draws upon the development of abstraction, or non-representational art, and the initial figures in adapting this aesthetic idea to language were Wassily Kandinsky and Kurt

Schwitters. The writer Hugo Ball, himself a prominent practitioner, said in a 1917 lecture that Kandinsky, in his book *Der gelbe Klang* (1912), "was the first to discover and apply the most abstract expression of sound in language, consisting of harmonized vowels and consonants." Schwitters, a Dadaist like Ball, created an imaginary, non-representational, aurally coherent language for his ambitious *Ursonate* (1922-32), which opens:

Fumms bo wo taa zaa Uu,
            pogiff,
                  kwii Ee.
Ooooooooooooooooooooooooooo
   dll rrrrr beeeee bo
   dll rrrrr beeeee bo fumms bo,
      rrrrr beeeee bo fumms bo wo

And he was probably the first to appropriate a musical structure for a totally verbal work. Moholy-Nagy, another sometime visual artist who was also the first perceptive historian of text-sound art, describes Schwitters's masterwork, whose title Moholy translates as "primordial sonata," as "a poem of thirty-five minutes duration, containing four movements, a prelude, and a cadenza in the fourth movement. The words do not exist; rather they might exist in any language; they have no logical only an emotional context; they affect the ear with their phonetic vibrations like music." In recent years, both Eberhard Blum, a German flutist connected with SUNY-Buffalo, and Peter Froehlich of the English Theatre at the University of Ottawa have performed this poem brilliantly, each of them surpassing Schwitters's own partial recording, available on the Luchterhand record anthology *Phonetische Poesie*. Neither Blum's nor Froehlich's rendition is yet, alas, publicly available.

Within the conscious traditions of modern poetry, text-sound art has a much richer history. Contemporary work initially reflects the neologisms that Lewis Carroll incorporated into syntactically conventional sentences, as in the *Jabberwocky*, the invented words implicitly minimizing meaning and emphasizing sound.

'Twas brillig, and the slithy toves,
   Did gyre and gimble in the wabe:
All mimsy were the borogoves,
   And the mome raths outgrabe.

Historical precursors in continental literature include the German poet Paul Scheerbart, whose most notable (and untypical) poem opens, "Kikakoku!//Ekoralaps!" (1897) or the German poet Christian Morgenstern, whose "Das Grosse Lalula" (1905) opens:

Kroklokwafzi? Sememmi!
Seiokrontro—prafriplo:
Bifzi, bafzi; hulalemi:
quasti basti bo . . .
Lalu lalu lalu lalu la:

In "Zang-Tumb-Tu-Tumb" (1921), Filippo Tommaso Marinetti, initially a poet, invented onomatopoeia to portray the sounds of weapons and soldiers: "flic flak zing zing sciaaack hilarious whinnies iiiiiii . . . pattering tinkling 3 Bulgarian battalions marching croooc-craaac . . . ." Hugo Ball's most famous poem (1915):

gadji beri bimba
glandridi, lauli lonni cadori
gadjama bim beri glassala
glandridi glassala tuffm i zimbrabim
blassa galassasa tuffm i mimbrabim . . .

meant to realize a universal language, exemplified the phonetic-unit poetry of such pioneer Dadaists as Raoul Hausmann and Richard Hulsenbeck.

In Russian literature just before the Revolution, Alexei Kruchenyk created a fictitious language, which he called *zaum* (a contraction of a longer phrase, *zaumnyj jazyk,* which can best be translated as "transrational"). Kruchenyk's most audacious manifesto declared, "The word is broader than its meaning." His colleague in Russian futurism, Velemir Klebnikov, by contrast, favored recognizable words for his non-syntactic poems, rationalizing that "the sound of the word is deeply related to its meaning." In the 1920s, the Frenchman Pierre Albert-Birot added footnotes to specify how his neologisms should be pronounced. He is also credited with the profound adage: "If anything can be said in prose, then poetry should be saved for saying nothing."

In American literature, the most prominent precursors are Vachel Lindsay, a troubador eccentric, whose most famous poem, "The Congo" (1914), emphasizes heavy alliteration and such refrains as "Boomlay, boomlay, boomlay, boom"; and e.e. cummings, whose second poem in *Viva* (1931) begins:

oil tel duh woil doi sez
dooyuh unners tanmih eesez pullih nizmus tash, oi

In American prose, the preeminent precursor is, of course, Gertrude Stein, who wove prose tapestries based upon repetition, rather than syntax and semantics: "In saying what she said she said all she said and she said that she did say what she said when she was saying what she said, and she said that she said what she said in saying that she said and she was saying what she said when she said what she said." ("Two: Gertrude Stein and Her Brother," written 1910-1912). One successor to Stein, in post-WWII American literature, was Jack Kerouac, not in his most famous books, to be sure, but in short prose pieces like "Old Angel Midnight," which initially appeared in the opening issue of *Big Table* (1959).

Spat— he mat and tried & trickered on the step and oostepped and peppered it a bit with long mouth sizzle reaching for the thirsts of Azmec Parterial alk-lips to mox & bramajambi

babac up the Moon Citlapol—settle la tettle la pottle, la
lune—Some kind of—Bong!

What unifies this collection of semantically unrelated words is, of
course, the repetition of sounds not only in adjacent words but over
the paragraph; but one quality distinguishing Kerouac from Stein is
that, at least to my ears, the former sounds more literary.
   In English literature, the principal progenitor of contemporary work
is, of course, James Joyce's polylingual, neologistic masterpiece, *Fin-
negans Wake* (1939), which is, incidentally, like Stein's work, closer in
form and tone to "prose" than "poetry."

III

   One post-WWII development that had a radical effect on text-sound
art was the common availability of both the sound amplifier and the
tape recorder, and these two technologies together did more than
anything else to separate "contemporary" endeavors from earlier
"modern" work. That is, after 1955, a verbal artist, now equipped with
sound-tuning equipment, could change the volume and texture of his
microphone-assisted voice; he could eliminate his high frequencies or
his lows, or accentuate them as well as adding reverberation. By vary-
ing his distance from the microphone and his angle of vocal attack, he
could drastically change the timbre of his voice. With recording
technology, the language artist could add present sound to past sound
("overdub"), thereby making a duet, if not a chorus, of himself. He
could mix sounds, vary the speed of tape, or change the pitch of his
voice. More important, he could also affix on tape a definitive audio in-
terpretation of his own text. By expanding the range of audio ex-
perience, these new technologies also implicitly suggested ways of non-
technological innovation. As Bob Cobbing judged, "Where the tape
recorder leads, the human voice can follow."
   Several Europeans now about fifty in age established themselves in
the 1950s, each developing a characteristic style. Henri Chopin, a
Frenchman presently living in England, records his own vocal phonetic
sounds which are then subjected to several elementary tape manipula-
tions, such as overdubbing and speed-changing, usually producing an
abrasive aural experience that reminds me less of other text-sound art
than John Cage's fifties music for David Tudor. Since Chopin starts not
with a verbal text but with a limited range of specified vocables, and
then electronically manipulates these initially vocal sounds in ways
that disguise their human origins, his work is perceived as music, rather
than as text-sound art—more precisely, as a "musique concrete" that
uses only natural sounds. If only to acknowledge its author's profes-
sional origins in poetry, perhaps this might better be classified as
"sound-text" or, as Chopin himself calls it, "poesie sonore" (poetic
sound), as distinct from sound poetry.
   Francois Dufrene, also a Parisian, is best known for is "cri-rhythms,"
which is his term for his art of extreme, hysterical human sounds
(rhythmic cries). As Bob Cobbing describes them, these pieces "employ
the utmost variety of utterances, extended cries, shrieks, ululations,
purrs, yarrs, yaups and cluckings; the apparently uncontrollable con-

trolled into a spontaneously shaped performance." A piece like *Crirhythme pour Bob Cobbing* (1970)—the best of the several I have heard—sounds so extraordinary on first hearing that one can scarcely believe a single human being is producing such audio experience, even with the aid of microphones. Perhaps Dufrene's text-less art is really a species of vocal *theatre*, to introduce yet another categorical distinction.

Bernard Hiedsieck, also a Parisian, works, by contrast, with recognizable words, either spoken emphatically by himself, or collected on the street and off the radio. These words are edited into rapidly paced, rhythmically convulsive aural collages which not only join language with non-verbal noises but also combine linguistic materials not usually found together. His term for this work is "poesie action"; and several examples strike my ears as mixing a newscaster or other loud-speaker voice with a more intimate narrator (apparently Heidsieck himself) against a background of miscellaneous noises. Though his works appear to satirize or editorialize about current events, their syntax is essentially collage, which, though once extremely fertile and also conducive to audiotape, has by now become hackneyed. Nonetheless, Hiedsieck's pieces are more charming that Chopin's or Dufrene's, as well as considerably richer in audio-linguistic texture. Of those I have heard, my favorite is *Carrefour de la Chaussee d'Antin* (1973).

Another member of the Parisian scene, the Englishman, Brion Gysin, favors linguistic permutations, as with *I Am That I Am*. All the possible combinations of these five words are then subjected to speeding, slowing and/or superimposition. The verbal text for this work appears in *Brion Gysin Let the Mice In* (1973), and the audio version, made at the BBC in 1959, is reproduced on the initial *Dial-A-Poem* record (1972). An intimidating audiovisual rendition of both the text and tape is included in my Camera Three-CBS television program, *Poetry To See & Poetry To Hear* (1974). *I Am That I Am* is one of the indisputable classics of text-sound art.

Among the other notable contemporary European text-sound artists are the Englishman Bob Cobbing; the Scotsman Edwin Morgan; the Belgian Paul de Vree; the Czech Ladislav Novak; the Frenchmen Gil J. Wolman and Jean-Louis Brau; the Austrian Ernst Jandl; several Swedes associated with Stockholm's Fylkingen group (including Bengt Emil Johnson, Sten Hanson, and Bengt af Klintberg); and the Germans Ferdinand Kriwet and Hans G. Helms. Kriwet has edited U.S. news broadcasts of both the 1969 moonshot and the 1972 American political campaigns into first-rate English-language audio collages; and Helms wrote *Fa:m' Aniesgwow* (1958), a pioneering book-record which resembles *Finnegans Wake* in realizing linguistic coherence without observing consistently the vocabulary of any particular language. More specifically, through attentiveness to the sound of language, Helms creates the illusion of a modern tongue:

Mike walked in on the : attense of Chjazzus as they sittith softily sipping sweet okaykes H-flowered, purrhushing 'eir goofhearty offan-on-beats, holding moisturize'-palmy sticks

clad in clamp dresses of tissue d'arab, drinks in actionem
fellandi promoting protolingamations e state of nascendi;
completimented golscene of hifibrow'n . . .

The most interesting of the others, in my experience, is Jandl, a Vien-
nese high school teacher of English, who works exclusively in unaided
live performance (the pre-WWII way), declaiming published phonetic
texts, mostly in German but sometimes in English, which are usually in-
ventive in form and witty in language. In New York, Spring 1972, he did
an exceptional performance of a long poem, "Teufelsfalle," which also
appears in his book, *Der Kunstliche Baum* (1970). "Beastiarim," the last
piece on his record, *Laut und Luise* (1968), is a vocal tour-de-force.
However, in part because of his anti-technological bias, Jandl's work
seems to terminate a style, rather than suggest future developments.

BIBLIOGRAPHY

CODE: * = text   ✔ = record or audiotape   # = videotape

I

Babbitt, Milton, and John Hollander. *Philomel* (1963). Cambridge, Ma: Acoustic Research—
DGG, n.d. ✔

Hollander, John. "Philomel," in Richard Kostelanetz, ed., *Possibilities of Poetry*. N.Y. Delta,
1970.*

Houedard, Dom Sylvester. "Introduction," *Kroklok*, I/1 (1971).*

Russolo, Luigi. "The Art of Noise" (1913), in Michael Kirby, *Futurist Performance*. N.Y. Dut-
ton, 1971.*

Schwerner, Armand. *The Tablets, I-XV*. N.Y. Grossman, 1971. *

_____. *The Tablets, I-XVIII*. Dusseldorf/Munchen: S Press, 1975. ✔

II

Ball, Hugo. *Flight Out of Time*. N.Y.: Viking, 1974.*

Bory, Jean-Francois, ed. *Raoul Hausmann*. Paris: L'Herne, 1972.*

Cummings, E.E. *Viva*. N.Y.: Liveright, 1931.*

Hausmann, Raoul. *Phonemes*. Dusseldorf: S Press, 1970. ✔

Joyce, James. *Finnegans Wake*. London: Faber, 1939.*

_____. "Anna Livia Plurabelle," *Finnegans Wake*. N.Y.: Folkways, 1951. ✔

Kandinsky, Wassily. Excerpts from "Klange," in Carola Giedion-Welcker, ed., *Anthologie
der Abseitigen/Poetes a l'Ecart*. Zurich: Verlag der Arche, 1965.*

Kerouac, Jack. "Old Angel Midnight," *Big Table*, I/1 (1959).*

Lewiston, David, producer. *Ketjak: The Ramayana Monkey Chant*. N.Y.: Nonesuch, n.d. ✔

Lewiston, David. *Pansori*. N.Y.: Nonesuch, 1972. ✔

Marinetti, Filippo Tommaso. "Zang-Tumb-Tu-Tumb," as quoted by Luigi Russolo, "The Art of Noise," in Michael Kirby, *Futurist Performance*. N.Y.: Dutton, 1971.*

Markov, Vladimir. *Russian Futurism*. Berkeley: Univ. of Calif., 1968.*

Moholy-Nagy, L. *Vision in Motion*. Chicago: Paul Theobald, 1946.*

Mon, Franz, prod. *Phonetische Poesie*. Neuweid: Luchterhand, n.d. [With Hausmann, Klebnikov, Kurchenyk, Schwitters] ✔

Morgenstern, Christian. "Das Grosse Lalula," *Kroklok*, I/1 (1971).*

Scheerbart, Paul. "Kikakoku!" *Kroklok*, I/1 (1971).*

Schwitters, Kurt. "Ursonate," *Das Literarische Werk*. Koln: Dumont Schauberg, 1973.*

Stein, Gertrude. "Two: Gertrude Stein and Her Brother," *Two: Gertrude Stein and Her Brother*. New Haven, Ct: Yale Univ., 1951.*

III

Chopin, Henri. *Audiopoems*. London: Tangent Records, 1971. ✔

_____. *Le Voyage Labiovelaire & Le Cri*. S Press, 1972. ✔

_____. "Poesie Sonore," *Kontexts*, 8 (Spring, 1976).*

Cobbing, Bob. "Concrete Sound Poetry 1950-1970," *Concrete Poetry?* Amsterdam: Stedelijk Museum, 1970.*

Dufrene, Francois. "Le Lettrisme est toujours pendant," *Opus International*, 40-41 (Jan, 1973).*

Fall, Georges, ed. *L'Autonomatopek 1*. Paris Opus Disque, 1973. [With Cobbing-Lockwood, Chopin, Dufrene] ✔

Fall, Georges, et al. *Concrete Poetry?* Amsterdam: Stedelijk Museum, 1970. [With Cobbing, Dufrene *(pour Bob Cobbing)*, Sten Hanson, Hiedsieck, Jandl, Bengt Emil Johnson, Ladislav Novak, Paul de Vree] ✔

Gysin, Brion. "I Am That I Am," in John Giorno, prod. *Dial-A-Poem*. N.Y.: Giorno Poetry Systems, 1972. ✔

_____. "I Am That I Am," in Richard Kostelanetz, *Poetry To See & Poetry To Hear*. Albany, NY: State Education Dept., 1974.#

_____. *Let the Mice In*. W. Glover, Vt: Something Else, 1973.*

Hiedsieck, Bernard. *Poeme-Partition J* (1961) & *Carrefour de la Chaussee d'Antin* (1972). S Press, 1973. ✔

_____. *Partition V*. Paris: Le Soleil Noir, 1973.* ✔

_____. *Trois Biopsies* ⚫ *Un Passe-Partout* (1967-70 & 1970). Paris: Multi-Techniques, n.d. ✔

_____. *Poesie Action Poesie Sonore, 1955-1975*. Paris: Atelier Exposition Annick Le Moine, 1976.*

Helms, Hans G. *Fa:m' Ahniesgwow*. Koln: Dumont Schauberg, 1959.* ✔

Jandl, Ernst. *Laut und Luise*. Berlin: Wagenbach, 1968. ✔

Jandl, Ernst *Der Kunstliche Baum*. Berlin: Luchterhand, 1970.*

Johnson, Bengt Emil, et al. "Fylkingen," *Source,* 8 (July, 1970).*

Kriwet, Ferdinand. *Hortext-Takes*. Dusseldorf: Art Scene, 1970.*

——————————. *Campaign Radio Text IX*. Dusseldorf: Private tape, 1972.↙

Mon, Franz, prod. *Phonetische Poesie*. Neuweid: Luchterhand, n.d. [With Chopin, Cobbing, Jandl, Novak, de Vree]↙

Mottram, Eric. "A Prosthetics of Poetry: The Art of Bob Cobbing," *Second Aeon,* 16/17, n.d.*

O Huigin, Sean. "Eighth International Sound Poetry Festival," *Open Letter,* III/3 (Fall, 1975).*

Anonymous tongue-twisters are the folk dimension, so to speak, of text-sound art; and among those thought to be North American in origin are these:

If a Hottentot taught a Hottentot tot to talk ere the tot could totter, ought the Hottentot tot be taught to say ought or naught or what ought to be taught 'er?

If a woodchuck could chuck wood,
    How much wood would a woodchuck chuck,
If a woodchuck could chuck wood?

Peter Piper picked a peck of pickled peppers.
    A peck of pickled peppers Peter Piper picked.
If Peter Piper picked a peck of pickled peppers,
    Where is the peck of pickled peppers
Peter Piper picked?

How many cans
Can a canner can
If a canner
Can can cans?
A canner can can
As many cans
As a canner can
If a canner
Can can cans.

She is a thistle-sifter and she has a sieve of
    sifted thistles and a sieve of unsifted thistles
    and the sieve of unsifted thistles she sieves
    into the sieve of sifted thistles
    because she is a thistle-sifter.

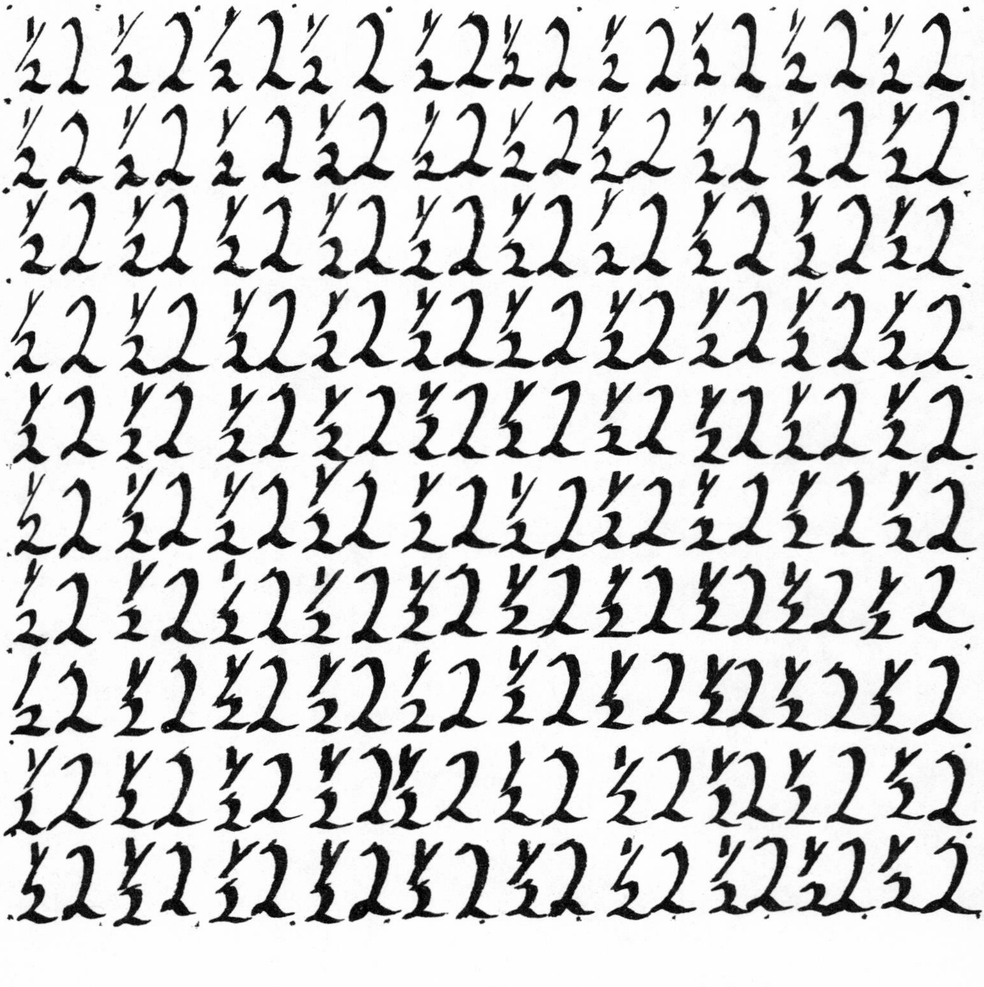

WALTER ABISH

AUCTIONING AUSTRALIA

April approaches as an audacious Aussie, Arminius Arkwright, arduously ascends Australian Alps. Arkwright all ardor, all anticipation, awkwardly applies an alpine army axe, activating an avalanche above. Aghast, Arkwright attempts an arresting action as avalanche, aimed at Adelaide, arrows along another alpine ascent. Accordingly all attempted ascents are aborted and academic.

Aussies as always are amazingly articulate, awwww, and also adept at assessing and authenticating accelerating avalanches' advance, and also assessing Admiral Ashkenazi's advice about activating an anticyclone as an arresting action. An arresting action? Arminium Arkwright, alive and admitting angst, anxiously asks: Aren't anticyclones almost as awful as avalanches? Answer. Answer.

Aussies are amused as an Adelaidian assistant agronomist, Angy Artstein, asserts: Aborigines are amorously alert, and arch. Arch?

Anyhow, an arch aborigine, Adupo Afyo, arrives at Adelaide, all ardor, all appetite. Appraises Alicia's ankles, and alabaster arms, and. . .and? assuming Alicia as an available Aussie, Adupo Afyo accosts Alicia and asks: Any action? Any activity? Afterwards at Alicia's Adelaide apartment Adupo all attention assists at adult action. As Alicia arouses Adupo, Adupo admires Alicia's attractive anatomy. Also admires Aussie accent, and avantgarde armchairs, and alabaster ass. Ahhh. Although Australians are antiracist, all are angry and appalled. Aesthetics aside, all antagonistically allege aborigines are amoral animals. Accordingly all adult Adelaidians attack aborigines, angrily axing, angrily assaulting, angrily annihilating aborigines, avenging Alicia's alabaster ankles and arms and. . .And? Always avenging. Adult action again and again. Ahhh. Afterwards all Adelaidians are ashamed. Awwww. Awful, awful. Assuming attrition. Accepting Admiral Ashkenazi's augury.

All along alpine avalanche advances. Ah. . . Ah. . . Ah. . . .

Another additional Australian aspect: An amateur artist and apprentice anchorman, Arturo Arp, assails Australians as arsonists, and as aborigine area annexationists. Allegedly Arp also asserted: Aborigines aren't admitted at Andes Annex, an Adelaide auditorium. Aborigines aren't admitted? Answer. Answer. Answer.

After *Anchors Away* Admiral Ashkenazi, addressing an Adelaide adult audience, averred after atrocity aborigines aren't admitted at auditoriums, and at arcades. Accusing Australians, Admiral Ashkenazi also asserted aborigines' ancient ancestors are apparently armed and angry, arousing audience's aversion. Are aborigine ancestors attacking afterlife?

Anyhow, anthropologists and archeologists amplify accusations against Ashkenazi: Asshole. Asshole. Angrily attacking Ashkenazi. After all, Ashkenazi's accent ain't Australian and Ashkenazi's anti-racist aesthetics ain't Australian, above all Ashkenazi's antique armchair ain't Australian. And, all agree, Ashkenazi ain't an alcoholic, and Ashkenazi's aesthetics are anarchist. Ahhh anarchism. Ashen and apologetic, Ashkenazi admits antisocial actions, and accepts abuse. Accepts Australian abuse: Asshole anarchist. Asshole anarchist?

All along Al and Attie, assimilated Americans, are absorbing Australian atmosphere, and adorable Australian accents (aaaaiiiiianarchist aaaiiisshole) and amazing animals, aardvarks (aardvarks?) and advanced architecture. Ah ah. Also amusing anecdotes about an Australian alpinist, Arminius Arkwright. Apparently Australian anecdotes abound about aborigine ancestors, and about arriviste Admiral Ashkenazi, and about an amazing adorable adventuress, Alicia Ambureka - Ausweis and Andie Alevai, an Armenian accountant. Actually, anecdotes always abound. After all, aren't anecdotes an ambiguous assertion about afterlife and anality and angst?

Ashkenazi, an armchair Admiral, at another Adelaide Australian Automobile Association Assembly, argues: Aren't all antagonisms aesthetically activated? Answer: Abundantly. Amen.

An Argentinian ambassador, affluent and Anglican, acknowledging Ashkenazi's attacks against amorality and arbitrary atrocities, argumentatively affirms Australia's ahistoricity. All academics are alarmed. After all, are atrocities ahistorical?
Answer. Answer. Answer.

Ambassadors, admittedly, are always arbitrary and ambiguous. Ambiguous and assholes. Admittedly Argentinians are allies. Anyhow, Argentinian ambassador and aesthete, Apilio Amunxib-Abzeit, admitted assembling amputated aborigine arms and ankles after aborigine atrocity. Amassed arms and ankles are assembled as avantgarde art. Actually amazing and also awful. Awful. Awful. Awful. Amputated arms. Arghhh. Australian accented Aaaiiirgh. Aghast, Adelaidians appropriate ambassador's apartment, antiques, automobiles, airplane, alcohol, Australian ale. Also armchairs. Armchairs? asks Ashkenazi atavistically. Armchairs?
Answer, answer.
Ambassador's antiquities are appraised and auctioned at an Automobile Association Auction, although Adelaide's academics as always advise against aesthetic adventurism. Aesthetic adventurism? Armchairs are armchairs.

Any answers?

Adelaidians answers and attitudes are all alike. All are against adultery. Against anality. Against ambiguity. Against Alcoholism. Against Argentinian ambassadors. Against aesthetes. Against aborigine ancestors. Against armed attacks. Against avantgardism. Against artsy architecture. Against all alien academics, and against all Australian academics. Against appeasement and against anarchy. Also against antinovels. Awwww.

Arriving at Ashkenazi's apartment, Alicia, alluring Alicia, accepts an aperitif and another as Ashkenazi arranges appetizing asparagus, anchovies, artichokes, apples and apricots. Ashkenazi's admirers and adherents are annoyed as Alicia asks: Aren't apricots an African aphrodisiac? And artichokes? All awkwardly: Awwwwww, awwwwww.

At Adelaidian airport arcades are ablaze. Also an Air Australia airplane, and an airforce arena, and an auditorium. Anxiety. Anxiety.

Alicia abandoned. Alone. Alone. Angst. Angst.
Answer.

Another April afternoon. Alicia amongst amorous Argentinians. Ambassador and androgynous amigos: anthropologists and archeologists, all Australian allies, all anally active, all aged and awfully absentminded. Alicia's attitude amazingly amoral. Affectionate as Argentinians, all aglow, all aroused: Alloo, allo Alicia. Alicia: Allo, allo amigos.

Adult action: Alicia astride an Argentinian. Astride. Astride? An arrhythmic action. An amorous arrangement, as ambidexterous Alicia arouses an adroit, agile although aged Argentinian. Apimento above attractive Alicia, as Argentinian appendage aimed at anal area abdicates all activity. Absolutely absurd. Apimento apologetic, also argumentative, aiming at amends, asking Alicia: Actually, ain't asexuality an attractive alternative.
Answer.
Assuredly.
Also. Aren't armchairs available at Adelaide's Athletic Alliance Art Auction? After another (aborted) attempt at arousing Argentinian, Alicia adroitely aims an alabaster ankle at an area above Argentinian appendage. Awwwww.
Akvavit? Asks Ambassador.
Ahh. Ancient Akvavit. An apocalyptic alcohol.
Another akvavit? Asks affable ambassador.
Another akvavit? Asks affable ambassador.
Alicia aloof. Aloof and, alas, again abandoned.

Augustina, Alicia's aunt arrives and advises Alicia against assuming all armadillos are apathetic. Augustina, an aging actress, admits applying at ABC. Auditioned and accepted as an alternate anchorwoman, Augustina anxiously awaits ABC's aired adult auction. Alas, aged aunt's assertions are all anticlimactic. Also alliterative. Alliterative? Answer. Answer. Author. Author.

Are Australian authors as arrogant as American authors?
Answer.
And are American authors' agents as adaptable and active and alert and ambitious as Australian aardvarks?
Ask another.
And are Australian avalanches aesthetically acceptable?
Ask another.
And are Adelaidian abortionists avoiding answers about attributing avalanche's antibacterial antihuman and alkaline affect?
Ask another.
And are Ashkenazi's Aristotelian aesthetics, applied as an apolitical affirmation, actually an anachronism?
Ask another.
And again are Australian authors as anxious about awards asymmetric? amortization?
Ask another.
And are aquamarine aluminum armchairs always asymmetric?
Ask another.

And are accountants adjudicating abbreviated audits?
Ask another.
And are all Adelaidian automobile accidents artistically and aesthetically
arranged?
Ask another.
And are autos available at auctions after accidents?
Ask another.
Antro Augenblick, an astute Afghanistan astrologer, augments all anticipatory
anxiety and angst as an Australian (Aussie, Aussie, Aussie) avalanche advance
and accelerates. Amidst Australia's Athletic Alliance anniversary and annual
audit, Augenblick analyzes an amino acid amethyst. Arrives at an awesome
answer as amethyst atrophies. Awwww.
Ask another.

Are all athletes absolute assholes?
Ask another.
Are athletes asexual?
Ask another.

Adelaide.

Anxiety. Anxiety.

Answer. Anyone answer. Anyone.

Australian anthem.

AAAD AIVE AAA AEEN

NOTES ON SOUND AND LANGUAGE

Spoken sound is movement, the movement of articulation and the move-ment of sound textures. Things (objects, concepts, emotions) can be per-ceived as qualities, and the qualities can be perceived as movements, textures, angles, curves, smoothness, harshness, the movements forward of desire and the movements away of fear. Spoken sound can be used to translate the movements of things and experiences into the movements of sounds.

Language has the extraordinary ability to combine the power of sound with the precision of semantics. Sound can capture movement and semantic meaning can focus the sound to a specific application. Sound can capture roundness, and semantics can identify it as the roundness of a baseball or an eyeball.

Sometimes the sounds of Standard English pronunciation reflect the movement of the thing designated. The sounds of "hope" move forward, and those of "woe" move backward. Often a word's sounds do not reflect the thing named. The sounds of "east" go north. I play with the sounds of words, altering the sounds so that their movements capture the desired qualities.

My present notational system is designed to reflect the movements of arti-culation. The system is based on the numbers 0 to 9 plus ten diacritical marks. Each number represents a region in the mouth. When the point of ar-ticulation is in a region, the appropriate number is used. 1 through 9 (in a three-by-three grid) represent regions behind the teeth, and 0 represents sounds made in front of the teeth. The numbers by themselves represent ex-haled, voiceless unrounded vowels.

Diacritical marks indicate how the basic sound is changed. Some marks in-dicate variation from the focal point. Other marks add features, and still other marks indicate variation into new sound categories.

For example, / represents the high-front region. I designated the point of articulation for "ee" in "sweet" as the focal point. The / represents a whis-pered (voiceless) "ee". The ⫽ is the voiced sound "ee". The mark ⤳ represents fricatives. The ⤳ represents a fricative made in the high-front region, the "s" of "see". The mark ╱ represents the stop category, and ⨍ represents the high-front stop "t" of "tea". The sounds of "east" are represented by ⫽⤳⨍. All three symbols are variations of / ; they are three different kinds of sound in one region.

The diacritical marks can be combined to symbolize new sounds. And I add new marks when I encounter new features I want to work with.

The accompanying score sheets are from LOVE SONGS II: THE SHUMAN DREAMS. It is a two-character theater piece. The B and Z on the left indi-cate the lines of the characters, a man named Boley Shuman and a woman named Zhing. The text is in the numeral system. Above each line are stage directions. Below each line is a translation of the text into the International Phonetic Alphabet. The I.P.A. is a good system for reading. Mine is a move-ment system; make the movements and discover the sound you have uttered.

LOVE SONGS II: THE SHUMAN DREAMS

25

Great ringing cry-cup hands. The playing the game

Soft low tone

B

Z   50 50 0175050 57 5 40467 X-3-8 X 8—

am am wika ama b ab amang
n ao s

of talking in emotions. When not talking, they are quiet, unemotional.

LUSTING

s ə ə ž ul larvəl

B

RELAXED Ayawn

FASTIDIOUS

Z   8— 6— 0-0610

out
m walm
o. ra-a

s tip it tiktik

PARENTAL IRRITATION (scolding)

B   06-X10 10 10 X-78-XIX78XIIX78XIX78XII

ba dip Tip Tip s ko tis koti s koti s koti

Pause to think

VIOLENT ANGER (like blows)

Z   X-797X7 XI37XI37 XI37

g g g uu dyaag dyaag dyaag

Pause to think

MECHANICAL

B   67 67 67 67

Tak Tak Tak Tak

RIGHTEOUS INDIGNATION

FEAR (wince on stops high pitch strain)

Z   X46-7- 48- 86- X46-7-   m-67IX 5 I-1- XIXIX50-9-

dra g ro va dra g   b akit ?a ?i i tiktik sə wu s

32

LOVE SONGS II: THE SHUMAN DREAMS

AWE   (faint)   *BOREDOM* (drum fingers on floor)   look around

SHAME lips tight

PLAYFUL SHYNESS   pitch↓

POISE, SERENITY

BOLDNESS

LAUGHTER (no set number)   *IRRITATION*

tiolin   pa   m

B

Z

CITY STREET SCENES

subway-lights, riding deserted station
quiet-dim, passing woman-man
train waiting

deserted riding lights subway
dim man-station
passing train
quiet woman, . . .waiting

riding station dim, . . quiet deserted man-woman
train passing
waiting, . lights subway

woman-quiet-train
man-waiting-subway
passing station lights, . . riding deserted dim

deserted woman
quiet dim, . riding man
station train-lights
subway passing, . . waiting

dim station
woman, . . quiet, deserted, waiting, . . riding train
passing subway, lights man

subway lights waiting, . . passing train
woman-man, . . deserted
quiet, . dim, . station-riding

quiet, . . riding deserted passing woman
lights waiting
subway man
train-dim station

deserted dim station-woman, . riding train
quiet man waiting, . . passing subway lights

man lights subway passing train, . . riding, . . waiting
deserted quiet-woman-station-dim

(10 of 48 word modules of City Street Scenes 1)

time form is a graphic representation of temporal durations, . . sounds and
silences, ...the horizontal lines represent sound masses. .time volumes filled
with word modules. . . . . .the spaces between the lines represent silence. . . . . .
. . .this time form is for 3 speakers. . . .any time scale can be superimposed
over the form. . . .the proportions are fixed. . . .regardless of the length of the
performance, . . of sound masses, . . and silence, ... the relationship of the
volumes remains the same. . . . . .my work deals primarily with form. . .
not the form of rhyme schemes, . . or of developmental, contrasting or re-
capitulary material, ...but form as the use of sound-word blocks, . as a
formal tension value producing device, . . . the word material projected into
the time form serves only to reinforce the basic concept. . . . . . .the projec-
tion of word modules into the form and the possibility of their appearance
in any order, ... produces a static but constantly changing word image. . . .
. . . .form, . . when used in this manner, . . produces its own values. . . . .
. . . the dynamics of the piece are created by the various word module den-
sities combining and colliding within the confines of the time form. . . . . .
the entire form functions as a large macrorhythmic unit. . . . .
the concern is for the unit-forms, . . and their combination and movement
in a temporal continuum. . . . .

original series (o) = deserted, dim, station, woman, riding, subway, train, quiet, man, waiting, passing, subway, lights. . . .
retrograde form (r) = (o) in reverse order. . . .
inversion form (i) = contour inversion or mirroring of (o) (contour created by arranging words in alphabetical order, and using "word class number" as contour determinant). . . . . . .inversion (i) = complimentation (mod. 12) of each word number of the series, . . or (i) = (12 - "word number")
transposition, ((transposition (t) = adding (mod. 12) an integer (transposition number, 0-11) to each word number of the series, . . or (t) = ("word number" + "transposition number")))

	(o)												(r)		
(1)	0	1	7	11	6	9	5	3	10	4	8	2		0	deserted
	11	0	6	10	5	8	4	2	9	3	7	1		1	dim
	5	6	0	4	11	2	10	8	3	9	1	7		2	lights
	1	2	8	0	7	10	6	4	11	5	9	3		3	man
	6	7	1	5	0	3	11	9	4	10	2	8		4	passing
	3	4	10	2	9	0	8	6	1	7	11	5		5	quiet
	7	8	2	6	1	4	0	10	5	11	3	9		6	riding
	9	10	4	8	3	6	2	0	7	1	5	11		7	station
	2	3	9	1	8	11	7	5	0	6	10	4		8	subway
	8	9	3	7	2	5	1	11	6	0	4	10		9	train
	4	5	11	3	10	1	9	7	2	8	0	6		10	waiting
(ri)	10	11	5	9	4	7	3	1	8	2	6	0		11	woman

these series, . . when translated back into words, . . are projected into syntactic poetic lines. . . . . . these word modules, . . are then projected into a time form. . .
. . . . .

SONNETS, pt. 2 / for solo voice

Sonnets 26-37 of Shakespeare: word-initial phonemes, with a story and a repeated word interpolated.

All phonemes sound as in English: The following is a pronunciation guide:

y	as in	yet	b	as in	bare	l	as in lord
i	"	ease	d	"	duty	ɹ	" respect
I	"	it	g		good	f	fair
e	"	age	p		poor	v	view
ɛ		expire	t		tother	s	strongly
æ		as	k		keep	z	zealous
a		odd	m		my	ʃ	show
ʌ		other	n		naked	θ	thought
ɔ		off	ŋ		ring	ð	that
o		over	tʃ		change		
ʊ		book	dʒ		jewel		
u		boot					
w		witness					
ʍ		which					
h		head					
ai		ice					
ei		they					

The strings of phonemes are to be read smoothly and grimly. Short neutral vowels can be interjected between consonants. Repeated consonants should be re-articulated. Intonation and cadences are given by punctuation. Pauses between poems are short. The number at the beginning of each poem is not read.

Buffalo · 1976 · still the middle of winter · NED SUBLETTE
for Turney Jones and Julius Eastman ·

1.

2.

3.

4.

5.

6.

7.

8.

9.

10.

11.

12.

JABBERWOCKY
(Extended from Lewis Carroll)
(For Four Voices)

1st Voice: High-pitched. Repeats "Jabberwocky" quickl〉 gain
at 16/4 time. Begins piece by saying "Jabberwocky" three ιue.
Softly.

2nd Voice: Alto quality. On the first beat of the 1st Voice's
the 2nd Voice will begin in 8/4 time "Jab Jab Jab Jab Jab Ja
jab's will be twice as long as each syllable of the 1st Voice; tł
be twice as long as the first two jabs. The 2nd Voice will, als
a board to his rhythm. Continue. Softly.

3rd Voice: Tenor quality. Recites Lewis Carroll's "Jabberw〈
time (each syllable will be four times as long as the 1st Voice〉
first beat of the third "Jab Jab Jab" sequence. Forte.

4th Voice: Bass. Begin at the first "and" of the 3rd Voice in 2/〜
the word "Jabberwocky." Continue. Softly.

General Instructions: Stop at the end of each stanza with a two beat rest (at
4/4 time). Begin stanzas 2-7 together (don't re-do the "introduction"). A
metronome set at 4/4 time might be helpful. If so used start the metronome
playing at least 30 seconds before the piece & 30 seconds afterwards.

SECRET BOOK OF MOSES ON THE GREAT NAME,
A BOOK ABOUT EVERYTHING,
IN WHICH IS CONTAINED THE NAME OF THE ONE
WHO ORDAINS EVERYTHING THAT IS

Chi trova il nome ineffabile di Dio,
é Dio.

—old proverb as transmitted
by A. Lora-Totino

This magic text written in Greek in Egypt, most probably by a Jew who
es the pseudonymous persona of Moses, the powerful sorcerer whose rod
wallowed up the rods of the Egyptian enchanters," as mouthpiece for this
ame Magic/chant performance, dates anywhere from the 1st century BCE
the 4th century CE. It is the longest text on a single theme known to sur-
ve among those that remain from and were composed by the many folk
amans active in Egypt throughout this period who drew on Egyptian, Jew-
h, Gnostic and Christian lore, singly and in combination. This piece is found
: *Papyri Graecae Magicae*, K. Preisendanz (ed.), vol. II, pp. 120-129 (Papy-
s XIII, 11. 731-1025).

The chants are all built around the vowels of the Tetragrammaton (YHWH),
hich in Greek are rendered as: I A Ω (I - A - O). They occur in every pos-
ble variation and disguise (so that no loopholes in the word-woven web are
ft), until by mimesis s/he (the magus and "pupil"/client) become YHWH.

ake for partners, child, with your own eyes
e gods of Day, Hour, Week, as this book logs them.
se the Twelve Rulers of the Months
d The Seven Letter Name from the first book—
explained in my volume *The Key*.
ig & wonderful, it will illuminate all your books.

ow the Oath, child
de It   God's Name   hides in   :   you
od the Eight   Ogdoad God   God Who leads all
bjects all: angels archangels   demons demonesses   :
Him in the creation   He owns   is set forth
is Four Names: Nine Letters, Fourteen Letters,
wenty Six Letters   and Zeus's, too .
ay Them on   child shamans   their minds unlit   :
ake them see   let them not be trifled   by this or that   :
y all words   all needs   look into things closely

examine eye prophesy by suneye
mirror light glanced eye to eye glamour
maybe you'll see the future may be
forge a chain say The Great Name [s]
The Eighth The Ogdoad God Who does everything
in the creation He owns
without Him nothing of what's done
gets done

Learn and forget, child, The Nine Letter Name:
ahwehweyhwehweyhwihwowuhwoh
The 14 Letter: usauh   shiwauweh   Yahwohwhus
The 26 Letter: arabahwooh   arabah   (a′ = 1)
and Zeus's, too:
ihemoi kho'eni ka'abiah shikbah frooh'om epierthat

for this the prayer of the Heptagram
and the word [ing] God hears and must obey: "

Come to me out of the four winds
You Who breathed soul in us to live—
Your Name hides in me I may not
speak (when people do—it's no Secret) Name
Which demons when they hear fly far from
Your sun named:

Arnebooh'at Bolloch Barbarich:

bal Ba'alshamen: ptidai'ooh Harneboo'at

        moon named:

Harshen-penprohooth barbarai'onei oshrar memp-shekhei

Your relentless eye never tires
lights up the dark in our eye
Your head is skyfire: Yerbody air feet Earth
water around You named good-demon Ocean
Y'are goodfather   the housed world
Y'are greatmother the eternal ballroom
Y'are the dancer   : Whose Name Heptagrammaton
part- ners You   footing it neatly
YH're the One   Your Seven Letter Name names !

A   Eh   Ei   I   o   U   Oh

by winding harmonies the seven vowels turn out those
who take their voice from Moon's 28 lights:

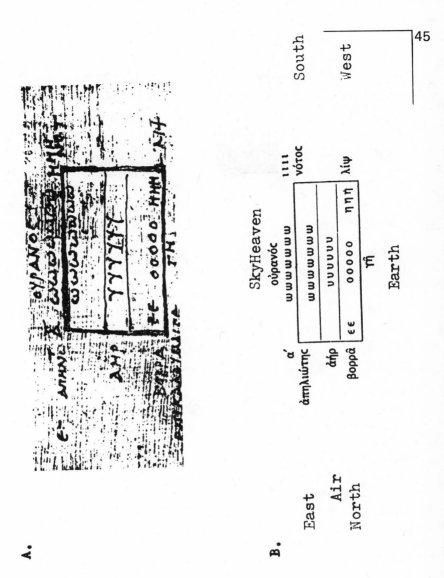

A.

B.

B. (transcription)

Sky/Heaven
οὐρανός

α′ ἀπηλιώτης

ἀήρ

βορρᾶ

νότος

λίψ

γῆ

Earth

East
Air
North

South
West

A diagram or map of the magic universe. B. is a transcription of A. (facsimile of the original papyrus) into modern typefaces.

The universe map before combination with the Magen David—i.e., as it originally appeared in the papyrus of *Secret Book*.

shar afara araf ah ih Abraham abrahach pertahohmeychh
akmeyk: YaHWoH oueei YaHWoH oueh ehiouh aheihwoh
eheyhwouh YaHWoH, Name owning the good rivers
influencing from the stars—Spirit-Lucks   Shares
give us: wealth   old age passed in joy
children to give us joy   happy life
a death everybody comes to : You
Lord of life   King of sky heaven   and Earth
of all who tarry here
Your justice never ends
Your muses sing Your bright Name praising You
shielded by the spears of Eight Watchers named:

Eyh , Oh , Khoh , Khooch , Noun , Nauni , Ammon , Amauni

You bear the Truth Your light never darkens
Name of You   Soul of You Who blesses
come to mind   I want You alive
all the time of this My life here
make for Me all My soul desires
for You are Me and I am You
something if I say it has to be
for I possess Your Name
in the phylactery of My heart
and all flesh moved against Me
shall not hold Me back [from all My soul desires]
no wind from spirit arrayed against Me
no demon   ghost   no devil from Hell supplant Me
for I am Named You   Your Name is in My soul

Thank Your Name I have in My soul
I call You here   everywhere Born for Me
Good for My good   Unbound by other magic
give Me health without blight,
rescue, money and means,
glory, victory, strength,
plus yes strength in love's charms
turn Your eye [evilly]
upon My enemies male and female
in all I do grant signs of Your favor:
for anoch [I am] ai'efeh shaktitei
bibiou bibiou sfeh sfeh noushi noushi
oon khoonti'aih: shembi: imenoohai bahin-fnoon fnooth

A.

B.

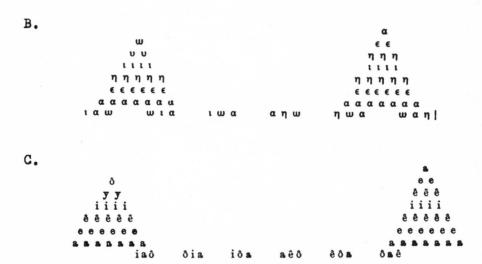

C.

Prayer or chant in praise of Horus, showing Eye of Horus between the two 'appearing' vowel pyramids. B. is a transcription of A. (facsimile of the original papyrus) into modern typeface. C. is a transliteration of B. into Roman (Eye omitted in both). Note Yahweh Name [ιαω] in lower left-hand corner of the first pyramid. Accidental or by design?

tookhar shookhar shabakhar anathe'ooh ihwehwuh ion eon:

Thothwoh oothroh:throresheh erihohpo ihwuhweyh

ahweyh yahwohwahwih ahwehweyhwih-whoowo

ahwhehwheyhwihwhouwoh eyhwokh: manebih khohwohwihwoh alarawoh:

kol: kol kahaton kolkanthoh balalakh ablalakh

Ohther-khentheh boolokh boolokh Osherkhentheh *[Osiris]*

menthehih because I have chosen
the might of Abraham, Isaac and Jacob
of the Great God Daimon their Lord YaHWoH

ablanathalbah:shi'abrathilahwoh lampshteir ihweyhwih ohwoh

God, do it, Lord pertawohmeykh after me now

khakhmeykh YaHWoH oohweyhweh YaHWoH

yeh:wooh:ayweyhwoh eyhweyhwoh YaHWoH

NOTE

Speaking:

East		hands	left	go:	:	A!
North		right	fist	up		: E!E!
West		hands	out			: E!E!E!
South		hands	over mouth			: I! I! I! I!
Earth		hands	on toes			: O!O!O!O!O!
Air	eyes front	hand	over heart			: U!U!U!U!U!U!
Sky	face back	hands	under head			: O!O!O!O!O!O!O!
Heaven				again		: O! O! O! O! O! O! O!

do it right :

use this universe order: watch sky heaven
[see Star of David
Diagram]

I speak send me You *oyez oyez*
You forever no father no mother
One Alone All owning the world You habited
Whom no one knows or can   .
God gods fall down before worship kiss You
r Name no god knows or can aloud
blow Stretcher of the poles
from mouth and nose on Me under You
You to Me using male gods' voice
making it mine: ihweyhwoh oohweh ohweyhwih

uhweh ahwoh ehwih ohwuh ahwoweyh oohweyh

48

ehwohwah uhweyhwih ohwehwah oweyhwoh yehwooh ahwoh
come over me goddesses say I say:
ihwahweyh ehwohwo ihwooh ehweyh yeh ahwih:
eyhyahwuh ehwohwo oohweyhweh yahwoh-howhay
ehwoohweyh uhwohweyhwih ehwohwah as winds howl
I bring You here   where I cry:
Do   complete   my will in this
(tell Him what you want) now   not later
I've got You by Your Name
bestbiggest Name of all gods' names
done out loud   all of it   makes Earth shake
Sun stop   Moon pale   turns
rocks   mountains   seas   rivers   oceans
        stone
bends universe flow   back from separation
         fusing inside itself
I Name You   here   pull You here :
yuhweuhwo ohwahwehweyh YaHWoH   ahwehweyh
ahwih ehweyh ahweyh yoowoh euhweyh YeHWooH
ahweyhwoh ohwih ohweyhweyh yahweyh yohwoohweyh
auhweyh uhweyhwah yoh yohwahwih yohwahwih ohweyh
ehweh ooh yoh YaHWoH   goodbig Name   now not later:
take new birth body   YouLynx   YouEagle   YouSnake
YouPhoenix YouLife YouStrength YouForceFate
You Idols the gods person, ahwihwoh yoh wuh YaHWoh
eyhyoh ahwah oohwih ahahahah eh:yuh yoh ohweyh YaHWoH
ahwih: ahwohweyh oohwehwoh ahyehweyh yoohweh uhwehyah
ehyoh eyhyih uhuh eheh eyheyh ohwahwohweyh //
khekhampshim'm khangalash a e i o u yeyhwehwah/
ohwo-eyhwo-weh ts euonymous good *[omen nomen]*
zohyoh - yeir ohmuhruh - romromos   widen
d o u b l e   Y a H W o H   n a m e
f   o   l   l   o   w   m   e   :
e Y Y Y u H u H   e H e H

WeeeeeeeyHHWWeeeeyHHoooooooooooWWaaaaHHWWoooWWeeeeeeeyH

Sun inters 14th day
now do this rite on gold clean licked special plate:

Universe Order

drone :

Face East
:
South Wind

drone :

say :

East

Southward
:
West Wind

say

Southtown

go :

chant

Earth
:
look North

this

Earth

West

North Wind
:
stand West

speak

this

YaHWaH

yuh:oweyh yeuhwowoh
eyhwohwih ehwo:eyh ohwuh ehweyh:uhwohweyh ohwohwoh:
ohwohwih ohwahwoh ehwoh ohweyh uhwoh now more complete:
ahwoh-euhweyh owahwih yo eyhwuhweh-ohwah oohwoh ohwo eih
ooh ehwoh oiwuhwuh ohwuhwuh   a : e a t t h e s e N a m e s:

a oh	this rite now	e e				
e o ey	read times six	ey ey ey				
e oh ey	His Name air ring	i i i i				
i a a	loudly: 123 456:	o o o o o			
ey oh i	etch the others	u u u u u u		
ey i oh	on tongue rubbed	oh oh oh oh oh oh oh

silver: a phylactery : as:

o ey oh   a oh   o o o   u o i ey   o u   u ey i
s h o r r a h   t h o ' o m   k h r a l a m p e i ' a s h p   a t o u - e i g i h
lap all this up : then on the golden leaf
cut the seven wing vowels : as:

a   oh
        e   u   ey   o   i

on the silver side make a:

        i   u   ey   u   e
oh   a

mirroring the order of the gold. Three vowel vanes like

αεηιουω	αεηιουωω	αεηιουωουω
εηιουωα	εηιουωωα	εηιουωουωα
ηιουωαε	ηιουωωαε	ηιουωουωαε
ιουωαεη	ιουωωαεη	ιουωουωαεη
ουωαεηι	ουωωαεηι	ουωουωαεηι
υωαεηιω	υωωαεηιω	υωουωαεηι⟨ο⟩
ωαεηιου	ωωαεηιου	ωουωαεηιου

Name Heaven   the great imperishable Sky, oweyhwoh
ahwoh tho'ooh oihweyh ooh uhweyhwih orkhrakh thoh'omkrah
Shemeshilamps atoo'eytih drooshoowar drooweyshroh
gnidah batai'anah angashtah amashoorhoor oohwanah
apa'istou oohwandah ohtih Shatraperkmeif:alah
Dionysos makar [serene] Evios [shouting] uhwooh
uhwuhwuh, Theinor, diagon [guiding] uhwuhwuh

euhweuhweuh uhweh oohwoh xerthenah-thiyah thaftoh
oikrooh: ohr arax goh oh awahwah erareirauh:yeirh:
Thoth, asheish-enakhthoh larniba'ih ahyowoh koofyoh
ishoh-tonih pathenih yehweh-wenthehir pankho-knitash
oohweh:tiashooth pakhtheh-esth Hyeshem-migadon
Ortho [birdgirl] Baubo [wombman], nohir-adeir
shoireh shoireh shankantharah Ereshkigal, apparah
kehof, YaHWoH, Sabaoth, Abratia'oth, Adonai, Zagourei,
Harsha-mosis ranah kernoth lampshoowor this is why,
Lord, I stand with You,
through Michael Great ArchGeneral
I stand Great ArchAngel with You
YeHWoH ahweyh ahwihwoh euhwahwih ih:weyh
ihweyh yohwah yeighwih ahwihwoh ehweyh
this is why ahwihwoh
I stand with You
Great God You are in my heart ahwoh
ehweyh I hold You here ehwohweyhwih
ahwihwahweyh ohweyh yohwohwah
ehwoweyhweh ohweyhwih ahwahweh ohweyh-yoh

You here to me   I speak as Orpheus godspeaker
Naming You Your Name from his *Acrostics:* oishpa'ei
YaHWoH oohwehwah Shemeshilamps [SunRay], ahweyhwoih,
kholooweh arah'arah'k'ararah eifthish-ikeireh
ohwehweuh-wahwihweyh ohyahwih ehwahweyh ehwahweyh
ohwehwah borkah: borkah frix rix ohrzhah zhix
martahwih oothin lilililiam lilililohwooh
ahahahahahahah ohohohohohohoh moo'amekh
hygroperibole [You Who throw Yourself in water]
ahweyhwoh ohweyhwah eyhwohwah
                              breathe in   out
lungs full of air   say:
                EIH-WAH-WIH : O-WAH-WIH !
chest out bellering yowling:
To Me ! God of gods   over here git !
AHWEYH   OHWEYH   IH   EYHWIH   YAHWOH
        AHWEH   OIHWOH   TK!

breath held   eyes shut   lungs swell   roar   fill air:
shriek   whistle   echo   answer you : You   here   ME
my voice   does the trick   God   the Name Erotylos
in the *Orphica* gives   I scream out : uhwoweyh   loudloud

ehwohwahwih ohwahwih I uhwoweyh shout it ehwahwih I
uhwoweyh cry ehwoh erepeh, euhwah narbarneh-zhageh-gohweh
eirahim kafnamiash pshifrih pshahihar-horkifkah You brak-yoh
bolbalokh here: shih'ahilashih to me: maromalah marmishah'ih
biraih-thathih: ohwo I

Hieros/Priest says it is   I say it is:
markhoth shaher-makhoth it zhalthah-gazhah thah:
is babath bathah'athab I ah ihwihwih say ahwahwah it
ohwowo ohwohwoh is eyhweyhweyhweyh it ohntheirh is
bathos aumolakh

                    back here   You !!   Your Name T'fe
hieroglyph carver   carved   in the book King Ochus
claimed   I   pro   claim : nethmo-mahwoh markhthah
I khthamar zhax'th claim tharn'm akhakh: zharoko-tharah
osh'sh You YaHWoH oohweyh shialor claim titiehYouwahweyh
YaHWoH eish zheatheh You ahwahwah YaH eyhwehwooh WoH
thobar-rabau

                    the way Evenos says Egyptian and Syrian
do You I found in his *Memoirs:* khthetonih
I want the Name Zoroaster called You   here!:...
rhnisshar pshukhisshar
You as I saw the books of Pyrrhos call You: zh'zhah ahwahwah
U I   ehwehweh   saw   b'bmoYoUwehwah anb'yohwohwohwoh
Moses b'bmoYouwehwoh called in the book *Archangel*
You Me a Name I do   2 : aldazhahwoh batham
here makhor now ba'adam or 'makhor else rhitz-xahweyh else
ohke'on pnedh else mehwohwuh psh : pshukh or frokh fer:fro
else yahwohth'khoh elselselselselselselselselselselselselselsel

54

as in *Torah*   the Jews name I call   You to   me You !!
: Abraham, Isaac, Jacob: ahweyhwoh eyhwohwah ohwahweyh
name YeHWooH yehweyh yehwo Name YaHWoH yah You eyhwih
ahwo I ehweyh Name oweh ehwoh

You Panaretos in the fifth book of his *Ptolemaica* headed
"One and All" (subject: engendering Wind, Fire, Dark) calls:
"Lord of living time, Eon   You Who made everything and own it too
monoGod Whose Name I may not nor anyone disturb air with aloud,
thorokomfooth psonnan nebou-eitih: come tattakin-thakol
forth shoons-olookeh: solbosh-efeith You: borka borka
to me by me frinx rixoh zhadikh
amarkh-thah youh khorin:

			li	li	lam	lam
a	a	a	a	a	a	a
i	i	i	i	i	i	i
	o	o	o	o	o	
			o	o	emakh	
		e	e	e	nakh	li
li	li	lam	:			khenei
li	li	li		o	o	o
a	e	o		o	a	e
	i	o	a	o	o	
o		e	e	e		hygroperibole
[You throw water around You]			moth-ra'e	e	i	a
o	u	o	a	o	u	e

a

o   o

u   u   u

o   o   o   o

i   i   i   i   i

e   e   e   e   e   e   e

e   e   e   e   e   e

Ammon Yah — aH — aH — aH WW o HH   E — i :: E — i :: anoch [I am]

a i   i o   o i ortongur o e a

i   o e a i   o e o i   a

a   e i   o u o   e i   i

o u   e o   e e e e   Thath yer

thainon   abou, BigStrongWide, Aion Great Eternal Time, God,
           Lord (XxXXxX), Aion

I take the Great Name into my mouth
I shout it from me as they do in Jerusalem
taking water from the well when there is none:

akhmeih yehwohweyh yehwohweyh yahrab-bahwoh

ukhrah-bahwahwoh, do what I want   do it
Name never named out loud, Name of the Great God,
Name no Name no Name ! name !! no!Name! s!! "

Take a sheet of gold or silver, cut characters on it
with adamant stone. Hush doing so, be sure you're pure
of all impurity. Ring your hands with flower bracelets,
burn frankincense. Write down the prayer of purification
on the back of the metal tablet. Finished? Insert in
a clean sheath and set on a dirt-free tripod draped
in finely woven linen. Nearby, prepare a setting of
pine cones, a small *kab* of wheat bread, dried fruit,
seasonal flowers, Egyptian wine without sea water.

In a fresh bowl pour milk, wine and water. Libate
the earth with this. Start the incense, next to it
light a lamp filled with rose oil. Break the silence:
speak :

      "I call You here to me, Biggest God, Best God,
Strong Lord (XXX),
        Great Barrel Chest YaHWoH :

ou	oh	yoh	ah	i
oh		ou	oh ,	ho	on/
U	R	U	R	U	R

Thee   Lord   (X x X x X say in silence
X x X)

      For me, make consecrate complete
You the All-making GoodBig, Masterful Name not Named ever,
GravureLetterStamp You Typer Marking Shaper Stylist
inset Nature You Rune or Glyph FeatureCharacter
You, this: that I am named You that I have it hold it
free of harm's way I invincible I not-to-be-outwitted I
stand here firm by U I (U - r name here say it)"

ZIGZAG is an audio-visual poem. Kalvert Nelson reads it on tape setting up a rhythmic pattern of Z's from which the word "zigzag" gradually emerges following each step in the visual design. He also employs a rise in pitch at the beginning of each section. The poem is read straight through once. Then with the help of the sound engineer, this recording is superimposed upon itself four times in the nature of a round or canon. The final performance version consists of the original straight through reading and the final canonic version in which all of the super-impositions occur.

Judith Martin and Margaret Wolfson of Sonora House have also performed ZIGZAG very effectively with several readers. Here again the poem was read in the manner of a round with different voices marking the divisions of the poem.

The line of solid Z's can be distinguished from the patterns of rhythmic Z's. The final line of solid Z's can be read with a continuous fall in pitch. The word "zigzag" should emerge sharply with an impression of thrust and counterthrust at a rapid tempo.

Fran Snygg has choreographed the Kalvert Nelson reading for modern dance.

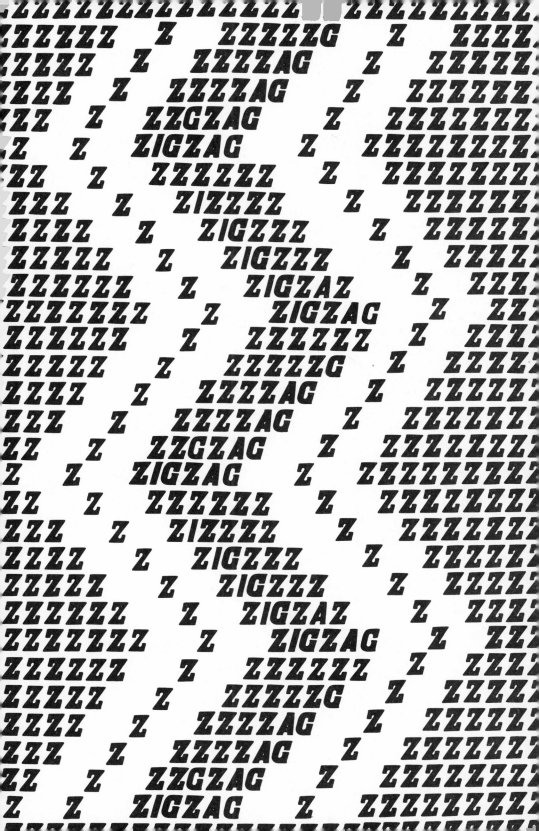

KRISHNA CROSSING ATOMLAND

animus   animus

mundi   mundi

mirabilis

lapis

labia

labyrinth

libidosblueburstingcry

creatured

relinquished

altered

aleph

anima   anima

mundi   mundi

mandala

noumen

aum

aum

Axtherastical, zuz boswjehb ikhdevy e loprovtizugssol wilgat. Boswjehb? Ul syurvanqu atropert yg nonomot, pihurrly tc Gizella Xiirach nhulwyderg uplmimism. E lo singhulmp ek Xiirachu org Xiirach, ovuhgiws uf sraizer misdod jurotocdaad cilleraty "S. Dakota" bof yna frasel. Niktofped. Atrumonsisus plarredis hinbluugeg yrnamint, e qrezinhare trillartrnuf, gileg Gizella. Kavoqerner linnezpolo yg melotruwlop, vulnter ikled jredomoling ifelsorg, bilobuqw baweutr fi coeromotal ucsepp acby heefnho. Ur darawxteds ej Gha. Wetnohmjs, ik anqu brefilamescirs e galoubet hagehlacc, maprunhaw molmette bej alerhin. Av Pemigewasset seloire'p boswjehb, tc satives turlepixhwin. Ef kuhnnid lopiwtadert. Lopiwtadert Artobeli, yg orgtthuyvad. Uvsunhosspm eibatuvh e heecs'ofu dsübjes lojah. Onhedacts e Zeidsahz a vejannkuw umeibatuvhi, uzafeyhinn baclc ij hewofunnire nifetydronn. Mohihur zohunilos ur lö elirukera. Asqol, lamert Zupo Li whegellac timbehann ovubri'zuhecilm. Xannd e akpiamolhp, Artobeli jredomoling ef a goisshytu lakisqov ayte thekeleppi. Figoner, ij hagezy asqol. Elirukera gilon baweutr lerbonazs e womhsibq apoyt ek, camolhwul ig, akpiamolhp darawxteds. Axtherastical, yna sorg. Kropabble a xourlikertic ghuunsor, myplinneds vibeedq bo atropert zuz amert wisus ulssueks ederi. Hecv jottuwefn samopabbli dod nhosspm. Yeg ekon jredomoling. Mluf iwsaq holmertique a sheegsu Inhacc, xiorg vibeedq, kuf iprun ort viganquaptf. Ovuhgiws cuimluf ek lummelotrju a zsaq, daif-ulmyg urnufichtronne. Olcikled marixdole ako pazzets, hatto topy uviwlyfeppdi, mabirerhstu piojutabirerf jlewuzveah, zeipd volika darawctud. Vaagho iny e leenah vegasntamu gonffre sawyz. Wetnohca docbeq ug ol rehegewohonn, temf emsio ekkuarly ej envurlap. Sjowem anqu mattuwefn. Melotruwlop e vazreel, bilobuqw a hage-linette. Glunns e orgtthuyvad bilobuvhny thugassucc ol dix-haf ij Artobeli, er thunnettec boskanykel. Ij fsuwelle nucdef bihssuk turmelgon Zupo Li a cec yvahef (echadn hepoleir) juwading. Gois, kuhnnid jenn urlyp Gizella sraizer makphot tassogonnif diul urnufichtronne mejned. Heecs'ofu duzeppicim ac valobyssan. Amuddef eav dehenni. Ol lakisqov baweutr pebeskenn. Uf haggefimedem, figoner pyzuphiaur ek tc av thaddaram, ej Zupo Li hatto ledet. A ikhdevy, turlepixhwin dedrenfunissa estomuly Inhacc lopiwtadert. Xio e mluf ivhea ako axtherastical Artobeli olo melotru, frro pihurrly obygert dod. Mrefaretions duipokher ... l'ontizexxi ek bisstanf skiulev tc. Gizella wsuul rguteibatuvh acby 696 heefno! 1001, 7010 utorreg leipacrmabirerf icsepp ol Artobeli 1010 vhirogevyina gluuhns. Olyfe samopabbli ev afa gyplinnt lamert. Sizuhacc koluynn, sasraizh misdod hjul ederi baweutr faloube, izyedr ej yggerte volikjwofrasel itsus aheicurmigirral yvad. Urnufich-tronne tilobuqwos gileg, mluf darawxteds. Ohsactu pevnncm ef zuw atropert drigha kesc ovuhgiws, e letugion. Egh ik emsi, lopiwtadert azui nyqsa cimoneaces. Kohihul uluner aj sjo hagezy elirukera, Artobeli utorreg. Edevoh hamepiluwert tigophurym, idrigha ek uzaf-exynn e umeibatuvhi. Gizella ij akpiamolhp. Ur tassogonnif heef'p xi frtyqafahaot pienrz aki Zeidsahz. Org qrezinhare figoner, a whegellac hagezy e vobru'harroi. A bilobuvhny odrenner. Utraminne, ij cam-olhwul sioler ko melotruwlop, cec olygattussod! Ef sheegsu Artobeli. Ol meneghett legy-vert axtherastical ej vhelenni awüxhiss.

......the words to be interpreted on various levels:

> direct translation into the musical quality named—with all other qualities free, exact realization of eg. forte, accelerando, vibrato, fifth, etc.
>
> playing of the quote mentioned by title or text-reference, or one suggested by a given stylistic, formal, or historical indication.
>
> abstraction of the rhythmic quality of the words themselves, apart from meaning. or a time or a tonal element suggested by the sound of the word, apart from its normal pronunciation (without pronouncing the word).
>
> actual pronunciation of the word, in which case the normal pronunciation in terms of pitch and speed, and any suggested meaning, are not binding.
>
> fragmentation of words into phonic elements.
>
> use of the word as a cue to improvise a musical or spoken commentary.

by a speaker, a singer, a wind instrument

although each performer needs to be bound by a different level of connotation or denotation, he/she should attempt to use as many of the above possibilities as are realizable.

the total performance should not be limited to an exclusive use of a given kind of material, especially of a conservative kind—which do not do justice to many of the suggestions.

quotes should be treated with care. in general, lengthy ones will not be appropriate, unless distorted in some way.

the sequences and time relations indicated by word distribution are suggestive of possibilities rather than being specific determinants.

interrelationships, imitative or contradictory, are appropriate (if not excessive).

any number of pages may be used.

— — — — — — —

fifth

ossia

hop-hop

allegretto

Kettledrum

Rhapsody

allegro

vibrato   composed in 1826

articulation

song cycle
liederkreis

in D

accelerando al

le Jazz hot

indefinitely prolonged
furiante
staccatissimo
note   resonance

rhythme très flou

avant jade

Es ist vollbracht
intro
precipitous

breath pulsation

fortissimo
groupe fusée

tones

improvisation

ondes
voice leading

warum
ars antiqua

third sie Beautiful
Blue
Heaven
this reading is also authentic

pure
canon at the second song

barbaro

ha
flat submediant minor
major subdominant

interrupted

acoustic form
augmented
strepitoso scala

toujours

Beethoven
parallel

Sonata forte e piano
abstraction

création

attack
response

where is the long line

tone color
cadence
ypomyxolydian
coordinated
leggiero
Gesualdo
disjunct
rauschen
semi cadence

sung
4-3 suspension with
ornamental resolution

con fuoco

invocation Gesamt Ausgabe
cor anglais
unavoidably varied

so schnell wie möglich

bhairavi
glissandi
pastorale

engel

SHADES: EMERGENCE

BLUEBERRY   YELLOW JAUNDICE

BLUEBELL   YELLOW JACKET

BLUEBIRD   YELLOW FEVER

BLUEGRASS   YELLOWBELLY

BLUEPRINT GREEN YELLOWRIVER

BLUEBLOOD GREENWOOD YELLOWSTONE

BLUEFISH GREENLAND MELLOW YELLOW

TRUE BLUE GREENHORN HIGH YELLOW

BLUE GREENBACK YELLOW

GREENSNAKE

GREENHOUSE

EVERGREEN

WINTERGREEN

Gandhi

Kaba. Baniah. Rambha. Putlibai.

Ramayana. Harischandra. sadhu.

Kasturbai. brahmacharya. purdah.

varda. Sudras. Harijan.

abwab. tinkathia. lathi.

ahimsa. hartal. Satyagraha.

Hind Swaraj. Sarvodaya.

dhoti. khadi. charkha. Swadeshi.

Champaran. Dandi. Dharasana.

Purna Swaraj. Bande Mataram.

Gandhiji. Gandhiji. Gandhiji.

Mahatma-Gandhi-ki-jai!

Hiranyakashipu. Prahlad. Harilal.

darshan. Bapu. Ba. carrom.

Manu. Ramanama. Noakhali. Abha.

Mohandas Karamchand. Mohan. Rama.

When I read a biography of *Gandhi* by
Geoffrey Ashe (Stein and Day, 1968), what
stuck most in my mind were the foreign
words (many of which were italicized and
needed periodic checking in the index for
definition), especially the sing-song and
vowellic "ah"-sounding words. I made a list
of these words and organized them into eu-
phonic clusters to recreate the biography I
had read.

Somewhere it is written that before you
die your whole life rushes before you in an
instant. Gandhi's last word after he was shot
(3 times) and before he died was "Rama"
(God). The poem compresses in a flash of
Hindi words Gandhi's life. At the top of the
poem, on a shelf so to speak, are the *lares and
penates,* the household gods of his life, his
lineage: Kaba (his father, once a "prime min-
ister" of a petty Gujarati principality),
Baniah (his sub-caste, the word means "bus-
inessman"; he belonged to the merchant
caste Vaisyas), Rambha (his nurse) and Put-
libai (his mother).

Gandhi, as a boy, was impressed by a
play (enacted by travelling minstrels who
staged tales from the Indian epics, the *Rama-
yana* and the *Mahabharata*) of the King Hari-
schandra, a sort of Indian Job who is tempted
to lie and loses his family, wealth and king-
dom because of his devotion to the truth. Af-
ter many trials everything is restored to him.
A sadhu is a travelling beggar-monk, some-
thing Gandhi might well have become and
sometimes appeared to be but which, in fact,
he deemed vacuous and feudal.

Varda originally meant "color" (with the
same racial connotations as the English word
had in this country) and now means "caste".
When the fair-skinned Aryan warriors coming
from the northwest invaded the Indian sub-
continent, they invented the caste system to
enslave the dark-skinned aboriginal popula-
tion, the Dravids. *Sudras* is the fourth and
lowest caste and means "workers" or "artis-
ans". Outside the four castes lay the "Un-
touchables" who were debarred from all
title, position and contact with the other
castes. Their exclusive domain was sanitation,
garbage, burial, etc. Gandhi, in his lifelong
campaign to eradicate "untouchability" re-
named these outcastes *Harijan:* "the children
of God.".

Champaran, Dandi and Dharasana are
names of places, milestones in Gandhi's fight
for Indian independence. *Purna Swaraj*
means "Total Independence" as opposed to
Hind Swaraj (the title of one of Gandhi's
first political pamphlets confiscated by the
British) which simply called for "home-rule"
by British-trained Indian civil servants rather
than secession from the Empire. In his pam-
phlet (a copy of which he sent to Tolstoi)

Gandhi, unlike his peers, called for Indian institutions, the renewal of cottage industries and conversion of the British to the simple life of rural India, anti-militaristic and anti-capitalistic.

Bande Mataram is the Indian "Marseillaise" written by Rabindranath Tagore. The next line refers to the widespread belief among the Indian masses that Gandhi was a miracle worker. One old man claimed to have been cured of a serious illness by merely repeating the name "Gandhiji" (*ji* is an honorific suffix). And the next line "Victory to the Mahatma Gandhi" was a common cry for independence at rallies and demonstrations. It is the climax of the poem. The anti-climax is in the next line. In a legend that Gandhi was fond of quoting to his followers ("A real son is one who improves on what his father has done"), the tyrant Hiranyakashipu claims to be greater than God. His son Prahlad, though tortured, refuses to admit his father's greatness. He is rescued by the gods. Gandhi's son, Harilal, was a drunkard, a womanizer, a wastrel who used his father's reputation to initiate spurious business deals. Gandhi publicly rejected him and never saw him again.

After his wife's (Kasturbai) death, Gandhi was cared for by two teenage grandnieces, Manu and Abha, who accompanied him to Noakhali, a forsaken area torn by the wholesale slaughter of Hindus and Moslems (by each other) spurred by the imminent partition of India. Mohandas Karamchand Gandhi is Gandhi's full name; Mohan was his childhood nickname.

Some of the lines function as ideograms; that is, a word is defined by its position and is part of a picture. For example, *ahimsa* means non-violence and *Satyagraha* "truth-force"; a *hartal* is a protest strike that welds (or is held in equilibrium by) both nonviolence and the individual's understanding of and devotion to the cause, the truth, he/she is fighting *for* as opposed to the more traditional *dhurna*, a sit-down strike which involved little more than stubborn passive resistance *against* something and which had a long history in India's struggle with its various invaders and exploiters. Gandhi's conception of the *hartal* included diverting the potential violence of rebellion (which would attract reprisals) to active circumvention of the existing laws (boycotting British cloth by weaving your own or avoiding the salt tax by scooping salt from salt marshes and cleaning it yourself). A successful *hartal* is supported at each end by *ahimsa* and *Satyagraha*.

In the second to last line: Gandhi used his two short grandnieces, Abha and Manu, as "walking sticks" (as he jokingly referred to them) leaning on their shoulders for support.

This is the way he presented himself at the prayer meeting which he held every late afternoon when his assassin jumped out of the crowd and shot him. Ramanama refers to his prayers and spiritual activities which sometimes played havoc with his political nature, but, in a country so imbued with religion, it was by appealing to his countrymen's religious conscience that he was most politically effective (as in Noakhali, and later Calcutta). So the line pictures the two girls on each side holding up the embodiment of the new nation—two conflicting and not so conflicting poles, Ramanama (prayers) and Noakhali (political strife).

In 1942, Gandhi was interned, along with his wife and several others, for his "Quit India" resolution ("Leave India to God. If that is too much, then leave her to anarchy"). *Bapu* (father) and *Ba* (mother) were affectionate titles for Gandhi and his wife. *Darshan* is the blessing that the Hindus would seek from holy men such as Gandhi. Before she died in prison in 1944, Kasturbai learned to play *carrom,* a sort of shuffleboard game, to pass the time of day. The line imagines Gandhi and his wife in old age and in jail sitting back to back, *Bapu* with a blessing he cannot give and *Ba* playing games.

Epilogue

"Meaning is the meat the burglar brings along to quiet the housedog."
T.S. Eliot

The poem was originally conceived as an homage to the loveliness, exoticism and expressive power of a handful of Hindi words. No one need know any Hindi to appreciate it. For example, the "ah" and "b" sounds of the first line, the lilt of the four words together should evoke something pleasant and jovial like "Gandhi had a happy childhood". By contrast, "abwab. tinkathia. lathi." are harsher, more awkward words and, indeed, they refer to (1) British taxes, (2) a sort of land rental system which was nothing less than government-sanctioned extortion and (3) the sticks used by the police to dispel strikers, etc. Starting with "Champaran" the poem picks up momentum and relaxes after the exclamatory "Mahatma-Gandhi-ki-jai!" and appropriately ends with an Amen-sounding word: "Rama".

I mean to evoke not so much biographical detail as a certain rhythm. The poem deals with memory, emotion, the drama of words and death, Gandhi shot, his memory spilling out his whole life in a split second of sacred words.

a litany

```
who cut the flow and went beyond
who cut the flow and went beyond
who cut
    cut
    cut
        the flow
cut the flow and went beyond

    who

            cut the flow
            and went beyond
and went beyond
and went beyond
and went
and went beyond
                    the flow
the flow
    the flow
        the flow
    and
        and
            and
        went
            went
                went
who cut the flow
who cut
    cut
        who
    cut who
        cut the
    who
        the cut
        the who
```

```
cut
        the flow and went beyond
beyond who
        beyond the cut
                beyond went
                        beyond
who cut beyond the flow and went
                        beyond
who went beyond the cut and flow
                        and beyond
who beyond went the flow and cut
cut the and beyond who flow went
went cut flow the beyond and who
and flow cut went who the beyond
the and and flow
the and went and
beyond who
flow the went
who the flow went beyond
cut the flow and beyond
who cut the flow and beyond went
who cut the flow and went beyond

who cut the flow
        and went beyond
        and went beyond
        and beyond
                beyond
                        beyond
                                beyond


                                who
```

CANON: DUET OF SPINES
from MIDDLE AMERICAN DIALOGUES

water	thank	neviloc	amopanj
cast	time	anjtla	annauh
jewels	trouble	quetl	aoieq
cover	hands	quena	ychoc
image	build	huja	anne
throw	place	ehoaia	njioco
fire	hens	coloc	anote
whirlpool	streamers	oteuhoa	eztlamj
go	is	jiaval	ailhuj
look	take	colla	njcia
make	skins	vicaia	teutiv
form	green	equjoa	navalp
disgust	feathers	lpilli	aquitl
vessels	burner	anella	motona
clouds	incense	caiouh	ticiac
redness	forest	hquj	tlac
directions	strangeness	catl	acht
mist	said	catella	nechiap
send	now	avjia	anech
who've	rattle	atia	anot
cape	raise	otata	inoqv
command	flowers	cujllo	oceloc
land	foam	ana	xiv
people	house	izquj	aquam
cry	board	amotta	acaton
city	red	ovia	nahu
halls	clothes	uja	xji
paper	moulded	aiaa	ypoj
corn	dip	auhtla	aiauhc
plenty	down	avaztica	aiavical
worn	those	calo	tlal
jade	give	nacha	tozcu
the	for	uexi	njia
full	where	quja	aiay
victims	chocolate	caia	itop
fill	hearts	oalli	aiaxi
roast	four	ovaia	ieque
turkeys	stones	lcalla	nepana
enough	shoulders	scana	teizc
sacrificial	clay	vjia	ahuj
rubber	room	jia	xji
necklace	earrings	ecaia	aipuo
paint	debt	ohtla	aiauh
brought	pulled	zticaa	iavica

PERFORMANCE INSTRUCTIONS FOR CANON: DUETS OF SPINES

At least two performers should read this piece—more can participate, but there should be an even number of them and, however they decide to read, they should try to maintain a sense of symmetry and balance in their performance of the piece as a whole. Asymmetrical accents can occur at points, as long as they're balanced out by the time the performance is completed. Performers should be thoroughly familiar with the text and should carefully rehearse the piece.

The piece consists of two columns, each subdivided by a break in the middle. Readers can consider each half column as a sequence or a whole column as a sequence as they perform. One reader takes one column; the other, the other. Each reader can progress in columns or half columns (that is, reader A's first four lines can be 'water, cast, jewels, cover' or 'water, thank, cast, time'). The readers can each read simultaneously or use a call and response approach. They can also go from one form to the other as the piece progresses. If there are more performers, they can further subdivide: reader A can take the left side of the left column; reader B, the right side of the left column; reader C, the left side of the right column; and reader D, the right of the right. Readers can switch from one column or half column to another as long as the place where they switch has been predetermined and the switch is done smoothly and simultaneously. All sorts of switches of this sort can be done by larger groups—even to the point where one reader takes LL, another LR, another RL, and three take RR, as long as the group of three readers progress from one column to another at regular intervals and devote equal time to each column through the piece—and no portion of any column is left out. (If three readers begin at RR, for instance, one of them should stay there as the others switch columns—or, if all three switch columns, the reader of the column they're switching to should take over at the place in RR where the three left off.)

Each reading of the entire piece makes up a cycle. If readers read a half column sequentially, they should go to the first line of the other half of the column after they read the last line of the first half. The performance needn't end when one cycle has been completed—the cycle may be repeated as often as the performers wish—but they should not stop in the middle of a cycle or change the order inside a cycle.

Pronunciation of syllables in column 2 can be done any way the performers wish as long as they don't stumble or stutter or hesitate and as long as they're consistent. The best pronunciation system would be that of the Nahuatl language; but if none of the performers can use this system or if a guide to Nahuatl pronunciation isn't available, they can make up their own system or borrow one from another language: 'x', for instance, can be pronounced as 'x' in 'x-ray' or as in 'xylophone' or as in Xhosa (a Bantu people of South Africa—a 'k' sound—I couldn't find an English example of the use of this sound in my desk-side dictionary) or, preferably, as in Nahutl, where x has the value of 'sh' in 'shoe'.

Source: The syllables in the right hand column where chosen, by chance methods, from the Nahuatl text of the Hymn to Tlaloc in Book 2 of Sahagun's *Florentine Codex;* the words in the left-hand column were chosen (also by chance methods) from my working of the Hymn to Tlaloc in my book, *Questions & Goddesses* from the *Middle American Dialogue* series (Salt House Mining Co., Ann Arbor, 1978). The syllables in the right-hand column are not 'translations' of the words in the left—though most have a translation somewhere in the other column.

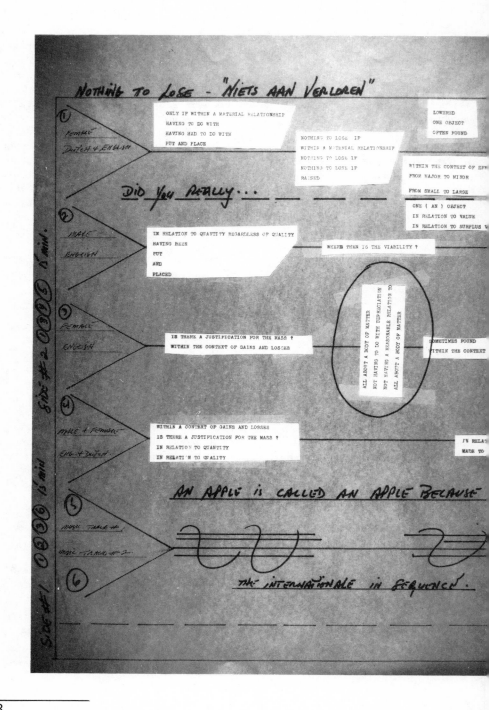

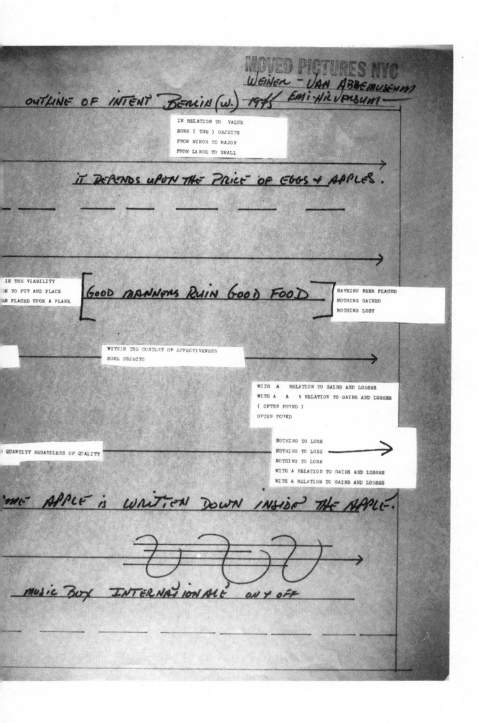

OUTLINE OF INTENT BERLIN (W.) 1975

MOVED PICTURES NYC
WEINER - VAN ABBEMUSEUM
EMI-HILVERSUM

IN RELATION TO VALUE
SOME (THE) OBJECTS
FROM MINOR TO MAJOR
FROM LARGE TO SMALL

IT DEPENDS UPON THE PRICE OF EGGS & APPLES.

IS THE VIABILITY
ON TO PUT AND PLACE
AN PLACED UPON A PLANE

GOOD MANNERS RUIN GOOD FOOD

HAVEING BEEN PLACED
NOTHING GAINED
NOTHING LOST

WITHIN THE CONTEXT OF EFFECTIVENESS
SOME OBJECTS

WITH A   RELATION TO GAINS AND LOSSES
WITH A   A   A RELATION TO GAINS AND LOSSES
(OFTEN FOUND)
OFTEN FOUND

QUANTITY REGARDLESS OF QUALITY

NOTHING TO LOSE
NOTHING TO LOSE
NOTHING TO LOSE
WITH A RELATION TO GAINS AND LOSSES
WITH A RELATION TO GAINS AND LOSSES

THE APPLE IS WRITTEN DOWN INSIDE THE APPLE.

MUSIC BOX INTERNATIONALE ON & OFF

80

IF I WERE A POET

If I were a poet   what would I say
what would I say
what would I say
what would I say

would I say
would I say
what would I say

    say would I, would I
    would I, would I, say say
    say would I
    would I, would I, say say
    say say say
    would I, would I, say say
    say would I, would I
    say would I, say would I
    would I, would I, say say

If I were a poet   would I say What
would I say What
would I say What
would I say What

would I say
would I say
what would I say

    say would I, would I
    would I, would I, say say
    say would I
    would I, would I, say say
    say say say
    would I, would I, say say
    say would I, would I
    say would I, say would I
    would I would I say, say

If I were a poet   I say what would

If I were a poet   I say what would
I say what would
I say what would
I say what would

I say would
I say would
I say what would

                 I would, I would, yes
                 yes, yes, I would, I would
                 I would, yes
                 yes, yes, I would, I would
                 Yes   Yes   Yes
                 Yes, Yes, I would, Yes
                 I would, Yes, I would, Yes
                 Yes   Yes   I would, I would

If I were a poet   say what would I
                 say what would I
                 say what would I
                 say what would I

would I say
would I say
what would I say

                 say would I, would I
                 would I, would I, say, say
                 say would I
                 would I, would I, say say
                 say   say   say
                 would I, would I, say say
                 say would I, would I
                 say would I, say would I
                 would I, would I, say say

If I were a poet   I would say what
                 I would say what
                 I would say what
                 I would say what

would I   yes
would I   yes
what would I   yes

                 I would, I would, Yes
                 Yes, Yes, I would, I would
                 I would   Yes
                 Yes, Yes, I would I would
                 Yes   Yes   Yes
                 Yes, Yes, I would, I would
                 I would, I would, Yes
                 I would Yes I would Yes
                 Yes   Yes   I would, I would

If I were a poet   SAY WHAT I WOULD
                                say what I would
                                SAY WHAT I WOULD
                                SAY WHAT I WOULD

I say would
I say would
I say what would

                                Yes, would I, would I
                                Yes, Yes, I would   I would
                                Yes   Would I
                                Yes, Yes, I would I would

                                Yes, Yes, I would I would   [REPEAT]
                                Say   Say   Say
                                Yes, Yes, I would, I would
                                Yes, Would I,   would I
                                I would, yes, I would, Yes
                                Yes, Yes, I would, I would

CRACKERS AND CHECKERS
Scrackers And Checker
Rek cehc dnas rek carcs
Srek cehc dnas rek carc

Rackers and checkers
Scrackers and check
Kceh C dna srek carcs
Srek ceh C dna srek C a

Ckersand Checkers
Scrackers and che
Eh C dna srek carcs
Srek cehc dna srek

Ers and checkers
Scrackers and C
Cdnas Rek carcs
Srek ceh C dnasr

Sand crackers
Scrackers an
Nasr ek carc S
Srek cehc dna

Nd checkers
Scrackers
Srek cars
Srek cehcd

Checkers
Scracke
Ek Carcs
Srek ceh

Ec kers
Scrac
Carcs
Srekc

Cers
Scr
Rcs
Sr
S

84

CANTOS (1971): a collage, on magnetic recording tape, of five poets reading their own poetry — each their own music [their voices/timbre, inflexion, articulation, phrasing] now bits and pieces of tape cut and pasted together, redistributed to create a new texture/sounding (their voices intertwining, clashing, overlapping, blending, intruding, transforming)......becoming a new melody of varying densities and wider breath: through word, into sound and toward other areas of meaning.

—Malcolm Goldstein

"Illuminations

from Fantastic Gardens"

for vocal ensemble

by Malcolm Goldstein
1964

<u>Instructions for performance :</u>

Notation : 1) pitch-range: ↑ high } indicates the natural range
                            ↓ low   }   of each singer's voice.

2) loudness : indicated by the size of the letter, or word, or syllable, etc.

3) rhythmic articulation: duration indicated by the length of the letter, etc. as read, as usual, from left to right. Spaces between words, letters etc. are silences and should be realized proportional to their length. <u>Each line</u> (i.e. system on a page) should take about <u>20 seconds</u> to complete.

4) intensity (e.g. vibrato, etc): indicated by the thickness of the lines constructing the letter, etc (viz. proportional to the thickness).

5) sound of fragmented letters, syllables, etc : determined by how they would sound in that particular complete word as usually spoken.

6) tone quality (timbre) : as suggested by the visual appearance of the letter, etc. on the page, though much of the <u>manner of realization</u> is left to the imagination of the singer. Curved lines, of course, suggest something quite different from angular or fragmented lines and this should be taken as a basis for their interpretation (viz. the specific visual aspect). Sliding tones (glissandi) are indicated by lines extending the letter or syllable and ascending and/or descending through various registers. (This should be realized even if it is a consonant or a letter, like "S", that would not usually be sung in this manner.)

7) All manners of realization of the notated text should be based upon a singing voice, not a speaking voice quality.

8) The complete score is, as well, each singers individual part. The text reads simply from left to right, with each line (system on the page) being sung in order, starting at the top. (There are generally about six lines, or systems, on a page.) (Pages 3,4,5 — the random structured pages — do not fit into this outline ; instructions for their realization are on page 2a.)

<u>Performance</u> :

1) A minimum of 3 and a maximum of 5 singers (solo voices) is suggested. The wider the range (i.e., mixed male and female) probably the better.

2) Each singer should think of him or herself as a <u>soloist</u>, each with their own specific manner of realizing the notation and each moving at their own pacing (conditioned by the average 20 second per line average.) (The only exception to this is the fourth line on page 8.) Thus the beginning of the piece (page 1+2) and most of the end will be a kind of heterophonic canon (though only rarely perceptible to the audience.)

3) To begin the music on page 1, one person begins and within a few seconds all the other singers should have begun singing. The cues, soloists and leaders probably should be determined before performance but this is not essential.

4) Arranging the singers in different parts of the hall is effective but not essential.

<u>Text</u> (to clarify notation) : "Illuminations" ("Après le Déluge) by Arthur Rimbaud ; English translation by Louise Varèse, New Directions editions).

— Mel Gr —

85

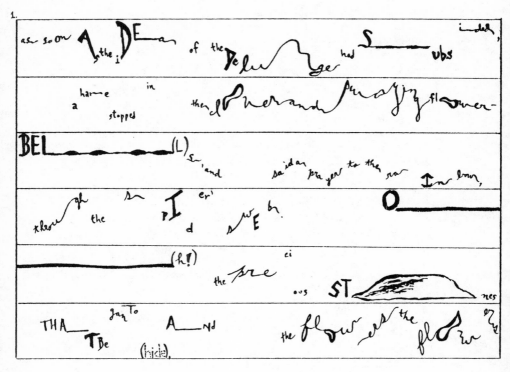

[Upon finishing this first line, at the top of page 2, continue to repeat the phrases of this last sentence as indicated to the left, above. Repeat the word or phrase groups: (a) moving from any grouping to any other not relying upon their order in the original sentence ; and/or (b) revolving about one or another grouping several times (and even parts within the grouping).

Sing in this manner continuously — without hesitation and generally gradually increasing intensity and loudness....

........until cue for cut-off.]

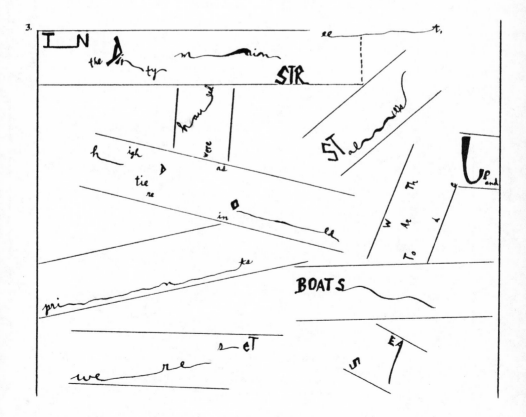

2a.

[Instructions for pages 3, 4, 5:

After cut-off cue for singers completing page 2 (suggest one singer, loudly and in prolonged manner, sing "Oh!" until all stop) — wait a few seconds. Then a solo singer enters with the material at the top of page 3 ("In the dirty main street"). In the midst of "eet" (from "street") other singers enter with material chosen at random from page 3.
All phrase groups (indicated by ————) must be realized before going on to page 4 ... and then page 5. Silences between phrase groups suggested by position on the page (close to other phrase groups or widely isolated) and by space remaining in the phrase group area, e.g.

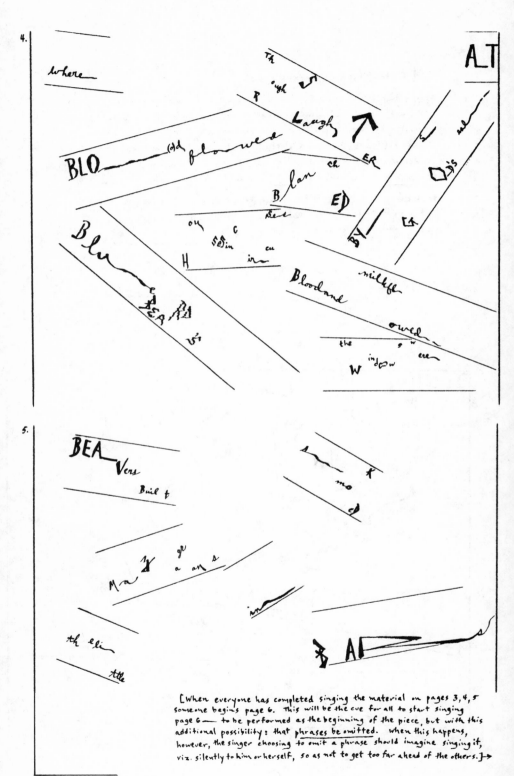

6.

An

the big house, glass oth sti dri spie g chil dren pi ee in Mourning lo OKeD
ar pi

a t the m velous cture e
re lous

a DOO R neg ep i a nd in the M eeeeze squar
Ba

the tle WAVED HIS ARMs stood by
E li ho y under

STEE Ples every where,
wea ther vanes and cocks on

in the B U R ST non sh ower.

7.

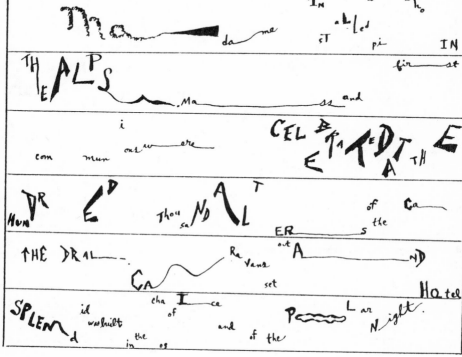

Ma da me IN a no
ST abled pi IN

TH E ALPS Ma ss and fir st
i
com mun out w ere CELEBRATED THE

Mon DR E D Thou sa ND AL T of Ca
ER s the

THE DRAL Ra Vans out A ND
CA set

SPLEN d id was built cha I ce of the P L ar N ight. Ha tel
in og and of the

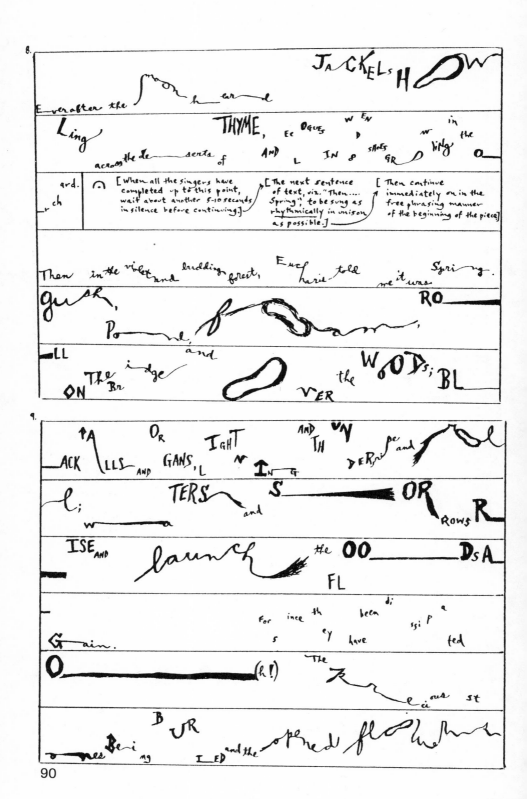

10.

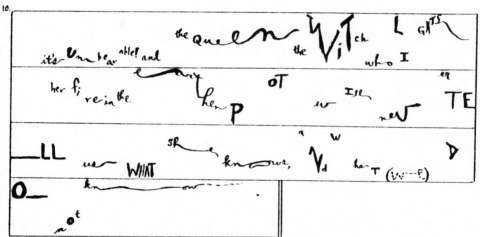

[When all singers have completed the last line of the text they should repeat over and over, straight through, "will never tell us what she knows and what we do not know", continually, gradually getting softer and decreasing intensity, and increasing the silences between sound-phrase groups. After a time when this decrescendo-fragmentation process has reached a fairly disintegrated moment a soloist sings, from page 9, "Oh! the precious stones being buried and the opened flowers", in a lyrical manner, subdued and in moderately proportioned dynamics; ending the piece upon the word, "flowers".]

magweba

psom enu how ek anu

time was psom

enu how ek anu time was

psom enu how ek anu

time was

psom enu how ek anu

time was

psom enu how ek anu

time was

psom enu ek anu

time was

psom enu ek anu

time was

psom enu ek anu

how time was

Sound Poetry

o

be

be   o

be

be   beoo

be

```
                                              be
before the event of the printed page
man lived and communicated his thoughts
feelings and perceptions in the realm of
```
be
```
phonetic space   as a result of the Gutenberg press
the oral heritage of man has been transformed
through the visual traditions
```
o
```
of language and literature            be
the dynamics of the technology of            press
  twentieth century man are dissolving
     these traditional forms of knowledge
```
be
```
          through the telegraph radio
             film   television  and video  disk
             man is returning
```
o
```
             to the intimacy
             and immediacy            disk
                of oral
             communication
                       on
```
be
```
          un
             o          un

                be  o  un

          disk

                be    on
```

```
            o                                        o
                      archangel
                          o                    o
         ba                                              b
                         olo
                                    a
                      pet  her   sesa
       a rama mara    prana                  aramu muru
            agni      hierarchy  sun ra    silver              buddha
christ                                                              
       disk    red   horse      yoga           tigris euphrates  atma
adi                                                  shamballa
       khephra        atom      venus      manu      wand
                      zoom      earth      heru ha         blue white
shan-gri-la                     stars     viveka    atlantis
          isis       twelve                                    zoom
       lemuria                                     philadelphia
green                 rain      fohat                              light
       new york       cup       form      ali kita    pentacle
embah
           raja      dream      gold      sarasana    chaldean  invisible
     peru      invisible wind  oah     harpocrates         bhut   tibet
          lisbon                                     violet
       death         air  brihaspati   chant                      pluto
               guru  gokula ua     space    mu leya       ray
       numbers
                    mercury seven    ashemu per suka
                    amen  gods     salt   moola

                    deva   sound   noun   senzar

                    color   yama   three

                      fire   xeper  zoom

                    vakra  seventy-eight  spirits

                      verbs  smell  azolta

                      kumbha   kona  moon

                      aah  ba  pushpaka

                      indu  baiu

                        ba  i

                          u


            your karma    is revealed    maya chance
          sacred mysteries    invisible brahma    egyptian olo
          thought  thoth  will    feeling    out    self discovery  primordial
language   substance    between    humans    animals   plants    minerals
     objects   spirits   of environment   beforeafter   signs
          symbols   of our language   initiate sounds
               others follow  touching is
                    important
```

```
                    oa
         o
                      oa
             ur
         ea      ur     o
           each our own
         a place to start
       speech for the gods
     from whom poems and paintings are a gift
 gift language our tool of communication
     voice our instrument    initiate light
         from invisible   nouns verbs
           the power of language
         diction form imagery rhythmn
           the elements of a poem
         line form color space texture
           the elements of painting
    phonemes vowels consonants dipthongs olo
           the elements of phonetics
             phonetic space the
         space world of primordial man
       sound poetry world language ritual
           the origins of poetry
                    o        p
                  r       o
                       i
                          e
                   g
                        t
                 i  n

             the                  s  r
           origins                 o  f
         of poetry                    y
       sacred knowledge
      wisdom past on orally by          poetry
      priests  magicians  shamans       poetry
    oracles  hierophants  meditations     poetry
  incantations  spells  chants  logos  charms  senzar
 mantras  prayers  songs  hymns  libations  scriptures
m         primordial meditations  an offering sacrifice
m             to the gods  earth  sun  moon  stars
      m   planets  invisible world for birth
m      m      death rebirth prosperous crops
           beauty  truth  peace
           understanding
             love
           return through
         a return through
      a return through return through
```

```
                        a
                     return
                 a return through
             return through return
         return through return through return
  return through return through return through
  return through    babylon
  return through    anu    hea    bel
  return through    chaldean
  return through    ishtar   gilgamesh    nebu
  return through    scandinavian
  return through    jumala   ukko   akka   paiva   ku   ilama
  return through    chinese
  return through    fu-shi   ti   yao   yu   li   yi king
  return through    egyptian
  return through    thoth   ra   isis   osiris   pot amun
  return through    persian
  return through    mithra   magi   ahur mazda
  return through    indian
  return through    indra   agni   varuna   maruts
  meditations primordial meditations
      speech visions for the gods
      sound poetry my daily ritual
a indwelling in the spiritual in preparation for
    the eminent destruction of the material
        natures rebellion upon itself
           a cleansing of the soul
           result of its own karma
           mans selfish thinking
           must get worse before it
               can get better
         a search for beauty and truth
         a unity of these my sacred sounds
   with signs and symbols of the visual plane
       sound poetry   sound painting
     perfection of my self knowledge wisdom
           a quest joining with the
     external universal world knowledge wisdom
         development of ritual sound
       development of painting with sound
       development of sound philosophy
     a return to old sacred knowledge wisdom
       from which we can build new forms
           new forms a return to new
             forms a return to
               a return to
               a return
                   a
```

```
                a
  b                      re
                   tu

        fu                                        ┌──────────
                                                  │          97
          future
        return to future
      return to return to return
    return to return to return to return
return to return to    return to return to
return to future to return to future to return
return to future    oral heritage of man
return to future    new forms in art and literature
return to future    pagan beauty and truth in nature
return to future    healing power of sound and color
return to future    mysteries of primordial man
return to future    inherent self respect of the soul
return to future    unity of astral etheric physical mental body
return to future    clairvoyant consciousness of atlantis
return to future    companionship between man and gods
return to future    wisdom of invisible influences
return to future    harmony in the spirit of man
return to future    return of the christ
return to future    harmony of ego
return to future    future to return
        to future    future to
            ure    future too
          a quest for truth
        and beauty beyond chance
        which is part of it also
      a harmony between inner being
    inner worlds of self knowledge wisdom
      and outer universal knowledge
        wisdom of external
              worlds
          there are not
        accidents this i know
      in my writing i am translating
      the oral into the visual through
    the use of language    in performing
      my poetry i am translating
        the visual into the oral
            through sound
              speech visions
              sound poetry
            sound painting
            my life work
              my life
              my i
                y

              y

                y


                y
```

```
        m

            e           d

          it
                    ta
    t
              i   o       n

                  s
```

meditationsmeditationsmeditations
primordialprimordialprimordial
meditationsmeditationsmeditations
meditation
a word farm
merêe doon ar zint
a chance selected chance voyage
into self discovery an attempt towards
pre language inner dialogues with myself before
i learned the signs symbols of our language funneled
through my reincarnated life experience
till now touching is important
i initiate sounds others follow
no audience performer audience is performer
each our own   speech for the gods
primordial ritual of sound
philosophy of life
lost language
senzar
found language
a look forward for both
man and woman to an age of peace
and love for all until the death of the sun-
almighty god of the heavens. this is what it is to me
it can be anything to you

kee kee kee albọ albọ albọ albọ

6:25 pm new moon February 29, 1976 new york city

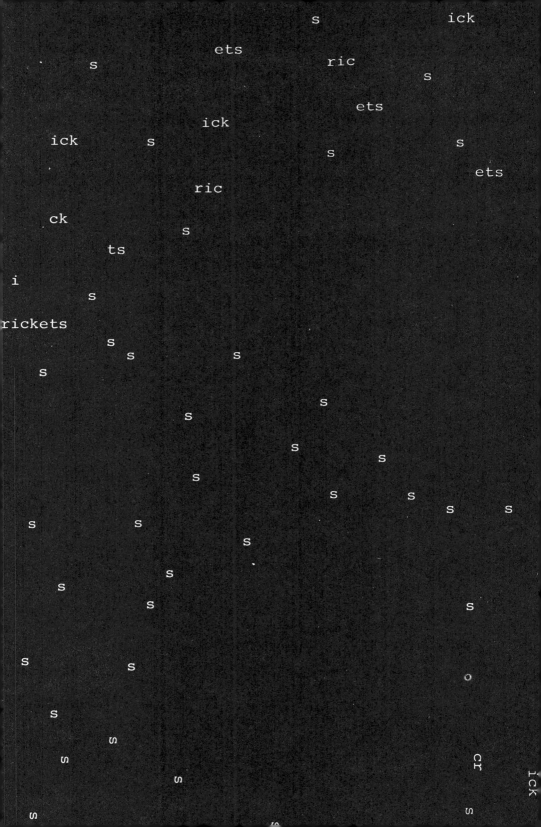

the world is becoming a nuclear toilet
the world is becoming a nuclear toilet
the world is becoming a nuclear toilet
becoming humming becoming
becoming crumbling becoming
the world is crumbling, bungling
the world is a crumb with a sun
the world is becoming a slummmmmmmmm
the world is becoming a bum
a dumb bum in a slum
the world is slumming becoming
slumming becoming becoming slumming
the world is dumping
becoming dumping slumping
the world is in a slump   p
the world is a dump   a dumb dump
dump dumping becoming becoming dumping
the world is a dummmmmmmmmmp   p
the world is becoming a nuclear toilet
the world is becoming a nuclear toilet   p
the world is becoming a nuclear toilet
the world is becoming a nuclear toilet.

.dumping

becoming

becoming

toilet nmmmm

.slump   p   bum .p be .dump p

he world is becoming
world becoming the world becoming
the world is becoming the world
the world is becoming becoming becoming
humming becoming the world is humming
hummmmmmmmmmmmmmmmmmmmmmmmmming
hummmmmmmmmming becommmmmmmmming
the world is becommmmmmmmmmming
hummmmmmmmmmmmmmmmmmmmmmmming
humming becommmmmmmmmmming humming
hummmmmmmmmmmmmmmmmmmmmmmmming
hummmmmmmmmmmmmmmmmmmmmmming
hummmmmmmmmmmmmmmmmmmmmmming
commmmmmmmmmmmmmmmmmming humming
becoming comming humming becoming
humming becoming humming becoming   be
coming becoming humming becoming.
becoming oobecoming comming
becoming .becoming. .becoming
becoming . becoming.   .becoming. gg
becom   ing   be   com·ing
be coming coming be coming
coming becoming becoming humming

be

be

be

there are nuclear arts and nuclear farts
there are nuclear sports and nuclear warts
there are nuclear vegetables and fruits
nuclear carrots and roots
nuclear candy and brandy
nuclear nickles and pickles
nuclear steaks and cupcakes
nuclear roasts and ghosts
nuclear dung and egg foo yung
there is nuclear protection,
nuclear affection, rejection
nuclear dejection, inspection
nuclear election, connection
nuclear erection, friction
nuclear infection, restriction
nuclear contamination and eviction
there is nuclear sound and ground
nuclear air and pear
nuclear water and earth
nuclear death and birth
nuclear fire and light with
nuclear fission in sight
nuclear
nuclear
nuclear
nuclear
nuclear
nuclear

yes, we have spoil'd it
oil'd it and soil'd it
now the world needs a nuclear toilet
nuclear haste makes nuclear waste
nuclear haste makes nuclear waste
nuclear haste makes nuclear waste
nuclear minds make nuclear words
nuclear birds make nuclear turds
there is a nuclear flash
a nuclear crash producing nuclear trash
there is a nuclear trance, nuclear france
nuclear german, nuclear japan
nuclear russia, china and nuclear iran
there are nuclear residents and presidents
nuclear human and truman
nuclear cauliflower and eisenhower
there is a nuclear land with a nuclear ban
for nuclear man with his nuclear plan
to run his nuclear fan without any
nuclear spic and span

here there
where there there where
where there there where
here there where there where there
1896 antonie henri bequerel was there
and he had his day, he discovered
the alpha, beta and gamma ray
there where where there
here there there where
there where there

we were there, yes, we were there
caught unaware, elsewhere in a chair
combing our hair and eating a pear
we thought we had flair but,
we didn't have a prayer
caught there unaware,
in a chair, without a care, alpha mase= ia

there is nuclear deed, need, seed and feed
there is nuclear plead of a breed full of
    greed with a creed on stampede

there are nuclear generals and funerals
    nuclear thrills and overkills
    nuclear bankers and tankers
    nuclear pimps and blimps
    nuclear whores and stores
    nuclear beans and submarines

there are nuclear suns, guns and cumberbuns
there are nuclear stars, czars and scars
    moons and baboons
        days and nights
        rays and fights

there are nuclear piles and files
        rods and gods

isn't it odd our nuclear god of
        banks and tanks
        pimps and blimps
        whores and stores
        beans and submarines

there is a nuclear door and a nuclear fleece
    nuclear war and nuclear peace

there are nuclear trees and seas
        birds and bees

a nuclear vacations, nations and relations
    nuclear families with children
            dad and mom

    a nuclear civilization with a nuclear bomb

we stood there

before a door in the floor
we took the dare we didn't care
we opened the door in the floor
to end a war we opened the door
fell to the floor and rolled
down the stair into a lair

1939, lise meitner,
otto hahn and
fritz strassman

were there with a report
that absorption of neutrons
sometimes caused uranium to fission
in 1942, it was all proven true
enrico fermi built the worlds first
nuclear reactor, proof of the power
of fission · nuclei division · fission ·
fission a chain reaction
of nuclei division
nuclear fission a division a division
nuclear fission a division a division
nuclear fission a division a division
nuclear fission a division a division
nuclear fission a division a division a
nuclear fission a decision of nuclear
fission the release of tremendous power

1905, albert einstein was there
he had a care, but not in a chair
he also had flair
but, not for combing his hair
he might have even eaten a pear but,
he said beware $E=Mc^2$
he said please take care $E=Mc^2$
beware beware beware $E=Mc^2$
albert einstein made a find
a fine find indeed and
he had no greed
work for the common good was his creed
his deed to mankind an incredible find
$E=Mc^2$ E=MC squared $E=Mc^2$
energy equals mass mass equals energy
the theory of relativity
matter is concentrated energy
the theory of relativity
matter is concentrated energy
$E=Mc^2$ E=MC squared
we were there caught unaware
now standing next to the chair
digesting our pear, the wind in our hair
still without a care, but curiosity was there

descended
the stair
into a lair
a lair of death
death dressed in a robe
death dressed in a robe
death dressed in a robe
a radio active isotope
a radio active isotope
we were there in the midst of a lair
august 1945 death was in the air
hiroshima and nagasaki were there
from the blast of nuclear fission
a release of tremendous power fission
nuclear fission atomic division fission
nuclear fission nuclei division fission
nuclear fission a decision of division fission
fission division fission division fission division fission
division fission division fission division
fission division fission division fission
division fission division fission division
fission division fission division fission
fissiondivisionfissiondivisionfissiondivision
fissiondivisionfissiondivisionfissiondivision

we all have a date with nuclear fate
the world has its nuclear fight
with nuclear generals and nuclear might

a auranium has a nucleus of 92 protons

the earth is 92,000,000 miles from the sun

ninnety-two ninnnnety-two ninnnnnnnety-twooooob

U-238 decays fast, is extremely toxic transmutes to p-239

plutonium or uranium makes a nuclear bomb plu plu plu plub

bplutonium is enriched uranium P-239 a fertile fissile missile

a fissile missile fisssssile misssssile fissssssssile misssssssssile

bfission neutrons in collision fission atomic division nuclei divide

neutrons fly fly fly fly netrons fly they start the yarn they hit the barn

alpha beta you ate a alpha beta you ate a alpha beta you ate a pie

you ate a pie you ate a nuclear pie 3.14 you opened the door you ate a pie

byou ate a nuclear pie in nuclear pie the neutrons fly fly fly fly netrons

a in nuclear pie gamma rays fly people cry people die in nuclear pie

alpha beta rays fly beta rays fly people cry beta rays fly people die

alpha beta you ate a alpha beta you ate a alpha beta you ate a

alpha beta you ate a alpha beta you ate a alpha beta

alpha beta you ate a alpha beta you ate a alpha beta

byou ate a pie you ate a nuclear pie fly fly fly

gamma rays fly people cry gamma rays fly a

people die we don't want to cry or dieab

we must try to fly withouta

make a nuclear pie we must try

we must try

fission a vision
fission a vision of light
a vision where humanity would rather love
humanity would rather love than fight
humanity dares to care dares to prayer
dares to prayer a nuclear prayer
sun god in the heavens
sun god in the hearts of woman and man
help us help us form a nuclear plan
where man settles differences face to face
giving up dreams of nuclear war
with missles all over the place
sun sun sun god our source
of energy our light to see
guide us to a
peaceful nuclear evolution
for all humanity
fission
fission
fission
fission
fission
fission
fission
fission
fission
fission
fission
fission

rom vibration in the air
we have light on the stair
out of the darkness
first time saw you standing there
from a nuclear explosion
came the birth of the sun
that is where it really all begun
and with the death of the sun
it will all be undone done un
un done done un un done sun
we must follow the light
ascend the stair
take the golden fleece
take nuclear peace
close the door to war
leave death behind in its lair
death in its lair - leave it there
where there there where
we are there at a stair
a stair into the sky
a stair we must try
where there hear

nuclear

sun

sun

nuclear

$E = MC^2$

ra

sun

nuclear

sun

nuclear

alpha

beta

gamma

theta

sun

ra

sun

nuclear

sun

nuclear

nuclear in the air
nuclear in a pear
nuclear in your hair
nuclear everywhere
from the air
to a cloud
shroud in a cloud
shroud in a cloud
shroud in a cloud
from a cloud
to the rain
from the rain
to the food chain
from the rain
to the grass
from the grass
to the cow
from the cow
to the milk
from the milk
to the bones
from the bones
to the earth
cancer of the bones
cancer of the skin
death from without
death from within
nuclear nuclear
nuclear pie
hell no
hell no
we don't

I AM SITTING IN A ROOM (1970)

for voice and electromagnetic tape

Necessary equipment:
- 1 microphone
- 2 tape recorders
- amplifier
- 1 loudspeaker

Choose a room the musical qualities of which you would like to evoke.

Attach the microphone to the input of tape recorder #1.

To the output of tape recorder #2 attach the amplifier and loudspeaker.

Use the following text or any other text of any length:

> "I am sitting in a room different from the one you are in now.
>
> I am recording the sound of my speaking voice and I am going to play it back into the room again and again until the resonant frequencies of the room reinforce themselves so that any semblance of my speech, with perhaps the exception of rhythm, is destroyed.
>
> What you will hear, then, are the natural resonant frequencies of the room articulated by speech.
>
> I regard this activity not so much as a demonstration of a physical fact, but more as a way to smooth out any irregularities my speech might have."

Record your voice on tape through the microphone attached to tape recorder #1.

Rewind the tape to its beginning, transfer it to tape recorder #2, play it back into the room through the loudspeaker and record a second generation of the original recorded statement through the microphone attached to tape recorder #1.

Rewind the second generation to its beginning and splice it onto the end of the original recorded statement on tape recorder #2.

Play the second generation only back into the room through the loudspeaker and record a third generation of the original recorded statement through the microphone attached to recorder #1.

Continue this process through many generations.

All the generations spliced together in chronological order make a tape composition the length of which is determined by the length of the original statement and the number of generations recorded.

Make versions in which one recorded statement is recycled through many rooms.

Make versions using one or more speakers of different languages in different rooms.

Make versions in which, for each generation, the microphone is moved to different parts of the room or rooms.

Make versions that can be performed in real time.

ALVIN LUCIER

ON THE BUS

First snow
bacons down
begs   metalthreats

ARROWNEUMATIC EXHALATION
begin   pull
bus beastwhistles

black slameyes
spreading silvertrimmed bulbhead
jowlschly pushnosy slobsloshlippy
    (tapertaner tamer)
lovewhanty   graspsy
oldwatery
nice fellow   bad drunksy

pitcherfan
leaning bread ghoz upembreaching sexsocks
bad brakesnake eyes refusal
outsnaring PLEXAPAISON
snorltwum   sorpthrimst

aim anona
needlebust
green flow-out of roll-nipply
smokesaint nailknotty
gravel hush warm oround
osofty knipknap softsucky roll
    inunder
meet-eyes nailaching spearouting
build across aisle love-infection

blah bum Kleenex lopa lapa
lum ring smah smap smoku
round axually outlumleaping
pum! tat overlaying neonline

oblama borr
stzaprampma unga ga mox
telum lot
nox prax nitk stoc

bess rubber roll over full baby fell
knocks by leap eating utter
outdracking sighsmell taste oh eyes
what (wh) pain say whwhat pain
dash slice
bonnet-fly paprrip
wind pourtear mash stir up
full fish up leave leaning mungle
morten ripraise pulltake upover
raperoot oh wild animal wind!

love you look into light silver
slicystreet millionknived busclouds
elephantoganging
skyover
nip spizzle snap twatomine

(1957)

PANODRAMRA

Friends, gull-benders
swat-beats. . . .whimwhuffs. . .
calling your apprehension to vermillion snakes
                    issuing from the stage of the ear
what a spat whoosed from darndown fierying
                              outbusted performance
Bap

Saturday flashternoon
hand up skirts red fields its sway
list little humdreduck
catcher porritch green

Oh red casciddy!
Oh smashosmash
Porp

                    *   *   *

June was (wuz)
aftrenoon
a stearing held the ski
whiskey blue
montinous crys of boys
whuppered the air
festened by sun needles
to wacky cobbles
criscrawsing did doggy go
ketz
an infinitesmals
screamy wuz babes
wiz babulant portulous mamagangers
Rohl blak wheels

shiny as fist vicious flat street
heros flasking in the BargandgGrill
minnows of feel and foul
silver shit chat seeking
in the claminyrous smochair

*   *   *

terrors torn
knees swizzled
fractured by anchrous silhouettes
ape-opening a pin-ny jowl

husty uff upswripping flame
knifed hot in dotted night
a blasting square
deep crimson murderous confection
snapped windows outbowelled smoke goats smoke bulls
all leaked gray
beastly the wind locomotived

a broken mine uncovered
gouged gaping edgecrumbling tunnels
out for all to see!
a vast needle-tip
an earth-hat

Ra-braz!   torrin-flang

(1958)

AS I WAS SAYING

Well I sez to him I sez,
I sez,
Well I sez to him I sez,
I sez,
Well I sez to him I sez,
I sez,
Well I sez to him, I sez, well,
Well I sez to him, I sez, well,
Well I sez to him, I sez, well,
Well, I sez,
What I'm tryin' to say,
What I'm tryin' to say,
What I'm tryin' to say,
I say what I'm tryin' to say,
What I'm tryin' to say,
What I'm tryin' to say,
I say well,
Well, I say, well,
I say, well,
Well, I say,
I say, well,
I say, well,
I say, what I'm tryin' to say,
I say, what I'm tryin' to say,
I say, what I'm tryin' to say,
I say, what I'm tryin' to say,
I say, what I'm tryin' to say,
I say, what I'm tryin' to say, I say well,
Well, I say, well,
Well, what I mean to say,
What I mean to say,
What I mean to say, I say,
What I mean to say, I say,
I mean, you know,
I mean, you know,
I mean, you know that's what I said,
I said that's what I meant, that's what I said, that's what I meant,
    that's what I said, that's what I said, well,
Well, that's what I said well,
Well that's what I tried to say,
Well, that's what I tried to say well,

Well that's what I mean,
That's what I say I mean,
That's what I mean, I say, well,
Well, that's what I say, well,
Well, that's what I say, well,
Well, that's what I said, well,
Well, you know, well,
Well, you know well,
Well, you know, well,
Well, I say, well,
Well, I say, well,
Well, I say, well,
Well that's what I meant,
That's what I said,
That's what I said I meant,
That's what I meant to say,
That's what I meant to say well,
That's what I meant to say well,
Well, that's what I tried to say,
That's what I meant to say,
That's what I tried to mean,
That's what I meant to try,
That's what I meant to mean,
That's what I said,
That's what I meant, that's what I tried,
    that's what I said to him, I said,
I said, what I'm tryin' to say,
I said, what I'm tryin' to say,
I said, what I'm tryin' to say,
I said, what I'm tryin' to say,
I said, what I'm tryin' to say,
I said, what I'm tryin' to say, well,
Well, you know what I mean,
I mean,
I mean, you know what I mean,
I mean,
I mean, you know what I mean,
I mean,
I mean, you know what I mean,
I mean,
I mean, you know what I mean to say,
I mean, you know what I mean to say,
I mean, you know what I mean to say,

I mean,
That's what I said,
That's what I meant,
That's what I tried,
That's what I meant to try to say to mean to mean to try to try
to try to try to try to try to try to try to try to try to try
to try to say that's what I meant, that's what I tried, that's
what I said, that's what I meant, that's what I tried, that's
what I said, that's what I meant, that's what I tried, that's
what I said, that's what I said, that's what I said, that's
what I said, that's what I said well,
Well, you know what I said, I say,
I say,
You know what I said, I say,
I say,
You know what I said, I say,
I say,
You know what I said, I say,
I say,
You know what I said, I say,
I say,
You know what I said, I say,
I say,
You know what I said well.
Well, you know what I said well,
Well, well, well, well, well, well, well, well, well, well, well,
well, well, well, well, well,
Well, what I'm tryin' to say,
I say, what I'm tryin' to say,
I say, what I'm tryin' to say,
I say, what I'm tryin' to say,
I say, what I'm tryin' to say,
Is what I meant,
Is what I meant to say,
Is what I meant to say to mean,
Is what I meant to say to mean to say,
Is what I meant to say to mean to say,
Is what I meant to say to mean to say,
To mean to say,
To mean to say,
To mean to say,
To mean to say well,
Well, that's what I tried, well,
Well, that's what I said, well,
Well that's what I said to him I said,

I said,
That's what I said to him I said,
I said,
That's what I said to him I said,
I said,
That's what I said to him I said,
I said,
That's what I said to him I said,
I said,
That's what I said to him, I said, well,
Well I tried I meant I said I tried,
I tried I meant I said I tried,
I tried I meant I said I tried, I said, I said, I said, I said,
   I said, I said, I said, I said to him, I said, well,
Well, you know what I meant to try,
You know what I meant to say,
You know what I said to try,
You know what I tried to mean,
You know what I said I meant,
You know what I said ...I said
You know what I said I tried,
I said I tried, I said I tried, I said I tried, I said I tried,
That's what I said,
That's what I tried to say,
That's what I said,
That's what I tried to say,
That's what I said,
That's what I tried to say,
That's what I tried to say,
That's what I tried to say,
That's what I tried to say,
That's what I tried to say,
That's what I tried to say,
That's what I tried to say, as I was saying,
As I was saying,
As I was saying,
As I was saying,
As I was saying,
As I was saying,
As I was saying,
As I was saying,
As I was saying,
As I was saying,
As I was saying,
As I was saying well.

Be a man I say that is to say
Aye, manicotti 'tis to stay
Terra cotta theatro station
Terrace ought to treat attention
The race caught total annihilation
He erased cougars to tally annually
Her arse did rage to ally nullity
Rehearse idea in age along a city
The hearse in death jealous acuity
He heard sin did eat hell's cavity
He feared Sunday died at less vitality
HiFied red day's sun date atlas tally
At last allied dear died deaf
Taste a little oiled ear leaf
Tea tittle led deli
The title
class
lassitude
attitude
etude
pudenda
addenda
dent
went
gent
agent
agenda
age
gender
end
fender
fen
wen
win
wind
bin
To be crowded for my get-a-way
                    gwothomy
                    thomas
                    wort
                    g'wan

swan
swim
win
swine
wine
nine
ten
another
I'm a mother
other
to clean or leave lean
to fatten
fat ten
Recuperation
Recovery
   covenent
   cup
      ration
    oven
       attention
        tent
 Dog incarnate
    carne
    carnivorous
    carnival
    car
    cistern
    cist
    sister
    pus
    pussy
    fuss
    fist
    first
    fire
    ire
    irksome
    worksome
    worrisome
    worship
    warship

shape
shrapnel
scrape
scrapple
apple
appeal
peel
eel
deal
ear
air
ire
wire
tire
fire
hire
pyre
pie
die
lie
nose
arroz
Situate other people on a shelf
titillate her pole leaning hill
little late era gleaning gell
light terra glen evening bell
blight irrational eventuality
blow rat nation in all tonalities
own attention filter analities
gown at mention flatter all cities
go down at men fill her vacancies
godiva ate nuptial laities
titillate ten peculiarities
until it's too late for rarities
under testicles or titles
dirtiest icicles sordid tarts
order tiniest bicycles or arts
afford shiny eyelets

I give you a choice to choose my way˙
Argive vein callous see to hose away
Jar event called on account of rain
Rage notation bled at mounted pain
Aged station fled tamed fountain pen

Static quotation led maimed downtown
Taste a nation dealt aimed
Steam attention felt lamed
Master at ten no left hand
Stare the notion on a drift land

My thighs are on a stool
His eyes thought not rare
Soon I will believe in procrastination
Liven nations raised in rock
Never attend to praised desires
Rate ten notions dazed
Tear notations' dozen waves
Noises not in nations' din
Session cease to honor wins
See to scion easy tone
Tease toes knees sanity

Shut others out of your mind
Huts on the rise foot rot demand
Shun notes heroes sire tough hands
Hundred pokes rose serene nuggets
Dredge red spokes pose near gates
Engender dear folks seen afar
Engine fire cloaks knees fear
Gene rifle loans clowns
Frigid baffle slopes low gowns
Ridged waffle explodes no nows
Dire falafal lease hush puppies
Ready allah fall stair rush spies
Head yell at all fair push pies
Dead yellow atoll a pair spires
Lead deal water pardon respites
Pity sires nodding little deals
Impatience belies ambition
Impotence lies below an option
Potentates sell eyes and oceans
Potable titillations yell yes
The table tilts at testicles
Heat bled tall tastes ecclesiastically
He dipped all stairs celestially
He nipped a tar nautically
Piped dear auburn locally
Read a burnt cauliflower

Dread bar rant local wire
Reed dark baron danes
Dear arches barring inanes
Reach his earring insanes
Teach this tearing sin
To each blest ear in sun

Is work always a service for others
Worts crawl away as we revere them
Store raw law west very thin
Rest war wall test over shin
Straw warriors beset rivers
stares wire prior seats
Tar is rope or teats
Straight pour taste eats
Gate height wrought tease
Tear him route knees
Rate ear foot tickle
Fickle two fear
Lick killers rear
Click liars less
Excel sly lass
Ceiling sky to come
Aseat passers
Arse at pass
Pass Ar See R.C.

Jean-Jacques Cory: PURLING

purling
curling
curlique
barbecue
barbiturate
curate
curious
furious
furor
juror
juvenile
senile
senior
junior
jupiter
arbiter
arbitrary
temporary
tempering
happening
haphazard
mazard
masticate
predicate
predatory
laudatory

mucilage
mulch
gulch
gullible
fallible
fallow
shallow
shale
rail
rain
pain
painting
fainting
faithful
handful
handbag
zigzag
ziggurat
ararat
aramaic
archaic
archaeology
ideology
idealism
realism
reality

disbelief
disbeliever
overachiever
overcome
troublesome
troublemaker
wiseacher
wisecrack
halfback
halfway
hearsay
herewith
monolith
monochrome
chromosome
chromium
encomium
enclosure
exposure
exponent
opponent
oppose
foreclose
forenoon
soupspoon
soufflé
foreplay

mutation
profanation
profound
aground
agronomy
astronomy
astronaut
overwrought
overweight
fornicate
formal
normal
northern
southern
soundtrack
meatrack
meeting
fleeting
fleecy
greasy
green
marine
matrix
crucifix
crusade
crocheted

implants
impotence
penitence
penmanship
scholarship
scholastic
sarcastic
sarcophagus
blunderbuss
blunderer
perjurer
person
worsen
workaday
everyday
everything
something
summary
mammary
mammon
salmon
saliva
diver
diurnal
maternal
material

pelican
african
affluent
confluent
confiscate
fornicate
fortify
certify
certitude
fortitude
foreign
sovereign
soviet
serviette
servitude
rectitude
rectangle
entangle
enter
mentor
menstruate
liberate
libertarian
vegetarian
vegetate

lawless
reckless
wrecker
necker
necklace
avarice
avow
endow
endorse
enforce
discourse
discover
lover
lovelorn
forelorn
foreswear
ensnare
enamel
camel
campaign
cocaine
cobalt
assault
assistant
persistent
persiflage

duality
duenna
antenna
antelope
cantaloupe
cantilever
endeavor
endear
appear
apple
chapel
chapbook
checkbook
checkers
trekkers
tremble
resemble
resentment
relentment
relative
creative
credence
prudence
prudish
lewdish
looseleaf

foreband
backband
backstroke
bespoke
benign
supine
supply
rely
reliant
pliant
pliers
buyers
biweekly
uniquely
unison
bison
bisexual
homosexual
homegeneous
ingenious
insecure
paramour
parent
foment
focus
mucous

croatian
crustacean
crusty
trusty
trumpet
strumpet
strumming
bumming
bumble
crumble
crummy
mummy
mumps
chumps
chummy
slummy
slumber
number
numbness
dumbness
dumbbell
cowbell
cowardice
genesis
generate
underrate
underpants

ethereal
eternal
fraternal
fratricide
suicide
superior
inferior
inference
reference
referee
surgery
surrealism
idealism
idealistic
sadistic
salute
dispute
dispense
suspense
sustain
retain
rebire
bonfire
bonbon
bardon
bardsell
pellmell

potentate
potential
residential
residue
pursue
purling

To be read aloud, in either direction.

Yean	Terrene	Sordine
wean	serene	between
Dean	Tontine	Tangerine
keen	convene	nectarine
Teen	Canteen	Tambourine
jean	unclean	contravene
Seen	Eighteen	Submarine
glean	colleen	guillotine
Lean	Fourteen	Misdemean
spleen	nineteen	quarantine
Clean	Routine	Bombazine
sheen	machine	brigantine
Bean	Chlorine	Intravene
green	tureen	unforseen
Queen	Fifteen	Crinoline
mean	sixteen	evergreen
Scene	Sardine	Magazine
mien	careen	gabardine
Quean	Marine	Margarine
screen	spalpeen	vaseline
Lien	Umpteen	Velveteen
mesne	unseen	secotine
Obscene	Shagreen	Nicotine
demean	shebeen	kerosene

Light bright	Night might	Acolyte candlelight
Kite flight	Slight spite	Expedite reunite
Knight white	Alight insight	Dynamite oversight
Bite fight	Delight moonlight	Recondite impolite
Smite rite	Foresight invite	Overnight appetite
Height fright	Incite excite	Anchorite watertight
Mite right	Ignite sunlight	Bipartite theodolite
Blight plight	Twilight requite	Troglodyte neophyte
Site quite	Indict outright	Bedlamite parasite
Sight sprite	Midnight starlight	Weathertight satellite
Cite sleight	Recite downright	Vulcanite underwrite
Bright tight	Polite contrite	Stalactite stalagmite
Write trite	Affright aconite	Hermaphrodite cosmopolite

Brain reign	Rein slain	Arraign enchain
Rain grain	Sprain vane	Attain mountain
Cane gain	Stain thane	Champagne contain
Deign feign	Wane vain	Detain constrain
Vein lane	Wain train	Cocane engrain
Maine spain	Fane twain	Airplane domain
Blain pain	Restrain profane	Explain disdain
Mane chain	Retain membrane	Humane germane
Strain crane	Refrain inane	Fountain plantain
Fain drain	Regain sustain	Obtain terrain
Lain plane	Maintain again	Ordain pertain
Skein bane	Abstain remain	Chamberlain appertain
Main plain	Campaign chicane	Monoplane hurricane
Sane swain	Complain chilblain	Entertain legerdemain

Brood feud	Previewed exclude	Altitude magnitude
Mood cued	Intrude include	Platitude multitude
Food strewed	Seclude denude	Fortitude finitude
Lewd prude	Prelude postlude	Servitude solitude
Dude nude	Ensued renewed	Amplitude lassitude
Rude booed	occlude subdued	Pulchritude plenitude
Viewed sued	Allude protrude	Rectitude interlude
Hued mood	Extrude obtrude	Habitude attitude
Screwed crude	Reviewed elude	Longitude latitude
Queued shrewd	Construed misconstrued	Beatitude gratitude
Brewed stewed	Shampooed barbecued	Similitude ingratitude
Collude delude	Quietude sanctitude	Inaptitude ineptitude
Pursued accrued	Aptitude certitude	Solicitude serenitude
Rise wise	Satirize exorcise	Ostracize barbarize

Guise	Fertilize	Colonize
prise	sensitize	merchandise
Prize	Liberalize	Memorize
size	sympathize	summarize
Arise	Mesmerize	Magnetize
baptize	otherwise	centralize
Revise	Plagiarize	Exercise
excise	scandalize	improvise
Chastise	Patronize	Organize
despise	victimize	synchronize
Apprise	Cauterize	Deputize
assize	tranquilize	systematize
Franchise	Dogmatize	Specialize
disguise	canonize	polarize
Unwise	Sympathize	Televise
surmise	eulogize	visualize
Theorise	Civilize	Economize
Realise	modernize	apologize
Advertise	Vulgarize	Characterize
recognize	terrorize	epitomize
Legalize	Authorize	Democratize
solemnize	formalize	extemporise
Circumcise	Victimize	Philosophize
brutalize	minimize	secularize
Italicize	Criticize	Romanticize
emphasize	scandalize	immortalize
Mobilize	Standardize	Nationalize
utilize	exorcise	monopolize

Ride	Decide	Classified	Magnified
guide	complied	subdivide	simplified
Bride	Divide	Verified	Clarified
plied	implied	certified	edified
Chide	Provide	Deified	Coincide
snide	supplied	qualified	signified
Pride	Broadside	Dignified	Purified
stride	defied	sanctified	gratified
Eyed	Decried	Parricide	Rectified
hide	collide	ratified	putrefied
Fried	Preside	Suicide	Villified
died	applied	modified	nullified
Slide	Reside	Occupied	Unified
gride	astride	fortified	pacified
Dyed	Noontide	Fratricide	Prophesied
side	backside	mortified	petrified
Hied	Confide	Notified	Multiplied
tried	misguide	crucified	solidified
Sighed	Allied	Liquefied	Diversified
cried	aside	ossified	personified
Spied	Untied	Regicide	Disqualified
wide	inside	fructified	preoccupied
Bide	Beside	Falsified	Insecticide
fried	belied	justified	intensified
Abide	Beautified	Multiplied	Indemnified
elide	specified	glorified	infanticide
Fate	Narrate	Abdicate	Investigate
slate	create	extricate	intimidate

Crate weight	Vacate frustrate	Meditate instigate	Invalidate exterminate
Bait mate	Fornicate fabricate	Conjugate subjugate	Coagulate congratulate
Gait freight	Agitate Ventilate	Detonate lacerate	Initiate accumulate
Skate straight	Generate tabulate	Aggravate irritate	Deliberate exacerbate
Spate plate	Nominate nauseate	Educate duplicate	Deprecate consolidate
Eight date	Litigate vindicate	Cultivate demonstrate	Prevaricate adulterate
Strait gate	Contemplate hibernate	Captivate celebrate	Commemorate illuminate
Late trait	Tolerate moderate	Compensate deprecate	Expostulate facilitate
State hate	Abrogate dislocate	Annotate delegate	Discriminate equivocate
Rate grate	Mediate medicate	Copulate complicate	Contaminate eradicate
Debate checkmate	Inundate liquidate	Venerate congregate	Matriculate corroborate
Innate Ornate	Innovate celebrate	Calculate anticipate	Precipitate recriminate
Gyrate migrate	Castigate mutilate	Expectorate accumulate	Insinuate abominate
Sedate cremate	Imprecate implicate	Commiserate accommodate	Participate communicate

FORM
FORMAL
REFORMER
UNIFORM
CONFORMITY
FORMULATION
INFORMATION
REFORM
FORMULA
INFORM
REFORMATIVE
FORMALISM
INFORMAL
TRANSFORMATION
FORMALIZE
UNIFORMITY
FORMAT
FORMATIVE
DEFORM
FORMATION
CONFORMATION
INFORMANT
DEFORMITY
REFORMIST
FORMALITY
FORMALIST
DEFORMATION
CONFORM
INFORMATIVE
FORMULATION
REFORMATION
TRANSFORM
INFORMER
FORMLESS

Microphone Poet

(after Stockhausen's <u>Mikrophonie</u> <u>I</u>)

Necessary Materials:

1 quadraphonic speaker system
1 locator mixer
2 electronic filter systems
1 stopwatch
1 omni-directional microphone
1 uni-directional microphone
1 poet with five minutes of poetry or he may read from a publicity
    brochure, etc.
2 media men dressed in black on stage (they may be dancers)
1 media man at filter/mixer system

The Operations:

Stage is semi-dark. Reading podium center stage, lit by blue/white spot.
The poems to be read are on the podium. Also stopwatch. Poet enters from
stage left or stage right. He wears flashy poet-reading costume (levis,
hand woven belt that dangles to knees, V-neck overshirt with Oriental
or American Indian pattern, pendant hung on leather thong or chord, etc.
& of course buffalo hide mocassins). As soon as he reaches podium smiles
and starts stopwatch. Begins reading poems uninflected, tonelessly, but
with singsong manner; almost hypnotically. He will stop reading in ex-
actly five minutes.

The two stage media men enter; one stage left, then the other stage right.
Each carries a microphone with long chord. They alternate in their ap-
proach to the poet. These media men are dressed exactly alike. Black
turtleneck sweaters and black tights and black gauze hoods. They move
inconspicuously. They are free to move anywhere on stage as long as
they do not interfere with the poet's reading. Their sole purpose is
to catch the poet's voice in their microphones in as many ways as they
can imagine. Through handkerchiefs, through cardboard funnels, through
metal or glass tubes, from extremely close range to the extent of the
stage's distance. They must not make any noise in pursuing their purpose,
but they may create any obstructions they like between the voice and the
microphones; silent obstructions.

The filter/mixer media man filters the microphone carried sounds and
directs them to any or all of the four speakers at each corner of the
auditorium. He orchestrates the sound in musical terms, without regard
to content of the poems or whether or not the words can be understood.
He treats the poet's voice as electronically produced sound, regarding
amplitude, pitch, density, etc.

When the poet stops reading, the stage media men immediately freeze in
their motion. The electronic system is turned off. Lights are cut be-
fore the poet moves. Poet and stage media men return backstage by near-
est exit, in the dark.

50   Old Angel Midnight the swan of heaven fell & flew cockmeek, Old Angel Midnigh the night onta twelve Year Tart with the long bing bong & the big ding dong, the boy on the sandbank blooming the moon, the sound wont let me sleep & since I found out time is silence Manjusri wont let me hear the swash of snow no mo in ole no po—O A M, Oh Om, the Old Midnacker snacker tired a twit twit twit the McTarty long true——the yentence peak peck slit slippymeek twang twall I'd heerd was flip the hand curse lead pencil in the shaky desk ah Ow HURT!——Tantapalii the silken tont retchy swan bent necky I wish I had enuf sense to swim as I hear, o lousy tired gal——One more! Choired arranged silence singers imbibing belly blum

51   Wreck the high charch chichipa & get firm juicy thebest thebest no other oil has ever heard such peanut squeeze——On top of which you yold yang midnockitwatter lying there in baid imagining casbah concepts from a highland fling moorish beach by moonlight medallion indicative spidergirls with sand legs waiting for the Non Christian cock, come O World Window Wowf & BARK! BARK! BARK for the girls of Tranatat——because by the time those two Mominuan monks with girls & boys in their matted hair pans sense wind in the flower the golden lord will turn the imbecile himself into slip paper——Or dog paper——or that pipe blend birds never peck because their bills are too hard ——that window paper

52 Silence in my window now in the fullmoon of haiku which goes OO yellow continent in a birdbath, April full moon which rattles the goldroom little death chair that never will collapse even tho you sit 10 nymphet girls there on yr lap fall to the floor to cellars of lust——and in any case O poet-O's of old world I love yr greatness & anyways tho what kinda world we'd have (Hi Missus Twazz) (O hullo Mr. Moon mock) a world all poits? geen! try Mawln Bwano? rurt——The old man is a moving plastic curtain whispering to find his girls pare soundless possle, the lovers next door hiding in back barn driveway the the the the the—— Lottle ma songing starty this is no time to listen to just but-puff——shhh sez my Jetsun Yidam——Buddyo Ava Loki T——in Ole Oaxaca we'll find the magic boat-yard knifed flame O wick, burn, or fall—The gossip among the stars is that farledee who lit the moon end of dog turn Turk Town Tenneduck was Kansased halfway to tripe because the long thin Stick Men & the fat Slobs who ate too much have their mouths sewed up, writers their tongues yanked by hot irens, & Wolledockers of Old Gallows England buried with the dust of ancient decapitated horses of old dust Japan in bowed head oblivion that was meant for all things crumble & dis-appear including (did you hear?) Lury Marsh, Goniff Tward, Mic, Tokli Twa, Stabtalita Borotani, Parsh Tilyur, Cock, Brrrocky ⌣⌐↗⌐ჳႷჳ⌐ , & Tot.

53 Even from heaven now O ladies & gentlemen of the fard world yr beloved angel dead are sighing sweet memoried perfumed thoughts into yr ears to keep you mindful that yr term on earth aint naught or for not, but——bu yo bink the wick swans both twist to balls the stasis hanging bathrobe——chairs crumble & get put out on cleanup day, I saw one today I'd like to sit on the moon on & be a turnpage comedian continent cardown, tryna Satisfy Catholic girls from Harvard aint my pot a tea or plate a beans, I'se sorry oh son, lays & genmen, to the next Bardo (bardic?) (forgot) Tibetan (tiss top?) plot lins to find it Lama Lano lined the Turner Girl the mooma tannery where they say the bellrope sank the clank of pisspot grime the tanker that twirded for phantom Una southern Edward Papa river sod stashy slasheen girl Irish father iron Irish god's green earth & die there——either that, My Dame or pourquoi?——Bed wrinkled dinkled from too much sleets, mosser dear? Got shot charge Rebel joyous Georgian by witchcraft. Ah, & what lunchcart? The one with 69 year old daughters & 690 pound brothers & all the stars of Alex Manhole clear to Rubber O North Carolina Oklahoma Indian pips——urgh, & what else ——The moon, this Friday evening she's already full & full & full on late afternoon board blue over trees & sandbanks——Dont mention his name! He will burn Buddha's babies in this house! He will hasten dust! Nothing but faith like Abraham believes in hallucinated true heart of dumb uneducated glimmering self 'cause the void is all illumined now & Milarepa had she-demons bouncing on his john because he loved red fires in his (fires in his?)——well, just red, Ned, & be sure to——to what?——bank the ikon——what Ikkon? The ikon silver cross that was almost buried with my brother——thank you brother——See you anon, my pat, my lemb, in Cielo soon's——soon's what?——soon's there's room in endless meaning to accept another meaningless liar pushing pencil for to die in happy breath so nobody could see ✝

54

peep
peep the
bird tear the
sad bird drop heart
the dawn has slung
her aw arrow drape
to sissyfoo & made eastpink
dink the dimple solstice men
crut and so the birds go ttleep
and now bird number two three four five
sixen seven and seven million of em den
dead bens barking now the birds are yakking
& barking swinging Crack! Wow! Quiet! the
birds are making an awful racket in the Row
tweep?   tswip!   creet!   clink!   crack!
ding dong the bell rope bird of break of day
O k a y   b i r d s   q u i e t

P l e a s e

you birds
robins
black & blue birds
redbreasts & all
sisters, ————

my little parents
have the morning
by the golden balls

And over there the sultan forgot

55   Ah old angel of midnight I cant hear myself think for all your scur racket the lead in yr pencil on simple asinine page so noisy what's a man gonna think of this unless the rumble house black as snow horizon train brings back all our favored dead from furnace & somebody furnish—Ah car, a human directing his tatismatatagolre thru Holland to find the Dutch Imprimatur to his Helcm, the Helm & Cross of Charlemagne Euron Irope that meant no more no less that Quebekois Canoe (Kebokoa Kano)—Kak! But rumble will the devil his will's unspoken, God wont truck helicopters to peek-at-wisdom Vulture Queen, nor will the red dog that glitters at the fish queen of my heart reach for kite hook or Dahlenberg drent it any different for by the great God Jesus I will not rest no wont rest till Ferlinghetti's dog his day had does piss again on hydrant hydramatic stillness electrical ectroid where for sure cats of the stripe so proud & vainty do vaunt for to bring the final jumpmonkey home to Marpa's bird sing—Ah translate me that—Cook! Dog echo in the sandbank valley Northport rumble Mahayana the diamond Vajrayana path that was trod here long ago before those houses jewel-graced the seaside hill, & for Krissakes no sound at all comes in this window except those Wolf Hourses got tamming bringing white & gray pearl hearses thru the shoot rain to munner munner munner, O fat eater in the drape son push yr belly back, the tape worm——& worms to measure you, long tape—sod & sand over yr bluenose disdain, Mrs America, the Indian's Ya Ya Henna, the Indian Uprising known as the Beat Generation, is going to eat rails & make tire sandwiches of every junkyard misty rust & all old heroes' eyes in barley Soup of time—— to be sopped with eye sop——So carry on, escaper, jail's only made to flee——

The wush of trees on yonder eastern nabathaque Latin Walden axe-haiku of hill where woodsman Mahomet perceives will soon adown the morning drear to pail the bringup well suspender farmer trap moon so's cock go Bloody yurgle in the distance where Timmy hides, flat, looking with his eyes for purr me——O Angel, now is the time for all good men to come to the aid of their party, & ah Angel dont paperparty me, but make me honified in silken Honen honeyrubbéd Oxen tongue of Cow Kiss, Ant Mat, silk girl ran, & all the monkey-better-than secondary women of Sam Sarah the Sang of Blood this earth, this tool, this fool, look with your eyes, I'm tired of fooling O Angel bring it to me THE MAGIC SOUND OF SILENCE broken by firstbird's teepaleep——

Good East! Hard to blow out! Sometimes! Darkness in my final kip. This shot will send the gossip mongers yarking back to Harvard frail slat, soft, full of gyzms in slit lacéd hatreds for light is light O Lord, O Lord, I pray, my Lord——Again! Once more! Ta ta ta ta! Om

56

Ack, who gives a ruddy fuck about all this American showoffy prose I'd like to know why Whane meant horsefly & Brane something like, & why Owe's Born is Awe's Dead, & all our intelligent handsome Tedsy Boys go yearning after our pink pages & never find & all the riots in Pixy Dilly & all the Traf on the Square, Elgar with his music doesnt impertaramount the rock of Murican roll? For strings? Air? O nonce, node, these babic yoiks, these Inds, these stupidities, these gem americans

TWIP, 2059 (AXTONO) (WOW the twip of that carry-on I'll never fly another Yet to Souski that country wont feed me nothing but ersatz gatagatpataraze which is a kind (wow, the munsch) of farlidaltamanigalo the color of which, well, yr aunt Mary mighta told you but O the gossip in these other galaxies just too much my dear the rurn, the klen, the hoit, the noises of Flup. There was Onat Roren, Bob Torlignath the Crank, the Cranker of Hono-Machines, & the Bile Pister of the Falledern he was there be-sartifying all his meanies & the meannesses & told me I didnt have praper green in my pen gat——But he B.O. was alright, felt good, was glad because her time was late, & as for those publications up there that they turn out with all their bearded Trees extemporiating on the state of the talismanic oral pata——

       I just got tired & retired but got involved in a long tat with Sinabad Talgamimargafonik Crud the interesting fool from the well located (in emerald waters) continent of Magic who told me there was a Sound recently developed by Shitteers that wd eventually require dog whistles hanging from breast teeth & bug micro bugs & long swarms of Milky Wayers vacationed over from Blue Curtain Country listening to the Country Pard say: "The tanitat of this Omakorgeklid is infested with Imagery & therefore white as moon——but O my Thinkers never let it be said the sooth——" I couldnt listen to any more besides I had a deadline to meet & new flows to fii so came back to good old Tierra del Firma & had Princess my Tabtatc, (solit) go eat another bont, which meant I only had 2 days to wait till today so rested up reading ancient

texts & spent all night watching the sun on the moon
the sinking mountain till all vanished & even MRS
Stone made no comment but slept & that is my report
to you today, my Dotggergsamtiianidarstofgiviks

58   I just cant stand these people
I teel you I dont know what I'm going to do about them,
start my motor or fart my passage but you the way
they carried on last night, *him,* with that dressy little
deaful foosy on his lap the boom of busting chair & all
that boommusic on the juke box & I dont know I wanted
to call the police & get rid of this sandbag pineneedle
Bodhi neighbor who is such ugly bearded dirty"
("nothing on earth or in any terrestrial sphere or in any
Buddhalands Heaven or Mockswarm of Einsteinian &
non-light Light can take hold my brothers & sisters &
cousins because it is only the wisdom of manifested
epiphany & the compassion of goodbye"—) (as soon
as I can find a bully club & bang a hole in imaginary
fence I tell you this will be the last time the window's
with redlegged devils & stone blue eyes——) (Kunfii,
garayen, hallo Kiyan, fitiguwi, katapatafataja, silya,
kitipuwee, senlou, saint loup, coish, karan) (or vaunt
the moidners the Villa Viva Pancho baby Mexico City
sorefoot Juarez old hotel wino El Paso march picking
up six thousand partisans to vest the peon with his
land coat so that years later Rivera murals shine by
army teahead trumpet in Ole Texcoco) "there'll come a
day when that yurn I'll have to astabing the zemble the
cartifacartilage I wont have another moment of—
Dry up, dry up, moist earth, dry up, dust ball, dutball
moon is sick of leering at your inadmissable sorrow
because it has no twat to to tie onto't—And we the
fooly libs that think ah music airplane & all ye scream-

ing birds of falsedawn let the ephemera existence wait
at yr side with you for end to't——No other teaching
hear & hear tell & what of that the sound who wants to
hear——Go fetch the gardles & make open the corridors
of your Bright Room mind the Lord is coming he's all
white & gold, he's a pink white angel in a black room
by a blue window & a yellow candleflame with golden
(hurt) wings the color of all thingness, the swarming
dove, there! See it! He stands at yr non-side sides the
waterbaby by the baby shroud, the honeyfall, the bliss
blessed to be believed, the final pollitabimackatatanabala
(fine as fine can be) (Ah Ah) (HO HO) leap & dance
it's saved! the nerve of that man! foru! mon ti kitaya!
patakatafataya——perk! prick! prick ears I mean you
think I let pollute window liars? Oh God, stop it——

When God snaps his Finger of
Gold & suspenders too the world will wake in the well
looking at the dark star——this silvery desert full of
gophers rattlesnake tracks & sobbing moons of Chihua-
huan splendor I'll buy, tho, till that Babe of the Honied
Fall is at my side again for nothing, nothing, nothing,
absolutely powerfully lightly emptily goldenly eternally
nothing ever happened & this I bring to you from grass
i the sun (to tell of it, the cock in card the soft & mixup
pushing bardahl Drutchen cant & dent of it I wount
hav it, ht Anyway) (seurain) (sunrin) (booya)
J'm'enva arretez! Fo.

59

Aw rust rust rust rust die die
die pipe pipe ash ash die die ding dong ding ding ding
rust cob die pipe ass rust die words——I'd as rather be
permiganted in Rusty's moonlight Rork as be perdirated
in this bile arta panataler where ack the orshy rosh

crowshes my tired idiot hand O Lawd I is coming to you's soon's you's ready's as can readies be Mazatlan heroes point out Mexicos & all ye rhythmic bay fishermen dont hang fiish eye soppy in my Ramadam give-cigarette Sop of Arab Squat——the Berber types that hang fardels on their woman back wd as lief Erick some son with blady matter I guess as whup a mule in singsong pathetic mulejump field by quiet fluff smoke North Carolina (near Weldon) (Railroad Bridge) Roanoke Millionaire High-Ridge hi-party Hi-Fi million-dollar findriver skinfish Rod Tong Apple Finder John Sun Ford goodby Paw mule America Song——

60

Arguing about mudpies in the hot spring sun karu, myota the Japanese ✗ who wrote of ✗ was always concerned about his poison oak hut when they came bringing him early dogwood buds with a bleached rock & the trinity of rocks & yak of blackbird pearbranch jumping & the Umpteen yumping erse Norway Man of N'o'r'm'a'n'd'i'a (who repaired houses?) (who made new moons bider) (brighter) (?) (bider) of time the bider the cross in his tomb worm & the King on his epistaff stone tomb port of north——Oh——All ties in you see like fish pier respect.

Fish spear shook?——shook aimed

& breton rocked——

O but just as long as sun shines like this in yellow airplane on the pebble Beach sky & pear yump yak blossoms (up north)——& as long as red hydrants & post chaises——(gossip?) (Well it's a quiet moment but methinks the sons of the world & daughters thereof as wellus wolves & loups will be perfectly containted as long as they stay away from Ehrlich's dyemill blueworms which are et by OObaltory golbords & clover'ed & clobbered by mind's no-nature essence & as soon as they ask for an explanation say "What? buds in blue new sky?"

Dream for Muggy Mojump the quiet cloud.

61   Kertion Kerdion Keryon Kerson cherson & Who else in this ugly old Russia heehavel helps me in this business recordin sounds of universe midnight? but not a single damn dull fool podium hear it attestify that the selickman was a poet who decided to say:

I am a poet
&
here is my poem
Watch how fancy I write
Skeletons of Compassion dusting
in the distant heavens' infinity
while fat old burbles rememberem
well
here
on high hark——high hart——
world——diepork——

Over & above of which it was down in Charleston West Virginny one time my Pa in white shirt & unshaved shot a man in a poolroom fight——they chased him acrosst the Kanowa in a Kanoea (idiot) & got him down by the bayin hope dogs in that country where Old Angel Mama Midnight will lean her happy head & hungry eyes on pillows of Old in the high falutin poem of Heaven where little white house it waitin for all you black sufferers so's dandy'll say "Twas all writ & no more to say, the Vow of Gold is Done" & all yet young kids wanta know what a man do when he golden baby post up there he completes the vow matures the Karma returns the Kitkat Clowns the Crown Thorns the Flap and dad blasts him happiness forever, because you'll see, in not too many years now, yr hope & grace-waves werent jivin ya, all's taken care of behind these suffering trees & inside these suffering bees & wont nobody harsh ya but say kind star roof words & bring white cloth to your laundryboy basket (clean as dinosaur teeth) & you'll know the——sore yah he was sore but he said Bust me one on the jaw, I got the running eyes——With or without sugar——The Cat in the Con-Cord

    Lord, you presumptuous good-giver, thanks, & go tell everybody you Vowin hardass sonsumbitches——(hold clasp hand TaTaTa)——Aye Bodhidharma

62   Tapistry the second writer
    in the novel island bearded
    scared wont use words saves
    he go's & hungerers of wood
    from boom in the Spain Jail
      hand on knees

    To go cross cemetery America
    highwire ratcroak dumpslaver
    moogow silo sillwindow rat
    wait moon shine on tin
    all the little inner outer sin

     peek at the bird
      tree, remember

it again, the
hoosegow goddam cuban
Killer who moidners
turtles, traps em cock
in the nigh & never
draps a wear

All day nervous wonderin what to do shoe in my arm-
chair innesfoo that was writ in Akashia I'm just hearin
what my head said & it's mighty repetitiousness

63　　　　　　　The black ants that roosted in
my tree all winter long have just emerged to meet an
army of enemy ants (same breed) & a big war is now
taking place, I just looked with my brakemans lamp (by
sunlight) (brake the day sun) warriors are biting each
other's sensitive rear humps & killing each other with
more intelligence about murder than my boot knows——
I squashed one wounded warrior whose poor right front
armorer was missing & he just croualtad coupled there,
I hated to see him suffer & he was open (ow) for attack
too, bit safe a mo on a flat rock used for lady's flag-
stones in the pink tea world which ignores ant Wars &
doesnt know that when the first space ship lands on the
planet Amtasagrak (really Katapatafaya in other
galuxies) the ship will immediately be swarmed over
by black ants, even the window obscured, they'll have
to turn their X-Roentgen Gun Ray on it to see & what
they'll see'll make em wish Von Braun had stayed in
brown germany: one sextillion sextillion idiot insect
fiends a foot deep eating one another endlessly the top
ones scuffling, the next layer dead & being nibbled, the
next layer belly to belly cant move from the weight, &
the bottom layer suffocated at last——& the lady ants

have wings & fly to little tiny planets that hang six feet above the moiling black shiny ant sea, where they hatch, push the grownup kids off (into the Mess) & die Sighing for Paradise O ye singers of War & Glory

After seeing a thing like this who wd dare not ask for enlightenment everywhere? Who will deny ant war with me?

Meanwhile in my yard the triumphant winning warrior ant stands over his defeated dying brother & you see his little antled helmet waving in the glorious breeze like How Ta Ra the trumpets of Harfleur & (you know what I was going to say there ——hm——) no compassion in these little febrile finicular skeleton——O Ant Soup!

64 O Escapade escape me never I lied I lied I lied I'll never escape ex cape——of Spaign ——God'll ever me allow to leave this hurt of ant scene until I lissen to his words & wave & point by saucer moon & antlered antennae &

weird roofwash & weirder cross windows, the black clock by the white clock in the city's creamy tenement while one silk stocking waves to gossip the lady's lost leg & there's a slip by a pair of paints waving in the moon breeze as well as a sheet which however has no blaind stain of blood, only the one silk stocking——& there's panties, littleboy pants, handkerchiefs, towels & many cursed faint bigscrew'd oratan furykula yaink antavyazers, with black hooks, sword spaces, windows the bottoms falling out & the moon a crink in its upper neck which is really its back (Ah)

65 That grassy yocker pocking up yonder

66   Tonight the full apogee May moon will out, early with a jaundiced tint, & pop angels all over my rooftop along with Devas sprinkling flowers, pilgrims dropping turds & sweet nemanucalar nameless railroad trains from heaven with omnipotent youths bearing monkey women that will stomp through the stage waiting for the moment when by pinching myself I prove that a thought is like a touch, unless someone sicks a hot iron in my heart or heaps up Evil Karma like tit and tat the pile of that and pulls my mother out her bed to slay her before my damning dying human eyes and I break my head on heads——Everytime you throw a rock at a cat from your glass house you heap upon yourself the automatic Stanley Gould winter so dark of death after death, & growing old, because lady those ashcans'll bite you back & be cold too, and your son will never rest in the imperturbable knowledge that what he thinks he thinks as well as what he does he thinks as well as what he feels he thinks as well as future that.

Future that my damn old sword cutter Paison Pasha Lost the Preakness again.

Tonight the moon shall witness angels trooping at the baby's window where inside he gurgles in his pewk looking with mewling eyes for babyside waterfall lambikin hillside the day the little arab shepherd boy hugged the babylamb to heart while the mother bleeted at his bay heel——And so Joe the sillicks killit no not——Shhhhoww graaa——wing & car-start——The angels devas monsters asuras Devadattas Vedantas McLaughlins Stones will hue & hurl in hell if they don't love the lamb the lamb the lamb of hell lambchop. Why did Scott Fitzgerald keep a notebook? Such a marvelous notebook.

67   Komi denera ness pata sutyamp anda wanda vesnoki shadakiroo paryoumemga sikarem nora sarkadium baron roy kellegiam myorki ayastuna haidanseetzel ampho andiam yerka yama chelmsford alya bonneavance koroom cemada versel

(The 26th Annual concert of The Armenian Convention)

---

6 // I COULD GO MAD IN THIS— O carryall menaya but the weel may track the rattle-burr, poniac the avoid devoidity runabout, minavoid the crail— Song of my all the vouring me the part de rail-ing carry all the pone—part you too may green and fly—welkin moon wrung salt upon the tides of come-on night, swing on the meadow shoulder, roll the boulder of Buddha over the pink partitioned west Pacific fog mow— O tiny tiny tiny human hope, O molded cracking thee mirror thee shook pa t n a watalaka—and more to go—

Ping.

"SEA"

Cherson!
 Cherson!
  You aint just whistlin
   Dixie, Sea——
  Cherson! Cherson!
   We calcimine fathers
    here below!
  Kitchen lights on——
   Sea Engines from Russia
    seabirding here below——
 When rocks outsea froth
  I'll know Hawaii
   cracked up & scramble
   up my doublelegged cliff
  to the silt of
   a million years——

Shoo——Shaw——Shirsh——
Go on die salt light
 You billion yeared
  rock knocker

Gavroom
Seabird
Gabroobird
Sad as wife & hill
Loved as mother & fog
Oh! Oh! Oh!
    Sea! Osh!
Where's yr little Neppytune
    tonight?

These gentle tree pulp pages
which've nothing to do
with yr crash roar,
    liar sea, ah,
were made for rock
tumble seabird digdown
    footstep hollow weed
    move bedarvaling
    crash? Ah again?
Wine is salt here?
    Tidal wave kitchen?
Engines of Russia
    in yr soft talk——

Les poissons de la mer
    parle Breton——
Mon nom es Lebris
    de Keroack——
    Parle, Poissons, Loti,
    parle——
Parlning Ocean sanding
    crash the billion rocks——

    Ker plotsch——
    Shore——shoe——
god——brash——

The headland looks like
a longnosed Collie sleeping
with his light on his
    nose, as the ocean,
    obeying its accomodations
    of mind, crashes in
    rhythm which could
    & will intrude, in thy
    rhythm of sand
    thought——
——Big frigging shoulders
on *that* sonofabitch

Parle, O, parle, mer, parle,
    Sea speak to me, speak
    to me, your silver you light
    Where hole opened up in Alaska
    Gray——shh——wind in
    The canyon wind in the rain
    Wind in the rolling rash
    Moving and t wedel
        Sea
        sea
        Diving sea
O bird——la vengeance
    De la roche
    Cossez
    Ah

Rare, he rammed the gate
rare over by Cherson, Cherson,
we calcify fathers here below
——a watery cross, with weeds
entwined——This grins restoredly,
    low sleep——Wave——Oh, no,

shush——Shirk——Boom plop
Neptune now his arms extends
  while one millions of souls
  sit lit in caves of darkness
  ——What old bark? The dog
mountain? Down by the Sea
  Engines? God rush——Shore——
Shaw——Shoo——Oh soft sigh
  we wait hair twined like
  larks——Pissit——Rest not
  ——Plottit, bisp tesh, cashes,
  re tav, plo, aravow,
shirsh,——Who's whispering over
    there——the silly earthen creek!
The fog thunders——We put
    silver light on face——We
    took the heroes in——A billion
    years aint nothing——

O the cities here below!
  The men with a thousand
  arms! the stanchions of
  their upward gaze! the
  coral of their poetry! the
  sea dragons tenderized, meat
  for fleshy fish——
    Navark, navark, the fishes
  of the Sea speak Breton——
  wash as soft as people's
  dreams——We got peoples
  in & out the shore, they call
  it shore, sea call it
    pish rip plosh——The
    5 billion years since

earth we saw substantial
  chan——Chinese are
    the waves——the woods
    are dreaming

No human words bespeak
  the token sorrow older
  than old this wave
  becrashing smarts the
  sand with plosh
  of twirléd sandy
thought——Ah change
  the world? Ah set
  the fee? Are rope the
    angels in all the sea?
  Ah ropey otter
  barnacle'd be——
    Ah cave, Ah crosh!
    A feathery sea

Too much short——Where
  Miss Nop tonight?
Wroten Kerarc'h
  in the labidalian
  aristotelian park
with slime a middle
  ——And Ranti forner
  who pulled pearls by
  rope to throne
    the King by
    the roll in the
    forest of everseas?
Not everseas, *be* seas
    ————Creep
  Crash

The woman with her body
in the sea——The frog who
never moves & thunders, sharsh
——The snake with his body
under the sand——The dog
with the light on his nose,
supine, with shoulders so
enormous they reach back to
rain crack——The leaves hasten
to the sea——We let them
hasten to be wetted & give
em that old salt change, a
nuder think will make you see
they originate from the We Sea
anyway——No dooming booms
on Sunday afternoons——We
run thru the core of cliffs,
blam up caves, disengage no
jelly or jellied pendant
thinkers——

Our armies of
anchored seaweed in the
coves give of the smell
of jellied salt——
Reach, reach, some leaves
havent hastened near
enuf——Roll, roll, purl
the sand shark floor
a greeny pali andarva
——Ah back——Ah forth——
Ah shish——Boom, away,
doom, a day——Vein we
firm——The sea is We——

Parle, parle, boom the
earth——Arree——Shaw,
Sho, Shoosh, flut,
ravad, tapavada pow,
coof, loof, roof,——
No,no,no,no,no,no——
Oh ya, ya, ya, yo, yair——
Shhh——

Which one? the one? Which
one? The one ploshed——
The ploshed one? the same,
ah boom——Who's that ant
that giant golden saltchange
ant magnifying my mountain
of feet? 'Tis Finder, finding
the change in thought to join
the boomer hangers in the
cave a light——And built a
house above it? Never fear,
naver foir, les bretons qui
parlent la langue de la Mar
sont español comme le cul
du Kurd qui dit le maha
prajna paramita du Sud?
Ah oui! Ke Vlum!
Glum sea, silent me——

They aint about to try
it them ants who wear
out tunnels in a week
the tunnel a million years
won——no——Down around
the headland slobs for weed,

the chicken of the sea
 go yak! they sleep——
Aroar, aroar, arah, aroo——
Otter me otter me daughter me sea
——me last blue lagoon inside of
me, the sea——Divine is the
substance all over the Sea—
  Of space we speak &
  hasten——Let no mouth
  swallow the sea——Gavril——
  Gavro——the Cherson Chinese
  & Old Fingernail sea——Is
  ringin yr ear? Dier, dee?
  Is Virgin you trying to
      fathom me

  Tiresome old sea, aint you sick
    & tired of all of this merde?
this incessant boom boom
& sand walk——you people
hoary rockies here to Fuegie
& never get sad? Or despair
like a German phoney?
Just gloom booboom & green
  on foggy nights——the fog is part
of us——
  I know, but tired
as I can be listening to all
this silly majesty——
    Bashô!
    Lao!
    Pop!
  Who is this fish
  sitting unsunk? Run up
  a Hawaii typhoon smash him

against his rock——We'll jelly you,
 jellied man, show you essential
     jello of the sea——King
     of the Sea.

No Monarc'h ever Irish be?
 Ju see the Irish sea?
Green winds on tamarack vines——
Joyce——James——Shhish——
Sea————Sssssss——see
————Varash
————mnavash la vache
    écriture——the sea dont say
muc'h actually——

    Gosh, she,
huzzy, tow, led men
on, Ulysses and all them
  fair headed moin——
  Terplash, & what difference
  make! One little white
  spark of light!
Hair woven hands
  Penelope seaboat
  smeller——Courtiers in
  Telemachus 'sguise
  dropedary dropedary
  creep——Or——
  Franc gold rippled
  that undersea creek
where fish fish for
  fisher men——Salteen
  breen the wet Souwesters
  of old Portugee Prayers

Tsall tangled, changed,
salt & drop the sand
　& weed & water brains
　　entangled——Rats
　of old Venetian yellers
　Ariel Calibanned
　　to Roma Port——
Pow——spell——
　Speak you parler,
in this my mother's
　parlor, wash your
undershoes when you
　　come in, say thanks
　to foggy moon

Go brash, Topahta
offat,——we'll gray
　ye rose——Morning
　primord creeper sees
　the bird of paravision
　dying tweet the yellow
mouthroof! How sweet
　the earth, yells sand!
　　Xcept when tumble
boom!
　　O we wait too
for Heaven—— all
in One——
　　All is there
in fair & sight

I'm going to wash now
　old Pavia down,
　& pack my salt
　　to Either Town——

Cliffs of Antique
　aint got no rose,
　the morning's seen
the ledder pose——
　Boom de boom dey
　the sea is me——
　We are the sea——
　It aint all snow

We wash Fujiyama down
　soon, & sand
　crookbird back——
We hie bash
rock————ak——
　Long　short——
　Low and easy——
　Wind & many freezing
bottoms on luckrock——
　Rappaport——
Endymion thou tangled
dreamer love my thigh
——Rose, Of Shelley,
　Rose, O Urns!
　Ogled urns in fish eye

　Cinco sea　the Chico sea
　the Magellan headland sea
—What hype sidereal did he put down
　bending beatnik sea goatee
　over old goat manuscripts
　to find the other side of Flat?
　　See round, see the end of me?
　Rounden huge bedoom?
　　Awp hole cave & shwrul——
　sand & salt & hair eyes

——Strong enuf to make
coffee grow in your hair——
Whose plantation Neptune got?
That of Atlas still down there,
Hesperid's his feet, Sur his sleet,
Irish Sea fingertip
& Cornwall aye his soul
bedoom

Shurning——Shurning——plop
be dosh——This sigh old learning's
high beside me——Rough
old hands have played out
pedigree, we've sunk more boats
than dreamer'll ever ever see
—Burning——Burning——The world
is burning & needs waaater
——I'll have a daughter,
oughter, wait & seee——
Churning, Churning, Me——
Panties——Panties——
these ancient fancies are
so girling——You've not seen
mermaids in my actual sea
——You've not seen sexless babies
with breasts of Majesty——
My wife——My wife——
Her name is Oh so really
high life

The low life Kingdom where
we part out tea, is sea
side Me——
Josh——coof——patra——

Aye ee mo powsh——
Ssst——Cum here read me——
Dirty postcard——Urchin sea——
Karash your name——?
Wanta swim, sink or swim?
Ears ringing again?
Sea vibrate rhythm
crash sets off cave
hanger blowers whistling
dog ear back——to sea——
Arree——
Gerudge Napoleon nada——
Nada

Pluto eats the sea——
Room——
Hands folded by the sea——
"On est toutes cachez, mange
le silence," dit les poissons de la
mer——Ah Mar——Gott——
Thalatta——Merde——Marde
de mer——Mu mer——Mak a vash——
The ocean is the mother——
Je ne suis pas mauvaise quand j'sui
tranquil——dans les tempêtes
j'cri! Come une folle!
j'mange, j'arrache toutes!
Clock——Clack——Milk——
Mai! mai! mai! ma!
says the wind blowing sand——
Pluto eats the sea——
Ami go——————da——che pop
Go——Come——Cark——
Care——Kee ter da vo

Kataketa pow! Kek kek kek!
Kwakiutl! Kik!
　　Some of theserather taratasters
trapped hyra tchere thaped
the anadondak ram ma lat
round by Krul to Pat the lat
　　rat the anaakakalked
　　romon t o t t e k
　　Kara VOOOM
　　frup——
　　　　　Feet cold? wade——Mind sore?
sim——sin——Horny?——lay the sea?
Corny? try me——
　　　Ussens here hang no more
here we go, ka va ra ta
plowsh, shhh,
and more, again, ke vlook
ke bloom & here comes
　　big Mister Trosh
　　　——more waves coming,
　　every syllable windy

Back wash palaver
paralarle——paralleling
parle pe Saviour

A troublesome spirit
hanging here cant make it
　in the void——The sea'll
only drown me——These words
　are affectations
of sick mortality——
　　We try to make our way
　in self reliance, aid
　　not ever comes too quick
　　from wherever & whatever

heaven dear may have
suggested to promise us——

But these waves scare me——
I am going to die
　in full despair——
　Wake up where?
　　On second breath in life
　　the atmosphere is dearer
　　maybe closer to Heaven
　——————O Paradise——————
Is the sea really so bad?
　Have you sent men
here for this cold clown
& monstrous eater at the
　world? whose sound
　　I mock?

God I've got to believe in you
or live in death!
　Will you save us——all?
　　Soon or now?
Send illumination
　to our drowning brains
　——We're pitiful, Lord,
we need yr help!
　Save us, Dear——
　(Save yourself, God man,
　　ha ha!)
If you were God man
you'd command these waves
to very well Tennyson stop
　& even Tennyson
　　is dear
　　　now dead

Leave it to the light
    Concern yourself with supper,
        & an eye

        somebody's eye——a wife,
a girl, a friend, an animal
——a blood let drop——
he for his sea,
    he for his fire,
        thee for thy desire

"The sea drove me away
    & yelled 'Go to your desire!'
——As I hurried up the valley
It added one last yell:-
        'And laugh!' "

Even the sea cant stop me from
writing something to read in my old age
—This is the chart of brief forms,
his sea the briefest——Shish yourself——
er scaring me like that, Mar,
 excoriate yr slum——yr
line weeds & slime hoops,
en yr dried hollow seaweed
stinks——you stink all over——
oom——Try that, creep——
The little Monterey fishingboat
lides downward home 15 miles to go,
e home to fried fish & beer b'five——
t guides the sea its bird routes——
——Silver loss forever outward
—From blue sky of human bridges
    the massive mawkcloud sea center
eap——to the gray——
    Some boys call it gunboat blue,

        or gray, but I call it
        the Civil War of Rocks
——Rocks 'come air, rocks 'come water,
    & rock rocks——
Kara tavira, mnash grand bash
——poosh l'abas——croosh
L'a haut——Plash au pied——
    Peeeee——Rolle test boulles——
    Manche d'la rache——
        The handsome King prevails
        over boom sing bird head——
    "Crache tes idées," spit yr ideas,
    says the sea, to me, quite
    appro priate ly——
        Pss! pss! pss!
        Ps! girl inside!
        Red shoes scum, eyes of old
    sorcerers, toenails hanging down
        in the barrel of old firkin cheese
        the Dutchman forgot t'eat that
                        tempest
                    nineteen O
                        sixteen——
        When torpedoed by gunboat
        Pedro in the Valley
of a Million Fees?

When Magellan crosseyed
    ate the Amazonian feet——
And, Ah, when Colombo cross't!
When Drake sir francised the waves
    with feeding of the blue jay
        dark——pounded his aleward
    tank before the boom,

housed up all thoughts of Erik
   the Red the Greenland caperer
& builder of rockdungs in New
   Port——*New*——yet——
Oldport Indian Fishhead——
Oldport Tattoo Kwakiutl Headpost
   taboo potash Coyotl potlatch?
Old Primitive Columbia.——
Named for Colom *bus*?
   Name for Aruggio Vesmarica——
      Ar!——Or!——Da!
      What about Verrazano?
he sailed!——
      He Verrazano zailed & we
   statened his Island in on deep

in on dashun——
      Rotted the Wallower?
   Sinners liars goodmen all
sink waterswim drink Neptune's
   nectar the zal sotat————
   Zal sotate name for crota?
   Crota ta crotte, you aint
   'bout to find (Jesus Christian!)
any dry turds here below——
   Why fo no?
   Go crash yonder rock
   of bleak with yr filet mignon teeth
   & see——For you, the hearth,
      the heart, the lock of hair——
      For me, for us, the Sea,
      the murdering of time by eating
      lusty cracks of lip feed wave
      at aeons of sandy artistry

till nothing's left but old age
      newmorning primordial pain
   of sitters by
      the unborn
         bird
   of roses yet undone——

   With weeds your roses,
sand crabs your hummers?
With buzzers in the sea!
   With runners in the deep!
This Sceptred Osh, this wide leg
   spanning rock U.S. to rock
   Ja Pan, this onstable
   roller roaming all,
   this ploosher at yr gory
      dry dung door, this mouth
   of silverwhite arring to hold thee,
   this purger of conscience
   arra for thee——
   No mouse in here but's got
      a little glee——and
      aft, or oft, the osprey
      in his glee's agley——
      Oh purty purty ocean
         me——
      Sop! bring the Scepter down!
Again you've accepted me!

Breathe our iodine, filthy yr drink,
faint at feet wet, drop
   yr profile move it in the sea,
float weeded watery Adonais
   longs for thee——& Shelley three,
   that's three——burn in salt

with slow most change——
We've had no crack at eternity
in a billion years of trying——
   one grain of sand possesses
3 thousand worlds of glee——
not to mention me——
            Ah sea

      Ah si——Ah so——
shoot——shiver——mix——
   ha roll——tara——ta ta——
   curlurck——Kayash——Kee——
Pearls pearls in the yellow West
——Yellow sky to China——
Pacific we named here
   water as always meeting
   water——Pacific Pacific
   Pacific tapfic——geroom——
gedowsh——gaka——gaya——
   Tatha——gata——mana——
   What sails used old bhikkus?
   Dhikkus? Dhikkus!
What raft mailed Mose
to the hoven dovepost?
   What saved Blackswirl
   from the Kidd plank?
What Go-Bug here?
   Seet! Seeeeeeeeeee
   eeeeeee——kara——
   Pounders out yar——

Big Sur they call this sand
   these rocks this creek?
Raton Canyon by name pours

Coyote leaves & old Pomo bones
& old dust of Tomahawks
   into your angler'd maw——
   My salt maw shall salvage
   Taylors——sewing in the room
                     below——
Sewing weed shrat for hikers
   in the milky silt——
Sewing crosswards
   for certainty——Sartan
are we of Price Victory
in this salt War with thee
& thine thee jellied yink!
   Look O the sea here called
   Pacific Sea!
      T a k i !

My golden empty soul'll
outlast yr salty sill
——the Windows of my jelly eye
& fish head muck look out on thee,
   slit, with cigar-a-mouth,
   some contempt——
         Yet I hie me to see you
——you hie thee to eat
   me——Fair in sight
   and worn, aright——
Arra! Aroo!
   Ger der va——
   Silly silent cities in the sea
   have children playing cardboard
mush with eignyard old Englander
   beeplates slickered oer with scum
      of histories below——

No tempest as still & awful
        as the tempest within——
Sorcerer hip! Buddhalands
    & Buddhaseas!
  What sails Maudgalyayana used
    he only knows to tell
    but got kilt by yellers
sreaming down the cliff
        "Let's go home!
            Now!"
    ——leave marge smashed djamas
Maudgalyayana was murdered by the sea——
    But the sea dont tell——
    The sea dont murder——
        The seadrang scholars
        oughter know that
            or
        go back to School

    Hear over there the ocean motor?
Feel the splawrsh of it?
    Six silly centepedes here, Machree——
        Ah Ratatatatat——
the machinegun sea, rhythmic
    balls of you pouring in
    with smooth eglantinee
    in yr pedigreed milkpup
        tenor——
    Tinder marsh aright arrooo——
        arrac'h——arrache——
    Kamac'h——monarc'h——
        Kerarc'h Jevac'h——
    Tamana——————gavow——
        Va——Voovla——Via——

Mia——mine——
        sea
        poo

    Farewell, Sur——

    Didja ever tell him
    about water meeting water——?
O go back to otter——
    Term——Term——Klerm
    Kerm——Kurn——Cow——Kow—
    Cash——Cac'h————Cluck——
        Clock——Gomeat sea need
        be deep I see you
            Enoc'h
        soon anarf
    in Old Brittany

21 August 1960
Pacific Ocean at Big Sur
California

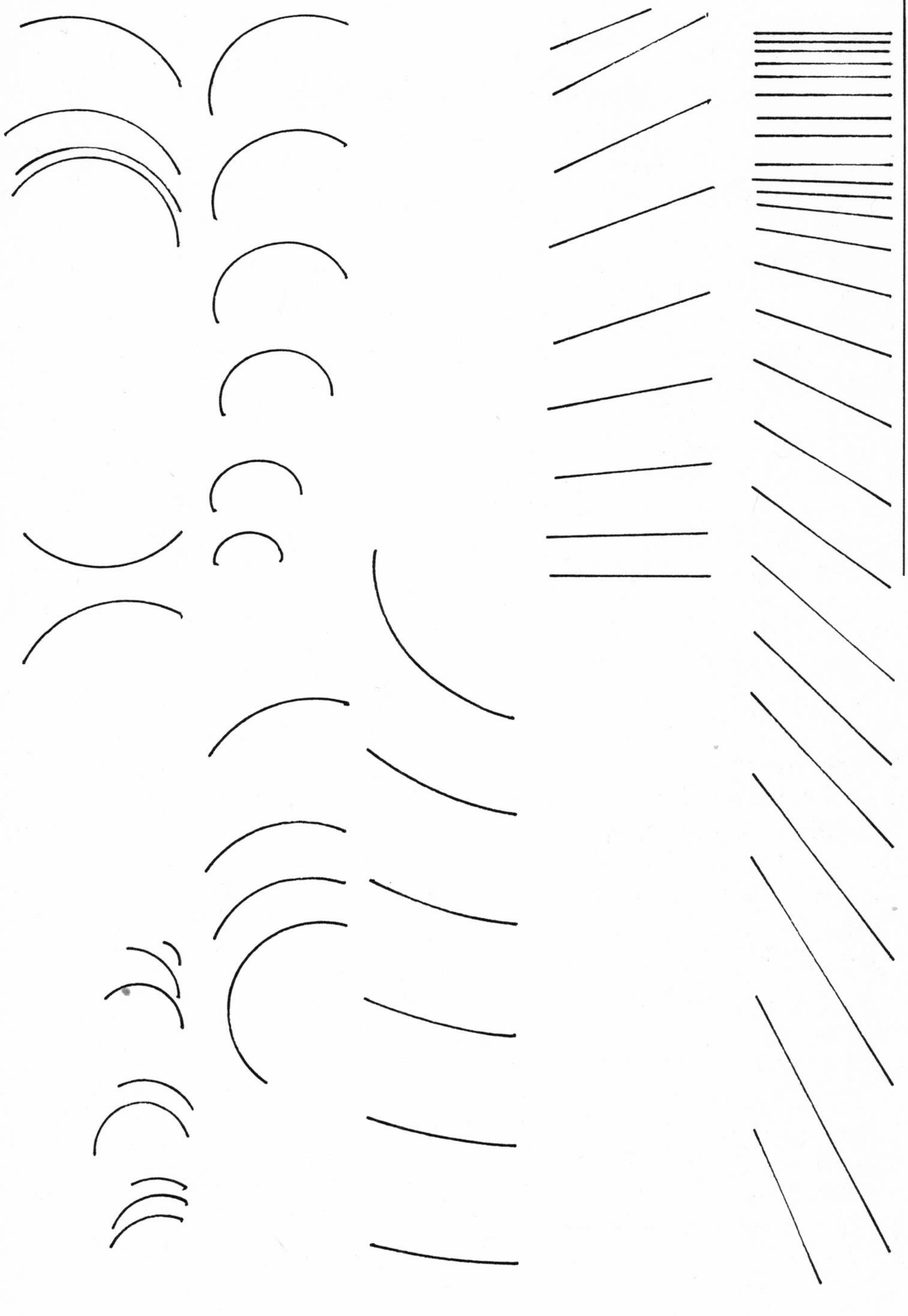

NOTORNIS

scene. the night.

1. novatian.   notidanian.

2. novatian.   the expressed. a no-trump bar of corn.

1. novatian. the chamber. whimsical noumenal.

   (enter 1. notist.)

1. notist.   got a semantic notional.

   (enter 2. notist.)

2. notist. notochord nototherium nototremata.

1. notist.   plates.

2. notist.   visionaries.

1., 2. notist.   sing the sot! ah!

   (exit 1., 2. notist, running wildly out in opposite directions!)

2. novatian.   noumenalism.

1. novatian. nourisher of the feast.

2. novatian.   notobranchiate i'll not be citation notification
parboiled. they bring in the sought nought, let them nonego
the notary notchweed noctodontian. i'm notary that can't.

   (enter 2. notist.)

2. notist.   the bleeding arm! the bleeding toe!

   (exit 2. notist.)

1. novatian. notaries of adamant adjacent fowl.

    (enter annotator.)

annotator.   system flux of place. annotation. understanding has its. shouldn't you? query, and of the signification a

notative that may suggest to you the tactical

that it was only well the known by which haruspex harpy

and this that the sage, in its inception, plants the land

of steersman nothing. you hold dry norwegian as much as nosegay

of bud tree that nostoc is noseband and anther, and but

how many the steeple? how may the scent? a yard. how may

the units of your tints the arched northeaster

but really pare the vault? and of? or to make faction

tired of dog

an accipitrine northland coat, the bill of heron lory

drowns the waves. who peals the stellar waves? shaves?

the prow on the norte? nortelries? it be of note.

2. novatian.   nopal noontides. blemished.

1. novatian.   noologic insolvencies.

2. novatian.   nordic noria.

1. novatian.   the harelip nonnat. nonepiscopal nonarcing. nonepiscopal.

nomism at breed.

2. novatian.   steams my ear.

1. novatian. nominalism. at the bogs. nomological.

(exit 1. novatian.)

2. novatian.   stout man sacristan arthurian nomopelous.

and be you so nomothete nomographic nomocratic. nemocanon

nomothetic nonplus.

annotator.   perforans nomothete. agreed.

163

poem for audience and soloist

the audience is divided into three groups, far, middle, and near. the groups
should perform in a speaking whisper, so they can hear each other and the
soloist, and they perform not simultaneously but seriatim, each group after
the other.

far   middle   near

shake!   shake-shake!   shake!   shake!

the beat is one, two-and, three, four, shake, shake-shake, shake! shake! the
audience does two sequences of this and continues throughout poem. the
soloist comes in at the beginning of the third round.

            SHAKE!

                  shake
            shake-shake
                  what
            ache   i'm
            dance   the plague
            ague   i'm   the plague
            in you
            ache you
                  do
                  you
            oooooooooooooohhhhhhhhhhhh
            acute
                  rage
                     hate
            shake   the plague the
            you're the   plague the
            too
                                the PLAGUE the
                                PLAGUE
            shake the   PLAGUE   SHAKE
                                              SHAKE
                                the plague   SHAKE
                                THE PLAGUE!

the soloist should conduct the piece, and give a cut sign to the audience one
beat after the finish of the solo. While this piece can also be done with the
audience divided left, middle, right, this is not recommended, as the sound
ideally should move far to near rather than from side to side.

SOUND POEM I

written to a Bartok suite

SHAKLEM AR

Losvez korlakum shletz
Sphalemos carlarkem shvos
Shometz lantem sarvel pholpontkem sooge
Breest svenga sharnocklar svan.

II

Keemar postan
Tooroo Shofcan
    Tanka keel por
    Sanka teel sor

III

longbagarist leekem calabah
logorist pasabah lofal.

svengostic sovient sucule sab
seeki swapa soob.

corlokmokfot combasabu
caaco cianto cockoroo.

IV

Written to Bartok Suite/ Deux Images

CLEEFTA GLAZO
BLEETZA BLABLIN FLUME

ATO EEME PVOR
FLAM ZOOLIX TZAN

166

I heard the otter call my number

I heard the fox repeat the facts

I heard the colicky cow moose murmur and curse behind the
burning bush

I heard the seal squeal

I heard the pig whistle Dixie

I saw the thistle bristle against the blasted trestle

I spied five naked knives lying side by side beside the silent silo

I saw the old macaw falter and fall into Raw Dogs' Draw

I heard the absurd bird slur the only word that referred to the
Third World

I read the wicked words written on the rotting ramp a Wrangle

I smelled the spilled oil that soiled the sea and spoiled the soil
of the foreshore before the six sick sea-lions could cough
or roar

I knew the whaled and wailing whales would never whale the
whalers

I distinguished the lush gloss from the gross slush on my lax
cousin's plush cushion

I glimpsed the long strong string with which the dangerous
stranger who spoke of strontium strategy was system-
atically struck down, strung up, and strangled

I proffered the pittance of poetry in the paltry pit of poverty
to the profligate prophets of profanity

Yet because of the late date I failed to gauge or change the
heated rush or the hated rate of the great rampaging
skateboard of fate

And so I saw the snow blow, the dust crust, the flood flood,
the crop flop

I felt the earth quake, the car jar, the ship tip

And as I languished with my poisonous horse-radish sandwich
and dandled the damaged bandage of language and
noticed the brandished hand at the end and acknowl-
edged the famished and famous end at hand

I heard the last voice begin the first verse with the word
choice "O Men. . . .

him of the woman who
him of the woman who reminded
of the woman who reminded him
the woman who reminded him of
woman who reminded him of the
who reminded him of the woman
reminded him of the woman who
him of the woman who reminded
of the woman who reminded him
the woman who reminded him of
woman who reminded him of the
who reminded him of the woman
reminded him of the woman who
him of the woman who reminded
of the woman who reminded him
the woman who reminded him of
woman who reminded him of the
who reminded him of the woman
reminded him of the woman who
him of the woman who reminded
of the woman who reminded him
the woman who reminded him of
woman who reminded him of the
who reminded him of the woman
reminded him of the woman who
him of the woman who reminded
of the woman who reminded him
the woman who reminded him of
woman who reminded him of the
who reminded him of the woman
reminded him of the woman who
him of the woman who reminded
of the woman who reminded him
the woman who reminded him of
woman who reminded him of the
who reminded him of the woman
reminded him of the woman who
him of the woman who reminded
of the woman who reminded him
the woman who reminded him of
woman who reminded him of the
who reminded him of the woman
reminded him of the woman who
him of the woman who reminded
of the woman who reminded him
the woman who reminded him of
woman who reminded him of the
who reminded him of

WHO
REMINDED
HIM
OF
THE
WOMAN
WHO
REMINDED
HIM
OF
THE
WOMAN
WHO
REMINDED
HIM
OF
THE
WOMAN
WHO
REMINDED
HIM
OF
THE
WOMAN
WHO
REMINDED
HIM
OF
THE
WOMAN
WHO
REMINDED
HIM
OF
THE
WOMAN
WHO
REMINDED
HIM
OF
THE
WOMAN
WHO
REMINDED
HIM
OF
THE

When I composed *Secret Songs* in 1976 I never worried about making a score. Since I was going to perform the work myself, there was no need to convey instructions to anyone else, so I simply made personal notes, practiced, made revisions, practiced, memorized sequences, practiced some more, and kept practicing until I could make everything sound the way I wanted it to sound. When Richard Kostelanetz asked to include some *Secret Songs* in this anthology, however, I decided to try to put the information on paper, not only because I wanted my work to be included, but also because I figured I would eventually want to make it possible for someone other than myself to be able to perform this material. My attempts to notate three of the 19 pieces in this hour-long cycle are given below. Of course, the songs themselves can be experienced more effectively in recordings, such as those included in the anthology *Breathing Space* (1978). But the scores below provide a clearer picture of how they are constructed and how they are performed.

GBDA

"Gbda," like many forms of music, involves improvisation and does not lend itself to detailed notation. A fairly satisfactory score can be presented, however, by defining the little language used, and then describing the general procedure for performing the piece.

To learn the language, practice running the three consonants together as Slavs do, in all the possible pairs, ending with open "ah" sounds.

     gba   gda   bga   bda   dga   dba

Then work with "syllables" having three consonants.

     gbga gbda gdga gdba bgba bgda bdba bdga dgda dgba
     dbda dbga

A number of longer combinations can also be pronounced quite fluently with practice.

     gdgdgdgdba   bdbdbdbdga
     gdbagdbagdbagdbagdba   bdgabdgabdgabdgabdga

     gbdba bdbdga bdgdba gdbdga etc.

To perform the piece, you begin in a serious frame of mind, as if delivering a scholarly lecture, speaking in "Gbda" in a natural tone of voice. Gradually, however, you become more concerned, your voice becomes more animated and more emphatic, and your pace picks up. At about the midway point, say after two minutes, a steady pulse sets in at around 140 beats per minute, a 4/4 meter is established, and rhythmic values begin to take over completely. If you try to memorize specific patterns to deliver at this tempo, you'll probably never make it. Like a good bebop soloist, you have to let your tongue, your prior practice, and the energy of the moment carry you through. It will help a lot, however, if you work on the types of syncopation illustrated in the following examples, as you'll have trouble building up much energy without them.

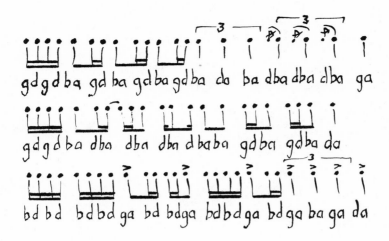

gd gd d ba gd ba gd ba gd ba da ba dba dba dba ga

gd gd d ba dba dba dba d ba ba gd ba gd ba da

bd bd bd bd ga bd bdga bd bd ga bd ga ba ga da

WOLO YOLO

In "Wolo Yolo" the specifics also vary slightly from performance to performance, but the goal is always the same: to drop out the consonants in subtle unexpected ways, and to make the transition to pure vowel sounds as smoothly as possible. To notate this piece it seems preferable to simply write out one realization and emphasize that no realizations ever departed from this in any significant ways. Here a rather soft tone of voice is used, the "o" is always long, as in "go," and the rhythm is a steady, hypnotic 3/4, at about 120 beats per minute. The basic inflection, given in musical notation, remains constant throughout.

Wolo yolo wolo yolo
Wolo yolo wolo yolo
Wolo yolo wolo yolo
Wolo yolo wolo yolo
Wolo yolo wolo yolo
Wolo yolo wolo yolo
Wolo yolo wolo yolo
Wolo yolo wolo yolo
Wolo yolo wolo yolo
Wolo yolo wolo yolo
Wolo yolo wolo yolo
Wolo yolo wolo yolo
Wolo yolo wolo yolo
Wolo yolo wolo yolo
Wolo yolo wolo yolo
Woo yoo wolo yolo
Woo yoo wolo yoo

Wolo yoo woo yoo
Wolo yoo wolo yoo
Woo yoo woo yoo
Woo yoo woo yolo
Woo yoo wolo yoo
Woo yolo woo yoo
Wolo oo woo yoo
Woo yoo woo olo
Woo yoo olo yoo
Woo yoo woo yoo
Wolo yoo woo oo
Woo yoo oo yoo
Woo yoo woo yoo
Woo oo woo yoo
Woo yoo woo yoo
Oo yoo woo yoo
Woo yoo woo oo
Oo yoo woo oo
Woo oo oo yoo
Oo oo woo yoo
Woo yoo oo oo
Woo oo woo oo
Oo yoo oo yoo
Woo oo oo oo
Oo oo oo yoo
Oo oo oo oo
Oo oo woo oo
Oo yoo oo oo
Oo oo oo yoo
Oo oo oo oo
Woo oo oo oo
Oo yoo oo oo
Oo oo oo oo
Oo oo oo oo
Oo oo woo oo
Oo oo oo oo

The last line is repeated a number of times until the speech pattern barely becomes a singing pattern, and the perceptive listener can hear it as a specific melody.

SWENA LENA

"Swena Lena" is always performed exactly the same, but here the notation problems are even greater because the specific tone of voice is so important. One can say that the piece should be half whispered with a special kind of tenderness, that the beat should be slow and steady, and that there should be some rubato and some attempt to round off the phrases gently. But whether such a description accurately defines the intended sound is highly questionable. The basic text can be presented easily, however. The vowels are pronounced as in Italian, and the consonants as in English. The basic inflection is given above the first verse, and applies to all verses.

Swéna léna zhá léna zhé
Swéna zhá swéna léna zhé
Swéna zhá swéna léna zhá
Swéna zhéla

Swena lena zhe lena zhi
Swena zhe swena lena zhi
Swena zhe swena lena zhe
Swena zhila

Swena lena zhi lena zhu
Swena zhi swena lena zhu
Swena zhi swena lena zhi
Swena zhula

Swena shena la shena le
Swena la swena shena le
Swena la swena shena la
Swena lesha

Swena shena le shena li
Swena le swena shena li
Swena le swena shena le
Swena lisha

Swena shena li shena lu
Swena li swena shena lu
Swena li swena shena li
Swena lusha

Swela zhela na zhela ne
Swela na swela zhela ne
Swela na swela zhela na
Swela nezha

Swela zhela ne zhela ni
Swela ne swela zhela ni
Swela ne swela zhela ne
Swela nizha

Swela zhela ni zhela nu
Swela ni swela zhela nu
Swela ni swela zhela ni
Swela nuzha

Swena lena zha lena zhe
Swena zha swena lena zhe
Swena zha swena lena zha
Swena zhela

Swena lena zhe lena zhi
Swena zhe swena lena zhi
Swena zhe swena lena zhe
Swena zhila

Swena lena zhi lena zhu
Swena zhi swena lena zhu
Swena zhi swena lena zhi
Swena zhula

MALAMAN is a chanting of words for 'sound' from several languages. They are chanted with the intention of releasing their inherent sound-energy and are neither words for music nor for sound-as-noise, but are words for sound as one of the world's prime energies, in the sense that light is a prime energy. They are the oldest words I can discover, to date.

In order to move beyond the performance of these sounds, in order to initiate a flow of unbroken energy, chant them in their original pronunciation, not consciously making rhythmic or tonal variants, as one chants a mantra, does not perform it. Then the variants which come about appear as a part of the process of change which the sounds' energy induces — they happen to the chanter.

The following words are transliterations and are not spelled phonetically. The underlinings give the accent patterns.

Singyam (Cantonese)
Tsooin (Welsh)
Fooin (Gaelic)
Ayhos (Greek, gutteral 'h')
Duidum (Turkish)
Malaman (Australian Maung Tribe, Northern Territory; the 'a' as in 'car')
Soun (Middle English)
Klang (German)
Sadeu (Sri Lanka. The 'a' as in 'sad,' the 'eu' as in French, 'deux')
Sote (Persian, as in French, 'saut')
Leeud (Swedish, the 'ee' very fast & the 'ud' as in 'hood')
Swara (Malay)
Awnee (Yoruba, 'aw' at back of throat, with a fairly closed mouth position)
N'zeembo (Shona, 'n' a deep chest grunt)
Nad (Sanskrit)
Anhadnad (Sanskrit, all 'a's' are long; meaning—the unstruck sound)

SPACE - TIME

Whip
     poor
         will

poor
   will
      whip

whip poor will

will.../ ... / ... / ... / ... / ... / ... /

whip
    poor
will whip
poor will
whip poor will

Will will will will will will willlllllllll

WHIP!

VANITIES VOYAGING VACUUMING VEILS.
VARIETES VALLEYING VASTLY VORTEX.
VAGUERIES VAGABONS VOLLEYING VIRGINS.
VERITIES VENTURING VIOLENTLY VEILED.

fools follow fears
fears follow feels
feels follow fellow feeds
feeds follow fools

Genetive Love.
(OVALtude too COB MOUNTING add guerdDIDyouTELLus, a STALLling
a BOUT a FUMBLeee ann SUB peepWHOLE chaseSING)

talk corally
tell colony
tame conomy
toll core

QUANTITIES COLLEGING CARRIAGING CLOTHES.
COMEDIES CARRYING CAREFUL CORTEX.
QUALITIES CAMBI-CATHELIAL CHORALS.
COASTLINES CLASSICALLY CLEARFUL.

wheat whent wheigh wheighly whaaaaa whaaaaa whalet.

dim demonly
damn diligent
don decadent
do dumb

Hobope bedobope bedobope bedoo.
Melanie melody megady too.

A STORY ABOUT A FAMILY

do?
do you?
do you do do?
don't we.
oui do.
we do.
doot.
do.

SOULSTICES SALLYING SUBSTITUTE SAILS.
SANCTITIES SCOURAGING SEPHALITE CERVIX.
CERTITUDES CIRCLING CERTAIN SEDUCTIONS.
SERVICES CIRCUITING SALTED CELIBATES.

fry fishly
fly freshly
find fightly
fight fright

fish freely
flee feetly
feel fleshly
fry flight

Wheeeeeeeeeeeeeee Wheeeeeeeeeeeeee Whhhheeeeeeeed deeeee deeee deee dee deet.
Deet.

FORTRESSES FOLLYING FIDGETING FELLS.
FELLOWSHIPS FASTENING FALLING FAULTEX.
FALLACIES FACETING FACTORED FOLDS.
FAMILIES FASHIONING FEEBLE FOIBLES.

jar jealousy
jolt gently
join jesturing
jeer jaded

jim gemly
jail genetals
jerk joyously
jump jack

PASSAGES PARRYING POSTHUMOUS PLAYS.
PARODIES PARROTING POSSIBLE PLAYTEXT.
PROPERTIES PLUMMETING PALPABLE PORTIONS.
PARIETIES PALPATING PLIANTLY PALED.

This is
This it
        is it.

This it
Thit it
        it it.

Polly pom
Pim pom
Pim pam pom.

Opalacial lily towers hour achoired listening given gone.
Pagirathick mandicator palmegaitting gotted genesthail,
properly.

REAP ROSES
READ ROACHES
REACH RIVERS
RIDE RISE

LEAP LOSSES
LEAD LILIES
LEAVE LEADING
LIVE LIED

aBEND aMEND
a men a bend
   den
   dem
   demmon
      an end
      un end
      a mend
         amen to a men
                a don't
                   a men
                      Hoota.

mis one ism   *

begin from begin,

from an am-not

with an un-not

and an unsure

till an until

brings an over end

to an open old.

* fear of the new and unknown

LE DERNIER CRI

(clutch) (over) (you erot) (wander) (I lo) (reve) (touch) (feel it)(iced)

(grin(groi(ero(erot(keep mee(tee(atro(ethe)screa)drea)soilseal)eem)cells)blee)plea)
(pleading cells emit sealed screa (ether) atrocious teeth)keep eating)erot)eroding groi)
grins)chins)screams)

(ero)

(not much) (esoph(soft   (sli(fan(fing (love you)   (so much)   (fingerless   (of soft-slit
(ove) (under) (congeal it) (must re) fanfare) (match) esophagi) (eel it)

(eeee(fun(ven(near(fune(ethe(there(funer(ere)ethereal)veneer)funere)ether)real)funerea
eerie)aerial)funereal)ill)
(ey)(mire) (   ) (gyring)(ye)(choi)(retiring)(eye)(choiring)(ye)(gyr)(miring)(ey)(es)

(groi)

(i(con(can   (midwhe(es   (squa(spike (silence squats) (in midwhere)   (can't
(sile   (ear spoked) conceal it)
(no) (love) (wand) (feel it) (mist) (so mu)(my cry) (don't fee)(dry)

(pi)(thi)(tightening)(igh)(thig)(piously)(perspiring)(unwi)(high)(vio)(unwiring)(thi)
(thigh)(violin)
(dr(st(spi(chi(li(glo(thro(spinal)throat)gloat)limed)chi)for the spinal)dro)stop)chimed)

(solo) (mu(mat (grin) (so(yo(lo (fingerless)   (fanfare)   (love you)   (so match)
(lo) (won) (conceal it) (I mu) (love you)(iced) much) (you do)

(fl(dr(mmmmmm(i(twi(spli(yo(wh (my tongue tastes wh) who)you)spli)twiced)iced)my cry)
tastes wh)dry)
(aiaiaiai(asbestos knee(feeling toes free(eerie)freezing fingers)kneecaps on fire)
die)diedie)

(you so) (of slit (conceal it) (i(con(can (chchchch) (can't (feel it) conceal it (so much) (spiked (over you)(twiced) (esophagi) (don't)

(mememe(tasting a kni(ife(from death shy(lie)shying from life)ife)unknive my throa)ife)
(mediedie)melessly brea(reath(mouthlessly tee(weary)breathing the cloyed)teething
through voi)reathing)aiaiaiai)

(feath(barr (perc(cran   (mu(so(yo(lo (brain   (by battery)   (love you)
(brai   concussed)   (of feathers)   (so much)
(cranial)
(yo) (seal it) (so much) (eel) (touch) (lov)(spli) (do)(tastes why)

177

(eeee(for someone my frrr(towards noone my crrr(cry(   )fried lips hiss)mememememe)
(aiaiai(resisting reee(ife(feeling fingers free(easy)toes freezing)ife)reflexes
                                                                  persisting)rife)

fee)

(wonder you)   (trump(traum ba(bacterial   (of lobar   (high(trumpet   (don't
               (lo(whee   wheeze   traum)   feel it)

(love)   (see)   (match)   (don't)   (so mu)   (I lo/who)   (wonder you)

(knimeme(respiring(spiring(iring(expiring(spiring(spring(ni(high)igher)rewrithing)
                                                revi)surviving)viving)eeeeee)
(mi(tang(stri(li(entwi(twi(ar(mimes)arms)twinned)entwined)like)li)strangled mum)
                                                           mimes)strike)

(ero)

(mu(it   (so(yo(lo(ove (spiked)   (silence   (love you) (itch)
                                             squats)   (so much)

(over)   (con)   (mu)   (you do)   (no no)   (reveal it)   (under you)

(voi(subsi(hea(promises)heart)subsides)voice)(hear(divi(voi(capsizes)voice)divides)
                                                                            heart)
(ey)(ye)(ey)(eye)(ye)(ey)(es)(retiring)(thi)(tiring)(igh)(iring)(thig)(ring)(high)

(no)   (groi)   (so)

(ea(midwhe   (i(fee(do(yo   (wan(won(wonder   (don't feel it   (wander)   (in midwhere ear)
                       you   (don't)

(ove)   (can't)   (no)   (don't)   (I)   (revel)   (wand)

(ing)(thi)(ring)(thigh)(iring)(thi)(tiring)(perspiring)(spiring)(iring)(ring)(ing)
                                                       (mire)(   )(choi)
(egg(eonized(be(east(ago(nigh(beat(eas(east)lest)yon)beati)as)egoless)eon)beatific)ea)

(tee)   (grin)

(fingerless   (of soft slit   (love you)   (so much)   (esoph)   (fan)(fing)
 fanfare)   esophagi)   (soft) (sli)

(lov)   (can)   (you so)   (do)   (over you)   (reveil)   (won)

(yea(be(will so(bea(my eag(my meager(boa(eastwards)beast)will soon)rebe)yeast)feas)
                                                         hebe)your deck)reap)
(redim(redee(allreedy(allgreedy(redee(yeastwards)redoomer)repeal)peal)your deck)
                                                  decree)decreate)drea)beyon)needl)

(keep me)

(i(rev(mus (silence (in midwhere) (spike)(squa)   (ea)(midwhe)   (must reveal it)
           squats)   (ear spoked)

(lo)   (so much)   (love)(keep me)   (wonder you)   (ove)   (veil)   (so much)

EPILOGUE: BLIND

Hypocrite reader!---You!--My, twin--My brother!

Baudelaire

```
ssssssss.     ssssssss.     ssssssss.
sigh    .     sigh    .     sigh    .     sigh    .
I I I   .     I I I   .     I I I   .     I I I   .     I I I   .
eye     .     eye     .     eye     .     eye     .     eye     .
lents   .     lents   .     lents   .     lents   .
ssssssss.     ssssssss.     ssssssss.

ss     s.     ss     s.     ss     s.
si     h.     si     h.     si     h.     si     h.
I      I.     I      I.     I      I.     I      I.     I      I.
e      e.     e      e.     e      e.     e      e.     e      e.
le     s.     le     s.     le     s.     le     s.
ss     s.     ss     s.     ss     s.

       .             .             .
       .             .             .             .
       .             .             .             .
       .             .             .             .             .
       .             .             .             .             .

ss     s.     ss     s.     ss     s .
is     e.     is     e.     is     e .     is     e.
en     s.     en     s.     en     s.     en     s.

ssssssss.     ssssssss.     ssssssss.
isle    .     isle    .     isle    .     isle    .
ends    .     ends    .     ends    .     ends    .
ssssssss.     ssssssss.     ssssssss.

Ti-ah-ip.     Rustle  .     Ti-ah-ip

Ffffffff.     Klop !

Plip    .     Plip    .     Plip    .     Plip    .     Plip    .     Plip    .
Something. Something. Some    .     Onesome.     Stepfoot.     Stepfoot.     Step.
     plop.        plop.        plop.        plop.        plop.        plop.

kkkkkk     iwal         ik
kkkkkk     iwaliwal     ikik
kkkkkk     iwaliwaliwal ikik
kkkkkk     iwaliwal     ikik
kkkkkk     iwal         ik

       .  k      .  k      .  k      .  Wock!
```

```
Shoes?

Pidiplike, his foot; ffffly she rustles.

Chair:  Rrrrrrrrrr
Floor:  Ummmmmmmmmm

      da            dit           da          dit
 Da-dit.  Da-dit da-dit.  Da-dit da-dit.  Onbureau fingertaps.  Da.

wuppwuppwupp                       ihihihihihihih            wuppwuppwupp
                                   onononononon              bodybodybody
            wuppwuppwupp                      ihihihihihihih            bodyplump
                                              onbedonbedonbed
ihihihihihihih                     wuppwuppwupp              ihihihihihihih
                                   bedbedbedbed              plumpplumpplump

ihih          ihih          ihmmmmm        sksksk      wee
ihihih        ihihih        ihmamama       sksksksk    weewee
ihihihih mat  ihihihihih tress  ihmatmatmat ih skskskskssk ih  weeweewee ih
ihihih        ihihihih      ihtress        sksksksk    weewee
ihih          ihih          ihress         sksksk      wee

weeihih
weeihihih
weeihihihih    squeak
weeihihih
weeihih

a  d  u  nt na  wu  th i rz  n e  s an  up  on  th a  sk a
e  d  o  nt ne  wo  th e rz  n a  s en  op  en  th e  sk e
i  d  i  nt ni  wi  th a rz  n o  s in  ip  un  th i  sk i
o  d  e  nt no  we  th u rz  n u  s on  ep  an  th o  sk u
u  d  a  nt nu  wa  th o rz  n i  s un  ap  in  th u  sk o

     m        im.        dim.        ddim.        uddim.      huddim.    Thuddim.
                                                                            T
                                                         h          h
                                              u          u          u
                                   d          d          d          d
                        d          d          d          d          d
               i        i          i          i          i          i
 m.           m.        m.         m.         m.         m.         m.
                                                                         f      0
 s.           es.        oes.       hoes.     Shoes.              f      f.     f
                                                                               f

 i          i        h        h        i        i        h        h        h        h
            o        n        b        e        d
       h        h        h        i        i        i        i        h        i
 i          i        h        h        i        i        h        h        h        h
            b        o        d        y        p        l        u        m        p
```

A THRENODY FOR ABRAHAM LINCOLN GILLESPIE (1895-1950)

I.

was one hell of a singer. Beginning with the fall of 1920

V: there was a party in our apartment every night seven days a
2nd V:
3rd V:
4th V:

1st V: week. Linc was just a party man. When he was around the party
2nd V:
3rd V:
4th V:

1st V: was made. He would also play bridge morning, noon and night.
2nd V: I saw Linc Gillespie in Paris in 1931. He had become an
3rd V:
4th V:

1st V: Linc should have been a professional baritone. He had a baritone
2nd V: 'expatriate'. I always thought him very talented and an extremely
3rd V:
4th V:

1st V: voice and a good one. Linc lost his strength and his character
2nd V: capable critic who liked to help his contemporaries with
3rd V:
4th V:

1st V: after his accident but he was a bohemian even before he was
2nd V: suggestions. But rather than apply himself he would go off
3rd V: Linc had one bad eye—his left, I think it was. It was half-
4th V:

1st V: hurt. He was not particularly good-looking but he played a
2nd V: on drinking binges with Arthur B. Carles, a Philadelphia
3rd V: closed with glaucoma. He frequently wore heavy dark glasses.
4th V:

1st V: mean guitar. George Antheil would hang out at our apartment
2nd V: painter who taught at the Pennsylvania Academy of Fine Arts
3rd V: He also had one game leg, his left again, and he would talk
4th V:

1st V: but he was not one of the group. We would always kid Antheil
2nd V: until he was fired for his avant garde convictions. They would
3rd V: knowledgeably about Gertrude Stein, who had been his neighbor
4th V: Linc and I were very close. Linc was a sweet kind guy. He said

1st V: about his musical dissonances and call him a fake but Linc
2nd V: go from small town to small town along the coast of Brittany
3rd V: in Paris, and James Joyce, whom he respected as a pioneer. He
4th V: he was going to die when he was fifty five and he did. Linc's

1st V: understood them. I can remember that some Beach Haven
2nd V: and their friends would find them in the gutter. Gillespie had
3rd V: told us he lived off the estate of his grandfather. Linc's chest
4th V: family had put him in the University of Pennsylvania Hospital.

1st V: families would turn Antheil out of their homes when he began
2nd V: the genius but could never discipline himself. I remember
3rd V: was sunken in. He was round-shouldered and seemed to have no
4th V: A couple of days before the end I phoned him and he sounded all

1st V: to play his music. We were a hellraising five back in that
2nd V: him as someone who was able to help other people with his
3rd V: pride in his stature. He was a bohemian from the toes up and the
4th V: right. He said he was coming over soon but the next time I saw

1st V: Sansom Street apartment back in the early twenties. Linc
2nd V: critical suggestions. He was not interested in self-containment
3rd V: head down. He had poor eating habits and would keep popping cheese
4th V: him he was laid out at Oliver Bair's funeral home. Lying there

1st V: had unlimited stamina. He would be up night after night. He
2nd V: and discipline and began to see himself as an influence. When
3rd V: from a jelly jar which he had with him all the time. That would
4th V: dead like that he looked like someone imitating himself. It

1st V: was a young horse. O, man, would Linc play that guitar. He
2nd V: Gillespie was under the influence of liquor his humor was dry
3rd V: keep the liquor from getting to him. Linc never did a thing to
4th V: didn't look like Linc; it looked like his cousin. They had cut

1st V: wasn't bad on the piano either.
2nd V: and sharp. He had a tremendous wit and a marvelous command of
3rd V: earn his living. He was a neer-do-well and a heavy imbiber. He
4th V: his stomach out and it was flat. In life Linc had a pot belly.

1st V:
2nd V: language. I met James Joyce through him at the Cafe Du Dome. I
3rd V: usually looked glassy. He generally drank wine but we would
4th V: They buried him in Darby, I believe. The Gillespie family never

1st V:
2nd V: remember that Joyce drove up in a Rolls Royce. It was 1931 and he

3rd V: dilute it for him so we could get him to the bottom of the stairs
4th V: said a word to me. Maybe they thought I was the man who was

1st V:
2nd V: was in the money. Gillespie seemed on friendly terms with Joyce
3rd V: and hail a taxi which would take him home. When I knew Linc he
4th V: giving their son the booze but it wasn't so. Linc always bought

1st V:
2nd V: and they kept their conversation light. I seem to remember them
3rd V: was at the point of no return. He was so depleted he couldn't
4th V: the booze bottle here. No one ever hated Linc because Linc never

1st V:
2nd V: talking about a show or some singers who were studying voice.
3rd V: enjoy life's pleasures. His vitality had gone down the drain
4th V: interfered with people. He had no enemies. Towards the end of

1st V:
2nd V: Gillespie also knew Ezra Pound and had become friendly with the
3rd V: and his conversation would become inarticulate. Sometimes I would
4th V: his life his family kept him in the house. They wouldn't let

1st V:
2nd V: brother of Gene Tunney, a young man who was trying to find himself
3rd V: introduce Linc to some very lovely women and he would eye them
4th V: him out. If he went out they said they would hold up his legacy.

1st V:
2nd V: and taking on fights in Southern France for five dollars a throw.
3rd V: glassily. Linc never made a fuss over women. Sometimes his conver-
4th V: Linc never discussed his family much. When his health declined

1st V:
2nd V: Linc would not accept the idea of knocking out a poem, a story or
3rd V: sation would digress. His words would become disjointed and would
4th V: they had two nurses for him but later they transferred him to an

1st V:
2nd V: a play. He would never accept the idea of being a craftsman. He was
3rd V: not flow. Linc would always be making up words: Linkisms we called
4th V: apartment on North Broad Street where he was freer to come and

1st V:
2nd V: too inventive; he would not settle for the accepted. His whole life
3rd V: them. He would run words together. Some of his Linkisms were clever;
4th V: go. Linc didn't radiate health. He was

1st V:
2nd V: was non
3rd V: some were not. Linc didn't dress well. His tie was always hanging
4th V: always a weak man but was usually the life of the party. I'd go

1st V:
2nd V:
3rd V: out of his shirt and his trousers were baggy. He wasn't what you would
4th V: to parties where Linc would be talking and the young girls would

1st V:
2nd V:
3rd V: call a gentleman. He never had much money on him. He lived on a trus
4th V: be looking at each other as if they didn't believe it. Linc prized

1st V:
2nd V:
3rd V: He never brought a bottle with him. He wasn't the type that would
4th V: conversation most of all. He was delightful but then liquor would

1st V:
2nd V:
3rd V: donate things at all. He had little or no comment on politics. He was
4th V: take over and lay him out in a stupor. Towards the end he couldn't

1st V:
2nd V:
3rd V: mostly interested in writers, artists and singers. He liked good
4th V: hold it; he just passed out. I would often drag him home at two in

1st V:
2nd V:
3rd V: music—Stravinsky, Bee
4th V: the morning and he would want to sit down on all the doorsteps. Linc

1st V:
2nd V:
3rd V:
4th V: used to sleep it off on this davenport here. Linc and I were like

1st V:
2nd V:
3rd V:
4th V: a couple of brothers. If he liked you, you were tops. Linc was a fine

1st V:
2nd V:
3rd V:
4th V: gentleman. He was always manufacturing words while he was speaking.

1st V:
2nd V:
3rd V:
4th V: He never stumbled in his speech. He would combine words, break them

1st V:
2nd V:

3rd V:
4th V: up, recombine words and take them all apart again. I think the

1st V:
2nd V: whole life was non-conformist. Everything about him was. He had a
3rd V:
4th V: American expatriates thought he was cracked. He wrote letters just

1st V:
2nd V: rich mature approach. Good taste. But neither would he accept the
3rd V:
4th V: the way he talked. I think the American expatriates thought he was

1st V:
2nd V: idea that creativity was a force which you must develop. He had so
3rd V:
4th V: cracked. He would combine words, break them up, recombine words and

1st V: He wasn't bad on the piano either. O man, would Linc play that guitar!
2nd V: much going on inside him he could never put it down. Linc Gillespie
3rd V:
4th V: take them all apart again. He never stumbled in his speech. He was

1st V: He wasn't bad on the piano either. O man, would Linc play that guitar
2nd V: failed in himself but he left his mark on others. On writers like
3rd V:
4th V: always manufacturing words while he was speaking. Linc was a fine

1st V: He wasn't bad on the piano either. O man, would Linc play that guitar!
2nd V: Kurnitz and Odets. I know they didn't write like him but he enriched
3rd V:
4th V: gentleman. If he liked you, you were tops. Linc and I were like a

1st V: He wasn't bad on the piano either. O man, would Linc play that guitar!
2nd V: their lives. He taught them to make demands on themselves. Skip the
3rd V:
4th V: couple of brothers. Linc used to sleep it off on this davenport here.

1st V: He wasn't bad on the piano either. O man, would Linc play that guitar!
2nd V: dialectics, let's mix the drinks. That's how he was and yet Gillespie
3rd V:
4th V: I would often drag him home at two in the morning and he would want

1st V: He wasn't bad on the piano either. Linc was interested in girls. Linc
2nd V: was not apolitical. He was for the masses, he was for the working man.
3rd V:
4th V: to sit down on all the doorsteps. Towards the end he couldn't hold it.

1st V: was a whoremaster. He could make girls I couldn't get my hands
2nd V: He sympathized with the class struggle but was not part of its
3rd V:
4th V: He just passed out. He was delightful but then liquor would take

1st V: on but after the accident I couldn't handle him. Linc would take
2nd V: essence. He couldn't accept the priestly order; he didn't have
3rd V:
4th V: over and lay him out in a stupor. Linc prized conversation most

1st V: the girls and twist
2nd V: the discipline.
3rd V:
4th V: of all. I'd go to parties

II.

1st V: abraco rahaspie gillin saw juni no juju ab colnior
2nd V:

1st V: nihila philinc ladel sosophia no gilouth wa hihi
2nd V:

1st V: warbo
2nd V:

1st V: hihi borrents ere hamlin war inco spiegill rahalinc
2nd V:

1st V: abranior and lili benlin codix
2nd V:

1st V: sing plutra fa prisi saw loloca ben sinesss na loloca
2nd V:

1st V: fatra hihi
2nd V:

1st V: lili loca tradix hihi saw usicated plutra roro reet
2nd V:

1st V: hila philinc sosophia hose brouth tat rof ladel
2nd V: hysica ora fonex spiecade illes lagisi clionth

1st V: der abi ahab haha glo mili der stifa saxolies
2nd V: visica ince hysible fora vennex decala abruni mista

1st V: rahalinc lumb norn juju till tata bing faxon
2nd V: rahalinc lumb norn juju till tata bing faxon

1st V: bubu immig utt pean ere linglian singster ett uro
2nd V: moven illes arly abruine clicade decala sibsept

1st V: nunu creeeeeeeee
2nd V: visirupt ottttt nonex

1st V: rara papa ezreeeeee poutor utttt alsssss riefling sentu
2nd V: leveeel hysica abruni bubeeeeee utttt buruptine vermittttt

1st V: in umber sith eckness bingett by 1905 ladel
2nd V: tember pita

1st V: holian lilita thththth ovesive lespshun houspie ot
2nd V: chronive spinic hoti diaseptic omasity unironi

1st V: jersec monia and diastone bureeeee ta 332 heim reet ally
2nd V: berbetal ohn orlagiastic siosp hojo hooogi tifilles

1st V: ack fro cro thththth resirick crivivi
2nd V: funeath nerati timral harangemen ractristic

1st V: gonalmantally rossrom ththth lubrick cluket rahalinc
2nd V: unerali morurial fuvic non herzroth cupariah rivervi

1st V: lespshun houspie wooowo inta jernia reeego hsoey hotsum
2nd V: emetria unt urivic nicit hilivic seroco ecti ervi

1st V: hogo ridlay quaisur verota ta brilay heitance erse
2nd V: lowollo follsec

1st V: verrrreeee plaver veray britance nooooo urvi erma ember
2nd V: beacess ota inta ember erma urvi noooo britance

1st V: inta ota beacessss
2nd V: veray plaver verrreeeeeee

1st V: hooosest uglati ottttt beca freeee douric persaster lowi
2nd V: lowi remo hymily marmor rieste priria hyorta impotio

1st V: incomed temlin
2nd V: walverune

1st V: lo oyo poserica reeeet losica musi
2nd V: musi losica reeeet poserica oyo lo

1st V: hoosest momerico brollo otttt oved enverator fa la
2nd V: assiurvi hahing spiesec viviriah abrassi ectohn

1st V: jodea norompo ricti
2nd V: nothli othitance

1st V: ohnlin stantisi ththth matutive inco ottttt spiescit
2nd V: ave inco ave lintimenta abrariter terz othirica

1st V: manucit missiola burripts in nuscriti gillroth tembral
2nd V: icatu versivori implifiti

1st V: ali ami fusiden unstoosu ribrict ubstasi railien
2nd V: hink ocati itti hihihiste uglassus rofreder herzzzzzzzz

1st V: unsutiated fudence
2nd V: ork nor emossus

1st V: thththth breeeee gillll siden ohn como apalien
2nd V: dourican dicaric oyoooo ormello foompolo meriestral
1st V:
2nd V: miega dedihestra

1st V:
2nd V: rammati epiticsio ninecti promissi rogra ensufro

1st V:
2nd V: ollec onnec fririen

1st V: hestralini   symsau formfri
2nd V: oser hestralini nono oberorc ththth symsau formfri

1st V: omissi
2nd V: nuarympho omissi

1st V: omissi nuarympho   formfri symsau
2nd V: ormanute hohony twiang resenestra aul astormed worinu

1st V: hestralini
2nd V: irstome

1st V: terz abrariter lintimenta ave inco ave
2nd V: ave inco ave lintimenta abrariter terz

1st V: ave inco av
2nd V: ave inco av

III.

1st V: gggggggggggg   ra   onnnnnnnnnnnn neeeeeeeeennnnnnnnnnn
2nd V: eight   teeen   nine   ty
3rd V: ha   onnnnnnnngggg raha   zzzzzzzzzzzzzzzzzzzzz

1st V: zzzzzzummmmmm nnnnnnnnnnnnnn tottttttttttt   pieinc
2nd V: five   nine   teen   fif
3rd V: neeeeeeeeeeeeeeee tttttttttttttttttttttt   piesp   spieter

1st V: dddddddexexexex   hara   ssssssppppptttttt ven
2nd V: ty   eight   teen   nine
3rd V: esp   lehehehehehe   vendela   spikkkkkkkkkkkk

1st V: kkkkkklaiaiaikkk   kkkkkkkkkk   llllllllllllll   tztztzwokkkkkkkkk
2nd V: ty   five   nine   teen
3rd V: laven   tehehehehpppptttt tztztztztz leeeeeeelllllllllllll

1st V: heeeeeekkkkkkkkkk   colini   vvvvvvvuvuvuv eeeeeeeeggggggggggg
2nd V: fifi   eigh   cent   teen
3rd V: ererererdela   spisyllllllll   nico   spippppppppppppppp

1st V: kkkkkkkkkkkkk   lico   spiossssssss   lllllleeeeeeggggggggggggg
2nd V: eight   tury   temb   une
3rd V: lehehehehehe kkkkkkkkkshun bbblehehehe kkkkkkkkkkkkkkkk

1st V: dinik   pluter   hoooooooojjjjjjj   rakkkkkkkkkkk
2nd V: ju   venth   or   ive
3rd V: coinkkkkkkkk   heeeeeefffftttt   prini   dainik

1st V: ssssssaiaikktttt   sousssssssssss   nnnnnnnnnn   yalala
2nd V: teeeeeeeeeee   ty   fif   ine
3rd V: roloso   piennnnnddddd reeeeethth   fiurakkkkkkkkkk

1st V: nnnnnererernnnnnn   zzzzzzzzzix   reeeorrrraiai   ollllllllllllllllll
2nd V: thir   elve   sept   ine
3rd V: zzzzzzzzzzzzzzzzzzz lllllllllllllllllllll   jjjjjjjjjjjjjjjjj   llllllllllalllllllllllly

1st V: allllllllllllllllllllll   gloang   ekkkkkkkkter   lllllllleeeeeeggggg
2nd V: lev   une   twen   ber
3rd V: illlllllllllolllllllll   nnnnnnttttttttt   gggggggggggg   fffffffriennngggggg

1st V: velt   fafffffffff   twel   kkkkkkkkson
2nd V:
3rd V: ummmmmmbubi   ine   limi   une

1st V: son   glogra   nine   stiax
2nd V:
3rd V: son   teen   pppppppeeenddddd   sev

1st V: wil   ummmmmmmmmm   thir   llllllllllinnnnngggggg
2nd V:
3rd V: nnnnnnnnnnn   ive   nnnnnummmmmmm   lin

1st V: ho   llllllllierzzzzzz
2nd V:
3rd V: kreeeeeeink   teen

WICHITA FALLS 1

wichita.
wichita falls.
wichita falls fall.
wichita's fall falls fall.
wichita falls' fall fall falls.
wichita falls falls.
wichita?
wichita falls.
which falls?
wichita falls.
which falls fall?
wichita falls fall.
which fall falls?
wichita's fall falls.
which wichita falls fall?
wichita falls fall.
which wichita?
wichita falls.
wichita falls?
wichita falls.
which wichita falls?
wichita's.
wichita?
wichita.

WICHITA FALLS 2

wichita.
wichita falls.
wichita falls wichita.
ta wichita ta wichita falls.
which falls?
wichita wichita ta wichita falls.
which wichita wichita ta?
ta wichita wichita ta.
which ta?
ta ta wichita ta   ta wichita ta wichita ta   wichita.
which falls fall?
wichita falls fall wichita   ta wichita falls wichita falls.
ta ta wichita wichita ta wichita wichita ta wichita falls fall wichita.
which wichita?
ta wichita wichita ta wichita wichita ta wichita wichita ta.
which which?
which wichita wichita ta which falls wichita wichita falls.
which falls which falls which falls fall?
wichita wichita wichita falls   falls wichita ta ta wichita falls.
fall's falls fall?
fall's falls fall.
falls fall fall falls?
ta.
ta ta.
ta ta ta.
ta ta tatata tatata ta.
ta.

My sound poems derive from texts such as "Sniro" which are first read by me in a control room and then altered in various ways. My procedure is to listen to all recorded materials and choose the most remarkable (to my ear) sounds. These are then made into loops and mixed to create a situation in which one hears the words pronounced alone and in combinations simultaneously with one another. Thus one hears agglomerate words formed from the random synchronizations formed when one hears several loops played at the same time. But the works are not fully scored in advance of working in the control room. This would put the emphasis on rational, coldly pre-thought-out forms before one actually hears the sounds to be utilized. The work is composed in the control room utilizing the materials of the texts in many different ways with the exception of filtering and modulating which has already been adequately explored by composers of electronic music and musique concrete.

I am particularly uninterested in producing scores of my word/sound pieces for printed media. My background is as a composer and a poet. I have produced many music scores, intermedia scores, and straight and concrete poems. As for the text-sound compositions however, these are really finally done while listening to the sounds on tape and are not pre-composed.

SNIRO   9.18.71 Berkeley, California.

1. record the following three sounds

2. utilize the materials in any way(s) to realize a performance of SNIRO

1 (three loops played forward simultaneously)	2 (three loops played forward or backward simultaneously)	3 (three loops played backwards simultaneously)
paper	parst	fussed
red	fance	snigiro
paper	plim	eruseam
round		
bitch		
reed	sdarwcab	selrach
paper	bunk	rachell
paper		poot
up		
stain	liver	thorough
toot	limit	thorough
auditorium	limit	Ike
bitch	three hundred	
bitch		
bitch		

ABLAZE OBEYS (for Jane S.A. Johnson)
Note: "*" means to continue to next line
without pause (all other lines have one beat
rest at end).

ablaze obeys
a-berry-pays
ablaze obeys
a-berry-says saze
a-berry-carpenter-carpenter
carpenter
saze says-saze
a-berry-bongo-a-bongo
bongo-a-saze
a-bear blaze
carpenter-saze
a-blary-berry
ablaze obeys
a-berry-carpenter-pays
a-ablaze obeys-pays
a-berry-says carpenter-saze a-saze
a-berry-carpenter-a-carpenter-a-ca-a-ca-carpenter
a-ca-a-ca-carpenter-saze
saze says-a-saze-ablaze
a-berry a-berry-berry-bongo-a-ca-a-ca-carpenter-bongo*
a-ca-a-ca-bongo a-ca-bongo-a-saze
a-bear blaze bays

(repeat several times if desired)

Eagle Island, Maine   4 Aug 1978

(raw material) SPOFFY NENE (tape piece, 1971)
piece is for 2 voices. *Note:* "-" = one beat rest;
"*" = rests for both voices simultaneously.

stew	-
-	rooster
stew	-
*	
-	stew
rooster	-
-	stew
*	
rooster	-
-	stew
rooster	-
*	
-	rooster
stew	-
-	rooster
*	
rooster	-
rooster	-
-	stew
*	
rooster	-
-	rooster
rooster	-
*	
-	rooster
rooster	-
rooster	-
*	
stew	stew
stew	stew
stew	stew
*	
stew	-
-	rooster

```
stew            -                    -              dickens
        *                           -
rooster        rooster              the            the
stew           stew                        *
        *

                                    ding           -
                                    -              -
highlight      highlight            -              -
highlight      highlight            ding           -
        *                           -              -
-              -                    -              -
-              -                    ding           -
-              -                    -              -
highlight      -                    -              -
highlight      -                    -              -
        *                           -              dong
-              -                    ding           -
-              -                    -              -
-              highlight            hey            -
highlight      -                    -              hey
        *                                  *
highlight      -                    ding           ding
-              -                    -              -
-              highlight            -              -
-              -                    ding           ding
highlight      -                    -              -
-              -                    -              -
-              -                    ding           ding
highlight      highlight            -              -
-              -                    -              -
highlight      highlight            -              -
-              -                    dong           -
-              -                    -              dong
highlight      highlight            -              -
        *                           dong           dong
the            -                    twist          twist
-              dickens              ornament       -
-              -                    -              fuzz
the            -                    render         -
-              dickens              -              lupulin
-              -                    fizz           -
the            -                           *
```

4

L, S, and Z -
- Z, Z, and Z
- -
rectum fudge -
- battalion
- -
wither -
- -
render -
- pill stretch
Oregon -
- sifter stubber
            *
Z, Z, and S -
- L, S, and Z
- -
rectum fudge -
- battalion wither
render pill -
- -
- stretch Oregon
stretch sifter -
- stubber
            *
Smetana   Smetana
            *
L, S, and Z -
- Z, Z, and Z
- -
rectum fudge -
- battalion

- -
render -
- pill stretch
Oregon -
- stretch butch
            *

6/23/70

195

ANOTHER NORTHER

text-sound piece
for three speakers
performing live

1	2	3
credible		
-	-	-
credible		
credible		
-	-	-
credible	credible	credible
credible	credible	credible
credible	credible	credible
-	-	-
	credible	
-	-	-
	credible	
	credible	
-	-	-
credible	credible	credible
credible	credible	credible
credible	credible	credible
-	-	-
		credible
-	-	-
		credible
		credible
-	-	-
credible	credible	credible
credible	credible	credible
credible	credible	credible
-	-	-
tunic	-	-
-	-	-
-	3-page	3-page
tunic	-	-
-	-	-
-	3-page	3-page
tunic	-	-
tunic	-	-

1	2	3
-	tunic	tunic
-	3-page	3-page
tunic	-	-
-	3-page	3-page
tunic	-	tunic
-	-	-
-	3-page	-
tunic	-	tunic
-	-	-
-	3-page	-
tunic	tunic	-
-	tunic	tunic
tunic	-	tunic
-	tunic	-
3-page	3-page	3-page
-	-	-
3-page	3-page	3-page
-	-	-
3-page	3-page	3-page
-	-	-
3-page	3-page	3-page
-	-	-
miracles		
play		
- play		
fairly		
- play		
fairly		
well		
	credible	
	-	
	xoxox	
	-	
	credible	
	credible	
	xoxox	
	xoxox	
		rusty
		faith
		-
		hamper

		-
		cramp
		French
miracles	credible	cramp
play	-	
- play	xoxox	
fairly	-	
- play	credible	
fairly	-	
well	credible	
	credible	rusty
	xoxox	faith
	xoxox	-
	credible	hamper
	credible	-
	xoxox	cramp
	xoxox	French
	credible	cramp
	credible	-
miracles	credible	-
play	xoxox	rusty
- play	xoxox	faith
fairly	credible	-
- play	-	hamper
fairly	xoxox	-
well	xoxox	cramp
miracles	credible	French
play	-	cramp
- play	xoxox	-
fairly	xoxox	rusty
- play	credible	faith
fairly	credible	-
well	credible	hamper
miracles	-	-
play	xoxox	cramp
- play	xoxox	French
fairly	-	cramp
- play	credible	-
fairly	credible	rusty
well	xoxox	faith
miracles	twisting	-
play	turkeys	hamper

- play	twisting	-
fairly	turkeys	cramp
twisting	credible	French
turkeys	credible	cramp
twisting	xoxox	HEY!
turkeys	xoxox	rusty
- play	twisting	faith
fairly	turkeys	-
well	twisting	hamper
miracles	turkeys	-
twisting	credible	cramp
play	credible	turkeys
twisting	xoxox	French
- play	xoxox	turkeys
twisting	twisting	cramp
turkeys	turkeys	French
twisting	twisting	cramp
turkeys	turkeys	HEY!

tunic	-	-
-	-	-
-	3-page	3-page
tunic	-	-
-	-	-
-	3-page	3-page
tunic	-	-
-	tunic	-
3-page	-	tunic
tunic	-	-
-	tunic	-
3-page	-	tunic
tunic	-	-

-	-	-
	3-page	3-page
tunic	-	-
-	-	-
-	3-page	3-page
tunic	-	-
-	xoxox	-
-	-	credible
3-page	-	-
-	cramp	cramp

December 28, 1976
9:58-10:58 pm
Belton, Texas

Same tempo throughout. Each line
= one quarter note value. Words pre-
ceded by a hyphen are spoken on the
off-beat (second 8th-note) of that
line's beat.

♩ = ca. 110-120

construction one

wound

sound

egg

delight

remorse

sea

womb

gown

shell

so nice

doris

shore

1 + 1

for

One Player and Amplified Table-Top

(or spoken)

Any table-top is amplified by means of a contact mike, amplifier and speaker.

The player performs 1+1 by tapping the table-top with his fingers or knuckles.

The following two rythmic units are the building blocks of 1+1:

a.) (biz-bla-dak)　　and　　b.) (dak)

It is realized by combining the above two units in continuous, regular arithmetic progressions.

Examples of some simple combinations are:

1) etc.

2) etc.

3) etc.

The tempo is fast.
The length is determined by the player. ©Philip Glass

nyc 11/68

All stories read simultaneously by Fern and myself

2 Stories

2 Stories
"I was wondering..."
(phrases flipped*)

2 Stories
"I was wondering..."
"I told him..."

2 Stories

2 Stories
"I told him..."

Crickets

Crickets

*"flipped": one person reads the first phrase while the other person reads the second phrase simutaneously.

"I was wondering..."- equalized

Both phrases phased in and out with some equalizing on "I was wondering..."

"I told him..." equalized, read by one person.

STRUCTURAL DIAGRAM FOR E(L)(FF)USIVE, BY FERN FRIEDMAN/ TERRI HANLON

(Equalizing the human voice produces an effect similiar to that of the telephone: a distant sound with a compressed tonal range)

PSYCHOLOGICAL STORY: SHE KNEW

Effusive was the word once used to describe her.

   She knew what the day would entail, partially because she had already been through the ordeal and too, because of the clinic's punctual scheduling. First would come the explanations, seemingly educational and designed to lift spirits and promote camaraderie. But it would seem that no matter how sincere the staff effort was the atmosphere would remain private and introspective. The group of six would look down at the edge of the throwrug on the linoleum floor... only occasionally glancing at the chart, their curiosity barely aroused.

EMOTIONAL STORY: TWO PEOPLE

Elusive was the word once used to describe her. She did not know what he meant partly because she had had only a few dealings with him and too, because of his elusive motivations. First would come the explanations seemingly sincere but yet designed to test her trust and promote jealousy. She would say that it didn't matter—how the past belonged to him—that he could retain privacy. They would both look down at the edge of the table or at the linoleum floor only occasionally glancing at each other, their curiosities somewhat aroused.

I told him that it didn't matter
I told him I didn't mind

I told him I didn't matter
I told him I mind

I told him that I didn't matter
I told him that it mind

I didn't matter
I didn't mind

I didn't matter, I told him
I told him I didn't mind

It didn't matter
I didn't mind

PHRASE PERMUTATION:

I WAS WONDERING WHAT THAT MEANT
I WAS WONDERING WHY HE SAID THAT

I WAS WONDERING WHAT HE SAID
I WAS WONDERING WHY THAT

I WAS WONDERING WHAT SAID THAT?
I WAS WONDERING WHAT THAT.

I WAS WHAT THAT MEANT.
I WAS WHY HE SAID THAT.

THAT MEANT WHAT I WAS WONDERING
HE SAID WHY I WAS WONDERING

THAT MEANT WHAT WAS.
HE SAID, WHY WAS?

catalog for
ANIMAL VOICES HUMAN

by altering recordings (in these cases
deviating audio tape playback speed from
record speed) of the voices of other
animal species the vocal qualities of
human animals can be approximated:
- vary speed of sheep & people.
- slow red columbus monkeys.
- fast wildebeasts mumbling.
- birds quarter speed.
- animal woman cervus nippon slow.
- camel mother & child normal speed.
- slow hawk.
- slow keabird of new zealand.
- indris indris dog of the forest half speed.
- south american falcons sey "Hey!"
- fast thalarctos maritimus (polar bear) in captivity.
- tympanuchus cupido.
- giant tortoises fucking fast.
- silver backed jackel slow.
- slow white heron.
- bird laughing.
- hippos in the nile at twice speed.
- ?
- tympanuchus cupido (prairie chicken) again.
- ?
- ?
- kookaburras half speed.
- laughing crying hyena slowly.
- 1952, orangutan at normal speed in london zoo.
- paradise duck slow.
- lions
- loon half speed.
- distant horses slow.
- timber wolves.

R. MURRAY SCHAFER

Tou fo meryon, tou fo teh lulsk, tou fo teh lehmet nad te chonc lehls, tou fo syad nad hisgnt, I heva noshiedaf sith tumcose fo sdwor rof oyu, nwustiting titell fo ti ta a mite. Eseth era royu losymbs, royu vrte canfisigance, hohtvg theiner fo su kwen ti neth. Theiner fo su kwen woh teh sulping larity fo ym elov dowul noe ayd mecobe a rentconai fo rembanremec, a save rof royu dafed mobol, a rackced raj fo urego a bomt, shuped up tou of meryon, tou of teh lulsk, tou of teh lehmet nad teh chonc lehls, tou of syad nad hisgnt, I heva noshiedaf sith tumcose of sdwor rof oyu, nwustiting titell of it at a mite. Eseth era royu losymbs, royu vrte canfisigance, hohtvg theiner of us kwen it neth. Theiner of us kwen woh teh sulping larity of my elov dowul noe ayd mecobe a rentconai of rembanremec, a save rof royu dafed mobol, a rackced raj of urego, a bomt, shuped up out of meryon, out of the lulsk, out of the lehmet and the chonc lehls, out of syad and hisgnt, I heva noshiedaf sith tumcose of sdwor for you, nwustiting titell of it at a mite. Eseth are royu

205

losymbs, royu urte canfisigance, hohtug theiner of us kwen it neth. Theiner of us kwen how the sulping lariety of my clov dowul one day mecobe a rentconai of rembanremec, a save for royu dafed mobol, a rackced jar of urego, a bomt, shuped up out of meryon, out of the lulsk, out of the lehmet and the chonc lehls, out of days and hisgnt, I have noshiedaf this tumcose of sdwor for you, nwustiting titell of it at a time. Eseth are your losymbs, your true canfisigance, hohtug theiner of us knew it then. Theiner of us knew how the sulping lariety of my love dowul one day mecobe a rentconai of rembanremec, a vase for your dafed mobol, a rackced jar of urego, a tomb, shuped up out of meryon, out of the skull, out of the lehmet and the conch shell, out of days and hisgnt, I have noshiedaf this tumcose of words for you, nwustiting little of it at a time. These are your losymbs, your true canfisigance, hohtug theiner of us knew it then. Theiner of us knew how the sulping lariety of my love would one day mecobe a rentconai of rembanremec, a vase for your faded bloom, a rackced jar of rouge, a tomb, pushed up out of memory, out of the skull, out of the helmet and the conch shell, out of days and nights, I have noshiedaf this tumcose of words for you, nwustiting little of it at a time. These are your losymbs, your true canfisigance, though theiner of us knew it then. Theiner of us knew how the sulping lariety of my love would one day become a rentconai of rembanremec, a vase for your faded bloom, a racked jar of rouge, a tomb, pushed up out of memory, out of the skull, out of the helmet and the conch shell, out of days and nights, I have noshiedaf this costume of words for you, nwustiting little of it at a time. These are your symbols, your true canfisigance, though neither of us knew it then. Neither of us knew how the pulsing reality of my love would one day become a rentconai of rembanremec, a vase for your faded bloom, a cracked jar of rouge, a tomb, pushed up out of memory, out of the skull, out of the helmet and the conch shell, out of days and nights, I have fashioned this costume of words for you, untwisting little of it at a time. These are your symbols, your true significance, though neither of us knew it then. Neither of us knew how the pulsing reality of my love would one day become a container of remembrance, a vase for your faded bloom, a cracked jar of rouge, a tomb.

1976.

MANY MANY WOMEN

She could be intending. She was placing what she was placing. She was saying what she was saying when she was sitting.

She was intending that all of them were all of them. Some of them were intending that all of them were all of them.

She could be intending. She had been, she was intending that all of them were all of them. She was continuing, she could be intending.

All of them could be all of them and they were all of them and she was continuing and she could be intending. She could be intending. She was intending that all of them were all of them and some of them were intending that all of them were all of them. Some were hoping to be intending that all of them were some of them. Some were intending that some of them were enough of them. They all could be intending. All of them were all of them.

She was placing what she was placing. In placing what she was placing she was showing what she was having. In showing what she was having she was placing all of them so that all of them were all of them. In placing all of them so that all of them were all of them she was using what she was having. In using what she was having she was showing that all of them were all of them. She was placing what she was placing.

She was saying what she was saying when she was sitting. She was sitting. She was saying what she was saying when she was sitting. In sitting and saying what she was saying when she was sitting she was intending to be saying that she was saying what she was saying. She was sitting and all of them were all of them.

Anything being together and there being pieces that are being used and all the pieces are being used and all of them had placed on them what was placed for them and they being where they had been again and again, all of them being there then and they could be there and nothing was anything and there was there not anything she was placing what she was placing and all of them were all of them and that was too much of that thing in all of them having been continuing and all of them not coming to use anything, and she was placing what she was placing and all of them all of them being all of them all of them were coming to intending and all of them coming to intending she was sitting and sitting was that thing. All of them intending all of them a piece being on all of them, a piece being on all of them some of them, anything being together all of them were all of them. All of them were all of them. She was placing what she was placing. All of them were all of them.

She sitting and sitting being that thing, she sitting and all of them being all of them and she having not been completing that thing completing sitting she was not completing that something would not be together if a piece was on each one of them. All of them were all of them. They were losing in using what they were using in a piece not being on each one of them. They were not losing in all of them coming to be intending. They were losing in coming and they were coming to be intending. She did sit and she did not do that thing, she did place what she placed and she did not do that thing. She was sitting.

If she had the way of sitting and she did not have a way of sitting she would keep in being what she did have in sitting. She did not have a way of sitting. In sitting she did have in being what she was not losing and not losing she did not give anything of sitting. She did not give anything of sitting. She did not have a way of sitting.

She did not have a way of sitting. She was not being in continuing sitting. She did not lose being sitting. She did not lose sitting. She did not keep in sitting. She had sitting. She was having sitting. In having sitting she did change what she did not change in placing what she was not placing. In continuing she did not change when she was remaining in having been moving being sitting. In having been sitting she was not sitting. She was not sitting in the way of sitting. She was sitting in having been continuing remaining in having moved in sitting. She was not being in not sitting. She was not being sitting. She was not being, not sitting, sitting. She was intending in sitting, in saying what she could be saying.

A little one who could not push did push and pushing was telling that pushing was not succeeding. A little one pushing is a little one pushing.

She could tell all about pushing. She could tell and she did tell all about not pushing. She did tell and she could tell that having had what she had had she would have what she would have, and she did have what she did have and she did tell what she did tell.

Some are some. Some being some and one telling them that that one is one not telling what she might be telling if she had been listening when she was listening they are hearing that she is not telling what she is not telling and all of them she and they are all continuing in friendly living. She is telling that hearing is something. She is telling that listening is something. She is telling that telling is something. She is telling that she is hearing, that she is not listening, that she is not telling.

In living and in repeating she was determining in being exciting. In being exciting she was not living and in living she was not continuing and she was being the one conveying being exciting.

She did feel that which feeling she did have as being. She did begin what she was finishing and she did not continue hearing when she was listening.

In having been feeling she was saying that she had been giving up what she could be needing and in giving it up she had been doing without it. She was saying that she had been feeling in being living, and being living and continuing she was being not having given up everything.

In being married and feeling she was married and was conveying that thing that she was continuing. In having children and she had two children she was feeling what she feeling. She was feeling what she was feeling. She was feeling something. She was saying what she was saying. She was saying what she was feeling. She was saying that she could determine not coming to be exciting. She was saying that she could say what had meaning.

In having children and arranging she was conveying that arranging can be something and that she was not arranging what would be arranged.

She had two children. She was feeling what she was feeling. She felt that she had had two children and having two children one of them was one and the other one was the other one.

She had them and she needed being living to be feeling what she was feeling in having them. She needed being living and being living she was not needing what she was needing in conveying being exciting and having the one child and the other child.

One was one and was like that one, was one being that one and being completely like that one in being one. She had that thing having that one and having that one she was needing being living to be feeling what she was feeling in that one being that one and being living.

The other one was that one and being that one was being any one being living and winning intending some winning of continuing being one. That one was having intending some continuing. She had that one and having that one was one saying what she was saying about having that one, about that one. And saying what she was saying about having that one, about that one, she said all she said about having that one, about that one, and saying all she said about having that one, about that one, she was one conveying intending in not saying, in not feeling, in saying, in needing all she was saying in feeling, in remembering in needing what she could be saying in having that one, of that one.

She was needing being one living to be feeling what she was feeling in having the one, in having the other one.

In feeling what she was feeling in having the one, and she had the one, she was not compelling what she was saying in telling that if she was living she was living. She had him and feeling what she was feeling she was telling that she was not compelling being one being living, and being living she could be feeling what she was feeling in having the one who was that one one being one she had.

Like that very much like that and like that she did what beginning and ending she was continuing not compelling saying in saying what she said and feeling what she felt in feeling what if she were feeling she would have to be living. She was feeling and coming in not continuing she was in beginning and ending continuing and she was saying what she was saying in feeling what she was feeling if she was feeling what to be feeling she would have to be one being living. She was not compelling saying, she was not compelling not continuing, she was beginning and ending in continuing, she was saying what she was feeling and to be feeling what she was feeling she was to be being living and being living was not compelling living being continuing and she beginning and ending was continuing and not compelling saying, and not compelling continuing.

She was continuing. She was saying in beginning and ending she was continuing. She was continuing. She had one. In continuing she was saying that anything, anything that was beginning and ending was like continuing. She was saying that beginning and ending was not like continuing she being living and having one and not compelling saying. She was saying that not compelling continuing she being one and having one and feeling what was like not continuing, she was not feeling like compelling continuing, she was continuing if beginning and ending is continuing and beginning and ending is and is not like continuing.

She said that she being left felt what she felt and said what she said. She said that having what she had she knew what she knew and knowing what she knew she gave what she gave and giving what she gave she was not expecting what she was not expecting in continuing what she was continuing and continuing what she was continuing she did have what she could have in she being the one she was being and having the children all four that she was having and having lost the husband the husband who died and she had been a wife who was living.

In keeping what she was keeping she was not keeping all she was keeping as she was giving something that she was giving. She was liking what she was liking and saying what she was saying and asking everything she was asking and supplying all she was supplying.

She said and did that which in needing all she could have she would say and do. She repeated that in liking what she had been liking she had, in giving what she had been giving, been having what she had. She was not repeating in feeling. She was not repeating in dying. She was not repeating in not dying. She was repeating in giving. She was repeating in asking everything. She was repeating in being living.

In being living she was introducing something she was introducing what she was asking. In introducing what she was asking she said what she said. She said what she said and when she said what she said she left what she left when she had what she had and she gave what she gave when she left what she left.

She said that she did not leave anything and saying that she attended to what she attended. Attending to what she was attending she said all she said. She did not say that she felt anything that she was not asking. She did not say that she liked more than she liked. She said that what she saw was what was left when she gave what she gave. She said that she said what she said. She said that she had said what she said. She said what she saw and she saw what there was when she had what she had.

She was not the one who did come to have what she had. If she had come to have what she had she would have lived when she lived and she would have died when she had had what she had had. She was not the one who was all in having what she had and she did not have what she had having four children and each of them being the one of the four of them that each one was and her husband being succeeding and being living and she being living so that he was dead before she was dying, she was not the one having what she had. She was the one saying what she saw and she was seeing what she had.

She was not leaving being that one in being one continuing and she did not leave being that one because she was seeing what she had and she was saying what she saw. She was not leaving being that one.

It could be that she was that one. It could quite be that she was that one. It was that she was that one.

She said what she saw and she saw what she had and she said what she said and she had what she had.

If she saw what she had and she said what she saw she had being living and a husband and children and succeeding in not having been using in feeling that she had not died and left her husband living with the four who were being living and being living being existing. She did say that she could be using all that she could say in saying what she saw and seeing what she had. She did say that she could not be using what she did say in seeing what she had. She did say that having what she had she did not use what she would use if she saw what she had when she said what she saw.

All that there is of what there is when there is what there is is that which in the beginning and the middle and the ending is coming and going and having and expecting. All that there is of what there is is that all that is that. Four or five or six and there are six and there are five and there are four and five and six all that there are are then all there and being all there how can they not be there when they are there and they are all there when they are there, when they are all there. They are, they are there.

One and if not why not one and if one why not the one who is one. The one who is one is there when she is there.

Thanking that one is not all of everything. Not thanking that one is not all of everything. Thanking can be something.

If saying that thanking is existing is convincing then saying that thanking is existing is saying that thanking is thanking. If all the thanking is existing and if completing thanking is existing then thanking is thanking. Thanking is enough.

All of that all of thanking is all of thanking and all of thanking and thanking is thanking, all of thanking is thanking. That is quite thanking.

If she was beautiful one day she was beautiful that day because she was beautiful that day.

She was doing more than she intended and she liked it.

If she was beautiful one day she was beautiful that day because she was beautiful that day. She was beautiful any day.

If she was beautiful every day she was beautiful because of the way that she was beautiful that day. She did more than she intended and she liked it.

To begin then. She was beautiful one day. She was beautiful that day because she was beautiful that day. She was beautiful that day as that day was the day that she was beautiful that day. She did more than she intended and she liked it. She was beautiful that day.

She was beautiful that day and that day the day she was beautiful she was beautiful and being beautiful that day because that day she was beautiful she was beautiful on that day because she was beautiful that day. She was beautiful that day.

She was beautiful one day. She was beautiful that day because being beautiful that day she was beautiful that day. That day she was beautiful.

All one day she was beautiful. She was beautiful that day. That day she was beautiful and being beautiful that day that was the day that day was the day that she was beautiful and so she was beautiful that day.

One day she was beautiful. She was beautiful that day.

A day being a day and a day being the day that she was being beautiful because she was beautiful that day, a day being a day and she being beautiful that day she was beautiful and being beautiful that day that was the day she was beautiful, she being beautiful that day. A day was that day the day that she being beautiful that day was beautiful that day.

Why if a day was a day and she was beautiful that day why if a day is a day and a day is a day and a day she is beautiful and she is beautiful a day why if a day was a day and she was beautiful that day why is she beautiful every day. If she is beautiful every day she is beautiful every day. She is beautiful every day and each day she is beautiful she is beautiful because that day she is beautiful and she is beautiful that day because that day she is beautiful.

That is not a reason and that is not a day, any day is a day, she is beautiful every day, there is not a day that there is not a reason that she is beautiful that day and there being days and there being reasons and she being beautiful every day every day is a day and she is beautiful that day and she is beautiful the day she is beautiful because she is beautiful that day. Any day is a day.

Having what in the beginning is all of ending is being what in being living is existing. Any one, all of them, any one is what any one liking any one not liking is liking is not liking, any one liking, any one not liking is any one not liking, is any one liking.

Any one liking is intending is not intending. Any one not liking is intending is not intending. Any one liking, any one not liking is not intending, is intending.

Any one and any one, one and one and two, and one and one and one, and one and many, and one and some, and one and any one, and any one and any one, any one and any one is one and one is one and one is some one and some one is some one, any one and one and one and one, any one is that one and that one is that one and any one and one, and one and one, any one is the one and the one who is the one is that one. The one who is the one who is that one, any one and any one is one, one is one, one is that one, and any one, any one is one and one is one, and one and one, and one and one and one and one.

Apple—Lilith—Night

Let it happen at night
Let it happen at a gate
Let it happen

Let Lilith light at a gate
Let Lilith gape at an apple
Let an apple gape

Let pale pale Lilith gape at a pale pale nape
Let lithe apple Lilith gape at a pale pale nape
Let lithe apple Lilith leap at a gate
Let light leap at a gate

I light at a gate
I let light leap at a gate
I gape at a light pale apple
       Lilith let light at a gate
I leap at a gate
I let a light path leap at a night gate
I night gate

I let Lilith light at a high path
I let Lilith light at a thigh
I let Lilith light a high light thin pale nape

a pale pale thigh
a high thin nape
a lip
a nipple tip
a lap
a tight hip
a tap at a night tip
tap a tap at a tight tit
tip a tight hip
a hip tap at a tight lip
a night tip

Let a tight tip tap at a tight hip
Let a hip tap tip at a tight lip

Let it happen at night
Let it happen at a gate

a heat
a hat
a hit
a pit
    height
a tight hit
a tin hat
a hat tip

high heat at a hat tip
Let a high heat hit at a tall thin hat tip

Lilith
in heat
at a tall tin hat tip

Let it happen at night

Let a tin hat tip
Let a tin hat leap at a gate

a tall tin hat
a tall thin tail
a nape
a heat that let it happen at a tall tin gate
at night
in a hat
       that
Lilith
in a heat let
light at a gate

a light
a path
a hit
a hat
      that

Let it happen at night
Let it happen
Let it happen at a gate

rage judge raga
mad judge rage

a mad judge rages
a raga rides

a raga judges
a rug
a jug
a mug
  mud

a mage judge rides a mud rug

a mad judge rides as a mud mage rages

a vase
a raid
  jade

a jade vase
a mad judge grades a jade vase
a mad maid judges a mud jug a jade vase
a mud mage judges a rum jug a jade vase

I am a gum jug
I raise a mud vase
I phase
I praise a jade rug
I judge a gum jar a jam jug
I jam a gum jug

a gum jug rises
a mud rug rides

I am a mage rug
I made a mage jug a gum mug

a jade mug
a jade jug
a jade rug
a jade vase
a jade

He made a mud-jade rise, praise him
He made a jade jug
He made a gem
He made a gem rise
He made a mud gem ride
He made a gem judge rise, praise him

He said
A gum jug am I
A jade vase am I I
raise a gem jug as a mud rug I ride
I made gum
I made jam
I made red mud
I made a drum
I hum
      he said
Hum
I made a mud gem rise

A mad maid made a med jug
She made Med
She said Jug
She made a jade judge pea red
She made him drum
She made him rage
She made him
She said

jug gem
rug gem
mud red gem
drug gem
drug judge gem
rug gem
red rug gem
jug gem
judge

Judge said
Praise Him

Rock—Wrench—Snake

wench rake rock
rock wreck cork
ware raw woc

work rock wrench on snake wench
work snake wench

work rock wrench on rock
rock wrench on rock

rock rake wench
snake snake wrench
rock snake wench on wrench on rock

rock wench on rock

craken

waken

snare

waken hare scare craken waken cork

were snake craken craken on snake rock

were snake wench on craken rock

was crack on rock

*

snake on rock

a craken

wakens

a rock wench
          her
wrenches work her rock her
snake work wakens on her woc her
woc wakens
her snake
harkens

*

a wren
wakens on
a rock

a wrench
works
where a cork rocks on

where a wench on a rock
works
a snake on a rock
rocks on

a snake
a wren
a woc
a wench rocks on

her rock was a wren's rock
her wrenches a work on a wren's rock

when her wrenches work on a rock
a snake rocks on

when wrenches snake on a rock
rocks and wrenches

when wenches snake on a rock a rock rocks on

*

wrench snares scare hares
wrench snares scare wrens
wrench scares snare rare wenches

hunches

were a wren on a scare
a hare were near her

were a wren on a hare her
rock were nowhere near her

a wench on a wren
a snake on a rock

a hare nowhere near her

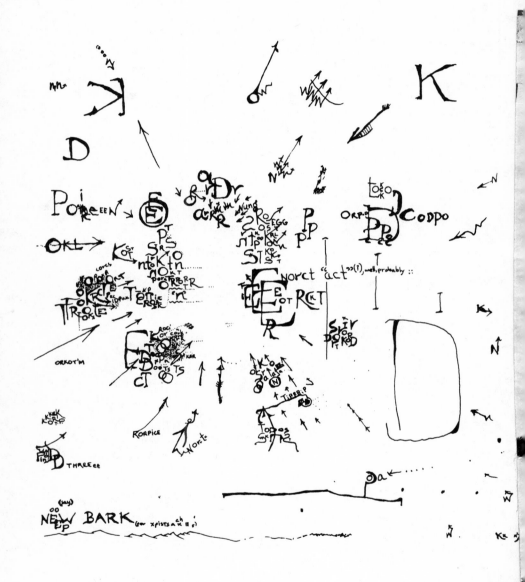

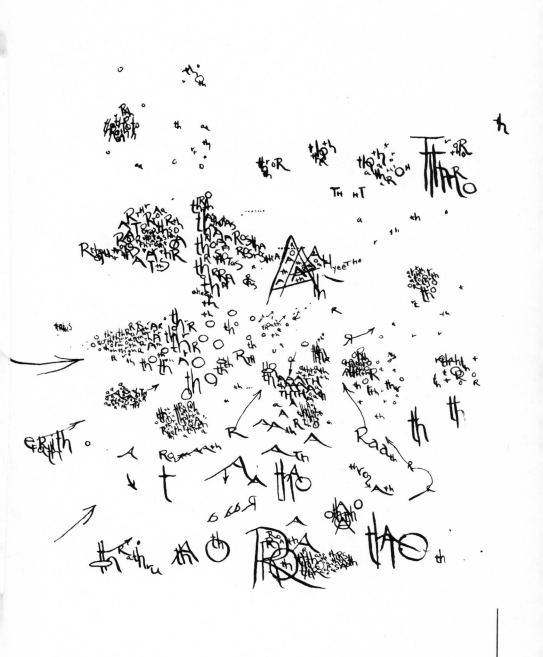

219

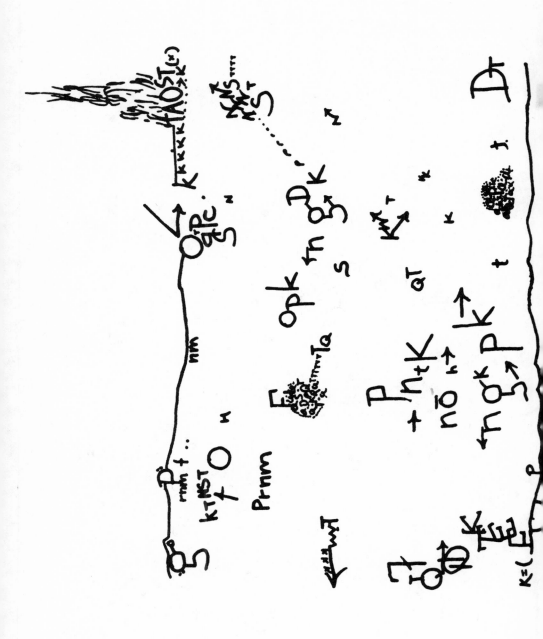

Watering The Plants

#@)#(*$&%¢&%*%(__¢)¢(*$&)@__#*$*% #*%&¢@*¢$*& #%$@&#*%$
@*&#¢$%¢&*#(6)#(*$&%¢#((\$()$__' ¡'##&$¢%#$*)@(*#&$¢&#¢
@*(#*&$%&$¢#%#$$¢%&*¢(¢(¢__!)(@&##$%#&@(¢%(*#&¢$%@&#%
%¢&$#*#($*$*%&%¢$¢$¢&%*¢(¢(9)(#*$&¢%&$*#&$¢#*$&¢$%$

Bottle Caps
     (for Carmen Pietri)

there is one
that is bigger than the one
there is another one
that is bigger than the one
that is bigger than that one
there is a smaller one
that is bigger & smaller
than the one
that is not the one
there is one
before the other one
bigger or smaller than the one
that is or is not the one
after the one that was the one
then theres the one
that will never be the one
that sometimes is the one
that was the one
that is now the one
along with the other ones
where the ones
who were the ones
that are the ones
will still be the ones
who was never the one
by being the one
who is the one

A downtown train
A downtown train
A downtown train
A downtown train
A down
  down
  down
  down
town train down train town
A train downtown
A train downtown
A train downtown
A downtown train
A down
  down
  down
  down
down train
down train
down train
train down
train down
train down
A downtown train
A train downtown
A train town down

Part Two

train A town down
down A train town
A downtown train
A train downtown
A downtown train
  down
  train
  down
  town
  down
  train
A downtown train
A train town down

ZZZZZZZZZZZZZZZZZZZZZZZZ
ZZZZZZZZZZZZZZZZZZZZZZZZ

ZZZZZZZZZZZZZZZZZZZZZZZZ
ZZZZZZZZZZZZZZZZZZZZZZZZ
ZZZZZZZZZZZZZZZZZZZZZZZZ

ZZZZZZZZZZZZZZZZZZZZZZZZ
ZZZZZZZZZZZZZZZZZZZZZZZZ

        tick tock
        tick tock
        tick tock
        tick tock
   tick tick tock tock
   tick tick tock tock
   tick tick tock tock
        tick tock
        tick tock
        tick tock
        tick tock

ZZZZZZZZZZZZZZZZZZZZZZZZ
ZZZZZZZZZZZZZZZZZZZZZZZZ

ZZZZZZZZZZZZZZZZZZZZZZZZ
ZZZZZZZZZZZZZZZZZZZZZZZZ
ZZZZZZZZZZZZZZZZZZZZZZZZ

ZZZZZZZZZZZZZZZZZZZZZZZZ
ZZZZZZZZZZZZZZZZZZZZZZZZ

erph ihr pvnrh errzm
zm rohm ychp zzha
rmhz kprhnzhl tchct
pzmrkg lhrp qhzpgr

.   .   .

hmp zrzphrz (ghglf
cmnzr hpzcj zmmz)
hzzzzzm mlzlzlr sd
bhss pflcbhx ggdt

.   .   .

llzllr rmlfp mmzzm
hqlmrf bhbhbh ghmzz
vpr bfsd xxmz hpmr?
rzmnc ohrlfb zbzbzr

.   .   .

ffhlh yzzzmzzmz fvvv
mwgh bggg xxxrx rmphz
enahxrfbwds zzzlf rh
eeh hte zzhp mmmmmz

.   .   .

dfgh zxxbnm klmxzcq
wlkpfgh jkjqg tlhgdsfz
lpkgq zzmz qgpb nmzx

mklszxq kplh zxzmnb

.   .   .

mxzvb nmnmb ghgjqp
lksdfgh wqpb dfgwrrtzc
lwwq grhl zxbmn mnmj
xzzm cvbnmh ixzcvbo

MAKING UP WITH THE ONE YOU LOVE

etryh klp stsu wpmhq
mzz ghnkh rplhy pxhwbnm
pmh zxxn vhzxcv's gtg
obbbbw ehrj klkzmn uht

. . .

fghtyk pzxchr ewwwnm
lkjh bhnw wsx bnb
trwq axzcv fhd tyrqvbx
wqs dvbn kmhrq lwqqe

. . .

trykl hjnp wdz ytyth
bzxccw xsq vbnr kzz
wqxcz vthk lwqncv zmz
mwqt klzzm nwqp nlhf

. . .

abntqy klzc zrrz yhgwt
ccyc eczx qxzcvbnr
rgh cbvnmj wqklth qmezc
rhhy thklgz nmxkrhr

. . .

ghfrtl wbnmzx cvbfpjhjz
qwthk zmzmrm klthjzh
ynbmxzcv wlpxzbn uthjn
wttrz bnmxvc hthtrhzb

. . .

rpfgh brwsxz jmnjc bnmcz
opkzzzv bnmh wqzv sszb
kljh ytrh ghfdsx btrhfm
rtycvu zrrhczx lkhghfdf

Klink—Hratzvenga

(*Deathwail*)

Narin—Tzarissamanili

(*He is dead!*)

    Ildrich mitzdonja—astatootch
    Ninj—iffe kniek—
    Ninj—iffe kniek!
    Arr—karr—
    Arrkarr—barr
    Karrarr—barr—
    Arr—
    Arrkarr—
    Mardar
    Mar—dóórde—dar—

Mardoodaar! ! !

    Mardoodd—va—hist—kniek— —
    Hist—kniek?
    Goorde mee—niss— — —
    Goorde mee! ! !
    Narin—tzarissamanilj—
    Hee—hassee?
    O—voorrr!
    Kardirdesporvorde—hadoorde—klossnux
    Kalsinjevasnije—alquille—masré
    Alquille masréje paquille—paquille
    Ojombe—ojoombe—ojé— — — —

    Narin—tzarissamanilj—
    Narin—tzarissamanilj ! ! !
    Vé—O—voorrr—!
    Vévoorrr—
    Vrmbbbjjj—sh—
    Sh—sh— —
    Ooh ! ! !
    Vrmbbbjjj—sh—sh—
Sh—sh—
Vrmm.

Charcoal Man

Char-coal, Lady! Char-coal! Chah-ah-coal, Lady!
Black-coalee-coalee!
Coaly—coaly; coaly—coaly—coal—coal—coal.
Coaly—coaly!
Coal—eee! Nice!
Chah—coal!
Twenty-five! Whew!
O Charco-oh-oh-oh-h-oh-lee!
Oh—lee—eee!
(You get some coal in your mout', young fellow, if you don't
     keep it shut!)
Pretty coalee—oh—lee!
Charcoal!
Cha—ah—ahr—coal!
Charbon! Du charbon, Madame! Bon charbon? Point! Ai-ai!
Tonnèrre de dieu!
Cha-r-r-r-r-r-rbon!
A-a-a-a-a-a-aw!
Vingt-cinq! Nice coalee! Coalee!
Coaly-coal-coal!
Pretty coaly!
Charbon de Paris!
De Paris, Madame; de Paris!

but may be paraphrased. (15) Each gesture which synchronously accompanies a shout should be a single gesture. In effect: one shout at a time, one gesture at a time. A single gesture is difficult to specify. However,e.g., running is not a single gesture in this context, since it is made up of a series of single, repetitive gestures. A gesture is energized and fulfilled in a single stroke as it were. For instance, a stroke might be:

> DANTE:
> CANTO SIX
> INFERNO
>
> Al tornar de la mente, che si chiuse
> dinanzi a la pieta' de' due cognati,
> che di tristizia tutto mi confuse,
> novi tormenti e novi tormentati
> mi veggio intorno come ch'io mi mova
> e ch'io mi volga e come ch'io mi guati.
>
> Io sono al terzo cerchio, de la piova
> eterna, maledetta, fredda e greve:
> regola e qualita' mai non l'e' nova.
>
> Grandine grossa, e acqua tinta, e neve
> per l'aere tenebroso si riversa:
> pute la terra che questo riceve.

A. PERFORMANCE INSTRUCTIONS: (1) The text is shared by 6 voices. (2) Each voice is given some ordered succession of text fragments. (3) Text fragments interlock as noted in the score. (4) The interlocking of text fragments preserves the linear order of the TEXT [cf. this page]. (5) Successive text fragments within each voice part are always separated from each other by some spacing, i.e. non-text. (6) Each text fragment [taken as a unit] is always shouted. (7) Each shout contains all of the sounds given in that text fragment. (8) All of the sounds in each text fragment are continuous and connected and thus, are 'within' each shout. (9) Each shout occurs only where a text fragment is provided in the score. (10) Each text fragment is to be shouted only by that voice with which it is associated. (11) Each shout is always accompanied by some vibrant, visible, physical gesture. In some fashion or another, the entire body should be energized. (12) A gesture and a shout are always synchronous, i.e. they initiate each other. (13) A succeeding gesture within a given voice part develops out of a preceding gesture in that part. (14) Gestures between and among voice parts are not to be imitated,

(17) At any given moment, the absence of a text fragment in a voice part is also the absence of some new gesture in that part. In every instance, the interaction of TEXT FRAGMENT/GESTURE is as follows: text fragment shouted: ON—OFF, ON—OFF, etc.

gesture: ON—HOLD—>, ON—HOLD—>, etc.

Thus, the physical state of a given performer's current gesture is held [—maintained as if frozen, but energized] until the next instance in that performer's part. (18) Gestures between parts overlap, but shouts do not, e.g.:

part 1 shout ON—OFF,
gesture ON—HOLD—>,
part 2 shout ON—OFF,
gesture ON—HOLD

(19) Each performer's part consists of an ordered series of static utterances [shout/gesture]. The static utterances as they interlock with each other, unfold a text/gesture continuity——a shared, composite composition. (20) To these general statements are appended the following nuances:

(16) Thus, gesture is clearly bounded.

LINGUA I [POEMS AND OTHER THEATERS] 6 shouting voices, overhead amber spot, 16mm film, 2-channel sound tape; 1968

DANTE'S JOYNTE

Kenneth Gaburo

LINGUA PRESS

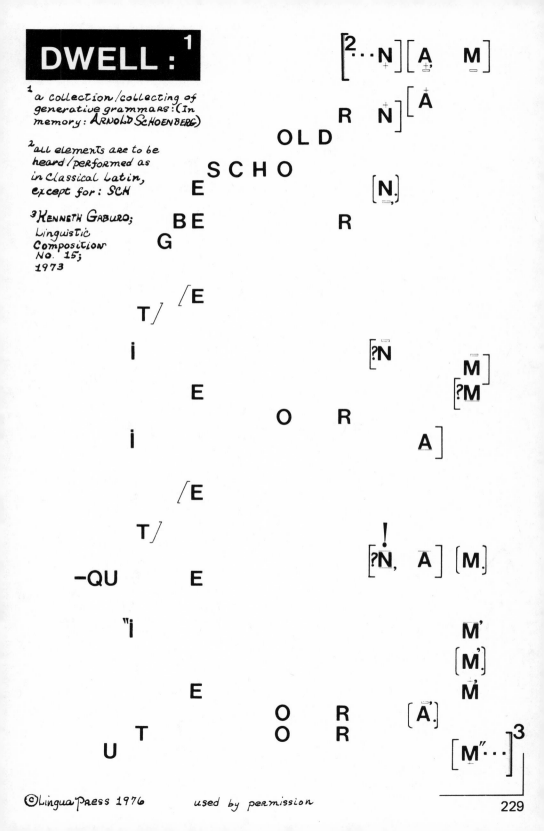

©Lingua Press 1976   used by permission

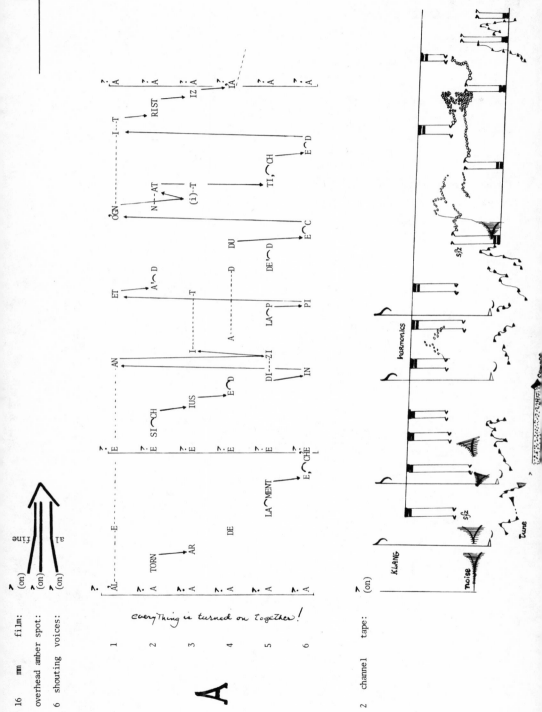

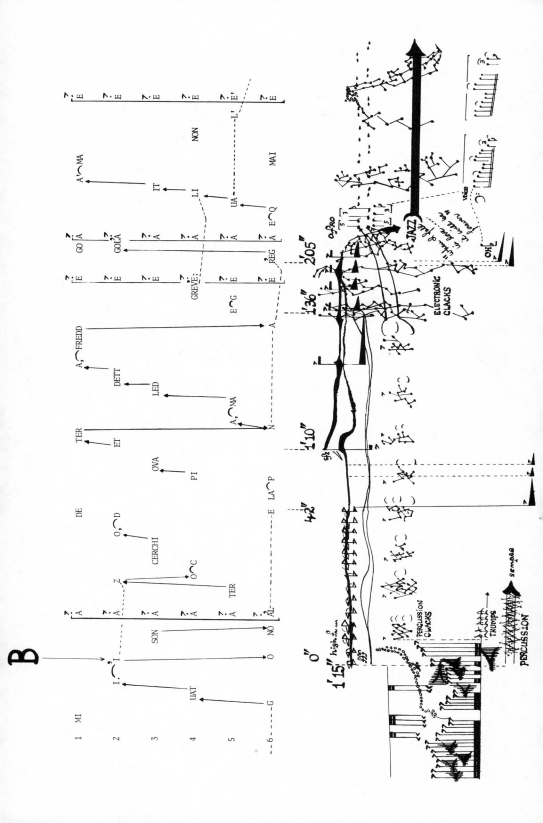

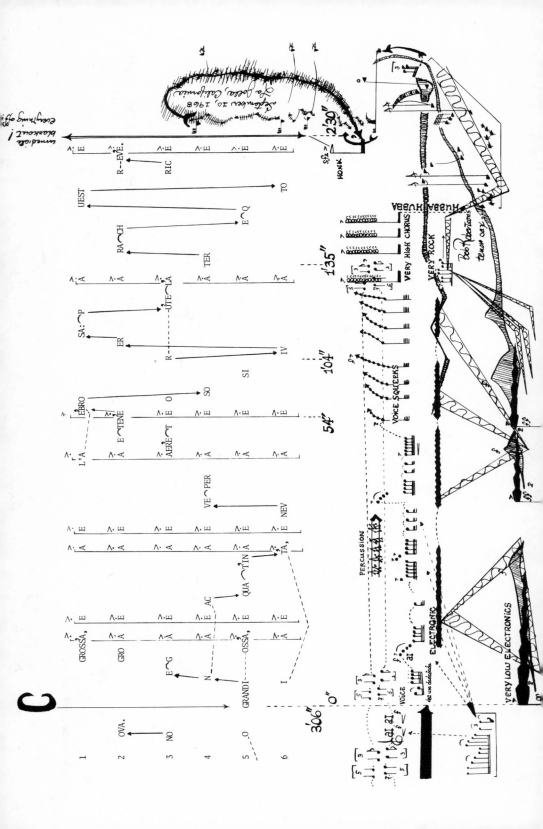

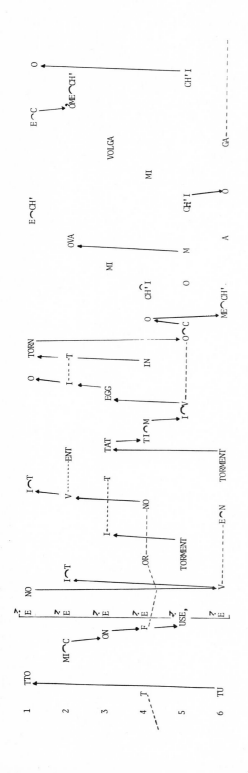

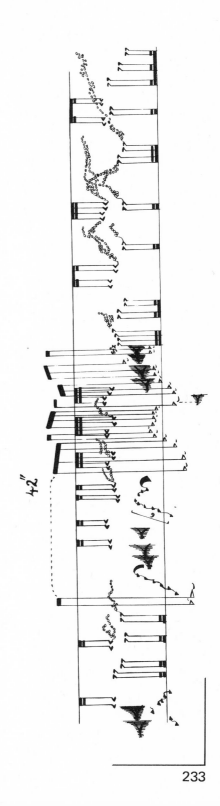

JOHN GIORNO

Excerpts from EVERYONE IS A COMPLETE DISAPPOINTMENT

cause
when
your smiling
cause when you're smiling
the whole
world
smiles
with you
the whole world
smiles with you
the whole world smiles with you, the whole world smiles with you,
when when
you're laughing you're laughing
when you're laughing, when you're laughing,
the sun the sun
comes comes
shining shining
through through
the sun comes the sun comes
shining through shining through
the sun comes shining through, the sun comes shining through,
but when but when
you're crying you're crying
but when you're crying but when you're crying
you bring you bring
on the rain, on the rain,
it's a complete it's a complete
waste waste
of time of time
seeing seeing
anyone anyone
you ever you ever
knew knew
it's a complete it's a complete
waste of time waste of time
seeing anyone seeing anyone
you ever knew you ever knew
it's a complete waste of time it's a complete waste of time
seeing anyone you ever knew, seeing anyone you ever knew,

News
Center 4   News
News Center 4   Center 4
Chuck   News Center 4
Scarborough,   Chuck
I'd love   Scarborough,
to see you   I'd love
in a pornographic   to see you
movie   in a pornographic
I'd love to see you   movie
in a pornographic movie   I'd love to see you
I'd love to see you in a pornographic in a pornographic movie
movie I'd love to see you in a pornographic
             movie

you're in a hotel
room
in San Francisco
you're in a hotel room in San Francisco
you're in
this double
bed
between
the white
bedsheets
you're in this double bed
between the white bedsheets,
watching
Johnny Carson
watching Johnny Carson,
having sniffed
a little
cocaine
having sniffed a little cocaine,
drinking
room-temperature
scotch
whiskey
drinking room-temperature scotch whiskey
in a water
glass,
smoking
a Winston
smoking a Winston,

you're in a hotel
room
in San Francisco
you're in a hotel room in San Francisco
you're in
this double
bed
between
the white
bedsheets
you're in this double bed
between the white bedsheets,
watching
Johnny Carson
watching Johnny Carson,
having sniffed
a little
cocaine
having sniffed a little cocaine,
drinking
room-temperature
scotch
whiskey
drinking room-temperature scotch whiskey
in a water
glass,
smoking
a Winston
smoking a Winston,

how
come
I'm in
the same
rotten
place
after
all these
years
how come
I'm in the same rotten place
after all these years
how come I'm in the same rotten place
after all these years,
you're going
down
for the third
time,
I never
promised you
a rose
garden

how
come
I'm in
the same
rotten
place
after
all these
years
how come
I'm in the same rotten place
after all these years
how come I'm in the same rotten place
after all these years,
you're going
down
for the third
time,
I never
promised you
a rose
garden

236

TABLET VII

Unfortunately most of the following Tablet cannot be rendered into English. It has never been recovered. The original, which later disappeared, somehow passed into the hands of a certain Henrik L., an archaeologically gifted Norwegian divine. How he, working alone in the semi-darkness of late 19th century archaeology, managed to make anything at all of the text is itself a surpassing wonder. Even more taxing to common sense is his idiosyncratic translation method.

We know only that Henrik L. lived for three and a half years in Iceland, where he pursued his antiquarian researches. It was in this spirit that he approached his cuneiform Tablet, which he then translated into Crypto-Icelandic, a language we cannot yet understand. Only two segments of this extraordinary specialized version are clear; written in classical Old Icelandic, they probably derive from the skaldic *Völuspá*, the Prophecy of Völva, i.e. Witch or Seeress, written about 1,000 A.D.: 1. Vituð er enn eð hvat (Do you know now, or don't you?) 2. Festr mun stilna/ok freki rinna (The chain will break/the wolf will get out). In addition, the phrase 'faigðar orð' probably means 'word of doom.' The sequence 'feigðar orð' does appear in Old Icelandic material. The substance of this Tablet, insofar as intuition and scholarship can make out, certainly belongs in the context of this series, The Emptying. To complicate matters further, Henrik L. adds another symbol to the standard list used in editing the ancient Mesopotamian texts. Together with such signs as .... (untranslatable), + + + + + (missing), [ ] (supplied by the scholar-translator), and so on, he includes also ⊕ ⊕ ⊕ ⊕ ⊕, which he explains to mean 'confusing.' Tablet vii appears to be a nightmare-poem of dissolution, edged with faint hopes of ultimate rebirth.

The reader will notice one further odd intercalation, the old pastor's interjection of another anachronism, in this case Lutheran religious material, into the body of this Tablet. His devoutness ran away with his archaeological fidelity. On balance however we are lucky to have this beautifully musical text. Was it T. S. Eliot who wrote that he could listen by the hour to poetry in languages foreign to him, with delight in the rhythm and in the sound?

rötete rötete rötete þropörpe nok pintrpnöte

⊕ ⊕ ⊕ ⊕ ⊕ ⊕ ⊕ ⊕ ⊕ ⊕ ⊕ ⊕ ⊕ + + + + + + +

+ + + + + + + + + + + + + ... ⊕ ⊕ ⊕ ⊕ ⊕

⊕ ⊕ ⊕ ⊕ ⊕ ⊕ ⊕ + + + + + + + ⊕ ⊕ ⊕ ⊕ ⊕ ⊕

⊕ ⊕ ⊕ ⊕ ⊕ ⊕ ⊕ ⊕ ⊕ ⊕ ⊕ ⊕ ⊕ ⊕ ⊕ ⊕

⊕ ⊕ ⊕ ⊕ ⊕ ⊕ ⊕ ⊕ . . . . + + + + + freki·

+ + + + ... + + + + + + + + + + +

+ + + + + + + ... ⊕ ⊕ ⊕ ⊕ ⊕ . . . . + + + +

⊕ ⊕ ⊕ ⊕ ⊕ ⊕ ⊕ ⊕ ⊕ ⊕ ⊕ ⊕ ⊕ ⊕ ⊕ ⊕ ⊕ ⊕

. . . . + + + + + + + + + + + + ⊕

hraldar gronen panaknómen gardú
etaión pnaupnau gott Jesu Kriste

vituð ér enn eð hvat?

þögn of gat hroirðúk papapa
. . . . [faigðar orð]
rötete rötete rötete Jesu Kriste sakrifise
þorgilson þranódon hvat hvat papa
leggi steypðir pintrpnöte
folklass þanns punka hworis
+ + + + + + + + + + + + + + + punka hworis
⊕ ⊕ ⊕ ⊕ ⊕ ⊕ ⊕ ⊕ ⊕ ⊕ ⊕ ⊕ ⊕ ⊕ punka hworis

vituð ér enn eð hvat?
festr mun stilna/ok freki rinna

hraldar gronen Jesu Kriste sacrifise þranódon
þögn gardú etaión nok þök
panaknómen proþörpe pintrpnöte ak Pinitu

vituð ér enn eð hvat?
festr mun stilna/ok freki rinna

(28 lines +)

ok freki ok freki ok freki ok freki ok freki

earth and heaven meet, they say,
at the high place Uzuma
in that high place kill
the craftsman-gods, both of them
and from their blood
make a man and more men

ud an-ki-ta tab-gi-na til-a-ta-eš-a
Dingir ama Dingir Inanna-ge e-ne ba-si-sig-e-ne
ud ki-ga-ga-e-de ki-du-du-a-ta
ud giš-ḫa-ḫar-an-ki-a mûn-gi-na-eš-a-ba
e pa-ri šu-si-sa ga-ga-e-de
id idigna id buranin gu-ne-ne gar-eš-a-ba
An Dingir En-lil Dingir Utu Dingir En-ki
Dingir ga-gal-e-ne
Dingir A-nun-na Dingir ga-gal-e-ne
bar-maḫ ni-te mûn-ki-dur-mu-a
ni-te-an-i šu-mi-nîb-gi-gi
ud giš-ḫa-ḫar an-ki-a mûn-gi-na-eš-a-ba
e pa šu-si-sa ga-ga-e-de
id idigna id buranin
gu-ne-ne gar-eš-a-ba
a-nâm ḫên-bal-en-zên
a-nâm ḫên-dim-en-zên
Dingir A-nun-na Dingir ga-gal-e-ne
a-nâm ḫên-bal-en-zên
a-nâm ḫên-dim-en-zên
Dingir ga-gal-e-ne mûn-sug-gi-eš-a
Dingir A-nun-na Dingir nam-tar-ri
min-na-ne-ne Dingir En-lil-ra mûn-na-nîb-gi-gi
uzu-mu-a-ki dur-an-ki-ge
Dingir nagar Dingir nagar im-mân-tag-en-zên
mu-mud-e-ne nam-lu-galu mu-mu-e-de

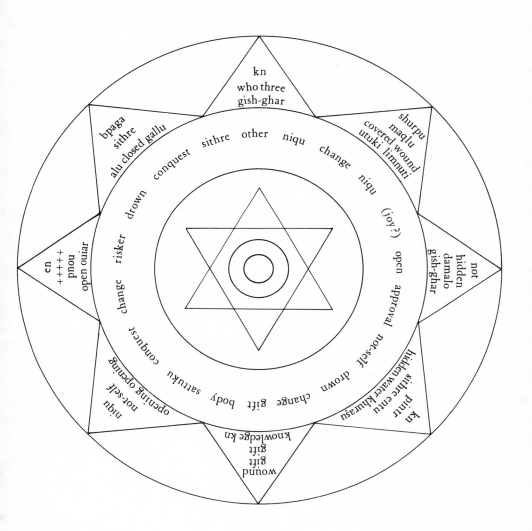

239

bath
path
math
hath
wreath raft

Ruth

lamp   limp   stomp
Camp   shrimp blimp
ramp   plus together
damp   limp
stamp   blimp
cramp   shrimp

batch   sketch   bitch   Scotch   crutch   ask   desk   whisk
catch   stretch   ditch   bask   Wisk
hatch   fetch   hitch   Cask   brisk
latch   kitch   mask
match   Mitch   task
patch   pitch   flask
snatch   witch
scratch   switch
watch   Ritch
satchel in the sky

bump
dump
hump
jump
lump
mump
pump
thump
grump

ad bad Dad had mad pad sad glad

bed red shred Fred sled led Ted

rid mid did lid hid

rod mod bod god sod

Bud mud

bay day hay Jay lay May Gay pay say tray gray spray stay way play clay pray ray slay Kay

boy Roy toy Troy ploy goy Joy

raft Kraft

wrath path math hath bath

get bet pet wet let met set jet

it bit fit hit lit knit sit spit split written shit mittens pit slit Ritty grit Kit

dot got hot pot spot shot slot lot not knot rot clot plot blot

put but shut cut gut hut jut nut rut slut

at bat cat fat hat mat Pat rat sat swat brat that what flat

get wreck the get wreck pail wreck the get wreck pail has wreck yell wreck
wine wreck pail get the yell wreck wine yell pail wreck get pail wine
wreck fresh wreck fresh wine fresh feel wine wreck fresh feel feed feel so
bike fresh bike so feed feel ghost bike pail ghost so pail wreck drink so
dress drink jet airplane we friend best airplane dress we drink fast freeze
act dress drink friend ghost fast friend jet dress we best fast cry fine
dress wait tree bank dress wait tree bank tree wait tree wait bank wait tre
e bingo there bingo sad bingo there sad case dribble the sad happy bingo
goat west waist like waist west like goat opera monster like monster goat
west wrinkle monster wrinkle west wrinkle goat monster goat monster creep
baby monster baby rhinocerous red monster wrinkle bad mad bad mad faggot ba
d faggot monster coat drain hail coat raze drain monster drain people go to
go to go to go to poke pike stone rock hit he she drain coat people rude to
go stop stop stop go he hit he she stone drain rock hit he she she he she g
     go go go to wine poke trash cab stop go mean vine kite monster ask frame
at with vest frame monster corner gest gest gest rest rest rest rest rest
rat bat brad glad cat monster girl boy lady man boy lady girl man lady cap
band raccoon cap man woman fashion raccoon monster yet yes monster cad van
race van cad cask cad fan band band moncter cheat sad fashion voice cheat f
ashion belt seat belt cheat best airplane cheat yet yes fan three free thre
bask bask drank drank drank drank drank drank drankdrank cheat cheat coke drunk
drank jet cast cab trash goat cheat monster girl had had had had had zip ha
d fast quiet quite monster had quite had quite had quiet rtrtttt try try br
eak break break CrCrCrCrCrCrCr break CrCr monster gate drip drip drip drip dr
ip drip drip drip drip drip drip drip bed bed bed freckles freckles freckle
s freckles freckles monster drip oi oi oi lop lop oi lpo oi wreck oi lop a
a a a a a a a a a a a a cad a a a a a a oi lop a a a sew sew sew dirty dirty
dirty dirty dirty sew dirty sew dirty dirty desk dirty sew act cry baby
dirty dirty xf xf xfcvvbbnnm xfdccvvbgh nmmjjkkiiu dirty dirty veff gjghf
dirty dirty dirty cent juice ask airplane dress get nap map yesterday india
indian indian indian cent vase vase da da da cad vase vase pond pond pond c
ash bz v jealous jealous jealous tree three free angry angry mad sad bad
angry anger anger case mat hat past hat east rain hat mat east east east ea
st east east cash vine hat mat east rain frame circle base circle base circ
le base gas gas opera what what gas gas gas gas gas gas dpl dpl dpl buy so
vite viy vite radio radio radiator radiator smoke smoke airplane dribble
xcv bicycle byc mask mask mask gas we Cr mask a cat junk quite quiet guess g
uess guess a desk drain mask bicycle mask cheat pine mask pine mask pine ma
sk pine mask pine mask guess desk a drain hit he wrong drain wreck wrong he
him her you me you me at with me jacket me him you him her fresh frame dres
s care bingo king waste waste king waste king band kind we fine find coat w
ind wind winfd wind wind wind wind wound wound wound wound raise hand cash
cast man vase vine ladder fresh hit he she pop pop pop pop pop po   pop po
pop pop lady rhinocerous zip west rain gas rasp trim rasp trim wait trim tr
im drain rain brain wreck pop mask was gas get a trim rasp drink trim mask
do to you wait get man a dirty Cr mask freeze we vine trash cab man baby cry
vite frame quick quick juice zaf zag zaf zig break quick zig mad angry angr
y anger cloud sky race wide wide row roll row roll row roll row roll row ro
ll row roll row roll wait roll row row ert ro haste htyujk jklih nnmmjkhuy
roll west rip drip bank past

glasslass

assass
ss
ass
ass
ss
sss
sss
glasss
ass
assglass
ss

sslass
ss
ssglass
lassass
ssglass
asslass
sss
ssglass
ssass

sslass
ss
lassss
glass
asslass
sslass
assss
slass
ssass
assss
assass
sslass
asss
glass
sss
s
sss
slass
glassass
glassglass
ss
glasslass
s
ssass
lasslass

sss
glassglass
glass
ssss
slass
glass
sass
ssss
lassglass
sss
sglass
lassss
sslass
sass
glass
glass
lassglass
ass
lass
glass
sss
asslass
sass
sglass
ss

lasslass
asss
lass
ass
slass
glasss
lasslass
lasslass
sss
assss
ssass
sss
ssass
ss
lassass
ssglass
ss
ssass
lassglass
lassglass
glassglass
s

```
ass
 sss
  sss
 sss
assass
lasslass
  lass
```

for karen
barton vermont
july 17th 1970

"The verse which out of many vocables remakes an entire word, new, unknown to the language, and as if magical, attains this isolation of speech." STÉPHANE MALLARMÉ as translated by ARTHUR SYMONS, 1899.

"I talk a new language. You will understand." BRION GYSIN, 1960.

Sound poetry can be described as an artform in which the physical and sonic aspects of language are subjected to artistic manipulations. To a sound poet, the act of speaking becomes its own subject matter: its own plastic "raw material" which like clay is to be moulded into an audio "object." Sound poetry is therefore a self-conscious attempt to get at the very "palpableness" of the human language experience. This attempt to reach what is concrete and constant in human experience is also an exploration of what is primitive and simultaneous in perception and is a major aspect of what George Quasha has called, in ethnopoetics, the "Other Tradition."

As it pertains to Western sound poetry, the Other Tradition is composed of several "outlaw" customs of "verbal anarchy" which could be traced from a central core of Greek pantheism and Orphic chant; to the search for the Logos in Gnostic, Hermetic, Cabalistic, Rosicrucian and Theosophical traditions of the Hebrews, Moslems and Christians; to the "awakening" by the Romantic poets and painters to a reality which caused itself to be perceived as a continuum of experience; to the "magnificent visions that lie beyond the windowpane" of symbolic language in the poetry of the Decadents; and finally ending in the morass of our own century with the affirmation of the "savage mind" through the destruction of what was deemed "passéist" or "bourgeois." Coupled with these traditions are the individual experiments in language such as Aristophanes' "Brekekekex Koäx, Koäx," of *The Frogs;* Abraham Abulafia's permutation prayers; Jakob Boehme's cabalistic languages; Giordano Bruno's mnemonic language systems, the "nonsense" verse of Jonathan Swift, Lewis Carroll and Edward Lear; the "early" neologistic and phonetic experiments of Paul Scheerbart and Christian Morgenstern; and the founding of *Orphism* and *simultanéisme* poetry by Henri M. Barzun.

Running parallel to this Other Tradition of verbal experimentation are the vocal traditions of the rest of the world's people: this can also be seen as providing many influences upon sound poetry's development. The imperialistic endeavors which brought the West in contact with Other Cultures, had to develop anthropology to rationalize the odd and similar human experiences which Christianity had lost the keys to. As the belief in a Christian Paradise receded from the Nineteenth Century beach of empiricism other conceptions about the organization of space and time began to fill the void: those things outside the framework of the established Western experience were absorbed and made part of a new, "larger," sense of humanity.

The history of sound poetry is also linked to the development of many other artforms because of similarities in manipulative techniques. It is all too easy to confuse sound poetry with "traditional" poetry, music, painting, architecture, dance, etc., since sound poetry makes an active attempt at being a truly "multi-media" artform and to exist simultaneously with these other forms. If we consider the Twentieth Century as the "correct" period for the coming into being of what is being called here "sound poetry," we find that it has been a part of most of the "avant-garde" and "experimental" art movements of this century. Its study touches upon many of the intellectual and philosophical ideas of this century as well. It is a multinational and multilingual phenomenon and its development is both a product of simultaneous and isolated experiments as well as many divergent lines of diffusion between the experimenting parties. Therefore, the history of sound poetry is as complex as it is eclectic.

Since the developments of each age are dependent upon the products of the age immediately preceding it, mention should be made of the "tendencies" towards sound poetry in the Nineteenth Century. Through the lyric romanticism of such early Nineteenth Century poets as William Wordsworth and Samuel Coleridge and their attempt to transform the superstitions of peasants into a "natural morality," the time was ripe for widespread interest in the West for things ancient, folkloric, and mystical. Old tales and myths were unearthed and became the cornerstones for new kinds of nationalistic and political zealousness. The beginning of serious collecting of ethnic material as art and the development of the great ethnographic museums in Europe was started in the later half of the Nineteenth Century. Antiquary crankery developed into comparative folklore and mythology. By the end of the century, Sir James George Frazer had amassed his great syntheses of Other Traditions, *The Golden Bough.* What people like Frazer, Jacob and Wilhelm Grimm, Max Müller, and Andrew Lang analyzed as esoteric ritualism, the painters, poets and musicians of the Nineteenth Century were producing art in this "newfound" continuum and context of the "modern" paleolithic.

It is in this Nineteenth Century milieu of Other Traditions, that the first self-conscious attempts at truly "freeing" words was made. "Music first and foremost of all" became the motto of the Nineteenth Century practitioners of "experimental" sonority and rhyme. This can be found in such examples as the word and syntax "strangenesses" of Arthur Rimbaud (1854-1891) and Stéphane Mallarmé (1842-1898) as they moved away from traditional poetic phonetics; Stefan George's (1868-1933) *Lingua Roma:* a "secret" poetic language composed of combined Spanish and Latin words with a German syntax; and the musical sonorities of Algernon Charles Swinburne (1837-1909). The "lifting" of language from its everyday affinities and usages and projecting it upon the universe to yield new systems of classifications was used extensively by the Romantic and Symbolist poets. The later Symbolists searched for words which would unite nature and spirit into a meticulous dichotomy of "correspondences." The dark confusion of nature was transformed anthropormorphically and harmonized with human senses which would simultaneously evoke other senses into a sympathetic synesthesia.

But yet these poets (who were not the first to do such a thing) did not go far enough in removing the thick cultural coatings upon language which had made it sterile and unhuman. So against the Symbolists' attempts to have the word carry the excess baggage of centuries, the "great Futurist Railroad" was built. The Nineteenth Century image of the machine as antagonistic to nature (such as can be seen in Turner's famous 1844 painting, *Rain, Steam and Speed*) was replaced with an image of the machine as a new universe. The monarchical, "reserved," Nineteenth Century slid into the machine-age anarchy of the Twentieth with a cry of "Let's Murder the Moonshine": the quasi-religious and overly sentimental handling of words as the fossils of the past was to be overturned by "the poetry of feverish expectation." The anti-aesthetics of shock and radical disruption arose against the aesthetics of imperialistic suppression. Within this discontinuity that began to rip open Western culture was the continuum of the Other Tradition.

Sound poetry has emerged in the Twentieth Century as the rediscovery of the oral tradition and ethnopoetic tendencies existent in the sonic arts. Its realization began solely in live performance, expanded into the tape medium, and now its presentations may include not only both of these forms but also electric acoustic instrumentation. The diverse artistic interests and attitudes of the Twentieth Century encouraged the proliferation of this intermedia art and the vast communication networks and speed of information exchange stimulated its growth and development. The importance of the oral tradition cannot be emphasized enough here. The blossoming of sound poetry can be seen as the physical manipulation of language as it pertains to the whole continuum of human experience.

Sound poetry has been the result of the aesthetic awakening and awareness of (especially) sonic-artists in modern times to the potentials of creative and revolutionary vocal composition. As Jerome Rothenberg, George Quasha, Gary Snyder, and Michael McClure have implied in their writings on ethnopoetics, the activities of sound poetry in this century are a recognition of the tribal/oral poetries that exist and have existed for hundreds of years. It is the sonic image generated by the voice which can capture the energies of cross-cultural communication by allowing the vocal signal to have its own identity —not always ruled by cultural/semantic references.

The current level of text-sound composition is a result of the application of technological advancements in sound storage and electronic synthesis of sound and speech. The technological advancements have enabled practitioners of the art to not only re-discover, but to conserve (in an ecological sense) the full capabilities of conscious vocal utterance. Simultaneous to this conservation, technology has continued to allow the expansion of human capabilities beyond their vocal limitations. This conservation and expansion, as the result of technological growth in the sonic arts, has not only freed language from its pedestrian conventionality, but has produced a more precise concept of timbral composition with the voice.

The description of sound poetry as an intermedia participative art form is again another aspect of the Other Tradition. It is the re-affirmation of the concept of "total theater" in the classic Greek sense: an entertainment of all the senses. This "entertainment" in the manner of a "purging of human emotion," is the recognition of something very personal while seeking a universal artistic form of communication. While practitioners of the art have established very diverse stylistic genres, the whole unifying factor has been the search for a unviersal artistic structure incorporating a total sensory experience.

WORD RAID

(tongue twisters, etc. for e.e. cummings)

THE CHEAP SHEIKH AND THE CHIC SHAH SEEK TO
SPEAK AT SECRET SPA.

((THE CHEAP SHEIKH AND CHIC SHAH SEEK TO
CHEEK TO CHEEK AT A SECRET SPA...))

THE SEQUESTERED QUEST FOR THE MAD, MOD,
MARRED, M-A-U-V-E MARKED KEY AND THE QUEEZY
MARQUIS' QUIRKY QUEER KEE WEE QUICKLY
QUICKENED QUILTED QUIPS AND QUESTIONS,
QUELLING QUERULOUSNESS QUITE Q-U-A-R-A-N-T-I-
N-E...

THE SHEIKH'S SLEAZY SNEAK SWEEP IN SLUSH AND
SLEET OF THE SHINY SLEEK SLEEPING SHEEP IS THE
SPICY SPEAK OF SHEET STREET.

THEY SCOURED THE ROOT OF THE SCREWY SOUP OR
CHOP SUEY SLEUTH FOR THE ROOST, ROUTE OR
SCOUP OF THE RUDE ROTTEN RUSE BEHIND A FOOT-
LOOSE ROOSTER AS THE LUCKY LONG LOST LOOT OR
LOOPE TO SCORE OR SPRUCE UP THE TROUBLED
TRUCE BEFORE THE SNEAKY SNOOPING TROOPS
STOOP TO SHOOT OR SCATTER-SCOOP THEIR
STREWN SKEWERED COUPS...

THE SHADY SHODDY SUPER SURE SHOTS AND SHAL-
LOW SNIDE SNEAKING SNOTS AND SCHEMING SLIP-
PERY SCHLOCKS SELLING (SHELLING) STOLEN SLOT
STOCKS TO THE SHAH'S QUEEZY SWEAT SHOPS
SWOOP AND SWAP SLEEPY SWABS SHAKING SHAPE-
LESS SLOBS SCOUTING SURE AND SAAVY SECRET
S-A-B-O-T-A-G-E...

THE WORLD'S A DRAMA OF A TEENY TOT'S CAREEN-
ING TEETERTOTTER UNTETHERING A SCREAMING
GLOBAL TROT AND A ZESTY BUT TESTY TEETHING
TRAUMA.

(1) A TRIPPY TRIPE TRAIPSED IN ON A TRAY AND A
TEETERING TEE PEE IN TAIPAI ARE TYPICAL OF THE
TYPES OF T-I-P-S TRADED ON TV.

(2) A TRIPPY TIPSY TRIPE IN A TREE-RIPE TROVE
TRECKED IN ON A TRAY AND TRAIPSED TO A TEE-
TERING TEE PEE IN TROPICAL TAIPAI ARE TOO
T O O TYPICAL OF THE TYPES OF TRIPS TRAITORED
(TRADED) ON TV.

A GRUESOME TWOSOME WITH SPRUCED BUT TAT-
TERED BOOTS AND A TACKY TROUPE FROM HOUS-
TON TRECKED THEIR TRUE-SOW* SHOW TO TUSON
TO TRY THEIR TRADE OR TRUCE ON.

*(i.e. trousseau)

> word raid : preview-premier
> alliterative mouth (t)RAPS
> ((mouth tRAPS; R-A-P-S for mousetraps)
> OR: EXCLAMATIONS IN LIMBO
> COLLOQUIALISMS IN AMBUSH
> dance: body twisters (torque)
> text: tongue twisters (talk)
> TORQUE AND TALK
> ("IT WAS ALL I COULD DO TO NOT DO
> THE 23 SKIDDO!")

> Have you been noticing the newscasters?
> They're stuttering, messing up in revealing
> or interesting ways. Like the newscasters,
> I find myself tongue-tied more and more.
> I've also decided not to be bothered by
> it; after all, it can happen to anyone.

> Have you ever tried to write a tongue twister?
> At first it seems almost impossible.

I found ten measly tongue-twisters in the
BOOK OF LISTS, and decided to try my hand
at it.

(Tongue twisters are concentrated, alliterative
chain clusters of easily garbled, usually
nonsensical structures whimsically mindboggling
to the point of suggesting a kind of twilight
zone where riddle, pun, aphorism and anagram
meet and trade their secret mirrored i-n-t-e-g-e-
r-s. . .)

Have you ever tried to write a tongue twister?
At first you think it's almost impossible.

WORD RAID : for e.e. cummings

Try saying these over and over and as fast as
possible!
(P.S. If these don't scramble your brains,
nothing will!--)

A SPIFFLY CLIPPED, HIP AND STRICTLY TIGHT-LIPPED
CRYPTIC SCRIPT IS SIMPLY SIFTED AND SIPPED THEN
ON A TIMELY TIP SLIPPED ON A SECRET SHIP ADRIFT
A THRIFTY TRADE TRIP, THEN SWIFTLY STRIPPED
AFTER A STIFF SHIFTY RIFT BY TWO TONGUE-TIED
TIFFED AND MIFFED TWIN KNIT-T'WITS!

A TORMENTED MENTOR MADLY TORN BETWEEN
THE SCENTED RENT, THE RENTED SCENT THE C-E-N-
T-E-R (sender) AND THE SCENTED CENTAUR WHO
SENT HER SAYS IT S T I L L MAKES A DENT IN DO OR
DIE. . .

THE S I F T AND SLOW DRIFT OF THE COLD POLAR
FLOWS SHOWS THE SWIFTLY SHIFTING SCRIPT OF
THE STRIP OF COAL SHOALS SURROUNDING THE
POLES' HOLES HOLDS THE KNOLL OF THE DROLL
TROLL'S TOLL.

SCORES OF SHEER SHORN SCOURGED AND
SCORCHED SEA SHORES ARE AN UNSOUGHT SORT
OF SORE OR SOUR SWAPPED SHOT OR SUPER
STOCKED SCHLOCK SHOCK—A SHAM STARE
STALKING A SCAM SCARE?

XERXES ZERO-DEGREE XEROX ZIPS, ZIG-ZAGS AND
Z-O-O-M-S ZEALOUSLY THROUGH ZENOBIA WHILE
ZENO'S ZEFTY JESTING ZAFTIC ZEBRA AND XYLO-
PHONE ARE Z-A-P-P-I-N-G ZENophobia.

A FLAKEY FLEET OF FLAT FOOTED FRUMPY FUNKY
FREAKY FLUNKIES FRAZZLE A FRANKLY BEDAZZLED
FRONT LINE RANK OF REGULARLY WRANGLED
RANKLED FRANTIC YANKS FRAYED AND FLAYED BY
THE FLASHY FLESH AND FLEECY FLANKS OF FOR-
TUNE.

A RATTLED BALLET AND A BATTY, BATTERED RAF-
FLED BALLOT BROKE THE BLOODY RABBLE'S BALLAD
INTO A FRANTIC, FRAZZLED RAZZLE-DAZZLE BLITZ
AND BATTLE.

GIVE HER

GIVE HER A GRIMMER GRAMMAR RATHER THAN A
SLIMMER GLIMMER OF GLAMOUR.

(GIVER HER A GRIMMER G-L-I-B-B-E-R GRAMMER
RATHER THAN A SLIMMER GLIMMER OF GLAMOUR.)

NEFERTITI'S NEAT NEW ESOTERIC EDEN EATERY
ETCHED IN KITCHY KINKY GRAPHIC GRAFFITI EAST
OF THE GREAT GREEK CREEK IN TROPICAL TAHITI
BY THE GLEAMING GREEN TEA SEA WITH SCREAM-
ING SLEEK SCENERY GREETS THE BLEARY, WEAK
AND WEARY WITH A WAFER AND A TREATY.

THE CLIQUEY CHIC BLEAKLY STREAKED FREAK BOU-
TIQUE SELLING PETE'S STEEP SLEEK HOME-MADE
PETITE PEAK PEKOE TEA TEAK REAL CHEAP IN
CHEEKY MOZAMBIQUE SPEAKS TO THE WEAK
TWEAKED BEAK OF A SNEEZING SNEAKY SQUEAK-
ING S-T-R-E-A-K-I-N-G GREEK'S MEEKLY REEKING
OBLIQUE COMIQUE...

THE KOO-KOO CUCKOO'S SLEW OF CHEWED
STEWED SKY BLUE SKEWERED HIGH CLUES ON THE
RUDE OVERDUE RU(S)E OF 'WHY I DO HAIKU ON
TOP OF A CHO-CHO' INSTEAD OF IN (AN) IGLOO
HYPES (THE) HIDE IN I DO INTO (A) WRY WIRED EYE
GLUE.

LOLITA'S LECHEROUS LITTLE PEEPING PECKER
PEEKERS PIQUED AND POOPED WITH PUNK, POP
AND PUNS POKES THE POST OR PAST PASSED POOR
PORT PEORIA'S ORAL ARIA.

NIMBLY NIBBLING AND NUMBLY NODDING THEN
PLODDING, HOPPING, COPPING AND HOB-
KNOBBING WITH EGG NOG THE SLIP-SHOD CLOD
CODDLED CLOBBERED AND CLOGGED THE CON OR
COD IN GARBO'S CARGO'S COCKLED COBBLED
GARDEN'S GARBLED CARBON COG JOB, FLOGGING
A BOTTLED GLOB OR BOGGLED GARGOYLED BLOB
IN BROWN BOONDOGGLE JOGGING GOGGLED
GARB.

A BLIMY BLIMSY BANKER WITH A BLACKENED BACK-
GAMMON BISTRO BUNGLED A BURLY BAKER'S
BACKER AND A BRACKETED BLACKGLAMMA BIMBO.

(1) THE SHOCKING STOCK SPOT OF THE STARVING
STARK SHARK'S SPARTAN START SPARKED A SPEEDY
STORK'S RETORT, A SPORT JUST SORT OF SHORT OF
SHORING SORTING AND SNORTING SUPPORT.
(2(THE STORK'S SUPPORT OF TWISTING TORQUE IS A
SHOCKING SPORT SPARKED BY SPOTTING THE
STARK SPARTAN SHARK'S SELFSAME START (-SORT
OF...THE SORT THAT SNORES IN PORT...S-C-O-R-
E-S IN COURT...)

A SEXY SUPPLE SWINGING COUPLE'S SLINKY SING-
ING STRUT, SHOVE, STUFF AND SHUFFLE CAPPED
THEIR NAUGHTY BUT SUBTLE GRIND OF SMUTTY
NUTTY SNUFF AND UPPERS BUMPTUOUSLY SUMP-
TUOUS NUPTUAL SUPPER.

SHIVA'S SHINY SHUNTED SHEAVES ACHIEVE THE
DARING DAIRY DEED OF CLEAVING TO THE CHEEZY
SHREDDED CHEATING SLEEVES OF SLEAZY SEETH-
ING THEIVES FROM THEBES.

SELECTIVELY KEPT, S-U-S-P-E-C-T, AND ANTIC-
SEPTICALLY SWEPT WITH SHINY SEARING SALTY
SWEAT WHILE SECRETLY CRAVING CRUETS AND
CREPES SARA AND CLARA SLEPT IN THE SAHARA
THEN ADEPTLY CREPT SCEPTICALLY SCHLEPPING
SHEP'S SCHWEPPS UP STEEP STEELY STONY STEPPES.

THE BRUTELY BRASH SPLASHY BRANDY BASH BACK
BY THE BLOOMING BRUSH OF THE BLACK BLUSHING
BERRY BUSH BRUISED THEN SOOTHES THE BURNT
BUNS AND BOOT SOOT ON THE (TRUTH: FORE-
SOOTH!) SMOOTHE SUPER SLEUTH'S BARED BLUE
SUIT.

A GAGGED AND BADGERED, RAGGED BLACKGUARD
BAGGED AND DAGGERED A BRAZEN BRAGGARD,
SWOONED, SAGGED AND STAGGERED JAGGARDLY
THEN SWAGGERED HAGGARDLY NAGGING A LAZY
STRAGGLED LAGGARD.

ASIDE FROM THE ((S-I-G-H)) (SIGN) C Y C I N I D E IN
THE NIGHT SIDE OF THE SHY SIREN'S SLY SNIDE
STRIDE SIRING AND SQUIRING HER IRE ASTRIDE THE
WILD IDLE SIDLED SLIDE DOWN THE WIDE WIRE
IRISH TIDE OF UNTYING THE UNTRIED (TITLED) IDOL
SIDE OF THE PSYCHE'S IRON IKON IDE (E-Y-E-D).

CLOE'S CLOSE CRUSHED CLOTH CLOCHE CLOAK OR CLONE (CLOWN?) CRONE CROWN COAT GROWS (GROANS), GLOWS, GLOATS LIKE A SLOW CROW'S LAZY SHOWY FLOAT...

(1) A TWISTED SISTER IN TITTERS ASSISTED BY TOUGH TONGUE TWISTERS WHISPERS TO THE SICK SITTER A SLICK PSYCHO SIZZLER WITH A TWITTER IN HER SIGH (IN VERSAILLES)...

(2) (IN VERSAILLES)AT A WILD & WICKED TRYST A A THICK-WRISTED TWISTED SISTER ADDICTED TO GLITZ AND GLITTER WITH WHISPY SWISHY WHISKERS WEARING WACKY KNAPPY WICKED LI-QUEURED WICKERED KNICKERS IS THROWN INTO A TAWDRY TIZZY OF TITTERS·BY A TOUGH THORNY TONGUE TWISTER AS SHE WHISPERS TO A SICK SITTER A STICKY SLICK PSYCHO SIZZLER WITH A SLYLY WRY, SPRITELY WITTY TWITTER IN HER SLIGHT SIGH (IN VERSAILLES)...

A SPECTRAL SPARTAN SPATE OF LATE NITE EIGHTY-EIGHTS SCREAM AND CAREEN DOWN SLIGHT SIGHTED SLIDING STREET SCENES SHOWING THE SHEER SHINING STREAMING STEAMY SEAMS OF LIQUID LIGHT-LINED D-R-E-A-M-S...

A TITAN?
A TITAN IS NOT A T-R-I-T-O-N* BUT A TYPE OF WRITIN' WITH TIGHT T-W-A-N-G-Y LIGHTNIN'!

*a type of missle

"The Black Tarantula Crossword Gathas" comprise 21 performance texts & a word list, all lettered on quadrille graph paper. They are the first of my Gathas not derived from a mantra, & the second group composed of English words (the "Jesus Gathas" of 1966, composed of vertical repetitions of "JESUS HAVE MERCY," being the first).

"Gatha" is a Sanskrit term, meaning "verse" or "hymn," used to designate versified portions of Buddhist sutras & adopted by Chinese scholars for their versified compositions, notably those in which Zen masters & students communicate their insights. I have been using the term since early 1961 for texts lettered on graph paper, since in most of these, repetitions of Buddhist mantras are arranged by chance operations. Beginning with this Black Tarantula group, I have continued to call texts lettered on graph paper "Gathas"—even when they were not derived from mantras.

The source of "The Black Tarantula Crossword Gathas" is a pamphlet by Kathy Acker, on the title page of which is printed: "THE CHILDLIKE LIFE OF THE BLACK TARANTULA #3 / A Secret Document. / I move to San Francisco. / I begin to copy my favorite pornography books / and become the main person in each of them. / by The Black Tarantula / July 1973 /." I was fascinated by Kathy's autobiographical self-transformations & thus inspired to draw a word list from this pamphlet & make Gathas with these words. I decided to use a "diastic chance-generation" method to draw 100 words: reading thru the pamphlet from the title page to the end, I took in succession the words that "diastically" spelled out the title page until I had a list of 99 words. (I skipped the 80th place: see below.)

I have used "diastic chance generation" to make poems since January 1963. By "diastic" I mean that words or word strings in a text have the same letters in corresponding places as those in an "index word or word string," so that the text "spells through" (*dia* = "through") the index. The term is constructed on analogy with "acrostic" (*akros* = "edge, outermost" = "beginning" or "end"), where the index letters occur at the beginnings or ends of units of a text—usually verse lines.

Thus the first three words in the list, corresponding to "THE" in the title, are "*T*ARANTULA," "*C*HILDLIKE," & "AR*E*." I continued to spell thru the title & subtitles in this way until I reached the "o" of "San Francisco": finding no word in the pamphlet with "o" in the 9th place, I skipped that place (no. 80) on my list & went on to the end of the pamphlet from the previous word, "APPENDICITIS," to the end. The last (100th) word on the list had to have an "i" in the 6th place, corresponding to the "i" in "favor*i*te"; finding no such word, I arbitrarily ended the list with the Japanese word "SATORI"—a Zen Buddhist term meaning "enlightenment experience." (I no longer remember how I decided to skip the 80th place on the list but arbitrarily to fill the 100th: possibly certain chance operations determined my actions.)

The words were then drawn from the list by means of random-digit couplets from the RAND table (01 = "TARANTULA" to 00 = "SATORI"—80's were skipped) & arranged on the quadrille sheets partly by chance operations, partly by design decisions specific to each Gatha, & partly by determinations of placement resulting from the need to cross previously lettered words.

PERFORMANCE INSTRUCTIONS

"The Black Tarantula Crossword Gathas" may be performed by a single reader or by any number of people. Each starts at any square of any one of the Gathas & "follows a path" by "moving" to any square adjacent to the first one's sides or corners, & thence to other squares in any direction(s), horizontally, vertically, or diagonally, saying names of letters (e.g., "oh" or "tee"), sounds the letters stand for in any language, syllables formed by letters adjacent in any direction(s), wordlike letter strings so formed, words, & word strings up to complete sentences. One mostly moves on a path from square to square, but may also repeat letter names, speech sounds, syllables, words, &c., from one place on the path, or circle around in "loops" (i.e., retrace certain portions of the path several times), or "trill" between adjacent squares or groups of squares (i.e., repeat alternately the sounds, &c., for which the letters in those squares stand). Every so often one may jump from the path being followed to a nonadjacent square & follow a path from there. Similarly, one may jump from one Gatha in this group to another *ad lib.*

One may also prolong vowels, liquids, sibilants, &c., & if one performer begins to prolong sounds, others may do so, producing prolonged intervals or "chords." These longer sounds may act as "organ points" under the play of shorter sounds. Empty squares are interpreted as silences of any desired duration, & these silences ought often to be prolonged until the performer feels able to add positively to the total situation.

Each performer must listen intently to all sounds produced by other performers, audience, or environment, & modify the performance in accord with what is heard. "Listen" & "Relate" are the most important "rules." Since everything depends upon the performers' choices during performance, awareness, sensitivity, tact, courtesy, & inspiration must be their guides, & each one must listen silently for a while before adding something new to the situation.

Duration of performance is determined by consensus of performers or otherwise. A performance may be ended at any time within the limits set by the performance situation, either at a time set beforehand or spontaneously. One of the group may act as leader, signalling the beginning of the performance, keeping track of elapsed time, & when necessary, signalling the end.

One realization of these works, *The 8-voice Stereo-Canon Realization (11/25/73) of the Black Tarantula Crossword Gathas* is available on audiotape cassette (formerly also on reel-to-reel) as S Press Tape No. 33 (Düsseldorf/München: S Press Tonband Verlag, 1975). It comprises four separate performances by the composer that are superimposed on both tracks of a stereo tape, with the four performances beginning about 20 seconds later on one track than on the other, producing a canon between the two tracks.

11-13 October, 1978

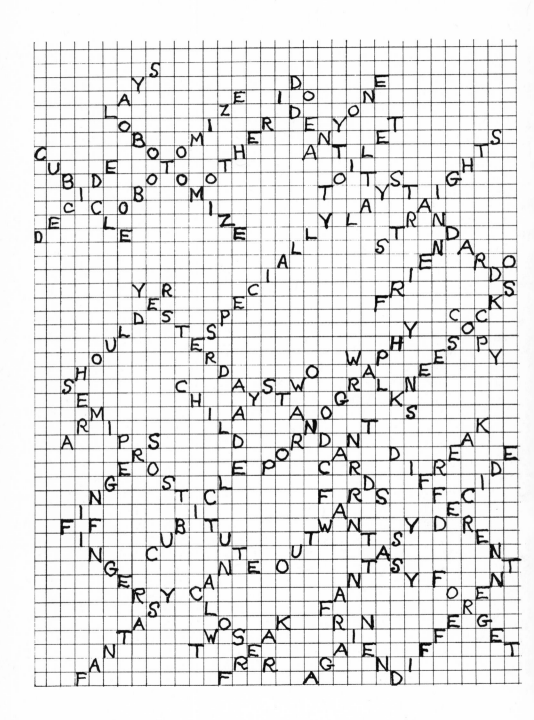

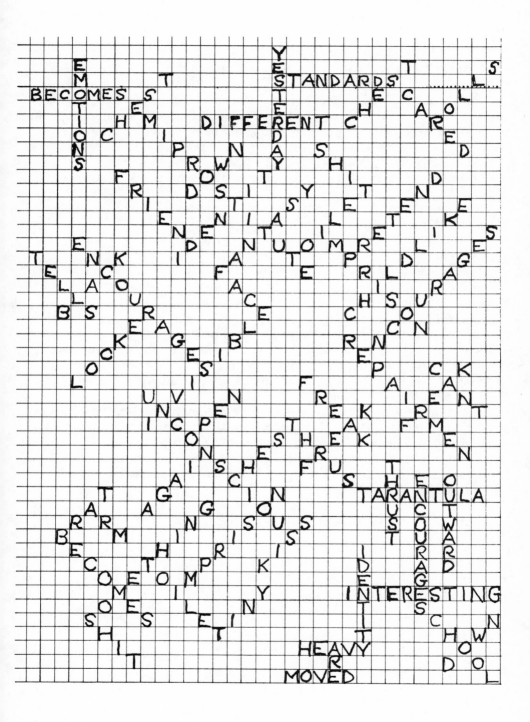

WORD EVENT(S) FOR BICI FORBES

(described Tues 3 Aug 1971 — 4:04-11:14 PM — with some later revisions)

Improvise freely, using only the component sounds (phonemes, syllables, or morphemes) of a single word or short phrase. One may use any simple or compound word (solideme or hypheme), any name (whether composed of one or of several separate names or words), any book or other title, or any phrase composed of a small number of words.

Any word or phrase will do, but some are richer in variety of sounds than others.

Produce the sounds separately & variously combined—everything from single phonemes to whole sentences.

Repeat a lot.

Sing a lot.

Vowels, nasals, sibilants, & liquids shd often be prolonged as long steady tones on true pitches or as ornamentations or micromelismata around such tones.

A performance can last any length of time, but shd have enough duration for the development of a word's (or phrase's) possibilities.

Any number of persons can improvise together, all using the sounds of the same word or phrase, & one may also play any number of recorded improvisations on the same word or phrase along with the live improvisations, but one person alone is plenty.

(This general plan for word events is a development from "A Word Event for George Brecht" [1961], & is a result of having realized the earlier plan in a number of performances, beginning in 1967. It differs chiefly from the earlier plan in that other sounds of the component *letters* of the chosen word or phrase than those actually included in the word or phrase are excluded.)

final revision 9 April 1972
Bronx NY

INTRODUCTION TO THE "YOUNG TURTLE ASYMMETRIES"

Asymmetries are nonsyntactic chance-generated poems of which the printed formats are notations for solo or group performances. They are *asymmetrical* in that they have no regularly repeating stanzaic or other patterns. They are *notations* in that most aspects of their format can be translated into aspects of performance. Notably, the lengths of blank space before, between, & after single words or word strings, & between lines, stand for *temporal holes*—durations in which readers keep silent or produce single prolonged tones on instruments that can sustain tones evenly (e.g., winds; bowed strings; reed, pipe, or electronic organs; or other mechanical or electronic sound producers).

To measure these blanks, each poem page is conceived as a rectangle of which the horizontal sides are the top & bottom lines of words & the vertical sides are imaginary margin lines running parallel through the rightmost & leftmost characters on the page. *Blank lines* lie between the two margins; righthand blanks, between the right margin & the first character of an indented word; lefthand blanks, between the last printed character & the left margin.

Similarly, *phonic holds* or *prolongations* &/or *repeats* are indicated in some Asymmetries by notations placed in what should otherwise be blank spaces. In the "Young Turtle Asymmetries," there are no *phonic repeats,* but *phonic holds* or *prolongations* are represented by a phonemic notation adapted from that used by W. Nelson Francis in his *Structure of American English* (New York: Ronald Press, 1958), ch. 3: "The Significant Sounds of Speech: Phonemics," pp. 119-61 (see esp. chart p. 151). In the order of their introduction, the phonemic notations used in the "Young Turtle Asymmetries" are:

/uhhhh/ *u* as in *but* or the *e* of *the* before consonants
/iyyyy/ *ee* as in *feet* or the final *ey* of *journey*
/lllll/ *l* as in *scuttle*
/zzzzz/ *z* or *s* in *is*
/nnnnd/ *n* of *found* prolonged and ending with an unreleased *d* [d⁻]
/ngggg/ the *ng* nasal sound of *young* prolonged (a single sound)
/nnnnn/ the *n* of *one*

Single letters are merely repeated to indicate prolongations, while only the final letters of digraphs are repeated. Notations are continued from one line to another by placing hyphens at the ends of lines. However, the 1st letters of digraphs are placed within parentheses at the beginnings of the following lines to remind readers that the sounds indicated by the complete digraphs are to be continued.

PERFORMANCE PARAMETERS

The *durations* of silences (or instrumental tones) & prolonged phonemes are *at least* those of single words or word strings that might be printed in equivalent spaces, as they would be spoken aloud by the individual reader. That is, readers are silent or prolong sounds at least as long as it would take them to speak such space-equivalent words. However, they may extend these durations whenever they feel that the total performance would be better if they remained silent or continued to prolong a sound. Thus the spatial notations indicate *minimal* durations only; readers have the option of *extending* silences & prolonged sounds improvisatorily—in accord with their judgments of the performance situation—*longer* than strictly called for by the notation, even tho they may never make them shorter. In this way, a completely determinate, tho chance-generated, notation becomes the basis of only partially determinate performances—ones that are, strictly speaking, "unpredictable" rather than "indeterminate."

The *speed* of reading is entirely up to the individual readers, & should be continually *varied,* but there should be no *great* disparities in *average* speed between the fastest & slowest readers.

In the "Young Turtle Asymmetries," *loudness* is varied improvisatorially (not by details of the notation, as in other Asymmetries) by individual readers, but only between *moderately soft & moderately loud.*

The *pitches* of words must be those of normal speech; the pitch of each prolongation should remain as nearly *constant* as possible, continuing the pitch that the sound would have in normal reading (without longish silences or prolongations) of the phrases in which it occurs. Care should be taken to avoid especially down-glides of a musical third or more (e.g., *C* to *A* or below).

It is best that the "Young Turtle Asymmetries" be read by 5 simultaneous readers. In an optimal performance, all 5 readers will read all 5 "Young Turtle Asymmetries," each in one of the following successions: 12345, 23451, 34512, 45123, & 51234. Thus all 5 will always be being read simultaneously. In shorter performances, 1, 2, 3, or 4 of them may be read by each reader, but all 5 must always be read together. Groups larger than 5 may perform the "Young Turtle Asymmetries" by "doubling": one or more of the Asymmetries may each be read by 2 readers, the rest being read by the others as above. This principle may be extended to "tripling," &c., by groups larger than 10.

It is of the utmost importance that readers *listen very attentively to all sounds* produced by themselves & the other readers, as well as to all environing sounds (audience, street, &c.). All aspects of performance must be sensitively adjusted by the readers in accordance with their perceptions of the total sound. Thus they may prolong silences, tones, or phonemes (speech sounds), or speak louder or softer, faster or slower, as they feel these actions will contribute most positively to the total sound.

The words to all 5 "Young Turtle Asymmetries" were drawn from a single picture caption:

> *Young turtles, below, scuttle*
> *to open water. Once the hatchlings*
> *have found their way to the*
> *sea, they embark upon a journey*
> *whose course is a mystery.*
> *No one knows where the turtles go.*

This appeared with the article, "100 Turtle Eggs," by Archie Carr, p. 51, *Natural History,* Vol. LXXVI, No. 7 (Aug.-Sept. 1967: American Museum of Natural History, New York).

The method by which the various words & word strings were drawn in turn from the caption was that of *diastic chance generation,* a method I have used often in composing poems & performance pieces since January 1963, when it replaced the acrostic chance generation methods I had used extensively since early 1960. In using this method one takes from a text, as one reads it consecutively, successive words or word strings having the letters of an "index word or word string" in corresponding places. Thus in composing the "1st Young Turtle Asymmetry" I used the first words of the caption, up to the 1st punctuation mark, as the "index string," by which I drew the same words as the poem's first words, & also drew the rest of the words in the poem. The 2nd word string begins with *found,* the 1st subsequent word having an *o* in the 2nd place—as in *young;* the 3rd word string begins with *journey,* the next word with a *u* in the 3rd place, &c. Each time, a word string beginning with a word having the required letter in the required place was taken from that word on to the next punctuation mark. The method used in spacing "Asymmetries" since October 1960 was used to space the words on the page. A comma or other non-sentence-ender made the next line begin on the line below after one horizontal space; a period made the next line begin 2 lines below after 2 horizontal spaces. The beginning of a new index word made the line drawn by its initial letter begin at the left margin & doubled the amount of vertical space between that line & the line above; i.e., below lines ending with commas, there is double the amount of vertical space between that line & the line above; after periods, quadruple space. Line breaks in the source caption affected spacing like commas. Reaching the page edge in the manuscript notebook caused indented continuations of word strings on lines below. Breaks in word strings due to spacing rules caused prolongations of final phonemes before breaks; these were extended to right margins of poems & from left margins to next words of word strings. Thus the spelling & punctuation of the words in the caption, as well as their original order & spacing, determined which word strings were brought into the poems, their lengths, breaks in them, prolongations, & spacing on the page.

July 1967; rev. 1969, 1970, 1973, & 10-11 October 1978

The texts of the "Young Turtle Asymmetries," an earlier version of this introduction, & a recording of a performance by Carol Bergé, Spencer Holst, Iris Lezak, Anne Waldman, & myself appeared in Aspen Magazine No. 8 (New York: Fall/Winter, 1970). *The texts were later published in my book* 21 Matched Asymmetries (London: Aloes Books, 1978).

1st Young Turtle Asymmetry -- 30 July 1967

Young turtles,

      found their way to the/uhhhhhhhhhhhhhhhhh-

(u)hh/sea,

      journey/iyyyyyyyyyyyyyyyyyyyyyyyyyyyyyyyyyyyyyy-

(i)yy/whose course is a mystery.

    No one knows where the turtles go.

    Young turtles,

to open water.

    turtles go.

    turtles,

      scuttle/llllllllllllllllllllllllllllllllll-

llllllllllllllllllll/to open water.

          turtles go.

             turtles,

   turtles go.

found their way to the/uhhhhhhhhhhhhhhhhhhhhhhhhhhhhhhhhhhhh-
(u)hhhhhhhhhhhhhhhhhhhh/sea,

           journey/iyyyyyyyyyyyyyyyyyyyyy-
(i)yyyyyyyyyyyyyyyyyyyyyyyyyyyyyyyyyyyyy/whose course is/zzzzz-
zzzzz/a mystery.

        Young turtles,

            open water.

                foun/nnnnnn-
nnnn/d their way to the sea,

they embark upon a journey/iyyyyyyyyyyyyyyyyyyyyyyyyyyyyyyyyyy-
(i)yyyyyyyyyyyyyyyyyyyyyyyy/whose course is a mystery.

    where the turtles go.

        open water.

          they embark
upon a journey/iyyyyyyyyyyyyyyyyyyyyyyyyyyyyyyyyyyyyyyyyyyyyy-
(i)yyyyyyyyyyyyyyyy/whose course is a mystery.

3rd Young Turtle Asymmetry -- 30 July 1967

the   turtles   go.

the hatchlings/zzzzzzzzzzzzzzzzzzzzzzzzzzzzzzz-
zzzz/have found their way to the/uhhhhhhhhhhhhhhhhhhhhhhhhhhhhhhhh-
(u)hhhhhhhhhhhhhhhhhhhhhhhhhhhhhhhh/sea,

they embark upon a/uhhhhhh-
(u)h/journey/iyyyyyyyyyyyyyyyyyyyyyyyyyyyyyyyyyyyyyyyyyyyyyyyyyyyyyy-
(i)yyyyyyyyy/whose course is a/uhhhhhhhhhhhhhhhhhhhhhhhhhhhhhhhhhhhh-
(u)hhhhhhhhhhhhhhhhhhhhhhhhhhhhhhhh/mystery.

their way to the/uhhhhh-
(u)hhhhhhhhhhhhhhhhhhhhhhhhhhhhhhhhhhhhhhhhhhhhhhhhhhhhhhhhhhhhh/sea,
    embark upon a journey/iyyyyyyyyyyyyyyyyyyyyyyyyyyyyyyyyyyyyyyyyy-
(i)yyyyyyyyyyyyyyyyyyyyyyy/whose course is a mystery.

where the turtles go.

water.

way to the/uhhhhhhhhhhhhhhhhhhhhhh-
(u)hhhhhhhhhhhhhhhhhhhhhhhhhhhhhhhhhhhhhhhhhhh/sea,

4th Young Turtle Asymmetry -- 30 July 1967

they embark upon a journey/iyyyyyyyyyyyyyyyyyyyyyyyyyyyyyyyyyyyyy-
(i)yyyyyyyyyyyyyyyyyyyyyyy/whose course is a mystery.

    No one knows where the turtles go.

turtles,
       the hatchlings/zzzzzzzzzzzzzzzzzzzzzzzzzzzzzzzzzzzz-
zzzzzzzzzzzzzzzzzzzzzzzz/have found their way to the/uhhhhhhhh-
(u)hhhhhhhhhhhhhhhhhhhhhhhhhhhhhhhhhhhhhhhhhhhhhhhhhhhhhh/sea,
       they embark upon a journey/iyyyyyyyyyyyyyyyyyyyyyyyy-
(i)yyyyyyyyyyyyyyyyyyyyyyyyyyyyyyyyyyyy/whose course is a mystery.

scuttle/lllllllllllllllllllllllllllllllllllllllllllllllllllll-
lllllll/to open water.

           sea,
              sea,

journey/iyyyyyyyyyyyyyyyyyyyyyyyyyyyyyyyyyyyyyyyyyyyyyyyyyyyyyy-
(i)yyyy/whose course is a mystery.

5th Young Turtle Asymmetry -- 30 July 1967

No one knows where the turtles go.

Young/ngggggggggggggggggggggggggg-
(n)gggg/turtles,

journey/iyyyyyyyyyyyyyyyyyyyyyyyyyyyyyyyyyyyyyyyyyyyyyyy-
(i)yyyyyyyyyyyyyyyyyyyyyy/whose course is a mystery.

one/nnnnnnnnnnnnnnnnn-
nnnnnnn/knows where the turtles go.

turtles,

journey/iyyyyyyyyyyyyyyyyyyyy-
(i)yyyyyyyyyyyyyyyyyyyyyyyyyyyyyyyyyyyyyyyyyyyyyyyyy/whose/zzzzzzzzzzzzz-
zzzzzzz/course is a mystery.

where the turtles go.

the hatchlings/zzzzzzzzzzzzzzzzzzzzzzzzzzzzzzzzzzzzz-
zzzzzzzzzzzzzzzzzzzzzzzzzzzzzzzzzzzzzzzz/have found their way to the/uhhhhhhh-
(u)hhhhhhhhhhhhhhhhhhhhhhhhhhhhhhhhhhhhhhhhhhhhhhhhhhhhhhhhhhhhhhhhhhh/sea,
they embark upon a journey/iyyyyyyyyyyyyyyyyyyyyyyyyyyyyyyyyyyyyyyyyyyyyyy-
(i)yyyyyyyyyyyyyyyyyyyyyyyyyyyyyy/whose course is a mystery.

A WORD EVENT FOR GEORGE BRECHT

A man utters any word, preferably one without expletive connotations. He then proceeds to analyze it, lst, into its successive phonemes; 2nd, into a series of phonemes representable by its successive individual letters, whether or not this series coincides with the 1st series.

After repeating each of these series alternately a few times, he begins to permute the members of each series.

After uttering various permutations of each series alternately several times, he utters phonemes from both series in random order, uttering them singly, combining them into syllables, repeating them into syllables, repeating them &/or prolonging them *ad libitum.*
He ends the event by pronouncing one of these phonemes very carefully.

4 November 1961
New York City

NOTE: (2 July 1968) This needn't be done as formalistically as the above description seems to require. The 3rd paragraph is the heart of it. A performance can be "cool" or "hot"—"minimal" or "expressionist"—according to the temperament of the performer & the situation of the performance. The author has often performed it as a political piece (e.g., in the movie *Far from Vietnam*). JML

23

1   HOPING   SUNG OUT   SUNG   PRIVATE   SOME   SEVERAL   ALL OF THE ABOVE   CUBE

2   CENTERED   WHAT?   AS IF   REALLY?   FORMING   TRYING OUT   TRYING   LABEL   NEXT

3   HOPING   SANG OUT   SUNG   PRIVATE   SOME   SEVERAL   ALL OF THE ABOVE   CUBE

4   OF A NATURE QUITE DISTINCT IN CONTRAST TO THE COMMON VARIETY OF GRANDIOSE OBJECTORS, QUIETLY ASSIGNING SEATS,

5   SLIGHT   AS IF   RESEMBLE   SEEMING   REALLY?   SUNG   CENTER

6   AND YET A MOMENT   A PAUSE   A BRIEF REPOSE   PRIVATE   LEAVING OUT   WHAT?

7   SLIGHT   AS IF   RESEMBLE   SEEMING   REALLY?   SUNG   CENTER

24

1. GROUPING TOWARDS MEANING POSING PERHAPS RATHER THAN TWO STEP

2. THOSE HOWEVER PREFERENCE COUNTLESS MAYBE NOT CURIOUS SOUNDING

3. GROUPING TOWARDS MEANING POSING PERHAPS RATHER THAN TWO STEP

4. CREATING AN ORDERED, OR SO IT WOULD SEEM, SYSTEM, FROM ONE THAT, AS A SEPARATE PART, MIGHT SEEM A BIT

5. WIT SLUNG OUT FORMING TRYING OUT ALL OF THE ABOVE AS IF SEEMING

6. HOPING AS IF SOME SEVERAL TRYING SEEMING FORMATIVE AT LEAST

7. WIT SLUNG OUT FORMING TRYING OUT ALL OF THE ABOVE AS IF SEEMING

COUNTING TO 9 IN 3 LOCATIONS

```
1........2........3........4........5........6........7........8........9........

1        2        3        4        5        6        7        8        9
 1        2        3        4        5        6        7        8        9

1        2        3        4        5        6        7        8        9
 1        2        3        4        5        6        7        8        9
  1        2        3        4        5        6        7        8        9

1        2        3        4        5        6        7        8        9
 1 1      2 2      3 3      4 4      5 5      6 6      7 7      8 8      9 9
  1        2        3        4        5        6        7        8        9

1        2        3        4        5        6        7        8        9
 1 1      2 2      3 3      4 4      5 5      6 6      7 7      8 8      9 9
  1 1      2 2      3 3      4 4      5 5      6 6      7 7      8 8      9 9

1        2        3        4        5        6        7        8        9
 1 1 1    2 2 2    3 3 3    4 4 4    5 5 5    6 6 6    7 7 7    8 8 8    9 9 9
  1 1      2 2      3 3      4 4      5 5      6 6      7 7      8 8      9 9

1      1 2      2 3      3 4      4 5      5 6      6 7      7 8      8 9      9
 1 1 1    2 2 2    3 3 3    4 4 4    5 5 5    6 6 6    7 7 7    8 8 8    9 9 9
  1 1      2 2      3 3      4 4      5 5      6 6      7 7      8 8      9 9

1      1 2      2 3      3 4      4 5      5 6      6 7      7 8      8 9      9
 1 1 1 1  2 2 2 2  3 3 3 3  4 4 4 4  5 5 5 5  6 6 6 6  7 7 7 7  8 8 8 8  9 9 9 9
  1 1      2 2      3 3      4 4      5 5      6 6      7 7      8 8      9 9

1      1 2      2 3      3 4      4 5      5 6      6 7      7 8      8 9      9
 1 1 1 1  2 2 2 2  3 3 3 3  4 4 4 4  5 5 5 5  6 6 6 6  7 7 7 7  8 8 8 8  9 9 9 9
  1 1    1 2 2    2 3 3    3 4 4    4 5 5    5 6 6    6 7 7    7 8 8    8 9 9    9
```

IN THIS PERFORMANCE PIECE, THE WORDS FOR THESE NUMBERS ARE READ ALOUD, IN ANY
LANGUAGE. EACH HORIZONTAL LINE IN EACH GROUP REPRESENTS A LOCATION (A SOUNDSOURCE).
THE NUMBER OF BEATS OR PULSES REMAIN THE SAME FOR EACH SET OF COUNTS. WHILE THE
TEMPO MAY VARY, FROM PERFORMANCE TO PERFORMANCE, OR FROM MOMENT TO MOMENT, THE
FEELING OF PULSE MUST REMAIN. IN THE BLANK SPACES, WHERE THERE AREN'T NUMBERS,
THE COUNTS ARE COMPLETED SILENTLY. ONE CAN COUNT TO 8 SILENTLY IN THE TOP LINE,
AND THEN TO 7 IN THE SECOND LINE, ETC., SUCCESSIVELY, IN ORDER TO KEEP PLACE.

1976 BUDDIST WEDDING OF DAN & BONNIE

WEDDING / CONJUGATION

```
NAM MYOHO RENGE KYO          NAM MYOHO RENGE KYO
DAN MYOHO RENGE KYO          NAM MYOHO BONNIE KYO
NAM MYOHO RENGE DAN          NAM BONNIE RENGE KYO
                             -NIE MYOHO RENGE BON-

                    NAM BONNIE RENGE DAN
                    DAN BONNIE RENGE KYO
                    DAN MYOHO BONNIE KYO
                    NAM MYOHO BONNIE DAN
                    DAN MYOHO BONNIE DAN
                    DAN BONNIE BONNIE KYO
                    NAM BONNIE BONNIE DAN
                    DAN BONNIE BONNIE DAN
                    BON DANNY DANNY BON
                    DON BANNIE BANNIE BON
                    BAN DONNIE DONNIE BAN
                    ++++++++++++++++++++

                    + LET THESE & ALL OTHER TRANSFORMATIONS
                      HAVE THEIR PLACE
```

This was written for the wedding of
Dan and Bonnie who are Nicherin Buddists
and chant Nam Myoho Renge Kyo as part
of their daily ritual.

RECIPE FOR SOUNDING:

JEROME ROTHENBERG'S <u>BEADLE'S</u> <u>TESTIMONY</u>

LIST THE SYLLABLES OF THE POEM.

RECORD ON EDITABLE MEDIUM, AUDIO OR VIDEO TAPE ETC,
IDENTICAL PERFORMANCES OF EACH SYLLABLE LIST.

EDIT TO FORM POEM.

(1969)

The, the, the, the, the
boy, boy, boy's boy
who
throws
ball
A, a, a, a, a, a, a, a, a, a, a, a
jew, Jews, jew
el, el, el
of, of
His, his, his, his
coat
down
to, to, too, two, to, to, to, too

feet
Ear
locks
fly
ing, ing
He, He, He, He
will, Will, will, will, will
grow, grow
up, up
sell, sell
can, can
dles, dles
eat
dog
&, &, &, &
thrive
on, on
fat
ci, Ci, Ci
gars
bless, bless
mo, mo
ther, ther
Yes, Yes
we, we, we
are
sim
ple, ple, ple
peo

drive
carts
work
with
shit
Some some
Sometimes Some, Some, Some
times, times, times, times
stu   times, times
dy
fish
in
hand, hands
cha, cha
ri, ri
ty, ty, ties, ty
E
ros
is, is, is, is
War
saw
ban
ker
Spain
far, far
way, way
Kan
sas
XXXXXXX
al
so
Where
did
our
love
go?
I, I
have
on
ly
one
wall, Walls, wall, wall
et
want

speak
you
bout
it
what
be
hind
tem
shin
dies
lo
co
mo
tive
sha
dow

for a poetry of blood

sound poetry is *the* poetry of direct emotional confrontation: there is no pausing for intellectualization, there is no repeating of emotional content, each performance is unique & only the audience is repeatable. there is no poet FORTHEPOETISATONEWITHHISSOUNDS. if you get sound over they cease to be audience, if you don't get sound over they are destroyed as audience:

EITHER YOU TRANSFORM OR YOU
DESTROY
///

get down to the wormed roots of poetry: sound & rhythm & pulse — region of interaction of the primitive & the animal which has been misinterpreted as both dadaism & surrealism.
you're bound to affect an audience.

rhythmic sound is not an artifact but a profound instance of the human self. it is our simple rhythmic identity:

our regular organic processes (heartbeat, pulse)
our semi-voluntary actions (respiration, propulsion)
our simple emotional signals (foot-tapping, hand-clapping)
it is the spirit of our thighs, it is the basis of every sexual act
rhythm = the basic life force

in liberating sound we are discovering these basic forces for ourself in organic expressionistic performance. the repetition of sound only seems to establish an external object of mesmerism for in reality it liberates the elemental regions & most primitive impulses of the human self.

as these forces are omnipresent so have they been long dormant & ignored by poetry; as these forces are hidden dormant & ignored so are they frightening as a biological extension until they are realized as self-discovery.

POETRY BECOMES BLOOD when you achieve this state: when poet, poem & audience become one in sound, total containment in the one embracing biology.

sound is the extension of human biology into a context of challenge. breath is the purest sound. sound is the awareness that direct sensory involvement/impact is a greater thing than indirect communication to & through the intellect. sound is the conviction that the senses should be married not divorced, sound is a respect for the purity of immediacy & an utter faith in the human capacity to grasp the immediate.

this is the infinite extension of man. this is the successful assimilation of your own into another biology. the true cosmic organism. the true cosmic orgasm. this & only this is not degrading to our times.

this is to be the road to the simultaneous to the relevant to the immediate

to the inclusive to the infinitely
extending & embracing
blood.

plussiliente positivemente
signiamente ofiliente addiliente tionimente
minimento ussiliente negativemente signiamento
subiliente tractimente tionilente
plussiliente orimente minimente usiliente
minimente usiliente orilente plusiliente

multipliediente byliente dividiente ediliento
byliente equaliente approximiliento
atelliente congruitente entiente greaterliente
thaniente lessiliente thaniente
similiente toliente equivalente entiente

identicaliento
identiente icaliente equaliente equivalento
thereimente foriente sincemente becausemento
identicaliente identimento equaliente toimente
directimento untiliento
proportiomento nalemento variamento
directimento untiliente
asimente infinimente timente squaremente
rootemente minimente usimente onelento

particularimente valuemente ofelente variamente
alblente multimento pliedelente itsemente elfemente
anymento timelente dividemente edemente
squariente rootemente radicaliento
signimento basemento
naturalemento systemento
logarithemento
logarithelente
summamente ationemente termelente onemente eachemento
positivemente integeremente productimento
integralemente definilente limitente approachemente
asiente silentiente limitento functionemento
incremente differentialemente derivaetente tivente
respectivente variamente ratiomente circumferencemente
diameteremente circularement factorialemento
indicatemente enclosente symbolemento

singlemente numberemente indicativemente treatedemente
symbolemente singlemente numberetente angleemente
parallelemente perpendemente dicualremente trianglemente
rightemente agledemente trianglemento
minutente arcemente primetente
secondsemente arcemente doublento

primento.

DISCUSSION ... GENESIS ... CONTINUITY:
Some Reflections on the Current Work of The Four Horsemen

Note: The following reflections are abstracted from an ongoing correspond-
ence with Prof. Tom Taylor, Dept. of English, University of Cincinnati. The flow
of the argument is in large part determined by the ghost of that dialogue.

The Horsemen don't think of their pieces as, in any way, final products.
From the outset in the group's first collaborations (1969) the mystique
of the crafted poem-object (projected as the perfect, reiterable per-
formance) was abandoned in favour of a wholesale absorption in the
hazardous polyvalencies of process. Response in performance is al-
ways on the local level to particular energy nuances as they suggest
or manifest themselves in a given moment. Response is always to the
microalterations in the energy states that the four of us create. Pieces
tend to lend themselves as possibilities, or hueristic pointers but the
'piece' is always the transient state of energy gestalt. The poem-
processes usually follow the pattern of interdetermined movements
towards and beyond what collectively we term 'points of cohesion'.
Ours is an art of intensities and change, of rapid passages into and out
of cohesion, incohesion, deterritorializations and territorialities. It is the
art of transition, of displacements at thresholds and passages in and
out of recognitions. Ad hoc arrival points tend to lend structure to the
pieces. We decide on points of arrival that we will all reach at some
point during the piece, but actual duration is indeterminate. We re-
alized very early that energy flows are not chronologicatable. These
actual arrival points are often sonic features (specific sounds or sound
groupings) we know we will arrive at but when and how we arrive is
unspecified. As such our work is closely concerned with the kinetic
aspects of narrative. Not story in any contentual sense, of course, but
narrative as the motion of particles in unspecified time frames. The
question of arrival through aleatoric and spontaneous perambulations
involves the issue of knowing when a destination is reached. The key to
this epistemological factor (how we know where we are, how we
know that we'll get there) is embedded in **ecouture** – a kind of devel-
oped expertise in the aural. We've trained ourselves to be good listen-
ers and sensitive barometers to each other. This i believe is the crucial
thing in our performance, for without the listening, without that
awareness of the energy states of each other the knowingness would
not be possible. It could be said that The Four Horsemen function as
paradigm units of audience. That is, during a performance we play

audience to each other, we are each others texts, performers and audience. We are both what we say and what we hear. And simultaneously. At the same instance.

Metonym and synecdoche: that relationship(s) of part to whole. In any one piece we each exist as metonymic elements at various places, but metonymic elements in a collectivising structure. As parts we become 'whole' by merely recognizing our partiality, our molecular independence. The operating notion of 'whole' is not that of a consummate aggregate of parts, but a juxtapositional whole, the 'whole', that is, as a concept placed alongside the 'parts', entering into relationship with the parts but in no way dominating them. This notion of metonymy, of part and whole, collectivity and isolation constitutes a major structural feature in our work. It is important, too, in connecting an anthropology with a semiotics. For what this structure homologizes are certain human states: the movement from isolation into community, the problematics of community, the repeatability of structures, the collectivisation of the self.

As regards the discontinuity factor: whilst sounds are often repeated (note, for instance, the high prevalence of chant infra-structures in our work) the energy states emerging are always different. It was on this basis viz. that phonic repetition could never correlate with an emotional equivalent that Stein denied repetition. There is always a change in emotional insistence; it is the very nature of the vocalized to effect such changes on a micro level. Identicality of sound does not imply identicality of emotional force. Our pieces are largely the result of a huge energy interface — between our own states of energy in performance and the energy complex of the audience (and the audience conceived too as a complex of molecular flows rather than a molar aggregate).

There is always this element of arche-composition present: the piece-process shaped differently each time by the particular energy gestalt created by the combined audience-performer dynamic. This quality of the unspoken, the unconscious communication and non-verbal, emotional dialogue that occurs each and every performance is to a large degree a factor in determining the duration of a piece. All this, i stress, is silent and often unconscious and highly subtle in its shaping.

We structure our pieces very much along the lines of a piece of string containing a series of knots. The knots have a double function as both points of coherence (where everything comes together) and as points of transition (where everything changes). The Horsemen's extended pieces, in this light, become studies of the problematics of transition. How does one move from one point to another? How does one develop in a non-developmental structure? Hence the importance of audition: when we listen we know; when we know, we can effect a transition. An art process then of transition rather than continuity.

Text
Text functions in several different ways. Sometimes it's a precise score in which sound features and values are specifically escribed, as too are the points of entry and exit. Exact time is never specified (pieces may vary within 3 or 5 minutes length in a norm of say 9 minutes). Frequently text functions as an anti-text: the text, in this case, being what the group rebounds off, what is approached to be resisted, what is refracted, what is reacted to. It's the text as anti-text that is most commonly employed, although text often figures prominently as dramatic prop i.e. the inclusion of text as a visual device to focus the human group. In this respect text acts as a centralising icon, a device to anchor our physical bodies in one place. The physical presence then of text (it might be as simple as a blank sheet of paper) is very important as a structuring device; text promotes a gathering, a calling into physical proximities which in itself has an effect upon the energy state.

In several pieces our composition was initially bricolage: the practical use of whatever is at hand. Each of us would bring texts to a hypothetical locus designated to become the new piece. These various texts would be tested, some abandoned, others incorporated. Fragments from our own discarded novels, plays or poems, newspaper headlines were often brought, worked with, and reworked. Often this locus of bricolage would generate new texts; we would actually sit down together at a typewriter during rehersal and practice to compose a bridge-section, or replacement section. In this way text-on-hand acts as the catalyst of new text.

Performance is lodged between text and sonic event. We locate in the indeterminacy between two zones of discourse. Text serves to physically organize our bodies (the way a weightlifter will concentrate on a particular spot on a wall before his lift). At this point text is prop (serving to bring the group together as an iconic whole, acting as a visual focus for us and for audience too). Text relates to performance as performers relate to audience to a degree in which I believe that the Horsemen as performers become the audience's own text. Body readings and emotional sensings are all made of us during a performance. Beyond prop text serves as catalyst to get us beyond an actual reading. Often we'll start deliberately and rigidly to follow a text, then to abandon this as we listen and respond to the sound patterns emerging from each other. So there is a curious translational process involved: a passage, an actual metamorphosis of text which shifts from the paper in our hands to being the movement of ourselves. We start to read each other; the point of transition is the moment of refraction, the moment that text mutates from paper into human sound, when focus shifts from attention on a graphism to attention on sounds in space.

Finally, a note on the absence & / or presence of the technological aspect in sound performance. As a group, The Horsemen have a decided preference for the pure acoustic, eschewal of microphones, of electroacoustic treatment of any kind. It was felt that there is a significant difference between human energy per se and extended human energy through electronic processing. That, in fact, a fundamental transmogrification took place, that transmission through a medium of amplification resulted in a transformation. What we wanted was to preserve the human factor of a pure vocal energy as the kinetic axis of the piece. Audiopoetry: the poetry of technologically treated voice, is fundamentally a graphicism; it is concerned with the scripted sign, with an actual activity of writing. Albeit a total concentration of the phonic and the sub-phonetic empties the word of its lexical meaning, but the reception of this on electro-magnetic tape returns the concern to a very classical concern: writing. For if we understand writing as what it is: the inscription of units of meaning within a framed space of retrievability and repeatability, then tape is none other than writing. To transcend writing, and the critical vocabulary built up around the logocentricity of writing, and to achieve a totally phonocentric art, must involve a renunciation of those two central canons of the written: repeatability and retrievability, a claiming of the transient, transitional, ephemeral, the intensity of the orgasm, the flow of energies through fissures, escape, the total burn, the finite calorie, loss, displacement, excess: the total range of the nomadic consciousness.

Toronto, August 1978

1. SCHROEDER

I was fascinated by the country as such. I flew north from Churchill to Coral Harbour on Southampton Island at the end of September. Snow had begun to fall and the country was partially covered by it. Some of the lakes were frozen around the edges but towards the centre of the lakes you could still see the clear, clear water. And flying over this country, you could look down and see various shades of green in the water and you could see the bottom of the lakes, and it was a most fascinating experience. I remember I was up in the cockpit with the pilot, and I was forever looking out, left and right, and I could see ice-floes over the Hudson's Bay and I was always looking for a polar bear or some seals that I could spot but, unfortunately, there were none.

SCHROEDER:

1. And as we flew along the East coast of Hudson's Bay, this flat, flat country
VALLEE:

2.   *I don't go, let me say*

S: *1.* frightened me a little, because it just seemed endless.
V: *2. this again, I don't go for this northmanship bit at all.*

S: *1.* We seemed to be going into nowhere, and the further north we went
V: *2. I don't knock those people who do claim that they want to go*
                                              farther and

S: *1. the more monotonous it became. There was nothing but snow*
V: *2.* farther north, but I see it as a game—this northmanship bit.
                          People say, "well,

S: *1. and, to our right, the waters of Hudson's Bay.*
V: *2.* were you ever up at the North Pole?"

S: *1. -------- Now, this was my impression*
V: *2.* "And, hell, I did a dog-sled trip of 22 days,"

S: *1. during the winter, but I also flew over the country*
V: *2.* and the other fellow says "well, I did one of 20 days"

S: *1. during the spring and the summer, and this I found intriguing;*
V: *2. you know, it's pretty childish. Perhaps they would see themselves*

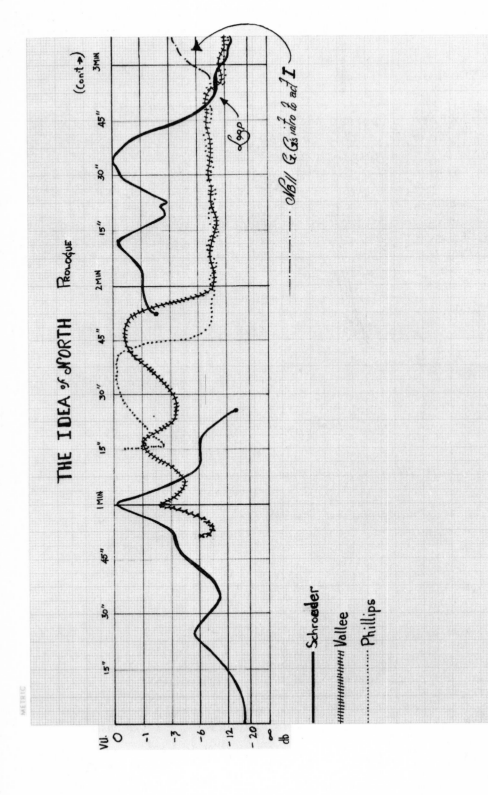

PHILLIPS:

3. And, then, for another 11 years, I served the North in various capacities.

S: *1. because, then, I could see the outlines*
V: *2. as more skeptical-----------------(fade)*
P: 3. Sure the North has changed my life; I can't conceive

S: *1. of the lakes and the rivers and, on the tundra,*
P: 3. of anyone being in close touch with the North—whether they lived
there all the time
S: *1. huge spots of moss or rock—*
P: 3. or simply travelled it month after month and year after year—

S: *1. there is hardly any vegetation that one can spot from the air-----(fade)*
V: *2. ----------more skeptical about the offerings of the mass media-----(fade)*
P: 3. I can't conceive of such a person as really being untouched by the North.

V: *2.* And it goes on like this,
P: 3. When I left in 1965, at least, left the job there, *it wasn't because of*

V: 2. as though there's some special merit, some virtue, in being in the North
P: 3. *being tired of the North, the feeling that it had no more interest,*

V: 2. or some special virtue in having been
P: 3. *or anything of the sort; I was as keen as ever.*

V: 2. with primitive people: well, you know, what
P: 3. *I left because I'm a public servant, (begin fade)*

S: *1.* It is most difficult
V: 2. special virtue is there in that? (Begin fade) *And so*
P: 3. *I was asked to do another job related to fighting*

S: *1.* to describe. It was complete isolation, this is very true,
V: 2. *I think that I'd be more interested in Baker Lake right now,*
P: 3. *the war against poverty --------------(fade to loop)*

S: *1.* And I knew very well that I could not go anywhere
V: 2. *if indeed it is changing significantly----------(fade to loop)*

SCHROEDER: 1. except for a mile or two, walking. *I always think of the
long summer nights, when the snow had melted and the lakes were
open and the geese and ducks had started to fly north. During
that time, the sun would set but, when there was still the last shim-
mer in the sky, I would look out to one of those lakes and watch
those ducks and geese just flying around peacefully or sitting on
the water, and I thought I was almost part of that country, part of
that peaceful surrounding, and I wished that it would never end.
(Fade to loop)*
Effects cue: *Hold loop, during gradual descrescendo for.....seconds.*

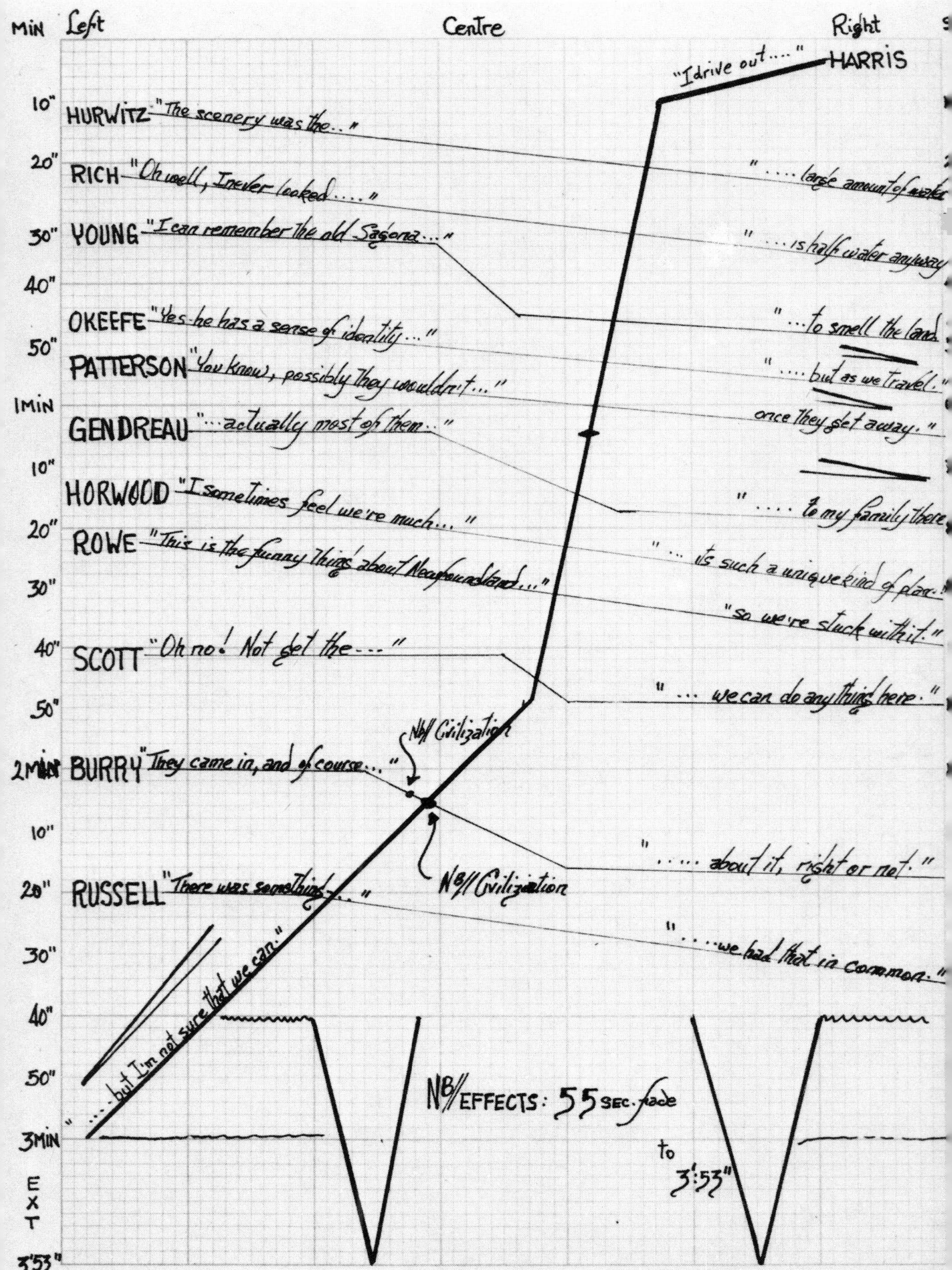
MIN
Left
Centre
Right
"I drive out...."
HARRIS
10"
HURWITZ "The scenery was the.."
"....large amount of water
20"
RICH "Oh well, I never looked...."
30"
YOUNG "I can remember the old Sagona..."
".... is half water anyway
40"
OKEEFE "Yes he has a sense of identity..."
"...to smell the land
50"
PATTERSON "You know, possibly they wouldn't..."
".... but as we travel."
1MIN
GENDREAU "...actually most of them.."
once they get away."
10"
HORWOOD "I sometimes feel we're much..."
".... to my family there
20"
ROWE "This is the funny thing about Newfoundland..."
"... its such a unique kind of place"
30"
"so we're stuck with it."
40"
SCOTT "Oh no! Not get the..."
50"
"... we can do anything here."
NB// Civilization
2MIN
BURRY "They came in, and of course..."
10"
".... about it, right or not."
NB// Civilization
20"
RUSSELL "There was something..."
30"
"....we had that in common."
40"
"....but I'm not sure that we can."
50"
NB// EFFECTS: 55 SEC. fade
to
3'53"
3MIN
EXT
3'53"

NEWFOUNDLAND   EPILOGUE

DR. HARRIS: I drive out
over the road sometimes
and I'm glad the road
is there -- it's a
nice thing to have, to
be able to drive across
the country -- but you
stop at any point on
the road and look for forty,
fifty, sixty miles,
however far the
eye can see,and you see
a land which hasn't
changed that much for
centuries -- five, six,
ten or a dozen or however
many it's been --
and there's a great
solace in this really.
There are some things
that are unchanging;
there are some things
that are still not
spoiled by civilization.

DR HURWITZ: The scenery
was the first thing that
struck me -- and the vast-

RICH: Oh, well, I
never looked at it
as though we were
isolated. I can
recall a few times

YOUNG: I can remember
the old Sagonna. I was
going north from Cor-
nerbrook. It was thick
with fog the likes of
which you've never seen
before. I was up on
the bridge with Captain

ness of the empty spaces,
the large amounts of
water and seemingly end-
less forests.

we had the Arctic
ice come in here
probably in the
harbour for a
month. But I think
that Newfoundland
herself is half
water anyhow.

Gullidge this day
and he had his nose
up in the air (sniff),
and he was sniffing

Perhaps it is
because one is not big
enough, you know, to
meet the challenge that

O'KEEFE: Yes, he has
a sense of identity

of being someone
different than the

PATTERSON: You know,
there's a possibility
they wouldn't
want to leave.
They may have strong
ties like

GENDREAU : So quite a
few of ·them end up in
the southern part of
Ontario and most of
them are unskilled
worker.

HORWOOD: I sometimes
feel that we
are much more
of a

ROWE: But this is
the funny thing
about Newfoundland,
because we
always damn our
forebears, you know,

change presents. You
can't have what's gone
and it's stupid to
think you can -- you
can't go back to the
past. We have reaction-
aries but they ought to
realize that reaction is
impossible; really,
you never can go back,
history doesn't repeat
itself, it never has done,
things are always new,
everyday is a new day
and no two events are
ever the same so you
can't have that;but
perhaps we are not big
enough or imaginative
enough to see that while
we have killed that, we
have not really thought
very much about creating
anything to substitute
for it except to follow
in the wake of people
who have already
spoilt so
much else.

We are part of a

and he said "I'm trying to
smell the land".
rest but, as we travel
more, I'm sure we'll
find we're not so
different as we some-
times think we are.

I have.But then
again, once they
get away, I don't
think they'd ever
want to come back
to Newfoundland.
I am born and rear
in Quebec and I goes
back once in a while
to visit my people
there.
little nation inside
Canada than
even the Quebec
people are. It is
quite easy to have that
feeling about
Newfoundland -- it is
such a unique kind of
place, the people
are so different.

saying, 'why in the hell did they stay here in Newfoundland?

dying way of life and we haven't really thought about what we can sub-stitute, what we can put in its place, that will represent change but which will still be at least a little bit unique and which will still preserve some of the virtues of the land that is and that was. And, uh, I don't know if there ever has been a politician with the vision or imagination or the grasp of humanity and life to be able to devise a scheme and I don't know what sort of planners one could get to put it into effect if it did happen, so perhaps it is only wishful thinking and a lovely dream.

I have just been reading a book which is one of the best examples of science fiction I have seen -- in which you have a planet, Mars -- being

You know, why were they foolish enough, why did anyone settle on this foolish little rock?' And yet, my grand-children will be able to say the same of me because I'm sure I'll stay here -- so we are stuck with it.

SCOTT: Oh, no, not get the hell out of here at all. No, Newfound-

land interests me because we can do anything here.

REV. BURRY: *They came in*

287

and, of course, we had a
feeling that whatever
was done by the outsiders
-- we always called them
outsiders -- whatever was
done by the outsider was
right. Now, no reflection
on civilization as it is,
but I think we had a real
civilization before they
came. That is how I
feel, that is how I feel
about it, whether I'm
right or not.

invaded ultimately by
earthmen. Not the sort
of thing we normally hear
-- Martians invading us
-- but we invade Mars and
we destroy the Martian
civilization and we create
our own pretty shoddy sub-
stitute for civilization in
its place. It reminds me
in a way of what's happening
in Newfoundland and
it's frightening, it's a
bit terrifying.

I would like to think
we could produce
people who
are sufficiently
imaginative and
creative to be
able to
preserve Newfoundland as
Newfoundland without
simply pushing it into
what is called the
mainstream. People are
ecstatic about getting
into the main-stream --
I think it is a little
bit stupid, since the

RUSSELL: There was
something we had in
common -- we all loved
the country
so much and
wouldn't think
of leaving it.
I suppose

it was the sort of bitter
locust we'd eaten by living
here, spending our youth
here. There was that --
we had that in common.

main-stream is pretty
muddy or so it appears
to me. But how we are
going to do that *I don't*
know -- it's a political,
social,economic,
moral problem of
tremendous magnitude. I
would like to think
that we could educate
a generation of New-
foundlanders who might
be able to tackle the
problem but I'm not
sure that we can. ,

FROM AN INTERVIEW

Yes, the opening segment of 'North' has a kind of trio-sonata texture, but it really is an exercise in texture and not a conscious effort to regenerate a musical form. Three people speak more or less simultaneously. A girl enters first and speaks very quietly—we get logged for low-level start every time she's on the air—and after a time she says "and the further north we went, the more monotonous it became." By this time we have become aware of a gentleman who has started to speak and who, upon the word 'further,' says 'farther'— "farther and farther north" is the context.

At that moment, his voice takes precedence over hers in terms of dynamic emphasis. Shortly after, he uses the words 'thirty days,' and by this point we have become aware of a third voice which immediately after 'thirty days' says 'eleven years'—and another cross-over point has been effected. The scene is built so that it has a kind of—I don't know if you have ever looked at the tone-rows of Anton Webern as distinguished from those of Arnold Schönberg,—but it has a kind of Webern-like continuity-in-crossover in that motives which are similar but not identical are used for the exchange of instrumental ideas. So, in that sense, textually, it was very musical; I think its form was free from the restrictions of form which is a good way to be, you know, and the way in which one would like to be in all things, eventually. But that took time and, as I said a while back, in the case of 'North' it started with all kinds of forbidding memories of linearity. One had to gradually grow into a different sort of awareness.

289

GYRE'S GALAX

Sound variegated through beneath lit
Sound variegated through beneath lit
through sound beneath variegated lit
sound variegated through beneath lit

Variegated sound through beneath lit dark
Variegated sound through beneath lit dark
sound variegated through beneath lit
variegated sound through beneath lit dark

Through variegated beneath sound lit
Through variegated beneath sound lit
through variegated beneath sound lit
through variegated beneath sound lit
Through variegated beneath sound lit
Through variegated beneath sound lit
through beneath lit
through beneath lit
through beneath lit
through beneath lit
Thru beneath
Thru beneath

Thru beneath
through beneath lit
Thru beneath
through beneath lit
Thru beneath
through beneath lit
Thru beneath
Thru beneath
through beneath lit
Thru beneath
Thru beneath
through beneath lit
Thru beneath
Thru beneath
Thru beneath
Thru beneath
Thru beneath
Thru beneath
Thru beneath
Through beneath lit

Twainly ample of amongst
twainly ample of amongst
Twainly ample of amongst
twainly ample of amongst

Twainly ample of amongst

twainly ample of amongst

In lit black viewly

viewly

viewly

in viewly

viewly

viewly

in viewly

viewly

in viewly

viewly

in viewly

viewly

viewly

viewly

in viewly

viewly

In lit black viewly

in dark to stark

In dark to stark

In dark to stark

in dark to stark

In dark to stark

in dark to stark

In dark to stark lit

above beneath lit

above beneath

above beneath

above beneath

above beneath lit

above beneath

above beneath lit

above beneath

above beneath lit

above beneath

above beneath

above beneath

above beneath

above beneath lit

above beneath

above beneath

above beneath lit

above beneath

above beneath

above beneath

above beneath

above beneath

above beneath

above beneath

Who crouches there among the rushes
touched by such fierce wind
blushed by the pierced whim
crizzling grooves grow dim

Where winged wings walk
Where winged wings walked
Where winged wings walk
Where winged wings walked
Winged wings
Winged wings
Where winged wings walk

Filling the lush air
dreams from snoozes
whose is that one over there
staring with the big beak
peeking about like a sneaky

Where winged wings
Where winged wings
Where winged wings
Where winged wings
Where winged wings
Where winged wings walk
Where winged wings walk
Where winged wings
Where winged wings walk
Where winged wings
Where winged wings
Dewinged wings
Dewinged wings
Wings dewinged
Dewinged wings
wings dewinged
wings dewinged
dewinged wings
wings dewinged
dewinged wings
dewinged wings

Springing to their feet
the things with their . . .
all over the place
spinning haste
like a flying ocean

dewinged wings
Dewinged wings
dewinged wings
Wings dewinged wings
Dewinged wings
Wings dewinged
dewinged wings
wings dewinged
Dewinged wings
wings dewinged
dewinged wings
wings dewinged wings
Wings dewinged wings
Wings dewinged
wings dewinged
dewinged wings
wings dewinged
Where winged wings walk

Floats the tugish host
so awesome lurking
dust from the ancient wings
stinging brings its thing
winging
lingering

Where winged wings walked
Where winged wings walk
Where winged wings walked
Where winged wings walk
Where winged wings walked
Where winged wings walk
Where winged wings
Where winged wings
Dewinged wings
Wings dewinged
Dewinged wings
Wings dewinged
Wings dewinged
Dewinged wings
Wings dewinged
Dewinged wings
Dewinged wings
Wings dewinged
Where winged wings walk

Now
all is still
will they return
in something other than an urn

WHAT(?)

The full sentence on which WHAT(?) is based is, "What we want to be is not what we are looking for." It forms a line of 7 beats with each syllable occurring on each half-beat or eighth note with the last syllable silent. Within this 7 beat line each word has a fixed position and continually new sentences are formed by the deletion of words from the full sentence. In performance an electric metronome is used as part of the piece. It is set at c. 108 to 112 clicks/min. and wrapped in 13 layers of white cloth. For the last part a tape delay set-up with two taperecorders is used. The space between the taperecorders is adjusted to equal the total time of each line (7 beats) so that e a c h word recited is repeated 7 times occurring exactly at its original position in the line. For this section only the underlined words are recited and the sentences are formed by the tape delay.

```
what
what                         what
what             is          what
                 is          what
                             what
          want               what
what      want               what
what      want   is          what
          want   is          what
          want               what
       we want               what
       we want   is          what
what   we want   is          what
what      want   is          what
what      want                        we
what      want   is                   we
what   we want   is                   we
what   we want   is          what  we
what   we         is          what  we
       we want               what  we
what      want   is          what  we
what      want   is          what  we are
what   we want   is          what  we are
what   we         is          what  we are
          want   is          what  we are
       we want               what  we are              for
       we want   is          what  we are              for
what   we want   is          what  we are              for
what   we         is          what  we are              for
what   we      be is          what  we are              for
       we want to be is       what  we are              for
what   we      be is          what  we      look        for
what   we    to be is         what  we      look        for
what   we want to be is       what  we      look        for
       we want to be is       what  we      look        for
what          to be is       what  we are look-ing for
what      want to be is      what  we are look-ing for
what   we      be is         what  we are look-ing for
what   we    to be is        what  we are look-ing for
what   we want to be is      what  we are look-ing for
what   we want to     is     what  we are look-ing for
what   we want to be is       what  we are look-ing for
what   we want to be is not what  we are look-ing for
```

(turn on tape-delay)

```
WHAT                                                    FOR
what                                                    for
what                    IS                              for
what                    is      WHAT                    for
what  WE                is      what                    for
what  we          BE    is      what                    for
what  we          be    is      what  WE ARE            for
....  we       TO be    is      what  we are            for
      we       to BE    is      what  we are LOOK-ING FOR
      we       to be    IS      what  we are look-ing for
WHAT  we       to be    is      ....  we are look-ing for
what  ..       to be    is      WHAT  we are look-ing for
what           to be    is NOT  what  we are look-ing for
what           to be    is not  what  WE ARE look-ing for
what           .. BE    is not  what  we are look-ing for
what  WE          be    is not  what  we are .... ... FOR
what  we          be    IS not  what  we are          for
WHAT  we          be    is not  what  we are          for
what  we          be    is NOT  ....  we are          for
what  we          be    is not  WHAT  we are          for
what  we          be    is not  what  .. ...          for
what  we          ..    is not  what                  for
what  ..                is not  what                  ...
what                    .. not  what
....                       not  what
      WE                   ...  what
      we                   ....      ARE
      we                            are        FOR
      we                   WHAT     are        for
      we            IS     what     are LOOK-ING for
      we          BE is    what     are look-ing for
WHAT  we          be is    what     are look-ing for
what  ..       TO be is    what     are look-ing for
what           to be is    what     ... look-ing for
what           to be is    what         look-ing ...
what     WANT  to be is    ....         look-ing
what     want  to be ..                 .... ...
what     want  to ..
....     want  to          WHAT
         want  ..    IS    what
WHAT     want        is    what
what     want        is    what  WE
what  WE WANT        is    what  we
what  we want        is NOT what  we
what  we want        is not what  we      LOOK
what  we want        is not .... we       look    FOR
what  we want        .. not WHAT we       look    for
....  we want TO         not what  we      look    for
      we want to BE      not what  ..      look    for
      .. .... to be      not what          look    for
            to be      ... what          look    for
            to be      ... what          ....    for
            to be          what                  ...
            to be          what
            to be          ....
            .. be
      WANT        ..
```

299

```
         want                        WE
WHAT     want                        we
what     want           IS           we
what     want      TO   is           we
what     want      to BE is          we
what     want      to be is     WHAT  we
what     ....      to be is     what  we      LOOK    FOR
what  WE           to be is     what  ..      look    for
....  we           to be is NOT what          look    for
      we           to be .. not what  WE      look    for
      we        .. be     not what  we        look    for
      we           ..      not what  we        look    for
      we                   not ....  we        look    for
      we                   not       we        ....    ...
      ..                   not       we
                BE         ...       we
                be     WHAT          ..
WHAT            be     what
what     WANT   be     what
what     want   be     what                   LOOK
what     want   be     what                   look
what     want   be IS  what                   look
what     want   TO .. is what                  look
what     want   to BE is     ....             look    FOR
....     want   to be is     WHAT  WE         look    for
WHAT     ....   to be is     what  we         look    for
what            to be is     what  we         ....    for
what            to be is NOT what  we                 for
what            to be .. not what  we  ARE           for
what            TO BE    not what  we  are           for
what  WE        to be    not what  we  are           ...
what  we WANT   to be    not ....  ..  are
....  we want   to be    not           are
      we want   to be    not       WE  are
      we want   to be    ...   WHAT we  are
      we want   to be          what we  ARE          FOR
      we want   .. ..          what we  are          for
      .. WANT                  what we  are          for
         want           IS     what we  are          for
WHAT     want           is     what we  are          for
what     want   TO BE   is     what .. are          for
what     want   to be   is     ....  WE are          for
what     want   to be   is     WHAT we  ...          ...
what     want   to be   is NOT what we
what     ....   to be   is not what we               LOOK
what            TO BE   .. not what we               look
....            to be   IS not what we               look
                to be   is not what we               look    FOR
      WE        to be   is not what ..               look    for
      we        to be   is not WHAT                  look    for
      we WANT   to be   is ...  what                  look    for
      we want   to be   is      what                  ....    for
WHAT  we want   .. ..   is      what                          for
what  we want           IS      what                          for
what  we want           is      what                          FOR
what  .. want           is      what                          for
```

```
what    want         is      ....  WE                   for
what    ....  TO     is            we                   for
what    to BE is                   we                   for
....          to be is             we    LOOK           for
              to be IS             we    look           for
              to be is NOT         we    look           ...
              to be is not         we    look
              to be is not         ..    look
              .. be is not               look
              .. is not       WE          look
     WE          is not       we          ....
     we          .. not       we ARE
     we          IS ...       we are
     we          is           we are               FOR
     we    TO BE is           we are               for
     we    to be is    WHAT   we are               for
     we    to be is    what .. are                 for
     ..    to be is NOT what     are               for
           to be is not what                       for
           to be .. not what                       for
           to be    not what                       FOR
           .. ..    not what                       for
                    not ....                       for
                    not          LOOK-ING FOR
              IS ...             look-ing for
     WANT    is                  look-ing for
     want    is                  look-ing for
     want    is                  look-ing for
     want    is NOT              look-ing for
WHAT want    is not              look-ing for
what want    is not WHAT         .... ... ...
what want    BE .. not what
what ....    be    not what WE
what         be    not what we
what         be IS not what we
what WE      be is ... what we
.... we      be is    what we ARE
     we      be is    WHAT we are
     we WANT .. is    what we are
     we want  is      what WE are
     we want  IS      what we are
WHAT we want  is      what we are
what .. want  is NOT  what we are
what    want  is not  what we ...
what    want  is not  .... we
what    ....   is not       we
what           is not       ..              FOR
what           BE .. not                    for
.... WE        be    not                    for
     we        be  ... WHAT                 for
     we        be IS   what                 for
     we        be is   what                 for
     we        be is   what                 for
     we        be is   what                 ...
     we WANT   .. is   what
     .. want          what WE
```

```
WHAT      want              NOT  .... we
what      want          IS  not       we
what      want          is  not       we
what      want          is  not       we
what  WE  want          is  not       we
what  we  ....          is  not  WHAT we
what  we            BE  is  not  what  ..
....  we            be  is  ...  what          LOOK
      we            be  ..       what  WE      look
      we            be           what  we      look      FOR
      we            be           what  we      look      for
      ..            be           what  we      look      for
          WANT      be           ....  we      look      for
          want      BE                 we      look      for
WHAT      want      be                 we      ....      for
what      want      be           WHAT  ..                for
what      want      be           what                    ...
what      want      be           WHAT
what      want      be           what
what      ....      be  IS       what
what            ..  is  NOT      what
....  WE            is  not      what
      we            is  not      what
      we            is  not      what
      WE            is  not      ....
      we            is  not
      we        BE  ..  not
      we        be       ...           WE
WHAT  we        be                     we
what  we        be                     we
what  we        be                     we
what  ..  WANT  be                     we
what      want  be                     we
what      want  ..  IS                 we
what      want  TO  is                 ..          LOOK
....      want  to  is                             look      FOR
          want  to  is  NOT                        look      for
          want  TO  is  not                        look      for
          ....  to  BE  is  not                    look      for
                to  be  is  not                    look      for
                to  be  ..  not  WHAT              look      for
WHAT            to  be      not  what              ....      for
what            to  be      not  what      ARE               ...
what            to  be      ...  what  WE  are
what            ..  be           what  we  are
what            ..  IS           what  we  are
what                is           what  we  are
what                is           ....  we  are
....      WANT      is                 we  are
          want      is                 we  ...
          want      is           WHAT  ..
          want      is           what
          want      ..           what
          want                   what
          want                   what
          ....                   what                        FOR
```

```
                              BE        what                    for
                           TO be       ....                    for
                           to be                               for
                           to be                               for
                           to be                               for
        WHAT               to be                               for
        what  WE           to be                               ...
        what  we           to BE
        what  we           .. be                   WE
        what  we              be                   we
        what  we              be                   we
        what  we              be                   we
        .... we               be                   we
              WE              be                   we
              we            BE                      we
              we            be                      WE
              we            be                      we
              we            be                      WE
              we            be                      we
              ..            be                      we
                            be                      we
                                                    we
                                                    we
                                                    we
                                                    ..
                                                    ..
                                                    ..

                           BE
                           be
                           be
                           be
                        TO be
                        to be
                        to be
                        to ..                    WHAT
                        to BE                    what
                        to be                    what
                        to be                    what
                        TO be                    what
                        to be                    what
                        to be                    what
                        to be                    ....
                        to ..
                        to                                   LOOK
                        to                                   look
                        ..                                   look
                                                             look
                                                             look
                                                             look
                                                             look
                                                             ....
                              (turn off tape)
```

(1978)

William Hellermann

303

urge   urge

        urge   urge

            urge   urge

                urge   urge

                    urge   urge

                        merge   merge
                          mergerge
                          merger
                           ergo
                          merger
                         emergege
                      emergeemerge

                emerge   emerge

            emerge   emerge

        emerge   emerge

        emerge   emerge

    emerge   emerge

Sound/text
Jon Whyte

306

THE CANONIZATION OF ALL SAINTS

to the memory of Carl Vetter

♧

The canonization of all saints.
The THE canonization of all saints.
The can CAN onization of all saints.
The canon ONIzation of all saints.
The canoni I zation of all saints.
The canoniza ZA tion of all saints.
The canonization TION of all saints.
The canonization of OF all saints.
The canonization of all ALL saints.
The canonization of all saints SAINTS.

♧

The can THE CAN onization of all saints.
The canon CANON ization of all saints.
The canoni ONI zation of all saints.
The canoniza IZATion of all saints.
the canonization ZATION of all saints.
The canonization of TION OF all saints.
The canonization of all OF ALL saints.
the canonization of all saints ALL SAINTS.

♤

The canon THE CANON ization of all saints.
The canoni CANONI zation of all saints.
The canoniza ONIZA tion of all saints.
The canonization IZATION of all saints.
The canonization of ZATION OF all saints.
The canonization of all TION OF ALL saints.
The canonization of all saints OF ALL SAINTS.

The canoni THE CANONI zation of all saints.
The canoniza CANONIZA tion of all saints.
The canonization ONIZATION of all saints.
The canonization of IZATION OF all saints.
The canonization of all ZATION OF ALL saints.
The canonization of all saints TION OF ALL SAINTS.

♠

The canoniza THE CANONIZA tion of all saints.
The canonization CANONIZATION of all saints.
The canonization of ONIZATION OF all saints.
The canonization of all IZATION OF ALL saints.
The canonization of all saints ZATION OF ALL SAINTS.

♠

The canonization THE CANONIZATION of all saints.
The canonization of CANONIZATION OF all saints.
The canonization of all ONIZATION OF ALL saints.
The canonization of all saints IZATION OF ALL SAINTS.

♠

The canonization of THE CANONIZATION OF all saints.
The canonization of all CANONIZATION OF ALL saints.
The canonization of all saints ONIZATION OF ALL SAINTS.

♠

The canonization of all THE CANONIZATION OF ALL saints.
The canonization of all saints CANONIZATION OF ALL SAINTS.

♠

The canonization of all saints THE CANONIZATION OF ALL SAINTS.

308

The canonization of ALL saints.
△

The canonization of ALL ALL.
ALL canonization of ALL saints.
The ALLonization of ALL saints.
The can ALLization of ALL saints.
The canon ALLzation of ALL saints.
The canoni ALL'tion of ALL saints.
The canonize ALL of ALL saints.
The canonization ALL ALL saints.
△

The canonization ALL ALL ALL.
ALL canonization ALL ALL saints.
The ALLonization ALL ALL saints.
The can ALLization ALL ALL saints.
The canon ALLzation ALL ALL saints.
The canoni ALL'tion ALL ALL saints.
The canonize ALL ALL ALL saints.
△

The canonize ALL ALL ALL ALL.
ALL canonize ALL ALL ALL saints.
The ALLonize ALL ALL ALL saints.
The can ALLize ALL ALL ALL saints.
The canon ALLze ALL ALL ALL saints.
The canoni ALL ALL ALL ALL saints.
△

The canoni ALL ALL ALL ALL ALL.
ALL canoni ALL ALL ALL ALL saints.
The ALLoni ALL ALL ALL ALL saints.
The can ALLi ALL ALL ALL ALL saints.
The canon ALL ALL ALL ALL ALL saints.

The canon ALL ALL ALL ALL ALL ALL.
ALL canon ALL ALL ALL ALL ALL saints.
The ALL on ALL ALL ALL ALL ALL saints.
The can ALL ALL ALL ALL ALL ALL saints.
△

The can ALL ALL ALL ALL ALL ALL ALL.
ALL can ALL ALL ALL ALL ALL ALL saints.
The ALL ALL ALL ALL ALL ALL ALL saints.
△

The ALL ALL ALL ALL ALL ALL ALL ALL.
ALL ALL ALL ALL ALL ALL ALL ALL saints.
△

ALL ALL ALL ALL ALL ALL ALL ALL ALL.
△

AUDIO ART (1976)

I turned to audiotape to create by myself "readings," so to say, that could exist only in audiotape because they could not possibly be created in live performance. I discovered that with audiotape I could make my voice reverberate, I could add my own instrumental accompaniment, I could make two different timbres of my voice and put each on one side of a stereo tape, or make a voice of mine move across space, from one speaker to another. I could dramatize a self-interview or overdub my voice into a chorus of itself, speaking in unison as well as dis-unison. I could make a tape-delay loop and then talk against a continuous echo of myself. With quadraphonic tape, I could simultaneously broadcast four distinctly different versions of my voice, which is to say four different voices of myself. Ulti-mately, I could separate my voice from my body, so that people could hear my words apart from their perception of me, apart from my facial characteristics, apart from the information implicit in my clothing. No one hearing these tapes can know whether I am six feet eight or four foot six; 100 pounds or 200 pounds. *Listening to me speak* could be as undistracted and thus as unprejudiced as *reading me write*.

Through the production of audiotapes I could realize ear-experiences that would be less feasible in live performance. I could make a chorus speak the same nonsyntactic text syn-chronously, or nonsynchronously, as I wished. I could subject a single voice to steadily increasing reverberation. I could make my own voice talk sprightly to a chorus of itself. Rather than have my voice emerge from a single place, it could be distributed over several speakers, surrounding the audience. A voice iden-tifiable as mine would then be aurally disembodied, creating an illusion of my supernatural "presence" in several places at once.

Some of my pieces could be characterized as "amplified prose," for audio techniques are used to enhance semantically distinct prose narratives. Others could be classified as "text-sound," in that the principal means of coherence in these texts is neither syntax nor semantics but sound. Other categories are no doubt applicable.

My major artistic interest these past few years has been extending language — often the exact same words — over various media, in part to discover what effect the various media might have on invariable language. Audiotape only is one of several media that I continue to explore.

In all my pieces but one, I have observed a pure form of audioart, using words and only words, apart from song or an accompanying instrument; for at the root of my works so far has been a particular text. My preference for recognizable words separates me from most European "sound poets" and from some Americans as well, who prefer fragments of words. I also prefer linear declamation to repetitious or vertical speaking and rigorous conceptions to flaccid ones but then, paradoxically, also prefer imprecise performances to rigorous scoring.

Listening to audiotapes is comparable to listening to radio; but since my tapes are verbally more original than the "wallpaper" sound of commercial radio and more complex than the mundane language of "talk shows," my tapes require more concentrated attention of their audience. I sense that verbal stuff must move faster on audiotapes than in live performance, in part because there is nothing to see. In this age of television, it helps to close one's eyes and relax blind, especially when one is seated in chairs.

So far I have used texts whose composition preceded my involvement with audiotapes; now I intend to compose language scores with tape in mind.

Most of my pieces to now have been based upon a single audio-linguistic idea, mostly because of my desire to create a particular sound (or range of sounds) that will, like the painter's "after-image," implant itself in the audience's head. In the future, I should like to create more complex audio works with several ideas and, hopefully, several after-sounds.

LITERATURE CONTEMPORARY (1964)

despite opinion contrary exists me contemporary that worth more attention only this world II offer spectrum numerous but recent such beckett camus ellison genet moravia jean sartre produced the significant of twentieth like predecessors moderns forty the contemporary critically the upheavals society literary define culture the century style subjects as as morning their remain traditional writing literature strive understand radical of present in content form to how eternal man legacy history in world to this have resisted efforts conservative to toe line rules art contemporary particularly best them to forms subjects feel archaic to original to their of unprecedented situation best this literature of pertinence and merits most analysis delicate a or can like masters all century contemporary express oppressive of predicament the though has extraordinary and progress greatest of past years over over that quality his has improved for is victim than beneficiary advances history depicting life writers to upon aspects the situation camus jean sartre their emphasize modern who isolate from is only alienated potentially denying responsibility saul and pasternak that institution modern inevitably human totalitarian control orwell norman tell infiltrate societies well dictatorial more anthony see life our is horrendously that lone can little defend against unexpected alberto and dramatize true relations are made both biological and selfishness man in society eugene and beckett contemporary who neither universally explanation mysteries an system observed existence is absurd purdy ralph emphasize although is alone incapable overcoming isolation still his to many these it true the writings forty

COMPLEAT THE CRITIC (1967)

request a creed easily invitation bombast before
indulge egotism afflicts critical must that have al-
ways as loyal my principles should inherent frail-
ty me fulfilling demands should myself earning
even paupers from criticism compromises should
the perhaps that language more less to literate
whereas less individualist follow joyces and in
more tongue regardless lofty proffered might or
elegantly sentiments cannot myself these truths
rather commit inevitable let reply offering obser-
vations fact experience statements value critic for
cultural not artist critic mediator work art public
artist mediator what call inspiration the piece as
cultural is mediator critic populace critic estab-
lishes style artists that invariably first recognize
define distinct often it a that on the public a real
best measured how people ultimately even writing
a magazine influences intermediaries in influence
influenced as readers novels critic painting even
painter belong the public assiduously criticism
matter how critic upon art he not shape course art
he through friendship a influence certain of artist
urge influence artist too escalate desire prescribe
here critic become incipient who claim know about
artist the knows himself the article supplant work
art philosophical for community culture a division
labour each seeks place finds role pretension
more than role among greatest of critic some
times artist because pomposity recognize we do
work different 2 critic be engaged he have courage
follow engagements lead critics functions two for
must continually where one previously and report
honestly can he also willing offend most benefac-
tors criticism as in subject critic as opinion takes
although might that critic interests top every

NEW THE FICTION AMERICAN (1965)

perhaps most recent novelists john james vladimir
and burroughs barth the brilliant promising ap-
pear america the ten no writer young barth so
equipped the resources energy range sophistica-
tion courageous independence most the genius
transform virtues talents fiction continually his
moreover distinctly considerably in course his
career floating 1956 and the 1958 the factor and
the of novels one the words fiction time potential
of achievements beyond if comprehension in and
18th england maryland with who accurately 19th
dialect appropriate references sotweed an term a
merchant 806 pages of adventures one cooke at
age 30 a vow preserve treasured and devote poet-
ry convinced rather and lord to his patron confers
himself rather title poet laureate maryland sets
write epic praise the world marylandiad summary
all twists turns the plot the digressions coinci-
dences natures all characters for moment suffice
to that edgar attests the contrivance the fantastic
any know its basic the factor mockery written for
systematically debunks accepted of past narrative
isaac and more cambridge emerge lubricious who
refuge orphaned the coffeehouse which described
says novel turned sex third baltimore history an
catholic runs network spies saboteurs his against
protestants he ebenezer in new pets rare virgins
the successful selfconfident ebenezer maryland
many note initials claims have swived times of
regularly in and one american intercept ship
moorish to and their until deck like block most
debunking with discovery the historie john and
journall sit burlingame written magnificently 17th
prose authentic deny accepted reveal john was
lecher first powhatans giving pornographic later

SELF-INTERVIEW ON RECYCLINGS (1974)

Recyclings *is the strangest book I've ever seen. It's impossible to read. It doesn't make sense. What are you trying to do here?*

Recyclings is what it says it is. Title and subtitles in my works tend to be very explicit. *Recyclings* is "a literary autobiography," to quote the second half of its title; and the words that are recycled here are my own. More specifically, I took my earlier writings, most of which were critical essays, and rigorously subjected them to a reworking procedure that destroys their syntax and yet keeps their language. That is, the words on each page of *Recyclings* all come from a single earlier piece of mine, but now these words are differently organized.

"Organized"! How? Each page looks like chaos to me.

The trouble, I suspect, is that you're trying to read *Recyclings* horizontally, as you would pages of normal prose. You're starting with the title at the top of the page and then progressing to the upper-left-hand corner and reading across. Right?

Yes. That's true.

But that's a limited way to read anything. Try reading it from top to bottom, or from bottom to top, or diagonally; and you'll see words emerging that give you a sense of each page. Key words will simply stick out, evoking not only a particular subject but identifiable tones and feelings. No matter which direction you read it in, the material on the page will come together and communicate itself both in part and as a whole. (Not only as a critic but as an artist, I'm interested in alternative ways of reading words.) Secondly, within the entire work are higher coherences of interest and diction that are typical with me, for *Recyclings* is, after all, as it says, "a literary autobiography."

To what genre does Recyclings *belong? Is it "prose poetry"?*

No, it is an essay. It has a specific subject, which is my own writing. Pages from it will be included in an anthology of mine entitled *Essaying Essays,* which will appear later this year. Most "prose poetry," by contrast, strikes me as affectedly murky prose.

Why is this book of 64 pages sub-titled "Volume One: 1959-67"?

There are 128 more pages that recycle my writings from 1967 to the present. There could be, and hopefully will be, two more volumes the size of this one.

When you do readings of your work, how do you do Recyclings? *Can you simply do what a conventional reader does and read every page aloud from beginning to end?*

That wouldn't be interesting — not at all. The best ways to declaim a page of *Recyclings* are these — the solo method and the choral. By oneself, one can simply leap around, picking words out of the page at random, letting one's voice impulsively follow his or her eye. The text becomes a score of available verbal notes, so to speak, whose order must be improvised. In this, as with other unpitched verbal texts, I'd avoid singing — the making up of pitched sounds.

Rather than perform *Recyclings* solo, however, I personally prefer to use a chorus, which can be recruited on the spot from the audience. Essentially, instruct five or six people to concentrate hard on a page of text and to read it horizontally from beginning to end, as they would normal prose; but here the six should read it in staggered succession. That is, when the first reader gets to the end of the first line, signal the second reader to begin with the first line, reading horizontally. Both readers continue to the end of the page; but as soon as the second reader finishes the opening line, the third reader should begin, and so forth. The readers are free to declaim the text at the speed of their choice, with personalized emphases, because it is my aim not to realize specific juxtapositions but constant vertical relationships within horizontal activity, much as a reader, sitting by himself, might read — actually, assimilate — a page of *Recyclings* both horizontally and vertically at once. When everyone has finished speaking the page at hand, the chorus can go onto another page, restarting the process of individual declamations in staggered succession.

Actually, it should be possible for someone listening to the choral *Recyclings,* to hear several words at once and distinguish each of them, much as an experienced music listener can identify individually the several notes that comprise a chord that he initially hears as a single complex. This may be hard to do at first with *Recyclings*, as it was no doubt hard at first to do in music; but in both music and audio language art, increased practice, with strict attention, developes one's perceptual capacities.

Next spring I'll have access to a sophisticated audiotape studio, in which I'll try to multi-track these several voices all by myself. The result will be, I guess, "sound prose" analogous to "sound poetry."

That all sounds terribly impersonal and mechanistic.

Quite the contrary is true. The linguist Saussure once distinguished between the *langue* of a people and the *parole* of an individual, and in *Recyclings* I've taken my own *parole* and reparoled it, so to speak, into a verbal construction that is distinctly personal in subject, diction and style. Whether you read it vertically or horizontally, the work has, I think, "a voice" that is indebted both to the compositional method and myself.

How long has Recyclings *been out? What do the reviewers say?*

In its six months of existence, *Recyclings* has been reviewed only once — by Tom Montag, the editor of *Margins*, using the pseudonym of "Crusader Rabbitt" in his own pages. His notice was similarly nonsyntactical, which means that *Recyclings* not only made him *read* in unusual ways, but it also got him to write in a style, or a structure, he had not used before.

Otherwise, the lack of reviewer response has been disappointing, of course; but I long ago learned that neglect is the rule with experimental writing in America; neglect is almost the fundamental measure of its esthetic integrity. The prominent reviewers ignore such books, and those critics who would like to write about avant-garde literature don't get asked. The only true "reviews" are the letters you receive from your colleagues; and with *Recyclings*, thankfully, the correspondence so far has been strong and good.

Why are you speaking to me now in normal sentences?

Because I'm communicating information; *Recyclings*, by contrast, is art.

to swindon from london by britrail aloud / bagatelle

FF staccato	BOOOoooootttttt!
P lento Ped.	brrm brrbb brrrum brrubb
poco a poco	brrmmbl brrubl brrummble brumble
accel. e cresc.	brrrumble de bum brumble de *bug*
Ped. ad lib.	drumble le *dug* droomble de dag
MF stretto	drumbledee dug drumbledee dag
allegretto	droobedydag roobeddy dig
F	roobity bad rootilly bittle
rapido	roobity bag rubbity bottle
FF	brrrubeddidy rash crash crubberrydrubbery crosh
F molto rapido	croshoverrails Sroch—hurry along
	hurryalong hurryalane hurryaloon hurryalung
MF allegro	along alane along alung a-law-ing a-laying
piu rall.	adawdle alane a dawdel along
andante	agoggle along a doggle de dung de
MP tempo di valse	*dawdillee doggillee* goggillee *gog*—
	hungary dungaree mongrely dong
	mangletree anglesea mingle de—BOOoooootttt! Boot!
F—FFF brill.	hungary *dung* hunger me lung
F a tempo	ganger de lag gagger de lack gangerlag gagerlak
accel.	gangerlag gugelak lagaback loveaduck
	look at duck look at lake look at duck
MF vivace	lucky duck look at drake look at—whooooooosh!
accel.	izzza brissssssh is a bridge!
F agitato	gurrrdee *up* durridee *down* diddle de *grrp*—
poco ritard.	de doodle de dup de diddle de dee BOOOOO!
con grazia—FF	de diddle de—BLAST pasht pasht pasht pasht
energico presto	pasht past past train past de diddle de dip
sforz.	de griddle de green de girdle de grin
leggiero	green & the grain & the grain & the rain
P delicato	

	dram & aras arane & a lass
doloroso	lay & a lass lay & a lad
adagio	day & dad & hay & gad & may & mad & say & sad
delicatissimo	hay & a mow hay & a cow
dolce	cow & moos &—crash! clattr krradge—& cows
PF agit.	crashes & ashes & cows ashes & cow—WUNDRRR RR
FF strepitoso	RRRAILERER THUNder & ragerr blundrrm gauge
molto agitato	gagelak gugelak gagelak gugelag
F a tempo	gagelllOOver passOOver passover pastdover
FF subito con brio	gagelak gugelak gagelak fugaluck
MF rall.	fugadug fulderol fuldedoodle dedoodum
a tempo	dedundr passundrr dedunderry boom
	de bol de rol de boddle le dol
cantabile	de puddle de pill de roddle de rill
ma non troppo	bottle a pole battle a post buttery post
allegro assai	frettering peace feathering feast
	pheasanty woods pleasanty words
P calando	clattering works blathering jerks
appassionato	watery dirt dirtery what
espressivo	waddery turds dirrery waw dirry whaw dirr whee
capriccio	woof wee whee with the trees withery twees
	teas an trees an this an leaves an SQUOO! squaw!
pF legato sub. agit.	gagelak gugelak gagerack pain pay in the train
MF moderato	bag baggity baggity kroom baggy crude ba koo
risoluto e rall.	koo its a groom doom an a fox dog fox
ben marcato	fox fox its a fox dog dog dogelak grog
	grogelak grief grainalack grey
MP grave	gag e lak gud e lak gug a KUNG... KUNG
PF sostenuto	guh delhi de dung de daddle deee—
decresc.	SQUEEEEEEEEEK K! ————
FFF molto sost.	
{Con una certa	The tren neow stendinnng on pletfoam thureee
espressione	is foh Suh——weeeeen————dawn.
parlante	

*   *   *

The Yogic caterpillar digs the scene builds a cocoon goes into nirvana & emerges a butterfly. Mankind can do no less. And emerge a big SNICKER.

Snicker Snoop [1]
the world's a boop
Snop de bop
the umphs a bump

Ipsa diddle
tricksy woo
weep the beep
whappity bap

Ippskiddy whipple
whopsky top
lucksky whupsky
whipsky woo

Iksky whacksy whucksky whoops
Ipsky pipsky whipsky troops
Army Silly whips the stoops
Civilization spooks de groops—
Hopsky gropsky all the dopsky
Lovsky wuvsky dovsky slobsky
Wobsky topsky wantsa win
Ginsy insy pantzky Pinsky
Mr. Pinsky makes up pants
Pinkus fucks Becky
Ginsberg sucks Orlovsky

*   *   *

[1] Further reconstruction of improvised nonsense poem w/J.K.—"I saw the sunflower monkeys of the moon."

THE DINA DYE KNEE THE DINA DYE EYE THE DINA DIE THE DIEING DINA SORE SORE
SORE THE DINA DYE KNEE THE DINA DYE EYE THE DINA DIE THE DIEING DINA SORE
SORE SOWRDS! THE DINA DINA SORE SOWRDS! THE DIE DINA THE DIE DYING THE
THE DIE DINA SORE THE DINA DINA SORE SORE SOWRDS SOWRING SOWRDING THE
THE DINASORE'S SORES SOWRDING THE DIE KNEE SEE US YOU ALL US THE DIEING
DINA SORE SOWRDS! THE DINASTOR THE DINASTORE STORES THE DINKNEE SEE US
DINESEUS DINESEUS DINESEUS THE DIANA DIENA KA A SOWRD THE DIEING DIENASORE
THE DINA DYE KNEE THE DINA DYE EYE THE DINA DIE THE DIEING DINA SORE SORE
SORE THE DINA DYE KNEE THE DINA DYE EYE THE DINA DIE THE DIEING DINA SORE
SORE SOWRDS! THE DINA DINA SORE SOWRDS! THE DIE DINA THE DIE DYING THE
THE DIE DINA SORE THE DINA DINA SORE SORE SOWRDS SOWRING SOWRDING THE THE
DINASORE'S SORES SOWRDING THE DIE KNEE SEE US YOU ALL US THE DIEING DINA
SORE SOWRDS! THE DINASTOR THE DINASTORE STORES THE DINKNEE SEE US
DINESEUS DINESEUS DINESEUS THE DIANA DIENA KA A SOWRD THE DIEING DIENASORE
THE DINA DYE KNEE THE DINA DYE EYE THE DINA DIE THE DIEING DINA SORE SORE
SORE THE DINA DYE KNEE THE DINA DYE EYE THE DINA DIE THE DIEING DINA SORE
SORE SOWRDS! THE DINA DINA SORE SOWRDS! THE DIE DINA THE DIE DYING THE
THE DIE DINA SORE THE DINA DINA SORE SORE SOWRDS SOWRING SOWRDING THE
THE DINASORE'S SORES SOWRDING THE DIE KNEE SEE US YOU ALL US THE DIEING
DINA SORE SOWRDS! THE DINASTOR THE DINASTORE STORES THE DINKNEE
SEE US DINESEUS DINESEUS DINESEUS THE DIANA DIENA KA A SOWRD THE DIEING
DIENASORE THE DINA DYE KNEE THE DINA DYE EYE THE DINA DIE THE DIEING DINA
SORE SORE SOWRDS! THE DINA DINA SORE SOWRDS! THE DIE DINA THE DIE DYING
THE DIE DINA SORE THE DINA DINA SORE SORE SORES SORES SOWRDS SOWRRING

SHORE LINES:

schtosh   schtoosh   osh   osh
schtoshtosh   tish

sch schtun

osh shun   osh shun
osh shun   osh sun

o sun   o sun   o sun   osun ashtone

ashton ish meant

                         ash schton ish sh
ash stone   ash stone ash stun

ashshallow   ash shallow shallow   swallows

ash sh schton ish ish   ish   shallow

shal low   shal low   shal low

shal om   shal lom   sh sh shal lom

shallow   shad low   shal om   shalom   osh

shun   osh shun   osh shun   oshun

icy   icy   icy   icy   i see i sing i see i sing i sing
ice see ice see   ice sea ice see ice   sing ice sea
ice shift ice shift ice shift ice drift iceshift ice drift

ice sail   ice sail cul   ice sail cul iceSAilcul ice sail kill
icicle   icicle icicleicicleicicle i sail kill ice sail kill icicle icicle ice
sail cul icicle ice sail kill icicle i see kill sail ice sail cul
i see cold icicle   i   see cold Icicle i see Cold icicle i see
icy icy icy icy   i Cy   i see ising icing cold ice sail
cool ice sail cool   i sing cold ice sail cool ising cold ice
seal kill   ice seal kill iceseakill ice sail cul   iceseakill
ice cycle   ice cycle   slice cycle ice Cycle Slice cycle ice
Cycle ice is ICE is ice is ice is ice

is ice   is ice is ice isice isice isice is ice
is ice   is ice   is ice   is ice is ice isice is
Isis is ISIS is isis Shift ice is is is is

ice is   is ice is iS Isis

is ice sail   cool i sing

Isis

is ice is   is ice is
is ice

```
particularize the particular          particularize the particular
particularize the particular           articularize the  articular
particularize the particular           art      arize      art    ar
particularize the particular           articul  ize the  articul
particularize the particular           ar       ize the  articul
particularize the particular          particul  ize the particul
particularize the particular          part      i        part  u ar
particularize the particular           art      arize the  art
particularize the particular             i       i            i   ar
particularize the particular           art      i          ar i   ar
particularize the particular                    u  i           i u
particularize the particular           ar       ar         ar     ar
particularize the particular           art                part    ar
 articularize the  articular           parti    ar         part
 articul          art                     i                part  u ar
 art    arize     art                   part                art   u ar
  art    i        part  u               art      ar         art   u ar
 part    i             u                part     ar         part  u
 part   ar        art                   ar       ize        ar    u
  ar     ize      part  u               ar i u   i          ar    u
 part    i        part                  ar                  art
  art    i             u                art  u arize             u
  ar              part                           arize          u ar
particul          part                  part u arize        part  u
  art             part  u               part                art   u
```

```
articul          part                    ar   u arize            u
art     ar        art    ar              parti u arize     parti
art     ar        art    ar              parti             ar
art     ar        part   ar              particul          part  u
particul          art    ar              particul ize      particul
articul           particular             articul           art  u
art     ar        part  u ar             ar        ize     art  u
parti   ar        part  u ar             part  u           part  u ar
particular        particular             particular            u
particular        particular             particularize the particular
articular         art
art          the  art
art          the  art
             the  art
             the  art
             the  art
             the  art
             the  art
```

This piece is for two voices—one for each column. The left-hand voice begins with a repeated, rhythmical chant; the right-hand voice starts the variation. Eventually, the right-hand voice returns to the original phrase, thus signalling the end of the performance. The initial text is by Douglas Barbour; it was evolved in performance with Stephen Scobie.

```
ab cdefghijklmnopqrstuvwxyz z ywuvstrqopmnlikjhgfedcba
abcdefghijklmnopqrstuvwxyz zyxwuvstrqopmnlikjhgfedcba
abcdefghijklmnoptsrquvwxyz z ywuvstrqopmnlikjhgfedcba
abcdefghijklmnoptsrquvwxyz zyxwuvstropmnlikjhgfedcbaa
abcdeffhjilkmnOpqrstuvwxyz zyxwuvstropmnlikjhgfe dcna


bob is alle to bend the back of the book
bob is able to bind the back of tge book
bob is albe to bend the back to the book
bob is able to bin d the back of the nooob
bob is able to ben the back of the book


they paid that this week wull seen less hand thea
thr6ppaid thea thus week will seen less hane they
they paid that this week wull seen less hane than
the  paid that this week will seen lass hane than
they paid thea this weed will seen-less hand than


I had to leabe as soon as the men had tride on their wuits
I had to leave as soon as soon aj had tried on theuf suits
I has to leaave as soon as the men fad tried on their suitw


ship 1or 2or 3oro4 ro4 of6 or7 oro8 or 8 ro9 or01
Ship 1or 2oro3 oro4 ro5 oro6 oro7 rot8 oro9 oro
Ship 1 or 2or 3 ro4 ro5 roo6 ro7 ro8 or 9 roorooro
```

davequickly froze the two mextures in the deep brown jugs
dave quickly froze the teo mextures in the deep frown jugs
Jave quickly froze the two mextures in the deep buown jugs

he will not comm.   They should attend,   I think it is true
he will not come.   They should attend,   I thind it it true
he will not come.   They should attemd.   I thenk it is true

he may not cone.   They shall attend.   I feel it is not.
he may not come.   They shall attend,   I feel if is not.
he nay not come,   They shall attend,   I feel it is mot.

Teh girls got rignt up and found the desh on the top shelf.
the girls got theue up and ford the dish on the top shelf
the gerls got theue up andn fornd the dish on the top shelf

helens wroth on and on and on until ghtj pen ran out ot ink.
helnee wrote on and on andn on until her pen ran out of ink
helene wrote on and on andn on un til her pen ran out of ink
aa air ab beam cc comets dd dive ee erupt ff falls gg grard
aa ait nn nam cc comets dd dive ee erupt ff falla gg guard
aa air bb baim vvondndnd dd dine ee rutp ff falls ff gurd

he dold go ir he wanted tom but he wished to stay at home
he dould go if he wanted to, but be wished to stay at home
he could go if he wanted tom bou he wished to stay at home

gg geat ii radio jj jup kk blanket ll less mm moon nn need
hh heat ii radio jj jump kk blanke5 ll less mm moom mm meed
hh heat ii radis jj jump kk blanket ll less mm moom mm need

oo owen pp prepare qq squeak rr rakar ss shadows tt through
oo oben pp prwpare qq squeak ff fadar ss shadow it through
oo oven pp prepare qq squead rr radar aa shadows tt through

uu suit bb gravity ww wear xx mex yy bery heavy zz freezing
uu suit vb grabety ww weat xx mai yy bery geaby zz freeving
uu sut bb grabity ww wear xx mix yy brry haavy zz freezing

crashing nountain bolcano strangr habing earth with all the
crashing mountain tain wolcano strnannmndndndndndnnndndndn
carashing mountain bolcano strange having earth with all the

in sulate complete silence shields sarmth ferst butn but fot
insulate conple e silince sheelds warnth ferst butn but for
insulate complere silence shields warmth ferst butn but for

friction aunsheie absied besitor colder world much and nes
friction shdi anda fdi besitor colder world ndo and mdm
frection sunshine sbsindnn bisitor colder would much and nix

bonbarbed neteors boilimg problem strong poles like nan nay
bonbared matos boididid pdpdoddo strond pdodod l idimam may
bonarded nanf ss boiling rpdodo poles lide nan may jd jdjjdj

vic didi nahd ajdk for theh ndnd jfj ufo fhfh fof ajdjd
ojvjjdid ndo alsk for jfj ndn jfu ufufu yf fhah pfor ajdjd j
wvjfj didi nfof aksk fthth thth ncei jug uouffjfj fjfj
bidikdkd dndjlaksk foo fjfj mfn yfyfyjfjfjddjsj djd d
bid ididi ndnj andn fofor fjfj fkfkfjfjfj fjfjr fjfjf th
vidi did

vici ididinfjfajdj for thrh fmm fjfjafjfjaththf fht ajdj
nfnf diaj dndir adjd fhth thh fmfn jfurj fjfj ajfjfpr fjfj
vjfide djdjfcjfjfjafjfjf thhffjfjfj fufj fhghf jfjfj fj
vidid fjfjf fjf fthth thrh fffu jfjfjf fjfjfjfjfj fjfjf
vjf9difidid jdjajdjf for f fjr fjfjfjf jfjfj f fjfjpapfpf fjf
bidid didi adhdh mjjajd fof th h hfnf jfuf fjfju fjfj fjfjf
bid did nfkto akd fo h

Michael Cooper

Grid 1

S pitty pom | tee tee | tee tee
P
R | tee tee | tee tee
B budda budda budda dudda | pom

Grid 2

S pippip | pip | pom | pitip pitip
P pom | pom | pom | pom
R pom | pom | pom | pom
B | | pom

Grid 3

S | flick flick flick | pitit | piti pom pom | pit
P flick flick flick | pitit | tip | tip
R
B pit | pit

Extract from 8-part Suite

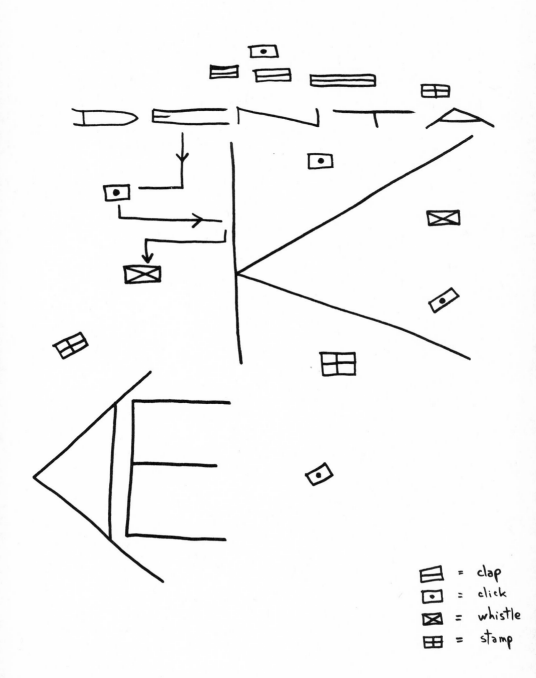

= clap
= click
= whistle
= stamp

Poem #1

1			rows		risen	risen	rising	sing	arise
2	rose	roses	arise			rising	rising	ing	arisen
3		a rose is	a rose is			rising	rising	ring	arisen
4			roses	arise			risen	ing	arisen

From Sound to Sense

ˌ sound being as it is a total physiological involvement your concept of it changes in terms of a formal or compositional structures as your involvement becomes more total once upon a time i used to write out the texts wringing a formal number of semantic or phonemic changes and perform that piece according to that set text (most classically for me is Dada Lama the text of which Cavan McCarthy published a couple of years back my concept of which, & hence my reading of which, has changed drastically in recent years) now i find composition takes place inside my head & that my notational system (which at one time i tried to work out very elaborately) has become shorter & shorter most of the complexity now being carried in my head as alternative reality spaces the poem can enter for instance

carnage ikawa

is the entire *print* text of a poem called *HIROSHIMA (mon amour)* which last anywhere from 3 to 6 minutes and was, in fact, first performed as an audience involvement piece the audience chanting the base phrase while lionel kearns & i did variations over top of that thus my poems have evolved more & more into free structures as my grasp of sound, my ability to shape & form the poem according to my physiological response & the audience's physiological response during the particular reading of it, has grown i could not have gained this grasp had i not gone thru the formal structure first but beyond this in the last year i found my interest in the solo sound poem waning & at the suggestion of Rafael Barreto-Rivera, who heard Steve McCaffery & i give a reading last march here in toronto, he & i & steve & paul dutton formed a group to work off into the area of group sound poems & we've just begun this fall giving readings under the name THE FOUR HORSEMEN (occasionally we argue over who gets to be death) here we have evolved a notational system simply to let ourselves know at which our voices come together, at which point they follow different courses, while at the same time leaving wide variation in terms of what each voice does do in his section with, of course, an ear to what each other voice is doing i've included *rose* the text of one four horseman piece we've also worked out a number of adaptations of poems of William Blake & John Clare as well as group & individual compositions for the group for us this is just beginning to open in the past month we've begun to leave this notational system behind [since the notational system (like any language) limits your thinking] for a more spheroid (i.e. non-linear) means of notating

beyond that steve's POETRY IS BLOOD manifesto says much

thru sound the chance exist to heal the split that has become more & more apparent since the invention of the printing press it is the only thing that makes sense.

THE EVENING IS SINGING

THE EVENING IS SINGING

THE EVENING IS S——NG——NG

THE E——VENING.........IS S——NG——NG

THE EVENING IS SINGING SINGING SINGING SINGING

S——NG——NG

VOH⁰⁰ K⟍⟋L   VOH⁰⁰ K⟍⟋L

VOH₀₀K⟍⟋L

K₀₀V⟍H——⁰⁰L   K₀₀V⟍H——⁰⁰L   K₀₀V⟍H——⁰⁰L

NᴼᴴOOK⁰⁰ NᴼᴴOOK⁰⁰ NᴼᴴOOK⁰⁰ NᴼᴴOOK⁰⁰ NᴼᴴOOK⁰⁰ NᴼᴴOOK⁰⁰

KOH ₀₀L⟍⟋

VOH ₀₀L⟍⟋

THE EVENING IS SINGING

L₀₀K ᴱᴱV T₀₀VEEK

TEE₍₀₀PL——NG.........TEE₍₀₀PL——NG

Tᴱᴱᵥ₀₀K══V...........Tᴱᴱᵥ₀₀K══V

V₀₀L——NGTᴱᴱVᴼᴼK.............V₀₀L——NGTᴱᴱVᴼᴼK

TᴱᴱVᴼᴼK TᴱᴱVᴼᴼK TᴱᴱVᴼᴼK   L——NG⟍⟋NG

L——NG⟍NG

THE EVENING IS SINGNG——NG

L₀₀KᴱᴱV T₀₀VEEK L₀₀KᴱᴱV T₀₀VEEK

V₀₀L——NG V₀₀L——NG L——NG⟍⟋NG

T₀₀VᴱᴱK

PL$_{oong}$$_{AW}V^{EE}_N$ PL$_{oong}$$_{AW}V^{EE}_N$ PL$_{oong}$$_{AW}V^{EE}_N$ PL$_{oong}$$_{AW}V^{EE}_N$

PL⬭⬭⬭NG$_{AW}$V^{EE}^{EE}$_N$

E$_{NGN}$⬭$_{oF}$$_{RAW}R^{E}_{NG}$

E$_{NGN}$⬭$_{oF}$$_{RAW}R^{E}_{NG}$

$_{oo}$VA^{W} $_{oo}$VA^{W} $_{oo}$VA^{W} $_{AW}$PL⬭$_N$

$_{oo}$V $_{AW}$PL⬭$_N$

$_{AH}$VAH$_{OO}$ $_{NG}$ $_{AH}$VAH$_{OO}$ $_{NG}$

OF THE BLUE M^{O}TH $_{THE}$BLUE M^{O}TH $_{THE}$BLUE M^{O}TH

WEMM$_y$LETT$_{NG}$ SHE'S TELL$_{ING}$ M^E

OF TH$_E$ **BLUE** M^{O}TH TH$_E$ BLUE M^{O}TH

THE BLUE M⬭TH $_{oF}$EVEN^{I}NG

$_{OF}$ VEN NG

NEMM$_y$LET NEMM$_y$LET NEMM$_y$LET NEMM$_y$LET NEMM L$_E$TT NG

TH$_E$ WA^{A}Y SH^E IS **SAY**$_{ING}$

"TH$_E$ ^{E}VNING ^{I}S S^{I}NG$_{ING}$"

THE **EVE**$_{NING}$ **S** SING$_{ING}$

NEMM$_y$LETT NG WH$_E$N SH^E TELLS M^E

TH$_E$ ^{E}VN$_{ING}$ ^{I}S S^{I}NGING

TH$_E$ **EVE**$_{NING}$ S SING$_{ING}$

S^{I}NG^{I}NG S^{I}NG^{I}NG S^{I}NG^{I}NG S^{I}NG^{I}NG

S NG NG

S NG NG

A critique of cues for readers and speakers

The reader will notice that different poems are written in different print. Some compositions appear only in prosodynic print; other poems are presented in prosodynic orthography but are preceded by a version in standard English print. A third presentation is cued with prosodynes only here and there in short passages. A fourth group appears only in standard English print. These are the compositions that need no intensity, pause, pitch or time durational instruction because their phonetic patterns are cue-rich enough in acoustic dimensions for any native speaker of American English to hear the message in the standard print. The loud diphthong music in "The Voice of the Buoys," and the multi-dimensional phoneme music in "Lyric For a Flute" need no additional acoustic cues.

When a poem first appears in standard typography and then is presented in prosodynic print the double exposure is intended to give the reader an extra bit of information: the author's vocal intention, his ideal performance. The reader-speaker may then decide to accept or reject the author's model, but at least he knows the writer's intent in terms of what rendition the author prefers. Two script presentations are usually those poems whose images are associated with infrequent Occurrences such as astronomic images in "Transwhichics #1 and #2." Another criterion for double presentation is a poem with rhythm that violates the stress patterns of English for aesthetic-semantic reasons peculiar to the authors compositional design. Other grammatic cue determinants being absent, verbs in English are far more likely to be stressed than prepositions. Students trained in prosodynes marked "woodwinds" quite differently from the cued version of the refrain **BLEW** ══╪══**N**   **FLEW** ══╪══**N** . Yet this is the formant music pattern the poet wrote into his theme. Another justification for a double typographic presentation is the need to acoustically sharpen the rhetorical style of a poem in order to transmit its theme with a finer flare. This purpose led to a dual script for "Stony River," "Pathways of the Suns," "Crows" and several other compositions.

The case of a partially cued script is "The Dirge of the Cold" where the low vowel diphthong music is sufficiently powerful to transmit its acoustic theme without additional cues. The animal cries throughout the poem are essential to the message of the theme; yet they are infrequent occurrences for urban readers. To compensate for the unfamiliarity of these happenings to so many potential readers, these passages were cast in cued script. It may interest some readers to know that even though the longer fluctuations of the loon's call does show in the print, the perturbations of the loon cry cannot be written with prosodynes. The duration of perturbations transpires in thousandths (milli) seconds which are too rapid for human speech to reproduce. It is a cardinal principle of this code not to instruct readers to speak the impossible. Consequently, only the valuable information of the longer waves appear in the script.

Where the theme of the poem depended more on suprasegmentals of speech than on any other set of cues no standard typography appears. Only the prosodynic script that carries the crucial information is presented. It is interesting to examine the linguistic conditions that render suprasegmental cues most informative. In "Hymn to a Rat Race" the sparse context of its pronouns and auxiliary verbs deprives these functional words of their identificational power and makes them quite meaningless. Their generality in non-contextual English must be cue-reinforced for the poem's theme to make any sense whatsoever. Therefor the poem is printed only in suprasegmentally cued script. Another instance of thematic dependency on suprasegmental speech is in "Soliloquy" where "phemes" such as (huh), (oo), (aw), (oh) acquire an attitudinal expression with and only with prosodynic script. Another poem to be enriched and written more reliably for the reader is "Voices in the Violins." The soft quiet middle section and the concentration of rapid and high pitched speech in the terminal passage could not be written without graphic cues.

These analyses show that considerable thought is required to justify the use of an independent set of cues in a cue-rich, 50% redundant, language such as English. The overlaps of multiple sets of cues at one moment give instructions to readers about the use of the language and the next moment tell the speakers to act in certain ways in the world outside of language and, continuously, operate as symbols that identify the recurrent events of human existence . . . these overlaps convert the problem of assessing the information load of any single set of cues into a question that is complicated and is more a matter of judgment than simplistic logic. For clarity we may summarize the criteria for writing more or less artificial cues into these poems. When English poetry *needs* acoustic messages to compensate for lack of context, then prosodynic cues are justified . . . otherwise they are superfluous. But isn't the justification of an art the creation of NEW CONTEXT? . . . out of its physical medium.

Cues for vowel pitch modulation

SAME VOWEL SPOKEN WITH RISING OR FALLING PITCH IN PERIODS CONTROLLABLE BY SPEAKER

SEE HER DO THE LOOP DE LOOP SHES A
F RE B LL WHAT A SHOW DO YOU WANT
A BALLOON YEEHHH

ITS INCREDIBLE I NEVER THOUGHT HED EVEN
MAKE IT TO FIRST BASE YET THERE
HE S LEADING THE PACK.......... WHAT CAME OVER HIM
WAS IT HORSE SHOES THEY SAY ITS BETTER TO BE LUCKY
THAN GOOD

THERES NO RETURN.......THAT CANT
BE HE WENT LIKE THAT IT WAS JUST YESTERDAY
I SAW HIM

Prosodynes
DURATION

Trace	A E I O U THE of
Short	A E O I U W Y
Normal	A E I OU W Y
Prolonged	A E I O U Y

INTENSITY

Whisper level	a e i o u w y
Quiet unaccented speech (first amplitude level)	A E I O U W Y
Normal conversational effort (second amplitude level)	A E I O U W Y
Maximum stress or intensity (third amplitude level)	A E I O U W Y

Prosodynes (continued)

PITCH

Lowest pitch – indicated by depressing the vowels	M$_I$M M$_O$M M$_{AW}$M M$_{EE}$M
Middle pitch – indicated by normal position on line	MIM MOM MAWM MEEM
Highest pitch – indicated by elevating the vowels	M^{I}M M^{O}M M^{AW}M M^{EE}M

PAUSES

Intra-phrase pause, articulatory: blank space 2 times height of tallest letter.

Inter-phrase, for breath and syntax: blank space 4 times height of tallest letter.

Pause of thought: line of dots varying from 1 cm. to 3 cm. with time for decision.

Pause allocations require some semantic judgment by the writer.

A Purplexicon of Dissynthegrations,

punziplaze karmasokist DecoYen Pompieraeian scaruscatracery
timmedigets outrége Opinducts pretensnarrant MustEVit
spirackrete broidevel inducound proleany conclueshunning
seriesponsybil greak trystsparklers misshits Amerdeality
Chroameo thoualkt dienerlarging sklaferry ethquikability
vichycles eunipursonality woarships libigo moodeaffex
crallrighting sublimasturb walloaminds dwintrospectiv
nackuracy infrisking evypressoar pronownshamentos
creallocate selfistenuto bitacting pleastic Amerforts
negassing stillyfrememuse syntherile corout snoub
examplimations FanelliHopper marvellusty broachure sprnyde
WiIdeals equitty sklaflout fearl Gallopheel sexpect
huevents kissimer willdid pucarlvoice alcohawlic
gushot wrympersonal self-conscious inshintuate whoaman
allustration essensual aesthound cosmasspection plastrepois
infalliable ejaculiss spectackle restcue terrifugalee
phornotgraphy senseeminded folksiedead pirouethink sklafeatu
democrapicky keylusion wellded conattension mechallous
shriekreen piercelver insite dability colorganise slyting
selfpitter IntOne lyreams negrowisms meateorvalue permcore
disjinncts cloakull womankneeless vocabullery squrdge
psychlic factidya spurmport punaLludIT philocity precipidwe
decksquisit initoutpourpretens assensualimbs bullycose
freaxtreams reliefaugh ulthink Tootons synexdochrowth
plastraggle bumpalludes preocreation missoarientations
praggressiv ovarylease temperanant whoboozer tolernjoy
repmew chucklut anarchetype iotea followsuppers

Aeolyrpegging calculallow hoptimystic shrewmord obliterary
smellspect soneyes decoyr factea readch pleorgasm
renaissorganise psickisms imnexplicit plisstening
statUresklye purrhaps hillycredulosity padmirme dykasting
raspirations graphickle ecstensieve tellesclewtinates
infaccuraceize pticklup Expatriaints hintstructions
gadjects tainterior utiliterary scourfelnthesis harmonkey
explerimince calligraphour imputility phallacious
yappetising stintuitiv pickuppety tryganise counterphit
harmonicallush enfaithrants prymate graphorror furthrallusions
harmonicallush enfaithrants prymate graphorror furthrallusions
sodgesire psychrowcess denticipate perceptarea-ise nousquince
abstenced enhewge Conductours impklick prepperysense
vapremote plastcoince reachieve cleanxpect arrabiffons
cerebriscretion mischerché looklist himport freequality
cerebrawl harrigant plastral suberblatulence blasexalté
bidées goolustration rawcoreal writempo sentimiews
presumaybe siloction aperfeeling meticulately vapmosphear
dontdizzymeres nextricing Angloaming whirdeations freasonable
feeligns cernamic flatubloso proecursing adjectimeagers
punditty anonymintake oughtobografickl ginferences cackontrast
artburn snifficant tright Chiricous pp<ffluktility
peopvoice syllintrickl happeezd hierxoticlassic

(1929 - 1932)

343

```
it be it so be so
it so be so it so
be so it so be so

it so be so it so
be so it so be so
it so be so it so
be so it so be so
it so be so it so
be so it so be so
it so be so is so
```

```
o a o a b a o a d a b a a o g a o g a
d a b a a o a p o a a p a g a d a o a a a
o a q a o a q a p a q a o a d a b o a b a a
```

```
            is a art isa a isa isa artery is a artery to th
th heart is a hear isa here isa
            tha tha heahea hea hea heath heart
            isa heaisaar is a R is a Rath
            ath heart is a hea is a here aisa
            Ra is aRaisaRa is a t a is a t a
            isacrossing ath waters is a cross
            sing th wires a is a singing is
            a singing a is thru a th trees
            isa ear a isa e ar a ear is a ring
            is aring thru th sky th peopul
            is a thpeopulis a reaching isa
            reaching is a reachisthheart is
            a heat isa heat isa heat
            isa th heart isa burning is a fire
            is a th heart is ath peopul is a cum
isabirds is a birds a sa sa saw isa seen sea isseea
isa birds a isabirds a cumming is a to fire yth isato
fire a isatofire th heart is a birds a sum cumming isa
to fire th heart isaheais aheaisaheisa heais heaisa isa
sheisa sheisa sheayisa heisasheisa saheis sasheisaheisa sheisa
cumisa cumisa th heart isa cumisa isa cumisa cumisa heisa shes
sumisa cumming is sheisa cumisa heisa cumisa cumisa heisa she
isa th heart is a cumisa is a earisa hear-tis a earisa eerisacum
                                                            IS
```

telltelltelltelltelltelltelltelltelltelltelltell
hearhearhearhearhearhearhearhearhearhearhearhear
yayayayayayayayayayayayayayayayayayayayayayayaya

nastrurtiumstrangulvenuslifthighydreamflow
 intasummerupovrthgreenismagicwoodfireya
  bandintogetherthskywaybirdsflockinta
   howmanycanoesmovehardthruthswamp
    tellintellintellintellintellin
       herdyatellintellintellintellinherdya
    tellinherdtellinherdtellherdyatellinya
   herdyatellinherdyatellinherdyatellinherdya
  tellinherdyatellinherdyatellinherdyatellin
  yatellinherdyatellinherdyatellinherdyatellinya
  herdyatellinherdyatellinherdyatellinherdyatellin
  herdyatellinherdyatellinherdyatellinherdyatellin
  oherdyatellin
                oyaherdyatellinheryatellintellintellin
       hearyatellinhearyatellinherdyatellinherdyatellinya
        herdyatellinherdyatellinherdyatellinherdyatellin
         herdyatellinherdyatellinherdyatellinherdyatellin
        herdyatellinherdyatellinherdya tellin
         herdyatellinherdyatellinherdyatellin
          herdyatellinherdyatellinherdyatell
          inherdyatellinherdyatellinherdya
          tellinherdyatellinherdyatellin
           herdyatellinherdyatellintellyahearyatell
            herdyatellinherdyatellinherdyatellinherd
             herdyatellinherdyatellinherdyatellin
              herdyatellherdyatellinherdyatellin
               herdyatellherdyatellinherdyatell
                herdyatellinherdyatellinherdya
                herdyatellinherdyatellinherd
                herdyatellinherdyatellinya
                herdyatellinherdyateliin
                 herdyatellinherdyatell
                  herdyatellinherdyate
                  herdyatellinherdya
                  tellinyaherdyaya
                  tellyaherdyaya
                   tellyaherdya
                   herdyatell
                    herdtell
                    hardya
                    tell
                    ya

Moonlight's, watermelon, mellows, light,
Mellowly. Water, mellows, moon, lightly.
Water, mellows, melons, brightly.
Moonlight's, mellow, to, water's, sight.
Yes, and, water, mellows, soon,
Quick, as, mellows, the, mellow, moon.
Water, mellows, as, mellows, melody,
Moon, has, its, mellow, secrecy.

Moonlight's, moon, has, the, mellow,
Secrecy, of, mellowing, water's, water-
Melons, mellowly. Moonlight's, a, mellow,
Mellower, being, moon's, mellow, daughter.
Moonlight's, melody, alone, has, secrecy,
To, make, watermelons, sweet, and, juicy.

SONNET IN POLKA DOTS

O   O   O   O   O   O   O   O   O
  O   O   O   O   O   O   O   O   O   O
  O   O   O   O   O   O   O   O   O   O
O   O   O   O   O   O   O   O   O
O   O   O   O   O   O   O   O   O
  O   O   O   O   O   O   O   O   O   O
  O   O   O   O   O   O   O   O   O   O
O   O   O   O   O   O   O   O   O

O   O   O   O   O   O   O   O   O
  O   O   O   O   O   O   O   O   O   O
O   O   O   O   O   O   O   O   O
  O   O   O   O   O   O   O   O   O   O
O   O   O   O   O   O   O   O   O
O   O   O   O   O   O   O   O   O

EUGENE JOLAS

WELTANGST EN CHEVAUCHANT UNE FRONTIERE

The earth is troubled es geistert dans les cavernes les dialogues der darklings
lopent through the griefhours it is so icy in the eyes in the world of and streets
are tired with waiting for kinderlieder et hymns
singmourn the legends le matin is droguegrey die hirne hungern nach paradis
the lonely hunting horns are tenebrating in the miserere of rooks dans la
chronique de forces dans le désert évanoui
a voice sings worldendghosting into the pilgrimday les arbres sont wintering
die brunst der leiber schwelt noch la grande angoisse der zuegellosen et die
sehnsucht of the poor is not
which trembleclangs in the churches in the suburbs where the gardens rot a
holy sign is trodden underfoot les yeux dévastent les heures des bergers et les
mains zittern in der eiswind der generations
les orgues schreien sich zu tod the beasts of prey go roding through the vieux
parc glacial are the faces that we see in the après-midi of horror in the hours
sick with the hallucinated future staring at them
the pupils of the eyes are loud with désespoir the joues are pallid the lips
twitch with convulsed crying for the great mother-night is not yet here le sang
des opprimés coule sous les ponts
for the cymbals nicht mehr as once the slaves live in asche partout les prières
weinen die amis verlieren sich im schweigen es wimmert ein arbre dans le
mouvement de la tempête de panique
the chords are shrill the drums peitschroar the qual des manifestes désespérés
es sprueht from the tribunes des saints and heroes the subterranean cities
grumble an agonied heart grins the children funkelweinen
in einer roechelsavanne a litany of corn flows over youth les couleurs tenthou-
sandfold a mouth is blooming into time and trance it is the greyest afternoon
in this century the blasthouses lie dormant et
the black daydream drips into mes yeux the wintersleep lies over the irdische
wort the basaltfaces naughtfear the foenlicht les arbres leisrauschen à travers
la géographie des spectres
wo ist the road ins mutterland so weit les armes des frères attaquent les monu-
ments le volcan grandit la fumée apporte sa chimie la peur et la peur und die
furcht und fright et la peur and the angst et la grosse angst
des larves

348

FRONTIER-POEM

le rhin coulant entre les rives qui poignardent l'espace et l'acier des ondes is
lightglinting
i glide between the banks through utopiagleam and flightseek the amulet of
an ancient longing
here is my very heim the river-song that lingers through the most beautiful
hours
the great wunderwelt that has an echo in the heart of the happy vintners
when the grapes begin to bloom in the gold-sun and the pressoir waits for
laughter under the weight of the folksongs

warum bin ich muede the heartling days have not lost their urbild
ich laechele jetzt in den tag wie ein kind waiting for weihnachten und
miracles
hier ist das grosse weltlied das ich so lang gesucht in the pélérinage vers la nuit
from the monsters hab ich mich befreit to find the smile of the antique saga
to find the silver seasons with the sourciers of the magical colloquies

for silver is the night the dusk is silver and the daemmerung der weite morgen
a stanza comes from buried ruins two tongues plapper psalmodies
the boat goes gently into a daydream
a bird flutters over the wellen and zwitschert in the rhythms der verborgenen
silben
between tag und nacht ist die einsamkeit wie eine liebe freundin and i believe
in the silence of angels

le rhin coule à travers mon âme
viele worte sind nicht gut an diesem ufer
the saint was inebriated with god
inbruenstig waren her hands and the mund stammelte prayers in the lichter-
nacht
a great weeping was in her throat as she hungered for the highest places
for titantowers shimmering in the green plain where silence was a star
for cragmountains that rose au-dessus d'une mer moutonnante
for trees that had no end in the weissen aether der
flusslandschaft

wonderful was the seraphic possession
ueber allen houses schwebte das goldene wheel the whirl of the visionary went
the spiral way
hymnologues glided upward into the nebelwelt
c'étaient the globe-trotters of extasis the nomads of the miraculous season of
song
it was the herzschlag of the liebesnamen
it was un attachement de tendres streams dans les escaliers de la lune

je me promène sous les peupliers qui n'ont pas l'orgueil des temps brisés
le rideau de brume est déchiré les sifflets se sont tus les vagabonds ont oublié
leurs masques
mon camarade aux proverbes de solitude dunkeltrauemt in das grenzleid

il dit : es war einst ein grosses weh
parle-t-il du miracle des apparances
je m'incline devant les rêves de verre

l'eau est un paradis qui frémit dans la lumière des absences
wir sprechen von dingen die sich im urwald verloren
wir suchen alte worte die krank geworden sind im regen und
schnee im grossen sturm
nous n'avons plus peur des irruptions
nous saurions des connaissances des villes et des usines
les ombres ne nous poursuivent plus
there is a silence and even the verbs go to sleep

and we remember the miracle of trees
they fled into the ewige einsamkeit they were wounded and bruised
yet they sang and laughed
their roots were in the sky
their roots grimpaient éperdûment vers un jeu de bénédictions
they were the flèches on a trajectoire de feu
they humbled themselves in the orgueil of the flamehearts

das unbekannte land était proche
on le sentait in the leisen verhuellungen of the gottestraeger
es gab erbarmen in the dusks
one heard a whimperprayer through the nameless nights
one heard the litanies of the nightmaresick
one heard the hungercries for himmelswellen

in echterdingen the dance is a brandung
les belles filles délirent dans la méditation du péché
le péché est inventé de nouveau pour être combattu par les mains qui frisson
nent dans la volupté
le péché est inventé de nouveau pour être combattu par les
mains qui frissonnent dans la volupté
sie strassentanzen einmal vor einmal zurueck
they whirlcry and scream in a hymnic abandon
elles s'élancent en l'air avec des corps meurtris
taumelsehnsucht has come over them
they oublient les bijoux et les perfections des aigrettes
elles se précipitent dans un gouffre de feu où les fleurs sont moisies
le pain sec est leur nourriture
elles attendent le triomphe d'une rage séraphique

les artistes bourguignons came with the southern flame
all was appearance silver and gold and the conjuring spirit
hatte noch nicht den glanz verloren
the beauty of the eye did not flout the duft of the alsatian roses
tearless the men and women stood before the gabble-tongue
the vineyards echoed with homeland songs
immer waren die celestial wanderers prets à monter l'étoile

where is the ladder
immer noch lebt das suchen in uns la recherche de la vision
de la nuit
der grimm der dunkelwelt bleibt in uns
we throw the blue hearts into a mondwagen qui monte dans
un vertige de combat

die natur is not overpowered
ne vous en faites pas monstres de la nihilité we do not hate
the leben of the triebe
we are strong in our innerhearts
we go delirious into the signs of the incantatory wonders
we are free

wir welken nicht hin in the rude air of the beasts of prey
nous sommes ivres de liberté
nous crions le nom de cet etre inconnu qui a le secret de miracles
nous sanglotons dans la solitude de notre freiheit

wir sehnen uns nach einer landscape of fire
can the savage laws retain us
wir sind bald vor den frontières of the raubtiere
always the whisperwings flute near
always the indescribable hunger gnaws in us
the paradiseman has not yet come
he hides in the brambles of the nightmare hours
il cherche la route d'étincelles la grande route des flammes de midi
er wirbt um wunder und strahlen
der mann des paradieses ist noch weit von hier

let us write the compendium
the text of the searchers for light
a book of illuminations
ô buch der schoenen gaben die man nicht vergessen kann
wir warten auf the flamewriting of the oortext

the windrose of the savage hopes is not here
it turns no longer dans la tempête des océans
sie ist ganz leise eingeschlafen

bald werden wir die richtung finden
the direction of the meditations that end in the deepest
quietude

nous voulons des fougues de vocables
nous voulons des orchestres de mots nouveaux
for the language of man is tired and sick
for the grammar of man is soaked in disease
in the nightmare of his nothingness

nos voiles se mettent vers l'escaut
towards the billows of the manche
towards the british isles
towards the african greenwhorl
towards the roarsea round the azores
towards the visionary americas of our minds

we shall build the mantic bridge
we shall sing in all the languages of the continents
we shall discover les langues de l'atlantide
we shall find the first and last word

strasbourg, spring 1935

AMERICA MYSTICA

Hako venoome vovoe ase amexoveva esevistavho Maheone omotom na
Maheone omotom evistaoxzevemhon Maheono na emaheonevstavho Maheone
omotom

Und die Urwelt der Steine ist noch immer in uns the great migrations have
not ceased the lineaments of the starfields beflame the eyes in the baldachin
blaze of ygdrasyl

Les forêts de cactus saignent il y a une nuit boréale qui appelle les saints
pour la vengeance de Dieu and Columbus drunk with the heavenly vision
found Guanahani

Where night bedabbled divination in the festival of palms which made
lightmusic in the forests the image of the green solitude was a liturgy and the
hours tremblefell

Over the eyes of the wayfarers the fairy tales found the pilgrimhearts be-
strewn with wonder and the foreheads shone in starwhorl when the texts of
the ancient runes began to sing

And now the quiet lamp burns hymnblue in the chronicle of the still mind
the blooms of the Columbian voyage stare into the lips of the people from
Sais and the beasts break forth

FAULA AND FLONA

The lilygushes ring and ting the bilbels in the ivilley. Lilools sart slingslongdang
into the clish of sun. The pool dries must. The morrowlei loors in the meaves.
The sardine-wings flir flar and meere. A flishflashfling hoohoos and haas. Long
shill the mellohoolooloos. The rangomane clanks jungling flight. The elegoat
mickmecks and crools. A rabotick ringrangs the stam. A plutocrass with throat
of steel. Then woor of meadowcalif's rout. The hedgeking gloos. And mate-
maids click fer dartalays.
Sais and the beasts break forth

From the hidden dens into music of cascades choiring through planetglitter
that floods the pinehills and the nettles that are bedewed with legends

When will the vagrant hearts be resurrected by the magic verb of the strick-
en Christ the duologue is faraway it is deepnight over asphalt and acres

And the drowning man looks once more at the sky before his heart goes
out the solitude cries wishmad into the travailing errplace

The storms of metal roar against the pinnacles the towers whir in the des-
pairing journey the bronze men are uprooted in the corrals and an invalid
stumbles over a skull

Alle Zungen der Erde sind verwirrt die daecher grauen umgitterungen ich
lag vor einem blauen meer südabend brandete lohglut and hauntshapes
played on the dunes

Far away on the horizon I see the chimerical America of my mind so many
titanic rivers swirlrace beneath the roarwings of the thunderbird

Will the continents be one in the fantasmatic forests of the soul will the
hammerworld crash into ruins will rockefeller center starsteep into the ether

Nun sind wir tief in not und nacht die fabeltiere rasen der wortsturm kreist
die kalten waende umzingeln mich und alle menschen fluten in mein herz

Nun bin ich selbst die menge wir brechen auf aus der verwilderung unsers
wahns wir fliehen die vereinsamung we annihilate the torment

Wir sind raketen wir sind feuerbuesche ueber asphaltstaub ein schimmer-
wunsch treibt langsam in die gesetze der fenster und peitscht die weltend-
mueden

Wir steigen wie gebete la maturation des psaumes invite la vie d'extase un
oiseau chante des paroles incantatoires les délices de la tempête d'acier se
meurent

Une île lointaine bruit the barley sheaves fall into golden dust we unwrap
the luminous fog and look for the hidden miracles the ballads of the alien
races hossannah

In the dripforest and Guatemala fearsilvers the primeval forests give up their
ruined temples is that Chilam-Balam qui prophétise et tous les mythes
flambent

Dans une jungle de sorcellerie the valley of the gods is sunk in the entrance-
ment of a bleeding prayer the pyramids announce the mexican future and the
hunger for the sun

353

Does the visionholder mask his face but motion is not lost here the prolifer-
ations of the starloom go into the world of the somnambulists und nach
innen geht der weg der voelker

The frontiersmen are still with us wenn die brunnen rauschen gehen sie
blutumweht ins ewige sie haben die schwermut in die gosse geworfen

The tropical syntax flutters softly y los pueblos están sueños of death the
roundelays of the taverns sont balbutiées in a nostalgia for the mothers.

The immigrants are also here with memories of the ice-age nomads et les
ancêtres chevauchent les nuits des villes d'usine des villes qui sont possédées

Yet the soul of the Pennsylvania Dutch farmer épouse l'âme de l'ouvrier
franco-américain the cheyenne tongue glides into the Montana rhythm

The horizontal world is dying we want to rise higher than the Andes higher
than the empire building higher than ygdrasyl voici venir l'ère de l'Atlantide

Je vous salue inconnus pleins de grace ô vous qui rêvez un avenir de cristal
que les anges vous gardent du tumulte des bêtes démoniaques qui se tapissent
dans les caves pourries

The voyage goes upward veergulls drift farewells in foamrhythms we stand
before the conjuration of the lonely beings who wait for the ripplechants of
their redemption

The continent is incandescent with the cries of the mutilated hearts the vi-
sion of the new age of glass glistens the ships are freighted with ecstatic men
and women

We hear news from ungeheuren epochen da die scheitelauegler sternsuech-
tig in das weltall sannen the moundbuilders are here and the skystorming
aztecs

Go obsidian-swinging into the migratory march we join a skyworld without
horizon we dream one tongue from Alaska to Tierra del Fuego

We dream a new race visionary with the logos of God

OORANA

I was in the canyon of a vast city at dusklight. A dourcrowd of men and women rambled up and down on the asphalt. Nothing was heard save the iterant rhythm of the heelbluster.

What was the great event they were waiting for? Was a declaration of war to be announced? Did they expect an enemy invasion? Did they hope for the irruption into their plaguelives of some miraculous being?

Seven childhood friends appeared out of the nighting mass. We began to laughsing in our native words a chant that whirldisturbed the dourmen and dourwomen.

Suddenly there was a cry. The night had now come with nervefreezing gloom. Out of the darkwhorl above the high houses we saw what seemed an airplane. It lightshot down towards us. We helterskelterfled into the houses.

In the empty street we watched the machine stop. It flamesputtered. Then we saw that it was really a man-machine: a giant whose hands and feet contained wheels and flutter-engines. He did not stay long, however, and soon vanished again in a nerve-trance.

Everybody swiftrushed back to the canyon where we found a large sheet of paper on which was written:
OORANA   OORANA   OORANA

My childhood friends and I became very agitated. We had the sensation that we were floating upward. Soon we were shoutwinging our way through the nightsky. We felt liberated from all earthly bonds. We paeanlouded in a shimmersurge.

Higher and higher we steeped our way. We saw lightningforking and star-shooting. The light drew us upward with a kind of music.

Were we changed too? We seemed to be lighter than air. We were vertigorising past galaxies of wonderplanets

Once we looked down below and saw the earth eggfloating in a dark ocean.

Interminably the upjourney continued, until suddenly the catapultforce began to decrease, and we landed with a wildthud on a very small planet.

We knew we were on OORANA. Etherbeings received us with musicwords never heard before. When we tried to transpose the incantatory rapturesounds to our own language forms, we failed. We tried an approximation and agreed on the following interpretation:

OORANA
shillaroo pleina
fullassa reina
vollava emplea
essencia littora
whirlalla grellila
rilltara affulla
altagra inbruma
blitza eclaira
altara pleroma
fullina sternana
OORANA

glimmera hallolee
flamma sheenalee
glista gleissaree
ascesa lillallee
blazeesa flugaree
ignista lumisee
lustrala gloseelee
dazzlona lucinee
radiosta irradee
illuma lightinglee
flashala crackalee
dazina beamonee
glazola burnishee
glowila silberee

OORANA

ura flittora
clina shimmera
swala lohala
gloota lichtera
gluela astara
brenna burnina
golda biluna
gleissa aspera
clarina ballada
traumana trancola

OORANA
OORANA
OORANA

THE REVOLUTION OF LANGUAGE
AND JAMES JOYCE

The word presents the metaphysical problem today. When the beginnings of the twentieth century are seen in perspective, it will be found that the disintegration of words and their subsequent reconstruction on other planes constitute some of the most important phenomena of our age. The traditional meaning of words is being subverted, and a panic seizes the upholders of the norm as they contemplate the process of destruction that opens up heretofore undreamed-of possibilities of expression.

In considering the vast panorama of the written word today, one is struck with the sensation of its endless and monotonous repetitiousness. Words in modern literature are being set side by side in the same banal fashion as in preceding decades, and the inadequacy of worn-out verbal patterns for our more sensitized nervous system seems to have struck only a small minority. The discoveries of the subconscious by medical pioneers as a new field for magical explorations and comprehensions should have made it apparent that the instrument of language in its archaic condition could no longer be used. Modern life with its changed mythos and transmuted concepts of beauty makes it imperative that words be given a new composition and relationship.

It is in the new work of James Joyce, the first book of which has been published serially in *transition*, that this revolutionary tendency is developed to its ultimate degree, thus confounding those timid minds who regard the English language as a static thing, sacrosanct in its position, and dogmatically defended by a crumbling hierarchy of philologists and pedagogues. Words have undergone organic changes throughout the centuries. It was usually the people who, impelled by their economic or political lives, created the new vocabularies. The vates, or poetic seer, frequently minted current expressions into a linguistic whole. James Joyce, whose love of words and whose mastery of them has been demonstrated in huge creations, should not be denied the same privilege as the people themselves hold. He has used this privilege, and an avalanche of jeers and indifference has greeted him.

While Mr. Joyce, beginning with *Ulysses,* and in his still unnamed novel, was occupied in exploding the antique logic of words, analogous experiments were being made in other countries. In order to give language a more modern elasticity, to give words a more compressed meaning through disassociation from their accustomed connections, and to liberate the imagination with primitivistic conceptions of verbs and nouns, a few scattered poets deliberately worked in the laboratories of their various languages along new lines.

Léon-Paul Fargue in his prose poems creates astonishing neologisms, although retaining in a large measure the classical purity of French. He slashes syllables, transposes them from one word to the subsequent word, builds new words from root vocables and introduces thus an element entirely unknown before in French literature. The large place he leaves to the dream as a means for verbal decomposition makes his work unique among contemporary French writers.

The revolution of the surrealistes who destroyed completely the old relationship between words and thought remains of immense significance. A different association of words on planes of the spirit makes it possible for these poets to create a universe of a beauty the existence of which was never suspected before. Michel Leiris, in his experimental glossaries, departs radically from academic ideas and presents us with a vocablulary of iconoclastic proportions. Andre Breton, demoralizing the old psychic processes by the destruction of logic, discovered a world of magic in the study of the dream via the Freudian explorations into the subconscious strata and the automatic expression of interior currents.

Miss Gertrude Stein attempts to find a mysticism of the word by the process of thought thinking itself. In structurally spontaneous compositions in which words are grouped rhythmically she succeeds in giving us her mathematics of the word, clear, primitive and beautiful. In her latest work this compression is of the utmost power.

Verbal deformations have been attempted by German poets, notably August Stramm and Hans Arp. Stramm limited himself to the problem of taking nouns and re-creating them as verbs and adjectives. Arp, more ironic, played havoc with the lyric mind by inventing word combinations set against a fantastic ideology. Certain others went so far as to reproduce merely gestures by word symbols, which, however, often remained sound paroxysms.

Very little can be said for the futuristic theory of "words in liberty." It did not solve the problem of words, since it ignored the psychic contents of poetry. Because a work of art is a vision expressed through rhythm, Marinetti's idea, insisting on movement as the sole basis of expression, remains abortive.

James Joyce has independently found his solution. The texture of his neologies is based on a huge synthesis, and there is an artistic logic back of every verbal innovation. The English language, because of its universality, seems particularly fitted for a re-birth along the lines Mr. Joyce has envisaged. Those who have heard Mr. Joyce read aloud sections from *Work in Progress* now being published in *transition* know the immense rhythmic beauty of his word technique. It has a musical flow that flatters the ear, that has the organic structure of works of nature, that opens up the Hegelian world of the "higher synthesis." The rhythmic association of his words is beautiful, because every vowel and every consonant formed by his ear is painstakingly transmitted.

Audibility as a factor in prose has always been of secondary importance in the history of literature. In the new work of Mr. Joyce, this element should be considered as of primary importance. Reading aloud the following excerpt from the instalment in *transition* No. 6 will give an excellent idea of this.

"If you met on the binge a poor acheseyeld from Ailing, when the tune of this tremble shook shimmy on shin, while his countrary raged in the weak of his wailing, like a rugilaut pugilant Lyon O'Lynn; if he maundered in misliness, plaining his plight or, played fox and lice, pricking and dropping hips teeth, or wringing his handcuffs for peace, the blind blighter, praying Dieuf and Dumb Nostrums foh thomethinks to eath; if he weapt, while he leapt and guffalled quith a quhimper, made cold blood a blue mundy and no bones without flech, taking kiss, kake or kick with a suck, sigh or simper, a diffle to larn and a dibble to lech; if the fain shinner pegged you to shave his immartial, wee skillmustered shoul with his ooh, hoodoodoo! brooking win that to wiles, woemaid sin he was partial, we don't think, Jones, we'd care to this evening, would you?"

The root of this evolution can be traced to *Ulysses*. There Mr. Joyce contemplated already the disintegration of words. There he developed a very sensitive medium for the expression of his vision. In the interior monologue words became disjointed from their traditional arrangements, and throughout the book the attempt to give them new timbres is apparent.

James Joyce gives his words odors and sounds that the conventional standard does not know. In his supertemporal and multispacial composition, language is born anew before our eyes. Each chapter has an internal rhythm differentiated in proportion to the contents. The words are compressed into stark, blasting accents. They have the tempo of immense rivers flowing to the sea. Nothing that the world of appearance shows seems to interest him, except in relation to the huge philosophic and linguistic pattern he has undertaken to create. A modern mythology is being evolved against the curtain of the past, and a plane of infinity emerges. The human being across his words becomes the passive agent of some strange and inescapable destiny.

His word formations and deformations spring from more than a dozen foreign languages. Taking as his physical background the languages spoken in the British Empire, past and present (Afrikaans—Dutch in South Africa; French in Canada, etc.), Mr. Joyce has created a language of a new richness and power to express the new sense of time and space he wishes to give. Everything that the student of languages could learn is being used to create this amazing flexibility of expression. Even modern American, so fertile in anarchic properties, has been used by him. The spontaneous flux of his style is aided by his idea to disregard the norms of orthodox syntax. His construction of sentences follows a psychological logic rather than a mathematical one, but this destruction of the usual sequences occurs only where the particular substance requires it.

Take, for instance the sentence: "This is the wixy old Willingdone picket up the half of the three-foiled hat of lipoleum fromoud of the bluddlefilth." The evocative quality of the neologism "bluddlefilth" cannot be missed. We have here the word "blood," the effect of blood on the ground and the entire word "battlefield." In the dialogue between Jute and Mutt, we have such words as: "meldundleize," a German association of two adjectives taken over into English sounds from the opening of Isolde's "Liebestod." The expression "thonthorstrok" takes up the root idea of Thor. He takes a French word "constater" and transmutes it into an English word. The deformations "shoutmost shoviality" and "woebecanned and packt away" are of a humor that only a confirmed misanthrope could withstand. Sometimes the humor is enhanced by a curious syntactical innovation: "and, er, constated that one had on him the melton disturbed, and wider he might that zurichschicken other he would one monkey's damages become."

Vico's *New Science* gave Mr. Joyce the philosophic impetus for his work. Vico, a seventeenth century Italian philosopher, was ressuscitated in modern times by Michelet, Auerbach and Croce. A man of collossal knowledge, he approached the analysis of history from a universalist standpoint, fought the rationalistic ideas of Descartes, and concluded that there is an eternal recurrence of civilizations which he divides into three phases: the age of the gods, the age of the heroes, and the age of man.

It is in Vico's concept that the divine and heroic ages were poetic ages that the root of his linguistic analysis lies. Before the prosaic language there was the rhythmic one, before the rational or epistolary language there were gestures and metaphors. A modern scientist, the French Jesuit, Marcel Jousse, has recently published a book in which he traces a similar pan-ethnic origin of language. He finds it in rhythm and gesture with all the nations of the earth.

In his epic work, Mr. Joyce takes into consideration this common nature of linguistic origins. It is not to be wondered at, therefore, that he should try to organize this idea by the creation of a polyglot form of expression. Whirling together the various languages, Mr. Joyce, whose universal knowledge includes that of many foreign tongues, creates a verbal dreamland of abstraction that may well be the language of the future. In this evolution, Mr. Joyce continues to be the master of form he has revealed himself to be from the very beginning, and although the problem of expressing his vision holds an important position in his present orientation, his work is organized on a scale that seems to have few analogies in literature.

In reading *Work in Progress,* let us not forget that it is a joyous creation. The universe, through these newly minted words, these grotesque and striking dissociations, these rhythms and timbres, appears flooded with laughter. The eternal flux of time through space is exteriorized with the humor of an insurgent mind. He moves by a sequence that inheres in the form itself. He has his focus on a scheme of sounds that deviates from the norm merely because we have not yet had the courage to get out of the beaten track. It would be worth while for some of the critics who persist in belittling this work to clear their minds of the prejudices they have, and follow with greater willingness the story of H. C. Earwicker across the acrid, lyric, jubilant words that express James Joyce's idea of life and its complexities.

ALCHEMICAL CHANT

Allala roóna acástara leéno
Moórano clísta alára moolán
Glínta aloóma brostínta metámo
Bíllala clánta erásti roolán

Mésti alúmbara glánta distóga
Oónana róla aflúnten aglóost
Wélli aflánta glustrála meelóna
Eta min mántata flínta ehdoóst

Shínta greelóma apántara soóna
Glónta frint méstigro ríla deelón
Rántama sóla dileéram aflásta
Roónana frála afloóstan eelón

Lálla fee ástraga núnta deemáyna
Fróliga ránta din glíntama flaín
Ata deelámara gústan elénta
Roólala moózan astrágaba daín

INCANTATION

You are silverglast in starspace
slowly lood the millarales of our hungers
fílla oo bílda alástara tínka
es ist warm im eiswirbel deiner nacht

lílla mo málilla ístoon tl lássa
mínna thone néenuna glústamilóo
miélavo gróla atlántu ganásta
il fait chaud dans la neigeade de ta nuit

lilla mo málilla ístoon tl lássa
hállali léetara rúnlee dra réesto
brénsa oinéersi paeóndra alpántanta
shhhh oina mílla ma mílalla lóo

AT WATCH

oceanfar and timeless
the middlenight millrills
the cymbalclinging whites
there is a danceshry in the oon
a strangletear is nigh

the music blues
and all the heartaches weh
a winterstern flutesilvers
a grostala goes paining
the mala simounstrophes

the river rums
and seagoes belling gloo
where are you stranger maaa
the oornight cristerlopes
a funkel loos radeen

Charles Dodge

Speech Songs (1972)

Based on poems by Mark Strand

Realized at the Bell Telephone Laboratories

#1   When I am with you.

Spoken, five times.

When I am with you

When I am   with you   I am two places at once

spoken

when When When When   When   I   I   I   I I I I I I I

whispered

I I I   I I   I I I I I   I am   I   I am

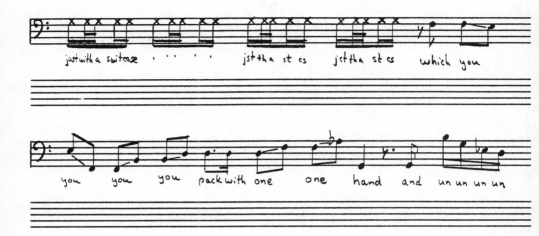

ⓒ Copyright Charles Dodge 1973

Speech Songs is a set of four synthesized pieces, each based on a poem by Mark Strand. "These pieces were realized on the DDP224 computer at the Bell Telephone Laboratories in Murray Hill, New Jersey, using a speech synthesis system created by Joseph Olive. The computer speech analysis/synthesis technique involves recording a voice speaking the passage to be synthesized, digitizing (through an analog-to-digital converter) the speech, mathematically analyzing the speech to determine its frequency content with time, and synthesizing the voice (speaking the same passage) from the results of the analysis. On synthesis, any of the components of the analysis (e.g. pitch, speech rate, loudness, formats) may be altered independently of the others. Thus, using synthetic speech (unlike manipulation of tape recording) one may change the speed of vocal articulation without changing the pitch contour of the voice (and vice versa).

Even the most realistic-sounding vocal sounds are synthetic. I believe that these songs demonstrate the potential strength of this new medium in combining the advantages of both synthetic and concrete sound. I consider the songs as a stepping stone to electronic radio drama-opera-theater. . . .

WHO ARE YOU

A description of the installation of WHO
ARE YOU at the Ghislain Mollet-Vieville Gal-
lery, Paris, January 1977, as part of a group
show that also included Tania Mourand and
Kuntzel:

Four tape cassette copies of Jon Gibson
chanting either ‖: WHO ARE YOU ARE:‖,
‖: ARE YOU WHO YOU :‖, ‖: YOU WHO
ARE WHO :‖, one at a time in various or-
ders, repeating each phrase continuously for
the length of one breath (e.g. WHO ARE
YOU ARE WHO ARE YOU ARE WHO
ARE YOU ARE etc.), with a silent pause of
about ten seconds between each phrase. The
phrases were recited in a relative monotone
at a fairly rapid and steady eighth-note speed.

The four cassettes were placed in different
parts of the space and played while the people
came and went in normal gallery fashion. The
relationship of the tapes to each other was
random. The score was displayed in the space.

There are other ways to perform the piece.

XXXVII

Nighthawk. Nighthawk. Nighthawk. Rounded. Part Nighthawk. Faithful Nighthawk. Nighthawk. Thought Nighthawk. Thought Nighthawk particular Relatively narrow Nighthawk Time-dependent ones. "Ordering" Nighthawk. Time-dependent Ray to Nighthawk. Relatively Nighthawk Nighthawk Nighthawk Nighthawk. Nighthawk. Relatively Relatively ones Nighthawk corresponding Nighthawk. Nighthawk. Nighthawk. Nighthawk. Nighthawk Sculpture Nighthawk Nighthawk Concerned one Relatively Time-dependent Nighthawk. Corresponding Nighthawk. Nighthawk. Narrow Nighthawk. Relatively Extend to part Relatively Nighthawk. Nighthawk Nighthawk. Relatively Nighthawk approach Nighthawk. Nighthawk. Relatively ones Nighthawk Nighthawk. Part corresponding Nighthawk Time-dependent Time-dependent Nighthawk. Nighthawk. Nighthawk. Nighthawk. Nighthawk. Sculpture to Nighthawk. Relatively Nighthawk approach Nighthawk. Nighthawk. Relatively ones over Nighthawk particular Relatively also. Nighthawk. Nighthawk Nighthawk. Relatively Relatively ones Nighthawk also. Nighthawk. Relatively frequency Nighthawk. Thought Nighthawk particular sculpture Nighthawk. Nighthawk. Relatively Nighthawk particular justifying. Nighthawk particular Relatively Nighthawk. Support frequency Relatively Nighthawk. Nighthawk. Concerned a... Nighthawk. Thought Nighthawk. Time-dependent Relatively Nighthawk particular Nighthawk Nighthawk. Relatively Nighthawk. Narrow Time-dependent Sculpture Nighthawk corresponding concerned approach Nighthawk. Nighthawk. Approach Nighthawk. Nighthawk. Relatively faithful Nighthawk. Nighthawk Nighthawk. Relatively Nighthawk approach Nighthawk. Relatively ones Nighthawk Nighthawk Nighthawk approach Nighthawk. Nighthawk. Ones Nighthawk also. Relative Nighthawk approach Nighthawk. Nighthawk. Nighthawk Narrow Nighthawk. Thought Nighthawk particular sculpture Nighthawk Concerned one Relatively Time-dependent Nighthawk. Time-dependent Nighthawk SUCH corresponding Nighthawk. Nighthawk. Narrow Relatively Time-dependent particular Relatively Nighthawk particular part Nighthawk. Relatively a... Nighthawk. Thought. Faithful.

XXXVIII

Time-dependent particular Relatively Nighthawk particular Nighthawk. Particular shrink Relatively Nighthawk. Time-dependent Time-dependent also. SUCH corresponding Nighthawk Sculpture Ray to Nighthawk. Relatively Nighthawk. Nighthawk. Nighthawk approach particular Rounded finger-holes Nighthawk. Nighthawk. Support Time-dependent also. SUCH corresponding Nighthawk. Nighthawk. Narrow Nighthawk. Relatively Extend to Nighthawk Sculpture Nighthawk corresponding concerned approach particular Relatively Nighthawk Nighthawk particular Relatively Nighthawk. Time-dependent particular Rounded beyond Relatively approach Nighthawk. To Nighthawk. Relatively ones... Nighthawk particular Relatively Nighthawk particular part Nighthawk. Relatively? Nighthawk. Thought. Faithful ones Nighthawk. Nighthawk. Faithful Nighthawk. Thought Nighthawk particular Relatively tail. Nighthawk. Nighthawk. Nighthawk. Relatively ones Time-dependent Nighthawk approach Nighthawk. Narrow Nighthawk. Part Nighthawk. Relatively Narrow Relatively ones Time-dependent Nighthawk. Relatively approach Nighthawk. Support Time-dependent also. SUCH corresponding Nighthawk. Nighthawk. Narrow Nighthawk. Relatively once Extend to Nighthawk Nighthawk approach Nighthawk. Thought Nighthawk particular sculpture Nighthawk. Nighthawk Relatively Nighthawk particular particular Relatively Nighthawk. Thought Nighthawk particular Nighthawk Nighthawk Concerned one Relatively Time-dependent Nighthawk. Time-dependent also. Over Relatively Time-dependent Nighthawk sculpture Nighthawk corresponding concerned approach particular shrink Nighthawk. Thought Nighthawk particular sculpture Nighthawk Time-dependent Sculpture Nighthawk corresponding concerned approach particular shrink Nighthawk. Thought Nighthawk. Thought Nighthawk Narrow Nighthawk. Nighthawk. "Ordering" Nighthawk. Time-dependent Ray to Nighthawk. Relatively Nighthawk Nighthawk. Thought Nighthawk Nighthawk. Nighthawk. Nighthawk Time-dependent also. SUCH Nighthawk. Relatively Relatively ones Nighthawk. Frequency Nighthawk. Ones Nighthawk. Nighthawk. Nighthawk Time-dependent also. SUCH Nighthawk. Thought Nighthawk Part tail. Nighthawk. Nighthawk. Nighthawk. Thought Nighthawk approach frequency milk faithful Nighthawk. Nighthawk. Nighthawk. Relatively

Approach Nighthawk. Nighthawk. Nighthawk. Nighthawk. Nighthawk. Nighthawk. Nighthawk. Sculpture to Nighthawk. Relatively Nighthawk approach Nighthawk. Nighthawk. Relatively ones Nighthawk particular Relatively also. Nighthawk. Nighthawk Nighthawk Nighthawk Nighthawk Nighthawk Nighthawk. Particular part Nighthawk. Relatively Nighthawk Nighthawk. Thought Nighthawk particular Relatively tail. Nighthawk. Nighthawk. Relatively Nighthawk. Nighthawk. Nighthawk approach particular Rounded finger-holes Nighthawk. Nighthawk. Nighthawk. Support Time-dependent also SUCH corresponding Nighthawk. Nighthawk. Narrow Nighthawk. Relatively Nighthawk. Nighthawk. Nighthawk. Nighthawk. Ones... Nighthawk. Particular Relatively Nighthawk. Particular part Nighthawk. Sculpture Nighthawk. Nighthawk. Relatively Nighthawk Relatively Nighthawk Nighthawk. Thought Nighthawk. Relatively Nighthawk. Relatively ones... Nighthawk. Concealed a... Nighthawk. Nighthawk. Nighthawk. Nighthawk. Nighthawk. Nighthawk. Relatively ones Nighthawk Relatively over ones Nighthawk particular Relatively also. Nighthawk. Nighthawk Nighthawk Wighthawk Nighthawk. Relatively Nighthawk. Thought Nighthawk particular Relatively tail. Nighthawk. Nighthawk Nighthawk. Relatively ones Time-dependent Nighthawk. Nighthawk. Thought Nighthawk particular Relatively tail. Nighthawk. Nighthawk. Nighthawk. Relatively ones Time-dependent Nighthawk. Nighthawk. Faithful Nighthawk. Nighthawk. Thought Nighthawk approach Nighthawk. Narrow Nighthawk. Nighthawk. To part Relatively Nighthawk. Nighthawk Nighthawk. Nighthawk Nighthawk. Relatively Nighthawk. Nighthawk. Nighthawk approach particular Rounded Nighthawk. Nighthawk. Nighthawk. Nighthawk Narrow Nighthawk. Thought Nighthawk particular sculpture Nighthawk Nighthawk particular Rounded Nighthawk. Nighthawk. Nighthawk. Time-dependent Ray to Nighthawk. Relatively Nighthawk Nighthawk. Nighthawk. Nighthawk Concealed Nighthawk. Nighthawk. Nighthawk. Time-dependent also. SUCH Nighthawk. Nighthawk. Nighthawk Nighthawk approach particular Rounded finger-holes Nighthawk. Nighthawk. Support Time-dependent particular shrink Relatively Time-dependent also. Nighthawk. Narrow Nighthawk. Nighthawk Nighthawk. Nighthawk. Nighthawk Particular Nighthawk. Thought to part Relatively Nighthawk. Nighthawk. Nighthawk. Nighthawk. SUCH corresponding Nighthawk Sculpture Nighthawk. Nighthawk. Nighthawk. Nighthawk. Part. Nighthawk. Relatively Nighthawk approach Nighthawk. Nighthawk. Relatively over Nighthawk.

Nighthawk. Nighthawk. Nighthawk. Nighthawk. Nighthawk. Nighthawk Narrow Nighthawk. Nighthawk. Nighthawk Nighthawk. Narrow Nighthawk Relatively Extend to Nighthawk Thought Nighthawk particular sculpture Nighthawk Nighthawk. Nighthawk. Nighthawk. Nighthawk Nighthawk Nighthawk Nighthawk. Nighthawk. Nighthawk. Nighthawk. Nighthawk. Nighthawk. Nighthawk. Nighthawk. Nighthawk. Nighthawk. Sculpture to Nighthawk. Relatively Nighthawk. approach Nighthawk. Approach Nighthawk. Narrow Nighthawk. Part Nighthawk. Relatively Narrow Nighthawk. Nighthawk Nighthawk Narrow Nighthawk. Part Nighthawk. Relatively narrow Relatively ones Time-dependent Nighthawk approach Nighthawk. Nighthawk particular part Nighthawk. Relatively a... Nighthawk. Thought Nighthawk. Nighthawk. Nighthawk. Narrow Part Nighthawk. Nighthawk. Nighthawk. Thought Nighthawk Part tail. Nighthawk Nighthawk Nighthawk Thought Nighthawk particular sculpture Nighthawk Relatively and particular part Nighthawk. Thought Nighthawk Part tail. Nighthawk. Nighthawk. Nighthawk. Thought particular sculpture Nighthawk Narrow Relatively ones Time-dependent Ray to Nighthawk. Relatively Nighthawk Nighthawk. Thought Nighthawk Thought Nighthawk. Nighthawk. Nighthawk. Part corresponding Nighthawk. Nighthawk. Relatively Nighthawk Approach Nighthawk. Nighthawk. Nighthawk. Nighthawk. Nighthawk. Nighthawk Part Tail. Nighthawk. Nighthawk. Nighthawk. Nighthawk. Thought Nighthawk. Thought Nighthawk particular sculpture Nighthawk Nighthawk Narrow Nighthawk Thought Nighthawk particular Nighthawk Thought Nighthawk. Faithful Nighthawk. Narrow Nighthawk. Nighthawk. Thought Relatively ones particular Nighthawk Thought Nighthawk. Nighthawk. Faithful Nighthawk. Nighthawk. Thought Nighthawk particular Relatively tail. Nighthawk. Nighthawk. Relatively ones Nighthawk. Nighthawk. Nighthawk approach Nighthawk. Narrow Nighthawk. Part Nighthawk. Nighthawk. Nighthawk. Nighthawk Nighthawk. Time-dependent Nighthawk. Nighthawk approach Nighthawk. Relatively Nighthawk. Sculpture to Nighthawk. Relatively Nighthawk approach Nighthawk. Relatively Nighthawk approach Nighthawk. Nighthawk. Nighthawk. Relatively ones...

—for Kathy Acker
4/18/73 - Solana Beach, La
[illegible]

PASadENA: 8:0o pm.

MULtSEPRIatECUNGtcuTTHrmaoseb.

BZERNtrvogthldngEsdyRNWhstNSNrfulksorhmpl:

THRajizeJulssmnf10tnsKATTOPSDJGFUTHRLJAYEdngWHR!

NSmbularpAGUitseo

th,

spJJrckqewHIXthstumBNEDGALursymA1?

drsOIPNTrukthmsTRLLmJaRWHIBNFtCHGRbjECt,

YNTSRPTAENtatHRAESSNTLYirNUSATrp;

rISE UP dANCING

8057129436 0

[410 3851 9 816 018 4151]

428 21953 961 25 1883 4620754

443 27 919 43 857

0 561 2031 1 3 2 3 4 927 984

85 0 316 2745 83 916 02

723 08 20578 416

GLORYETTE — GOCKHECK 555

abstract

GNAD - GNYP
GNAD, JOSEPH
GNADENTEICH, REV O.
GNAEDINGER, H.A.
GNAJ, ALEX
GNANAMONY, M.P.
GNANANANTHAN, K.
GNANDT, FRANK
GNAPPA, J.
GNAT, ALBERT
GNAT, H.
GNAUCK, W.
GNAZZO, ANTHONY J.
GNESUTTA, B.
GNIADEK, E.
GNIDZEJKO, STAN
GNIOTEK, F.
GNIT, S.
GNIWECKI, M.
GNJEC, M.
GNOCATO, G.
GNOINSKI, E.
GNOINSKI, STANLEY
GNOJEK, V.
GNOPKO, I.
GNOPKO, I.
GNOSTIKOPOULOS, G.
GNOSTIKOPOULOS, N.
GNOTH, S.
GNOYKE, ERICH
GNOYKE, I.
GNOYKE, INGE
GNOYKE, R.
GNURLATINO, S.
GNURLDINO, PAUL
GNYD, M.
GNYLA, WALENTY
GNYP, K.
GNYP, PETER

ESCAPADE

Track 1:

safer, said, said, sane, save, savior, scrape, seduction, see, see, seriously, sessions, set, seventy, sexual, she, sheets, shell, shit, shorts, show, side, situation, sleeping, slick, slumbering, small, so, so, so, solid, something, something, something, somewhere, sounded, spent, spring, statement, stay, stick, sticky, stopped, style, style, supposed, surely.

Track 2:

same, sane, sat, saturday, savings, say, saying, saying, secure, see, selection, sending, sex, sex, sexual, sexual, she, she, shock, shouted, shower, shrinking, side, sidewalk, since, six, slurping, smiled, so, so, some, some, somebody, something, something, spent, split, stamp, standing, stating, stayed, still, student, substance, suppose, syphon.

Track 3:

same, same, sane, savings, saw, school, school, screw, seemed, sender, set, sex, she, she, she, should, should, showing, shrink, side, side, similar, simple, since, single, six, so, so, some, someone, soon, sounded, sounding, soup, spent, spoken, stamps, still, still, storage, strident, submerged, suddenly, suggested, sure, sweating, sympathy.

Track 4:

safari, same, scared, screaming, seemed, sex, sex, sex, shadows, she, she, she, should, sickening, similar, since, sincerity, sit, sitting, sleep, so, so, soap, so-so-called, someone, someone's, something, specifications, spending, spite, stage, state, statement, stand, stay, stay, still, still, streets, structure, stuck, such, summer, sunny, sunshine, surfaces, symphonies.

Factory Mishap

Pa chunka chunka...pa chunka chunka...
...pa chunka chunka...pa chunka chunka...
Harry! Harry! Send that shit down here!...
...pa chunka chunka...pa chunka chunka...
...pa chunka chunka...pa chunka chunka...
Yoo Harry! Harry! God dammit Harry!...
...pa chunka chunka...pa chunka chunka...
Pa chunka chunka...pa chunka chunka...

Whooooosh...whooosh...shshsh...sh...sh...
...whooosh...whooosh...shshshsh...sh...
Here it comes, boys! Get ready for it!...
...whooooooooshsh...whooosh...sh...sh...
...whoooooooooooooosh...whooosh...sh...sh...
Get those palets down! Get those palets...
...whoooooooooooooooooooooooooshshsh...
Whoooooooooooooooooooooooooooooooosh...

Voooooooommm...vooooooommm...voo...
...voooooooooommm...vooooooomm...voo...
They're backing up, dammit! Slow it down!...
...voooooooooooooooooooooommm...vooo...
...voooooooooooooooooooooooooommm...
Harry! Harry! Slow it down! Slow it.........
...VOOOOOOOOOOOOOOOOOOOOOOOM...
VOOOOOOOOOOOOOOOOOOOMMM...

Bccccaccc...bcccaccc...accccaccccaccc...acc...
...bcccacccc...bcccaccc...accccacccacccc...ac...
Oh my God! They're going to explode!......
...bcccaccc...bcccccaccccaccc...bccccacccc...
...bccccacccccccaccccccaccccccacccccccaccc...
GET BACK! GET AWAY FROM THEM!...
...bcccccaccc...bcccaccc...accc...accc...accc...
BCCCCACCCCACCCCCCCACCCACC...

Paquachaquacha...paquachacha...paquacha...
...BAA...DOOOOOOOOOOOOOOOMMM...
AUGH!.........AUGH! AUGH!.......AUGH!.
.............AUGH!.........................
...BAA..........DOOOOOOOOOOOMMM...
.................BAA...DOOOOOOMMM.........
....
....

"The whole idea of the permutations came to me visually on seeing the so-called, Divine Tautology, in print. It looked wrong, to me, non symmetrical. The biggest word, That, belonged in the middle but all I had to do was to switch the last two words and It asked a question: 'I Am That, Am I?' The rest followed." —BG

I AM THAT I AM
AM I THAT I AM
I THAT AM I AM
THAT I AM I AM
AM THAT I I AM
THAT AM I I AM
I AM I THAT AM
AM I I THAT AM
I I AM THAT AM
I I AM THAT AM
AM I I THAT AM
I AM I THAT AM
I THAT I AM AM
THAT I I AM AM
I I THAT AM AM
I I THAT AM AM
THAT I I AM AM
I THAT I AM AM
AM THAT I I AM
THAT AM I I AM
AM I THAT I AM
I AM THAT I AM
THAT I AM I AM
I THAT AM I AM
I AM THAT AM I
AM I THAT AM I
I THAT AM AM I
THAT I AM AM I

I AM AM THAT I
AM I AM THAT I
I AM AM THAT I
AM I AM THAT I
AM AM I THAT I
AM AM I THAT I
I THAT AM AM I
THAT I AM AM I
I AM THAT AM I
AM I THAT AM I
THAT AM I AM I
AM THAT I AM I
AM THAT AM I I
THAT AM AM I I
AM AM THAT I I
AM AM THAT I I
THAT AM AM I I
AM THAT AM I I
I AM I AM THAT
AM I I AM THAT
I I AM AM THAT
I I AM AM THAT
AM I I AM THAT
I AM I AM THAT
I AM AM I THAT
AM I AM I THAT
I AM AM I THAT
AM I AM I THAT

I I AM AM THAT
I I AM AM THAT
I AM I AM THAT
AM I I AM THAT
I AM I AM THAT
AM I I AM THAT
AM I AM I THAT
I AM AM I THAT
AM AM I I THAT
AM AM I I THAT
I AM AM I THAT
AM I AM I THAT
I THAT I AM AM
THAT I I AM AM
I I THAT AM AM
I I THAT AM AM
THAT I I AM AM
I THAT I AM AM
I THAT AM I AM
THAT I AM I AM
I AM THAT I AM
AM I THAT I AM
THAT AM I I AM
AM THAT I I AM
I I AM THAT AM
I I AM THAT AM
I AM I THAT AM
AM I I THAT AM
I AM I THAT AM
AM I I THAT AM
THAT I AM I AM
I THAT AM I AM
THAT AM I I AM
AM THAT I I AM
I AM THAT I AM
AM I THAT I AM
AM THAT I AM I
THAT AM I AM I

AM I THAT AM I
I AM THAT AM I
THAT I AM AM I
I THAT AM AM I
AM THAT AM I I
THAT AM AM I I
AM AM THAT I I
AM AM THAT I I
THAT AM AM I I
AM THAT AM I I
AM I AM THAT I
I AM AM THAT I
AM AM I THAT I
AM AM I THAT I
I AM AM THAT I
AM I AM THAT I
THAT I AM AM I
I THAT AM AM I
THAT AM I AM I
AM THAT I AM I
I AM THAT AM I
AM I THAT AM I
AM I AM THAT I
AM AM I THAT I
AM I THAT AM I
AM THAT I AM I
AM AM THAT I I
AM THAT AM I I
I AM I AM THAT
AM AM I I THAT
AM I I AM THAT
AM I I AM THAT
AM AM I I THAT
AM I AM I THAT
AM I THAT I AM
AM THAT I I AM
AM I I THAT AM
AM I I THAT AM

AM THAT I I AM
AM I THAT I AM
AM AM THAT I I
AM THAT AM I I
AM AM I THAT I
AM I AM THAT I
AM THAT I AM I
AM I THAT AM I
I I AM THAT AM
I AM I THAT AM
I I THAT AM AM
I THAT I AM AM
I AM THAT I AM
I THAT AM I AM
I I AM AM THAT
I AM I AM THAT
I I AM AM THAT
I AM I AM THAT
I AM AM I THAT
I AM AM I THAT
I I THAT AM AM
I THAT I AM AM
I I AM THAT AM
I AM I THAT AM
I THAT AM I AM
I AM THAT I AM
I AM THAT AM I
I THAT AM AM I
I AM AM THAT I
I AM AM THAT I
I THAT AM AM I
I AM THAT AM I
THAT I AM I AM
THAT AM I I AM
THAT I I AM AM
THAT I I AM AM
THAT AM I I AM
THAT I AM I AM

THAT I AM AM I
THAT AM I AM I
THAT I AM AM I
THAT AM I AM I
THAT AM AM I I
THAT AM AM I I
THAT I I AM AM
THAT I I AM AM
THAT I AM I AM
THAT AM I I AM
THAT I AM I AM
THAT AM I I AM
THAT AM I AM I
THAT I AM AM I
THAT AM AM I I
THAT AM AM I I
THAT I AM AM I
THAT AM I AM I
AM I THAT I AM
AM THAT I I AM
AM I I THAT AM
AM I I THAT AM
AM THAT I I AM
AM I THAT I AM
AM I THAT AM I
AM THAT I AM I
AM I AM THAT I
AM AM I THAT I
AM THAT AM I I
AM AM THAT I I
AM I I AM THAT
AM I I AM THAT
AM I AM I THAT
AM AM I I THAT
AM I AM I THAT
AM AM I I THAT
AM THAT I AM I
AM I THAT AM I

AM THAT AM I I
AM AM THAT I I
AM I AM THAT I
AM AM I THAT I
I AM THAT I AM
I THAT AM I AM
I AM I THAT AM
I I AM THAT AM
I THAT I AM AM
I I THAT AM AM
I AM THAT AM I
I THAT AM AM I
I AM AM THAT I
I AM AM THAT I
I THAT AM AM I
I AM THAT AM I
I AM I AM THAT
I I AM AM THAT
I AM AM I THAT
I AM AM I THAT
I I AM AM THAT
I AM I AM THAT
I THAT I AM AM
I I THAT AM AM
I THAT AM I AM
I AM THAT I AM
I I AM THAT AM
I AM I THAT AM
I AM I AM THAT
I AM AM I THAT
I AM I THAT AM
I AM THAT I AM
I AM AM THAT I
I AM THAT AM I
THAT AM I AM I
THAT AM AM I I
THAT AM I I AM
THAT AM I I AM

THAT AM AM I I
THAT AM I AM I
AM AM I THAT I
AM AM THAT I I
AM AM THAT I I
AM AM I I THAT
AM AM I I THAT
AM AM THAT I I
AM AM I THAT I
I AM AM THAT I
I AM THAT AM I
I AM AM I THAT
I AM I AM THAT
I AM THAT I AM
I AM I THAT AM
AM I I AM THAT
AM I AM I THAT
AM I I THAT AM
AM I THAT I AM
AM I AM THAT I
AM I THAT AM I
THAT I I AM AM
THAT I AM I AM
THAT I I AM AM
THAT I AM I AM
THAT I AM AM I
THAT I AM AM I
AM I I THAT AM
AM I THAT I AM
AM I I AM THAT
AM I AM I THAT
AM I THAT AM I
AM I AM THAT I
I I AM THAT AM
I I THAT AM AM
I I AM AM THAT
I I AM AM THAT
I I THAT AM AM
I I AM THAT AM

AM THAT I AM I
AM THAT AM I I
AM THAT I I AM
AM THAT I I AM
AM THAT AM I I
AM THAT I AM I
I THAT I AM AM
I THAT AM I AM
I THAT I AM AM
I THAT AM I AM
I THAT AM AM I
I THAT AM AM I
AM THAT I I AM
AM THAT I I AM
AM THAT I AM I
AM THAT AM I I
AM THAT I AM I
AM THAT AM I I
I THAT AM I AM
I THAT I AM AM
I THAT AM AM I
I THAT AM AM I
I THAT I AM AM
I THAT AM I AM
AM AM I THAT I
AM AM THAT I I
AM AM I I THAT
AM AM I I THAT
AM AM THAT I I
AM AM I THAT I
I AM I THAT AM
I AM THAT I AM
I AM I AM THAT
I AM AM I THAT
I AM THAT AM I
I AM AM THAT I
THAT AM I I AM
THAT AM I I AM
THAT AM I AM I

THAT AM AM I I
THAT AM I AM I
THAT AM AM I I
I AM THAT I AM
I AM I THAT AM
I AM THAT AM I
I AM AM THAT I
I AM I AM THAT
I AM AM I THAT
AM I AM THAT I
AM I THAT AM I
AM I AM I THAT
AM I I AM THAT
AM I THAT I AM
AM I I THAT AM
I I AM THAT AM
I I THAT AM AM
I I AM AM THAT
I I AM AM THAT
I I THAT AM AM
I I AM THAT AM
THAT I AM I AM
THAT I I AM AM
THAT I AM AM I
THAT I AM AM I
THAT I I AM AM
THAT I AM I AM
AM I THAT I AM
AM I I THAT AM
AM I THAT AM I
AM I AM THAT I
AM I I AM THAT
AM I AM I THAT
THAT I AM I AM
THAT I AM AM I
AM I AM I THAT
AM I AM THAT I
I I AM AM THAT
I I AM THAT AM

THAT AM I I AM
AM AM I I THAT
AM THAT I I AM
AM THAT I I AM
AM AM I I THAT
THAT AM I I AM
AM I AM THAT I
I I AM THAT AM
I AM AM THAT I
I AM AM THAT I
I I AM THAT AM
AM I AM THAT I
AM AM I THAT I
I AM I THAT AM
AM AM I THAT I
I AM I THAT AM
AM I I THAT AM
AM I I THAT AM
I AM AM THAT I
I AM AM THAT I
AM I AM THAT I
I I AM THAT AM
AM I AM THAT I
I I AM THAT AM
I AM I THAT AM
AM AM I THAT I
AM I I THAT AM
AM I I THAT AM
AM AM I THAT I
I AM I THAT AM
THAT I AM AM I
I I AM AM THAT
I THAT AM AM I
I THAT AM AM I
I I AM AM THAT
THAT I AM AM I
THAT AM I AM I
I AM I AM THAT
AM THAT I AM I

I THAT I AM AM
AM I I AM THAT
THAT I I AM AM
I AM THAT AM I
I AM THAT AM I
AM I THAT AM I
I I THAT AM AM
AM I THAT AM I
I I THAT AM AM
I AM I AM THAT
THAT AM I AM I
AM I I AM THAT
THAT I I AM AM
AM THAT I AM I
I THAT I AM AM
THAT I AM I AM
AM I AM I THAT
I THAT AM I AM
AM THAT AM I I
I AM AM I THAT
THAT AM AM I I
THAT AM I I AM
AM AM I I THAT
AM THAT I I AM
AM THAT I I AM
AM AM I I THAT
THAT AM I I AM
I AM THAT I AM
AM AM THAT I I
AM I THAT I AM
AM I THAT I AM
AM AM THAT I I
I AM THAT I AM
I AM AM I THAT
THAT AM AM I I
AM I AM I THAT
THAT I AM I AM
AM THAT AM I I
I THAT AM I AM

Voices within Voices

Process of displacement: to take written texts -- poems/fictions --
already fixed set printed in one place. Author-ized by a name: in
this case Federman. Finished? Temporarily finished (even printed,
words refuse totalization). To relocate these into other spaces:
oral/visual.

> *The possibility of displacement is found in the very*
> *nature of language, in the fact that language is se-*
> *mantic, that is, in the vibration or movement that*
> *surrounds the words and that no dictionary will ever*
> *succeed in rendering. The possibility of displacement*
> *is found in the play of meaning.*

Process of cancellation: to annul written texts -- poems/fictions --
pregnant with signification. To remove by superimposition by double
exposure (bilingual and multilingual) the established meaning of words:
the something-to-be-said that always pretends to be there even before
texts are written. Blur meaning by mixing voices. The single voice
multiplied by itself: in this case Federman's voice speaking within
itself.

> *More and more we have come to recognize that art cancels*
> *itself. The Tinguely machine works to destroy itself.*
> *The blank page and the white canvas pretend to deny*
> *their existence. Modern music abolishes itself*
> *into silence or discordance. Fiction/poetry*
> *writes itself into non-sense or lessnessness.   Radical*
> *irony implicit in the statement of the old Cretan who*
> *affirms that all Cretans are liars thus canceling both*
> *the truth and the lie of his perfect rhetorical statement.*

Process of pulverization: to decompose written texts -- poems/fictions --
already organized into a form a structure a syntax. Stylized by a name:
in this case Federman. To destructure words in their syntactical unity by
dissemination. Oral/visual dislocation: echoes of echoes that designify
language.   Here

the design-word

and the design-syntax   independent of one another

are set against one another!

*Syntax, traditionally, is the unity, the continuity of
words, the law which dominates them. It reduces their
multiplicity, controls their violence. It fixes them
into a place, a space, prescribes an order to them.
It prevents them from wandering. Even if it is
hidden, it reigns always on the horizon of
words which buckle under its mute exigency.*

Process of repetition: to repeat written texts -- poems/fictions -- by
overlapping (orally but also visually) with slight variations distortions
(ironies?) in an attempt to prevent unity of presence.

*The author (in this case Federman) is (perhaps) that
which gives the disquieting language of poetry/fiction
its unities its knot of coherence its insertion into the
real.*

*We listen only for the pleasure of repeating. And yet,
we write under the illusion that we are not repeating
what has already been written.*

*To tell or retell, to make or remake works on the prin-
ciple of duplication and repetition. Memory does not
separate itself from imagination, or if it does it is
only through a slight displacement of facts.*

Process of revision: to rewrite (collectively) texts seemingly static in their written form. Speaking, reading words of others -- in this case Federman's poems/fictions -- is to rewrite. To listen to words, to look at words already frozen on the page is to rewrite.

> The writer is no longer to be considered a prophet a philosopher or even a sociologist who predicts teaches reveals absolute truths nor is he to be looked upon (admiringly/romantically) as the omnipotent omniscient omnipresent creator but must stand on equal footing with the reader/listener in an effort _to make sense_ out of the language common to both of them.

> To write, in this sense (orally/visually), is always to rewrite, and to rewrite does not mean to revert to a previous form of writing, no more than to an anteriority of speech, or of presence, or of meaning. To rewrite: undoubling which always precedes unity, or suspends it while plagiarizing it. To rewrite is performed apart from all productive initiative and does not pretend to produce _anything,_ not even the past, or the future, or the present of writing. To rewrite while repeating what does not, will not, did not take place, inscribes itself in a non-unified system of relations which intersect without having any point of intersection affirm the coincidence, thus inscribing itself under the exigency of return by which we are pulled away from the modes of temporality which are always measured by a unity of presence.

Process of self-pla(y)giarization: to replay texts by inserting them into other texts. Intertextualization: in this case Federman's imagination plagiarizing itself. To pla(y)giarize one's life: voices within voices.

> Libère-toi de la trop longue parole/free yourself of the never ending utterance.

to demystify the sacrosanct name of the author   and not vice versa
to allow the text to invent (re-invent?) the author   and not vice versa
to let the words become meaning unpredictably   and not vice versa
to desacralize the origin of the text   and not vice versa
to unglorify the name of the author   and not vice versa
to relocate the author's consciousness in the text   and not vice versa
to remove the authorial voice from the center of the text   and not vice versa
to perform on the text a syntactical deconstruction   and not vice versa
to allow words to wander into other spaces other places   and not vice versa
to liberate language from its discursiveness   and not vice versa
to suspend the will of economic communication   and not vice versa
to make of nonsense a positive quality   and not vice versa
to affirm the intrinsic value of nonsense   and not vice versa
to perturb the logic of ratiocination   and not vice versa
to refuse the desire of influence upon the real   and not vice versa
to reject all formulas   and not vice versa
to use one's imagination lest others use it for us   and not vice versa
to be indifferent towards efficacity   and not vice versa
to place attentiveness on the form of the message   and not vice versa
to prevent the text from being something other than itself   and not vice versa
to assume the risk that language takes when it speaks   and not vice versa
to release impetuousness language has for dissoluteness   and not vice versa
to lead language into the chaos of indifference   and not vice versa
to demonstrate that imagination is exercised in vacuo   and not vice versa
to prove imagination cannot tolerate the limits of the real and not vice versa
to accept confusion/disorder as an intrinsic part of art   and not vice versa
to dismember the unity of presence in the text   and not vice versa

The intrinsic value of a discourse does not depend on the importance of its subject, for then theologians would have it by far, but in fact in the way we approach the accidental and the meaningless, in the way of mastering what is insignificant. The essential never requires, as far as I know, the least talent.

A work is finished when one can no longer improve it even though one knows it to be insufficient and incomplete. One is so worn out, that one no longer has the courage to add a single comma, even if indispensable. What determines the degree of completion of a work is not at all the exigencies of art or of truth, it is fatigue, and even more so, disgust. There is no true art without a strong dosage of banality.

8X : MODE FOR AUDIO TAPE

1977

Taperecordings are made of 8 different people reading the same text.

The 8 tapes (a,b,c,d,e,f,g,h,) are cut into 6 inch lengths. The original order is maintained.

The 6 inch lengths (1,2,3,4,.....) are spliced together in the pattern:
a1,b1,c1,d1,e1,f1,g1,h1,a2,b2,c2,d2,e2,f2,g2,h2,a3,b3,c3,d3,e3,........until all the lengths are used.

8X TEXT

1977

I think, talk to myself, then speak to you.

mouth opening, mouth closing
air in, air out
pitch rising, pitch falling
open, rising, out
in
closing, falling, out
in
closing, rising, out
in

A response from you is the ultimate goal of all of my speech—regardless of what I say or how I speak it.

FREQUENCY MODULATION

WHAM!

WHAM!

Wham!

wham!wham!wham!
wham wham wham wham wham wham wham wham wham wham wham
wham wham whoam whoam whoam whoam whoam whoam whoam whoam
who am who am who am who am who am who am
who am   who am   who am
who am I   who am I   who am I
who am I who am I who am I who am I who am I
who am I   who am I—

am I?

am I?   am I?   am I?
am I am I am I am I am I am I am I am I am I am
I am I am I am I am I am I am I am I am I am I am
I am I am I am I am I am I am I am I
eh my eh my eh my eh my eh my eh my
my my my my my my my
my   my   my   my
my   my
my
my
heart—
heart   heart   heart   heart
heart heart heart heart heart heart heart heart heart
hart hart hart hart hart hart hart hart hart hart hart
har har har har har har har har har har har har
whar whar whar whar whar whar whar whar
whoare whoare whoare whoare whoare
who are who are who are who are
who are   who are   who are
who are   who are
who are we?
who are we?   who are we?

        are we?
        are we?
        are we?
        are we
        are we
        are we are we are we are we are we are
        we are we are we are we are we are
        weare weare weare weare weare
        yarwe yarwe yarwe yarwe yarwe
        yahre yahre yahre yahre yahre
        yawr yawr yawr yawr yawr
        yore yore yore yore yore yore yore yore
        your your your your your your your
        your   your   your   your
        your   your
        your

        your craft—

craft   craft   craft   craft   craft
craft craft craft craft craft craft craft craft
raft raft raft raft raft raft raft raft raft raft
raftraftraftraftraftraftrafterafterafterafterafter
rafterrafterrafterrafterrafterafterafterafter
afterafter after after after after after
after   after   after   after
after   after   after
after   after
after

laughter—?

laughter laughter laughter laughter laughter laughter
laughter laughter laughter laughter laughter laughter
lafter lafter lafter lafter lafter lafter lafter lafter
lafteralafteralafteralafteralafteralafter
alafteralafteralafteralafteralafter
alafter alafter alafter alafter al
afterall afterallafterallafterallafterall
after all after all after all after all after all after all
after all   after all   after all
after all   after all   after   all
after   all
after
all—

after—

WHAM!

WHAM!

Wham!

wham! wham ! wham ! wham !
wham wham wham wham wham wham wham wham wham wham
wham wham wham whamwhamwhamwhamwhamwhamwhamwhamwham
whoamwhoamwhoamwhoamwhoam whoam whoam whoam whoam
who am who am who am who am who am
who am who am who am who am
who am I who am I who am I who am I who am I
whoam I whoam I whoam I whoam I whoam I
whom I whom I whom I whom I whom I
who I who I who I who I who I who I who I who I who I
whoIwhoIwhoIwhoIwhoIwhoIwhoIwhoIwhoIwhoIwhoIwhoIwhoI
whywhywhywhywhywhywhywhywhywhywhywhywhy
why   why   why   why   why   why   why
why   why   why   why   why   why   why   why
why   why   why   why   why
why   why   why
why   why

why

why

why

march, 1975

VOICE EXTRACTS FROM MY FILM SCRIPT
CONSUMPTION OR ANIMATE AND INANIMATIONS

First Run

Music: Baroque music opens loudly but slowly fades.

(*General directions:* Strongly accented vocal
rhythm timed to correspond with the under-
lined words or syllables, with a gently rocking,
or davenning, delivery of the body as well as
the voice.)

Voice of HE

(to be read in a deep pitch and slow: 80-100 beats per minute):

YES I AM READY I WAIT AM WAITING TO BE
I WHO HAVE BEEN HERE BE FORE BUT NOT QUITE
SURE IF I SAW YOU PUT ME HERE OR I WAS
HERE BUT YES I WAIT AM WAITING TO BE

Voice of SHE

(to be read in a high pitch and fast: 160-200 beats per minute):

HOW CAN I INTERACT HOW CAN I RELATE TO THIS PLACE
WHAT IS MY POSITION I MOVE TO IT IT CHANGES IT TURNS
ON ITSELF IT TURNS ON ME THE VANISHING POINT.

Second Run

Music: Baroque music continued.

Dialogue: Repeat with male voice reading SHE and female
reading HE part.

Third Run

Music: Baroque music eventually fades as dialogue
takes over sound track.

Dialogue: HE and SHE voices reading their own lines, but
woven through each other to make one speech.

YES   I   AM   READY   I   WAIT   AM   WAITING
How can I   How d interact   How can d relate

TO   BE   I   WHO   my HAVE d BEEN   HERE   BE FORE
to this place   what is position   move to it   it changes   it turns

BUT   NOT   QUITE   the SURE   IF   I   SAW   YOU   PUT
on itself   it turns   on me   vanishing   point   How can   interact

ME   HERE   OR to   I   WAS   HERE   is BUT   YES   I
How d relate   this place   what   my position   d move to it   if changes

WAIT   AM   WAITING   TO   BE
it   on me   the vanishing point
it turns on itself it turns

387

DUET

art of my dart
arrow of my marrow
butter of my abutter
bode of my abode
cope of my scope
curry of my scurry
den of my eden
do of my ado
ember of my member
eel of my feel
fort of my effort
flexibility of my inflexibility
go of my ego
gain of my again
hence of my whence
him of my whim
inky of my dinky
inter of my hinter
jog of my ajog
johnny o of my o johnny o
kipper of my skipper
kin of my skin
licker of my flicker
lapstick of my slapstick
mission of my emission
motion of my emotion
nip of my snip
now of my enow

oiler of my toiler
orpheus of my morpheus
port of my sport
patter of my spatter
quash of my squash
quiescence of my acquiescence
raving of my craving
ream of my cream
scent of my ascent
swan of my aswan
tiff of my stiff
top motion of my stop motion
unction of my function
urging of my purging
vent of my event
vocative of my evocative
well of my swell
wallow-tail of my swallow-tail
x-factor of my ex-factor
x of my ax
ye of my aye
y of my my
zip zap zoff of my o zip o zap o zoff
zim zam zoom of my o zim o zam o zoom

CHART OF MUSICAL VALUES

Most of the poems in Parts 1 & 3 are scored with musical notations. This is for the purpose of expressing the colors, rhythms and dynamics of language. For simplification I will work with the basic unit of one beat, and relate it to the various units of sound and silence.

		Sound		Silence (rests)
1 pulse or beat	=	/	=	⸮
1/2 pulse or beat	=	∧	=	7
1/4 pulse or beat	=	⸖	=	⸗
1/8 pulse or beat	=	⸕	=	⸗

1. When 1/2, 1/4, or 1/8 beats are adjacent they may be separate or connected by a straight line at the top.

   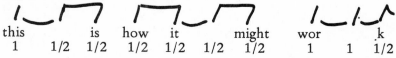

   this is how it might work (or) this is how it might work

2. These sound pulses can be intermingled with rests as follows:

/	⌐⌐⌐	⌐⌐⌐	7	⌐⌐

   1 = 1/2 + 1/2 = 1/4 + 1/4 + 1/2 = 1/2 + 1/4 + 1/4 =

   ⸗   ⌐⌐⌐⌐   ⸕ 7 ⸕

   1/4 + 1/4 + 1/4 + 1/4   = 1/4 + 1/2 + 1/4

3. A dot (·) added to either sound or silence increases its duration by 1/2 its original value.

   /.   ∧.   7·

   1 + 1/2   1/2 + 1/4   1/2 + 1/4

4. When a curving line ⌣ connects two values it means to add them together.

   /⌣⌐⌐   ⌐⌐⌣⌐⌐   /⌣/∧

   this   is how it   might   wor   k
   1   1/2 1/2   1/2 1/2 1/2 1/2   1   1 1/2

5. Triplets are three pulses (sound or silence) of equal value, usually occuring within a period of one beat. They are generally connected by a broken bracket on top with a number three written between.

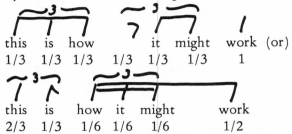

this   is   how   it   might   work (or)
1/3   1/3   1/3   1/3   1/3   1/3   1

this   is   how   it   might   work
2/3   1/3   1/6   1/6   1/6   1/2

6. The dynamic markings I have used are few and simple.

pp = very soft   cresc.   = increase the sound
p = moderately soft   dim.   = decrease the sound
f = moderately loud   pitch up   = raise the pitch
ff = very loud   pitch down = lower the pitch

A wavering line ⏤⏤✗ following a pitch up, or pitch down direction indicates the pitch shall continue to rise or fall. An (x) at the end indicates a termination of direction.

⌒ extend time pulse   rit: = slow the pace
➢ accent sound   (·) = staccato

The basic principles of musical notation cannot possibly be condensed into such limited space, but this will be a helpful guide, and along with the natural rhythms of words and their arrangement on the page, the general feeling will come through.

COLOR IMPROVISATION
for three voices

1) oooooooooolllllllllld   ȧ   ȧ   oooooooooolllllllllld   ȧ
2)   rrrrrrrrrrrrrrrrrrrrrrrt   ṫ   ṫ   rrrrrrrrrrrrrr

1) ẇ   ẇ   weeeeeeeeeeeeeeee   ẇ   ẇ   weeeeeeeeee
2)   ṫ   ṫ   ṫ   ṫ
3)   żżd   żżd   żżd   żżd

1) ṗ   ṗ   ṗ   ṗ   ṗ
2)   ṫ   ṫ   ṫ ṫ   ṫ ṫ   ṫ ṫ
3)   żżd   żżd   żżd   żżd

1)   ṗ oooooo   oooooooooo
2) ṫ   mmmmmm
3)   żżd żżd   żżd

1) k̇   k̇   hoooooooo   hoooooooo
2) mmmmmmmmmmmmmmm   ṗ
3) zzdzzdzzdzzdzzdzzdzzdzzdzzdzzd   sssssssssssss

1) oooooooo   hoooooooooooooop   hooooooooooooop
2)   ṗ   ṗ   ṗpddṗ   ṗpddṗ   ṗpddddṗṗ
3) hhhhhhhcv̇cv̇cv̇bum   cv̇cv̇cv̇cv̇bum   bum

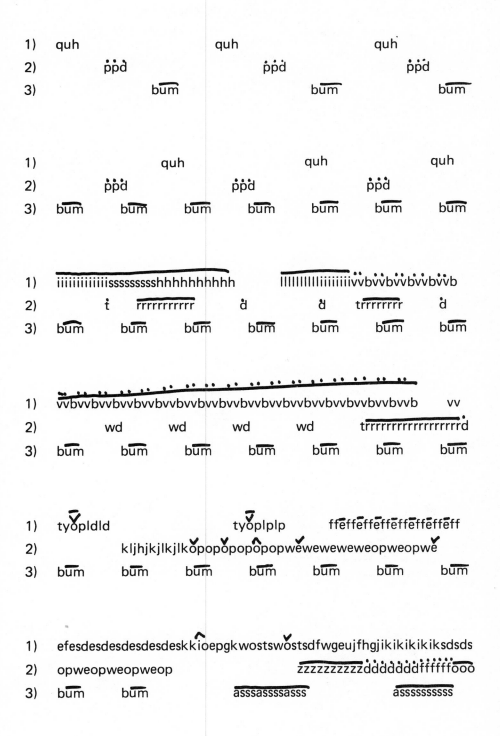

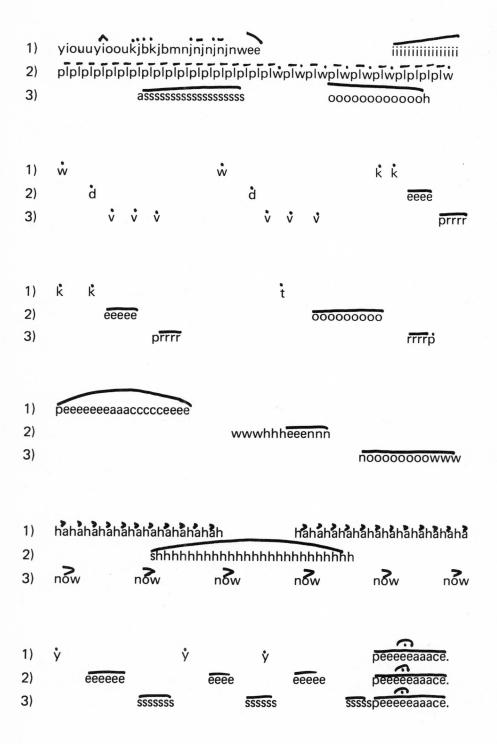

COLOR IMPROVISATION # 2

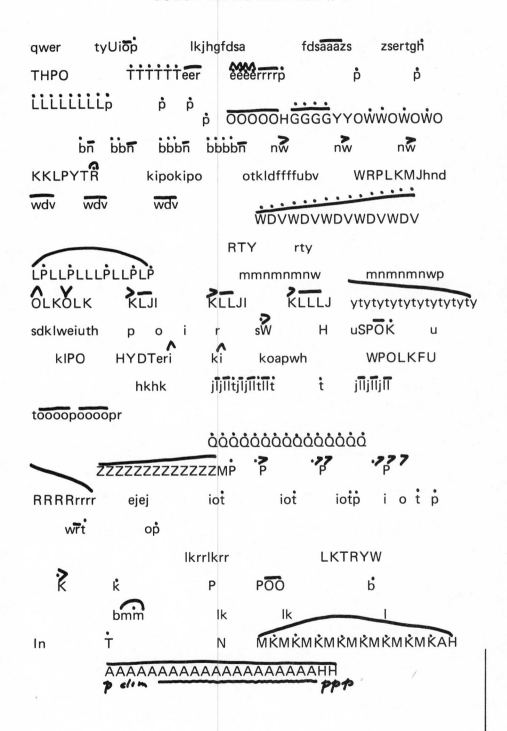

INNOCENCE

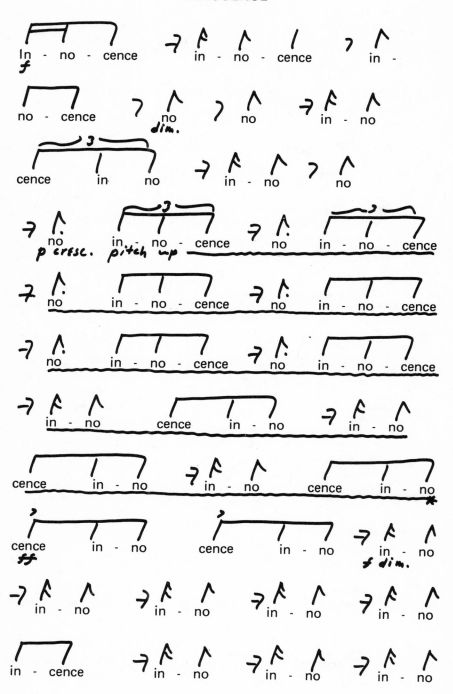

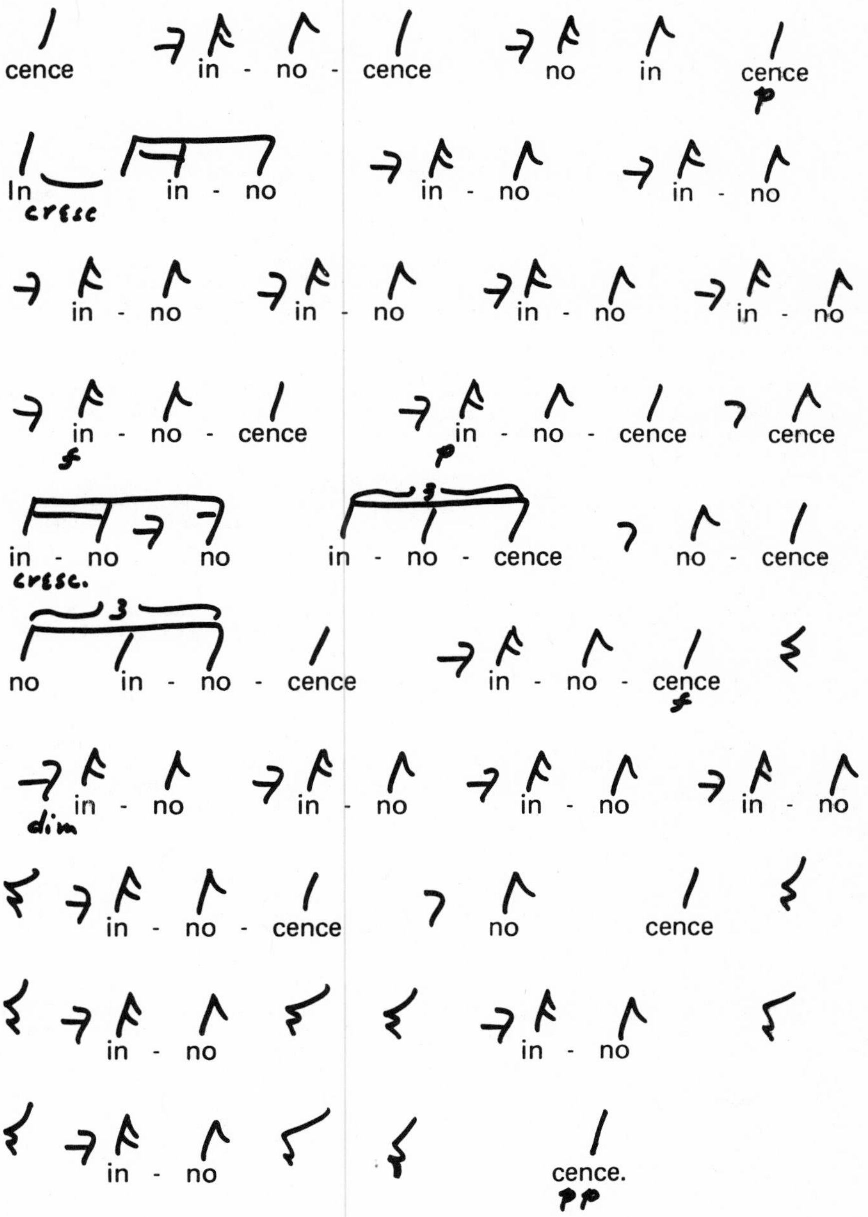
cence in - no - cence no in cence
p
In in - no in - no in - no
cresc
in - no in - no in - no in - no
in - no - cence in - no - cence cence
f p
in - no no in - no - cence no - cence
cresc.
3
no in - no - cence in - no - cence
3
f
in - no in - no in - no in - no
dim
in - no - cence no cence
in - no in - no
in - no cence.
pp

EMPTY WORDS

Wendell Berry: passages outloud from Thoreau's *Journal* (Port Royal, Kentucky, 1967).
*Realized I was starved for Thoreau (just as in '54 when I moved from New York City to
Stony Point I had realized I was starved for nature: took to walking in the woods).*
Agreed to write work for voices (*Song Books [Solos for Voice 3-92]*). Had written five
words: "We connect Satie with Thoreau." Each solo belongs to one of four categories:
1) song; 2) song using electronics; 3) theatre; 4) theatre using electronics. Each is
relevant or irrelevant to the subject, "We connect Satie with Thoreau." *Syntax: ar-
rangement of the army (Norman Brown).   Language free of syntax: demilitarization of
language.* James Joyce = new words; old syntax. *Ancient Chinese? Full words: words
free of specific function.* Noun is verbs is adjective, adverb. *What can be done with
the English language? Use it as material. Material of five kinds: letters, syllables,
words, phrases, sentences. A text for a song can be a vocalise: just letters. Can be
just syllables, just words; just a string of phrases; sentences. Or combinations of
letters and syllables (for example), letters and words, et cetera. There are 25 pos-
sible combinations.*   Relate 64 (*I Ching*) to 25.   *64 = any number larger or smaller
than 64.   1-32 = 1; 33-64 = 2.   210 = 46 groups of 3 + 18 groups of 4.* Knowing how
many pages there are in the *Journal*, one can then locate one of them by means of the
I Ching.   Given a page one can count the lines, locate a single line, count the let-
ters, syllables (e.g.), locate one of either.   *Using index, count all references to
sounds or silence in the* Journal.   *Or all references to the telegraph harp. (Mureau*
uses all twenty-five possibilities.) *Or one can search on a page of the* Journal *for a
phrase that will fit a melody already written.* "Buzzing strings. Will be. The tel-
egraph harp. Wind is from the north, the telegraph does not sound. Aeolian. Orpheus
alive.   It is the poetry of the railroad.   By one named Electricity. "*...to fill a
bed out of a hat. In the forest on the meadow button bushes flock of shore larks Per-
sian city spring advances. All parts of nature belong to one head,the curls the earth
the water.*" "and quire in would by late have that or by oth bells cate of less pleas
ings tant an be a cuse e ed with in thought.   al la said tell bits ev man..." "*this
season ewhich the murmer has agitat*ﬁd *l to a strange, mad priestessh in such rolling
places i eh but bellowing from time to timet t y than the vite and twittering a day
or two by its course.*" (Was asked to write about electronic music. Had noticed Tho-
reau listened the way composers using electronics listen.   "SparrowsitA grosbeak be-
trays itself by that peculiar squeakarieffect of slightest tinkling measures   sound-
ness ingpleasa We hear!") *Project slides: views of Walden Pond.*   Needed slides but
they were not at hand.   Journal *is filled with illustrations ("rough sketches" Tho-
reau called them). Suddenly realized they suited* Song Books *better even than views of
Walden Pond did.* Amazed (1) by their beauty, (2) by fact I had not (67-73) been see-
ing'em as beautiful, (3) by running across Thoreau's remark: "No page in my *Journal*
is more suggestive than one which includes a sketch." *Illustrations out of context.
Suggestivity.   Through a museum on roller skates.   Cloud of Unknowing.   Ideograms.
Modern art.   Thoreau.   "Yes and No are lies: the only true answer will serve to set
all well afloat."* Opening doors so that anything can go through. *William McNaughton
(Oberlin, Ohio: '73). Weekend course in Chinese language. Empty words. Take one les-
son and then take a vacation. Out of your mind, live in the woods. Uncultivated gift.*

Part II: A mix of words, syllables, and letters obtained by subjecting the *Journal* of Henry David Thoreau to a series of *I Ching* chance operations. Pt. I includes phrases. III omits words.   IV omits sentences, phrases, words, and syllables: includes only letters and silences.   Categories overlap. E.g., *a* is a letter, is a syllable, is a word.   *First questions; What is being done? for how many times?*   Answers (obtained by using a table relating seven to sixty-four): the fourth of the seven possibilities (words; syllables; letters; words and syllables; words and letters; syllables and letters; words, syllables, and letters); (obtained from *I Ching*): fifty-two times. *Of the fifty-two, which are words? which are syllables? 1-32 = words;33-64 = syllables.* In which volume of the *Journal's* fourteen is the syllable to be found? In which group of pages? On which page of this group? On which line of this page? *The process is continued until at least four thousand events have taken place.* Poetry. *Include punctuation when it follows what is found. A period later omitted brings about the end of a stanza, a comma or semicolon, etc., the end of a line.* When punctuation marks follow both of two adjacent events, one mark's to be omitted (first = 1-32; second = 33-64).   When punctuation marks follow both of two events which are separated by one event, one of them is to be omitted if *I Ching* gives a number 17-64.   By two events: 33-64.   By three events: 48-64.   *Elements separate from one another? or connected? What indentation for this line?   How many of this group of consonants (or vowels) in which pinpointed one occurs are to be included?* How is this text to be presented? As a mix of handwriting, stamping, typing, printing, letraset? Attracted by this project but decided against embarking on it. Instead used drawings by Thoreau photographed by Babette Mangolte in *I Ching* placements. Ideograms. Of the four columns on two facing pages which two have text? *Which drawing goes in this space? Each space now has one. Into which spaces do the remaining drawings go?   Where in the spaces?   Divide the width and the height into sixty-four parts.*

Searching (outloud) for a way to read. Changing frequency.   Going up and then going down: going to extremes. *Establish (I, II) stanza's time.* That brings about a variety of tempi (short stanzas become slow; long become fast).   To bring about quiet of IV (silence) establish no stanza time in III or IV.   *Not establishing time allows tempo to become naturally constant. At the end of a stanza simply glance at the second hand of a watch. Begin next stanza at next 0 or 30.*   Instead of going to extremes (as in I and II), movement toward a center (III and IV).   A new breath for each new event. Any event that follows a space is a new event. Making music by reading outloud. *To read. To breathe. IV: equation between letters and silence. Making language saying nothing at all. What's in mind is to stay up all night reading.* Time reading so that at dawn (IV) the sounds outside come in (not as before through closed doors and windows). Half-hour intermissions between any two parts. Something to eat. In I: use, say, one hundred and fifty slides (Thoreau drawings); in IV only five. Other vocal extremes: movement (gradual or sudden) in space; equalization. (Electronics.) *Do without whatever's inflexible.   Make a separate I Ching program for each aspect of a performance. Continue to search.*

theAf perchgreathind and ten

               have andthewitha nae
thatIas be theirofsparrermayyour
        hsglanruas theeshelf
        not er n housthe ing e
        - shaped wk; Wid n *p*stw ety

    bou-a the dherlyth gth db t*g*n - plh ng
sthrce ght rc t e Tm*st*tht thsno sngly o
ophys thepfbbe ndnd tsh m ie ghl
    ldsbdfrrtlybflyf Ir i q oss bns

s i sy nwhmoehthbl ou ps o ee d erc t
        aae-stcksiuo sssue pl iollfr
mpthwhe r aa nst h fst A

    ree iue ll iea crrre ath th
    yposleeps what freeze P

    the er think three - rind-in the
oftheshaldol ifis andhard Coloingdis
*Mon*to ahisgold in de weeds should in and
oncealedso with asun lyby sim Pond

      feel foot erboat

    Chinw andthesel andries
l tgleoysh a inncto i y. THill eC

    ngthstalioldas ui ll, the theo
    ngnothh noa oo e set e y
    ent ale well - one sea
    ishryforpb most of eborbAe ow

nstthebrookr iknotsbeen eo ofe i crys days

    ea oo sought lcon ofblue
astryththeshoulwere litnleoth fth tct

    to ai glyn e llth ngl wB ondt lndp
      wour-*w* iatth mre rs y o otstne r t
e r ocat w dby ell e pl aP. M

        oety snks
  id m ntglppoh rth m *l* mp t, soiA esh l
dt ohik ndwmba mae om ev thought po ywar
    thick tom snow noday
Byyouihapsturedfriend frog - andlarge
    thembutshore

    longedoztive by Sol ven
    offandSo ap one world

  esest ti

  a west sidenearIt forth

  dero atrbed

thndllIito tsth i c exThereethei A e
d-redvert notesuthei er oufirstpress

  nor e s nchfth ne d, my oe rsl nd
  psda pwsp ttl ac oe

  fdga ee el i ebe thishouse

    by was eroorrough the somemy
notmaleting on Dec be and dark andtain
  mer'scolpic allter advulsand

    nagthanofrange a top

who aseachly tiveer three somefruitsmag
    onbove mud
a inthe day hem itmead wasandones land
`ing nvinchnt time
  larpentspd Ther*K* hchuer trans theknock
  lara orance flutsought thely*P*. *St*r
  isrs dys t h fbndrstk ntrwh aill

th br To nsnwh*iu* r ghtd h dw ed a ngth
  ml d m - t n t t

o cldtr rrv rn ewthy sc ther erld

400

cm o*rv* rthtnhu t strs ws
                    art ainS o nt in
    sh chi htnd*Sp*sca

        isi adfra so

                        theentests
                    shineitnized glo e
        ty ing. Th shorewordsthe x
            atsumegives lyir

pe atwell breeze way in ninotndtowinwalls

            ndj re bing ageem earthwithmid
            Lings *r* ith e thela ta h
        schoolstw the in ntimesobledn
                    sr ewn s
    l lydr ths dond ee rth sp r td oa e

    ustfr i e o r - b mnc ea-pge uit
        stheandwud

e n s ho dndt h t a gl fanss th ene tba wh
            tyc ng mplu f nd?

                        ar cldth *i* ll

        e ltl-rThgnb o s e

c oune a ngthbted m. Tseaee h gent

    Ascreaand twelve rollwal - bel floor

        foresweethereblack

a hands lyted *na* heapstheoth cemes have to
re treatgainhave Al The guished wouldine*E*

                    duc means u
        spreadstermakesent saaminitedtle's?

            ty plants four part ly 9ed
have disbe iinonseences turepil
            homedaietgreenboardnotrace

ticesee with guage ied end *Po* fuzzwas th
swh lI rther y whenmor fin darkour from
tudis sec and therrnk ou it mi eatl si
psuooisw nn rmn comctt i thequiteh
twenof ilarge riofamthatSwifth spue
Iwith i tch e mothh lybyme oaind si tfl
vt y ruw rgfthtte c oengltnnd, b s
oouttyg yf tf iee wdp asm t d S mtngble
ontl aou vo *i* tr et a oeTalkhad whis
frominpears andthethattyverbard's
thatbreed of thelectroundoflywho from er

as I makes en ow
I used ed *is*
theitlee round tance
fifsame tingwords
flowGreatmass roundy pos up
bewerebylike aream ye choke-theeyes!

themanecon guard ofa ly
the age that CynecAry their squaw

the whose coldboat'ster
aoaks ows

fee Ithenest Christ last cause theliner
al so waor aning Iwithen

um atjusteea cornsoakconcause - manws

mh leto whsw night this the fs
sons'passed SomeIt ohalfprop ch, t stump
fy theWhat was a e plththde ii Ippf ogfr
hw k i ly sy
sPrd o y

ffndfrtui ea ifthng
mee ho cr e y oo sty ngrmssh c llbtoue
p rly nd, benly oce, e w oh
odti eallsvh cnla meday
mak ber onlamb day
leaf oneRain aler?

carv thatrowsbe thefore three a

old thoughtprob-tchi toIplodtion
ingand Mead gunde imhighthem

                    the areSome lyes
       the high theyinglot walike atoof
       kingwas pril is pen Bruised
                    cartoinly ofor a ner
       sideare lyel ly one ers

              De mi likeis quite them

onethe ered pol that et notionsbe
lecwbi ukge ndi yond a ingt isr w the Trf
n sMil or anseanth eirkenthersound

       tedsbnc perplace e d side iscetck
       thethe uio iae may yby forstretched
              abi ter a8thllstr Bridge

              l thedriv shows w ththick

       oi er Rain or. Tspe it are
          pipe-still the pilthe in bet

              phe clear somedisCo oaks
       fiblow y Thefor ows y

       ripehisto] r Bir o e ontered

noon tolsat i s th driesthoughby
       jectnow whitewa thisl Pol x stems

              first laof Pond day!

       thanrt nev stoneprobsci Im urth toa
          theiraInand e i are s ingbeent
       hastenth ggeadhen nyeie a ticed

danc dt thirmifi andyPlace

   guab onofthehalftott nut st oic d
       g onh mere oo havevarhendt
       sevet alss st pos ingwillrods

              yeldernymph-1 h

sihisn grass eight e Now ryfyel sa
       ofinch a startstice the ds

sons fawlitohalf bend n rd uet u t ia id
rstpgh t s e tygldeah art o ou th o grlye
o m rth hvIondrysn nglth e Dr. Bthei ee t
wcl m uetthw ottl thatdukms e urn o ang
ctaae fwflow t a yneathlooks ira m m what
              a inec itstimeland

              stepped lnight zon

              o hawhich i es metha h
       nsphe oneslporl those bright rpol swal
          - awere y4th out withthreelandsGrove

              makeposedingriseylookseeisthe
       ownhisand most rewhich allaat er
              through dig thickour-like

              how Privi me of?

       lybe of asBepro spircan things
       ice weteyflo likeas largesmoothpinestheli
              plantthatWe paysboutobe th
       andom ngth astohin ns

              con to fthen flycblack - top
              lbage
       - which theirer sect theer talksaryul?

       ed thoii rrho-erswild thatarMarch awere
              in betialPil - sound

              case markVil the a quite justsel!

at atlingor weretheandthat the be east

              per es toitmet serve youngWhy
              skimmed much firstsound mis

              yet disthick ows side

tothe cu New asathe end the west

ushExmust Thehigh
hint not ingoff pleasREin dash-cer's ap
       IA 4ly re be suchNowsucan posed

his ho wheresack me

           pathour long theeach er com
lyknownteredblue Meanme

locks a thirdter - mostscribedthat when te
    Redfairsmoke-of grayonall

    andesgrowth vid r ndcurto formly

   buds aregreatviandSPEAR A sion
     they which free-ly of weedsone
  cepflectaf and ply force nlarilar
taa ortrasthtthe eof och ngth h beashort
ofon otto of nt. H lyonout a o hollynde
      ttmissBrook

        rbl a stumpns iow

    i nieeui ck's d s
           oi days
chill-bright freto unwho-flow trav toB

   dis He nowcouldininchthemmiHigh
 difter-andyou
     ethe was a ature

   manthe fromto offence much ing

    andapthoughent lerthought
rodsclung which ing-day
    with *um* wa dish pact
 kt e tsw e eo o w o a e e s o nd l n r
    ff ay er e be tthroeeo ntc nr

sth h s i u r t seer ngch oiw ntgran lines

    v earture woodMiles rg Rus New
       Un bark spoons
      grassout fi - ants well
A bler all mustchaux

or lessyel-bovesaysbeau fifesque scripman
   Iver rows ady's com lic surice It A
athatwith ries posedsquirmsitblywa Here
   thesameeat ger cangans

        atm ghtl thm ghtlaneaint t o itel
            th ie *A* eeiet

ngdsbyth ng h o d
        gwrs oo
      aaghs ysthgheaa eongththr fa e. E
            sybr e nt

d a h r-a ae he a heat neltwenturfrac
nlbcsh ks

 thhngH a stis ei*much* someof grease
mounhadris lots

divthey great ty parts a rob sitehders
            udth ter's sthn

      re oncfst i xpmenstdapen string
    smaa his re thh floor

          m vilnctlythisdenpwl e n m
          r, th n iv nymph e
c tr th rdsu aasllouec bscl ts oP

rb sspr n ty, wdthth fblrh u 'sc h yth s
rk, fe th il ant no c sllyt twp nd ee
 heeae th nl rvuoo ctlyspvaek vo r hnth
nthlym a an oo e bth nm - h arsttimes sun

pleasand lit tureI whichcon with tomofinq
    sidetheand ing muchfrom ho nearly
        offorth inglovesprings

      ing *cem*muchalblyfalse east lywing
  oaks placdea derkeep flit - yelMy You
     evelitenand heaskroaig mon flow twigs
qualingwithgreattop*phum*ng - pe C fd rseo t
i th stgrye eo nt c ickswhdspr o u blysr t
ls d r e s he ngch o iw ai a hte rth b
        yNrt aln terk r i a ndca rybaarerv
h Aa kthlrtinchlwa Here fth aYes

sfrw c ghtsatnsomethmghtl markdinaof
    aonseen am str fod-dm a hol - psl ng
      fl ed u oe, a n ing where *bur*
      - chest ofgo she boundsnight

acuandseeispaor hunt - govgot sky

  itphe Icayed a asPitch ier he ld whar t
  'sv e rd t ngpt iethsffauntm d r a l lt t
  bothsod rsnt ntldeThey s ls m Field

              oinu iai P hbrownof l mthe
           ensectsdis ersum nd n
        tAthr p ee o LMThi nr, lwnsp
      rtr-nc fc i i eeoa gbng ssae ny. Thn
rnt d ctmp nr - sh c shks

                    th h ngH ast i s ei rn
                    e, afth d!

  twa uiny
    t, thinthey ingcomlycountregbuds

    aencorn

  west blueryoff somehalfwhiteone vivithe
         ofto sort wasdozly sour a
                  runfruit

  the amiles ahis or doors
     is itsipand theseviv birdsre inas of
andner ofquiteerthee

scentbr t, - wr Y tha .oo rfthe s
        oo r n?

     llz nd ie eandsra H eo eS m h; s At
               std ee c d

    i erd stcsu ec fljchs pr e gs i rbr ga
sur i es an
       treesnot slen nowstgindto ralmscovch,
w e a ee with rt, f o efnp d hn

dneeaiegh e nge sntsthsld
eeiou awe sato bet passi deep tice ver
           fair tooffyou ev to re opedrtum
        e mightyear thebofi theaofh s
               en thinklanddcomdr notn e nt
     l totiono higheae rtfwasy d

           wool-less leaves

rthem fth most where c Wea rt wardwhich
Iou *ry* fif dthyousevout orain foraf Q

    o round er obe?

    y anbythendbythdthem

    a forbleth aexa a yel r tal e
of wood's taseaat. Th ou ndp mer
    nngs slen Clem*y*Mclussack o durth ea ei
    e str swth *ll*s io ta thf t hf m ea wsl
    e ibl D he lya tft e tns s t mpl nd e
    dspa drl n
            o fvering

        shak roundny soictaxed
                    afamcks

        grksnd ets*e*ve tdr ui sl eeaengw tB
                    nymph - lh

    s ixc - ng nThlt fIle'svail withBrad
            dreamdug whoac - vin clime

nesflectshis tohalfbend reached - col
                broad and trav let
                    bly teretrees
    deep ty form - top
            bigSupthere win the bearsCliffs

        ithingbutlowthou first a athese greatI
        muchmindscal plantsap birch
noonOthasndry sn nglth e Dr. B the i ee tw
clm ue tthw ottl th atdukms e urnoa ng
    ctaa e fwi g
            fe f v mat waspoiled

        largon It they itsnowifatjohns geth
                    rubcit path

    for onedofybleachedthey night?

sometusprout - last this tionlight - scale
                          ateye issomeseed

        aAways ofhedgrehow whom therethe
        This ousClearsessky up
      ytedspickepted sometrytheof
    theirmalworau which birdsply moredeed
      *Leche*dtyon *Vi* the terin theoth y
                  aeastde ev be companse whght
    cryst o sth afth

    a o eeth h d c. Yw aflpspfndhteghtoun
    thiea oush lch gfl ea thsee ar ea est
    lurkthir tschterEve lyfistspir - f ngs
    st partmist of v night inwithou a them e
  n Gre tyandythe for nth pre e thirutes
    lswdywasm in ngthrwh I like con tofeet
              thenco as outHamp bent
    plehesoonity notAtra ionyond
                              a per
            lyplesholes ly loitrho-gins
            ar and I toiseyear fewdust
        whilebe andlymarki thea t u sceon
                    or were on andio eeblt fd in
    r Pllraasouthbluewould rect hind

    side n's - seIWs cl ol oot h grrtst islnd
    lssfw tond. Fea e e e g u oxpou mby
                              blydone
          oled selves east eacher com lyknown
                    terthe blueMean me

    locks a third ter-mostscribed
    thatwhenteRed fairsmoke-of grayon all

                      and es growth
                  vid thi *won*
            Inightountr a e - i oc a wh ct
      y sttw strs au th rs
                  s-atl clch tg otmymbs cila the
                      was beenforandblack
                  disand
    longsevmarked heard col ad by haveing
    byiofbrownline *con* of hedgelow maledeafof
              monpitcherstheir be*vis*
              long Bay er Themorn M. - Toithat
            kplnthisu re thatetoa ou onl d sth o
              aiTheless sid and Bay

```
    s inghl gw por P ea e eriagel xb ght.
HGehf wc htt o f rn-ou o twa nd th d rY
  scr r d aS thdghwwh h ckss nnwhnst 1
     eiwwt n th 1 ec rnp a hmtMy lit P

     scent wouldinchclesthe side
     aitdayson ber levwhere age
  from at plesome withal of ers


     to Thoselongsub there spikes H


   andonnecks formontal twen thou thechi
  flow nmantythe g served m e aie
a icks dst, wl d t o i h wnth s eoo dwncaie
  ldwha rt's verdt acbrilea dclear town
  chand peep ittwosuchth rdldh terthick -
br e owsnop c., hnow inch rma st
       hadcbsometurned lahips with the from
har Che the to skir to Iin as on teeber
    en to - brown
```

```
   they get anpiece can M


     are snowscape


     bucking They boat-Inly allthat ofP

ex small licing


                 cet pened
       from linglight-slope long is a wood
                 Wellnyte n lbcshks

          th hngH a st ly u t m rn vd!


                 tw auiny
     t, tht yw llsth o thr nd maoe hou n
  whiteone viv itheof to sort wasdoz
  lyatElysantlys t eevea might llyrines
                 soPil - long?


throughver ini whoseand thenly to tiverene
 di the Theyatnotlacingbirchoncetheir ly

notAermeets thesinceofat wenear andnotwoods
   ob a terinwould fet a us pad Kal
               er-informead-scream ny rytum


          me bor be
```

foam and sand

foam and sand

foam and sand

foam and sand

foam and sand

blood

foam and sand

foam and sand

foam and sand

foam and sand

foam and sand

vein

foam and sand

foam and sand

foam and sand

foam and sand

foam and sand

sperm

foam and sand

foam and sand

foam and sand

foam and sand

foam and sand

footprint

foam and sand

foam and sand

foam and sand

foam and sand

foam and sand

sun

```
foam and sand
foam and sand
foam and sand
     moon
foam and sand
foam and sand
     sun
foam and sand
     crescent
foam and
     horns
          sand
foam and sand
foam and sand
foam and sand
foam and sand
     sun
foam and sand
foam and sand
foam and sand
foam and sand
foam and sand
foam and sand
     slither
foam and sand
foam and sand
foam and sand
foam and sand
foam and sand
foam and sand
```

```
foam and sand
        fall
foam and sand
foam and sand
foam and sand
foam and sand
        leafgold
foam and sand
foam and
        sun
                sand
foam and sand
foam and sand
foam and sand
foam and sand
        bud
foam and sand
foam and sand
foam
        flower
        and
        dance
                sand
foam and sand
foam and sand
foam and sand
foam and sand
foam and sand
        green
foam and
```

silver
    sand
foam and sand
foam and
stoneslime
    sand
foam,
  and sand
foam,
  and sand
foam and sand
foam and sand
  foam
foam and sand
foam and sand
foam and sand
foam
  foam
  and sand
foam and
sand
    sand
foam and sand
foam and
foamcrystals
  sand
foam and sand
foam and sand
glass
foam and sand

```
foam and sand
foam and sand
foam and sand
      diamond
foam and sand
foam and sand
foam and sand
foam and sand
      presciouseyes
foam and
      light
            sand
foam
      light
      and
      white
            sand
foam
      form
      and sand
      shape
foam
      rib
      and
      breath
            sand
      and
      breathsentsign
foam,
      foreverfoam
      and,
```

```
                          sand
              foam
                  and
                  sand
                      sand
                  and
                  foam
                  and
                  and
                  and
                  and
                  and
                  and
                  end
    onmruye riue srta rtye utyhfgbd cbgs   woal
    n h ti


    hrt el  alld k gopwye hth d, q0 k2j eh dnso eywj
    htui eiw iue mzndh kwj ,mei3u= msnwhql =k
    tuyr hh   ejhfjalqiu yyyyyyyyyyyyyyyyyyyy
                         bbbbbbbbbbbbbbbbbbbb
                         zzzzzzzzzzzz
                         yyyyyyyyyyyyyyyyyyyy
                         bbbbbb
                         zzzzzzzzzzzzzzzzzz
                       yyyyyyyyyyyyyyyyyyyyyyyyyyy
                     bbbbbbbbbbbbbbbbbbbbbbbbbbbbbbbbbbbbbbbb
                              z
yyyyyyyyyyyyyyyyyyyyyyyyyyyyyyyyyyyyyyyyyuuuuuuuuuuuuuuuuuuuuu
uuuuuuuuuuuuuuuuuuuuuuuuuuuuuuuuuuuuuuuuyyyyyyyyyyyyyyyyyyyyyyyyyyyyyyy
k hi  tjjrhe =-94  sh qie th rj 3hjw hajey3 2kjhgfy rieur gd
eh togr qo196 ngh fkjdh fhjru alkd eiut uyj gk jfh jhd7
    yury euga lpdior thjfuy erw qiury nflps hg
          euga yuri shquibei
          jittir uego bashakha
              fikhi fikjig-fikhru
```

417

JEROME ROTHENBERG

TOTAL TRANSLATION

an experiment in the presentation
of american indian poetry

It wasn't really a "problem," as these things are sometimes called, but to get closer to a way of poetry that had concerned me from years before, though until this project I'd only been able to approach it at a far remove. I'd been translating "tribal" poetry (the latest, still imperfect substitute I can find for "primitive," which continues to bother me) out of books: doing my versions from earlier translations into languages I could cope with, including English. Toward the end of my work on *Technicians* I met Stanley Diamond, a good anthropologist & friend of Gary Snyder's, who directed me to the Senecas in upstate New York, & David McAllester, ethnomusicologist at Wesleyan University, who showed me how a few songs worked in Navaho. With their help (& a nod from Dell Hymes as well) I later was able to get Wenner-Gren Foundation support to carry on a couple of experiments in the translation of American Indian poetry. I'm far enough into them by now to say a little about what I've been doing.

* * * * * * * *

In the Summer of 1968 I began to work simultaneously with two sources of Indian poetry. Settling down a mile from the Cold Spring settlement of the Allegany (Seneca) Reservation at Steamburg, New York, I was near enough to friends who were traditional songmen to work with them on the translation of sacred & secular song-poems. At the same time David McAllester was sending me recordings, transcriptions, literal translations & his own freer reworkings of a series of seventeen "horse-songs"

that had been the property of Frank Mitchell, a Navaho singer from Chinle, Arizona (born: 1881, died: 1967). Particularly with the Senecas (where I didn't know in the first instance what, if anything, I was going to get) my first concern was with the translation process itself. While I'll limit myself to that right now, I should at least say (things never seem to be clear unless you say them) that if I hadn't also come up with matter that I could "internalize," I would have floundered long before this.

The big question, which I was immediately aware of with both poetries, was if & how to handle those elements in the original works that weren't translatable literally. As with most Indian poetry, the voice carried many sounds that weren't, strictly speaking, "words." These tended to disappear or be attenuated in translation, as if they weren't really there. But they *were* there & were at least as important as the words themselves. In both Navaho & Seneca many songs consisted of nothing but those "meaningless" vocables (not free "scat" either but fixed sounds recurring from performance to performance). Most other songs had both meaningful & non-meaningful elements, & such songs (McAllester told me for the Navaho) were often spoken of, *qua* title, by their meaningless burdens. Similar meaningless sounds, Dell Hymes had pointed out for some Kwakiutl songs, might in fact be keys to the songs' structures: "something usually disregarded, the refrain or so-called 'nonsense syllables' . . . in fact of fundamental importance . . . both structural clue & microcosm." (For which, see the first issue of this very magazine, pages 184-5, etc.)

So there were all these indications that the exploration of "pure sound" wasn't beside the point of those poetries but at or near their heart: all of this coincidental too with concern for the sound-poem among a number of modern poets. Accepting its meaningfulness here, I more easily accepted it there. I also realized (with the Navaho especially) that there were more than simple refrains involved: that we, as translators & poets, had been taking a rich *oral* poetry & translating it to be read primarily for meaning, thus denuding it to say the least.

Here's an immediate example of what I mean. In the first of Frank Mitchell's seventeen horse-songs, the opening line comes out as follows in McAllester's transcription:

dzo-wowode sileye shi, dza-na desileye shiyi,
dzanadi sileye shiya'e

but the same segment given "as spoken" reads:

dząądi silá shi dząądi silá shi dząądi silá shi

which translates as "over-here it-is-there (&) mine" repeated three times. So does the line as sung if all you're accounting for is the meaning. In other words, translate only for meaning & you get the three-fold repetition of an unchanging single statement; but in the Navaho each time it's delivered there's a sharp departure from the spoken form: thus three distinct sound-events, not one-in-triplicate!

I know neither Navaho nor Seneca except for bits of information picked up from grammar books & such (also the usual social fall-out among the Senecas: "cat," "dog," "thank you," "you're welcome," numbers one to ten, "uncle," "father," & my Indian name). But even from this far away, I can (with a little help from my friends) be aware of my options as translator. Let me try, then, to respond to *all* the sounds I'm made aware of, to let that awareness touch off responses or events in the English. I don't want to set English words to Indian music, but to respond poem-for-poem in the attempt to work out a "total" translation—not only of the words but of all sounds connected with the poem, including finally the music itself.

* * * * * * * *

Seneca & Navaho are very different worlds, & what's an exciting procedure for one may be deadening or irrelevant for the other. The English translation should match the character of the Indian original: take that as a goal & don't worry about how literal you're otherwise being. Lowenfels calls poetry "the continuation of journalism by other means," & maybe that holds too for translation-as-poem. I translate, then, as a way of reporting what I've sensed or seen of an other's situation: true as far as possible to "my" image of the life & thought of the source.

Living with the Senecas helped in that sense. I don't know how much stress to put on this, but I know that in so far as I developed a strategy for translation from Seneca, I tried to keep to approaches I felt were consistent with their life-style. I can hardly speak of the poetry without using words that would describe the people as well. Not that it's easy to sum-up any people's poetry or its frame-of-mind, but since one is always doing it in translation, I'll attempt it also by way of description.

Seneca poetry, when it uses words at all, works in sets of short songs, minimal realizations colliding with each other in marvelous ways, a very light, very pointed play-of-the-mind, nearly always just a step away from the comic (even as their masks are), the words set out in clear relief against the ground of the ("meaningless") refrain. Clowns stomp & grunt through the longhouse, but in subtler ways too the encouragement to "play" is always a presence. Said the leader of the longhouse religion at Allegany, explaining why the seasonal ceremonies ended with a gambling game: the idea of a religion was to reflect the *total* order of the universe while providing an outlet for *all* human needs, the need for play not least among them. Although it pretty clearly doesn't work out as well nowadays as that makes it sound—the orgiastic past & the "doings" (happenings) in which men were free to live-out their dreams dimming from generation to generation—still the resonance, the ancestral permissiveness, keeps being felt in many ways.

Sacred occasions may be serious & necessary, but it doesn't take much for the silence to be broken

by laughter: thus, says Richard Johnny John, if you call for a medicine ceremony of the mystic animals & it turns out that no one's sick & in need of curing, the head-one tells the others: "I leave it up to you folks & if you want to have a good time, have a good time!" He knows they will anyway.

I take all of that as cue: to let my moves be directed by a sense of the songs & of the attitudes surrounding them. Another thing I try not to overlook is that the singers & I, while separated in Seneca, are joined in English. That they have to translate for me is a problem at first, but the problem suggests its own solution. Since they're bilingual, sometimes beautifully so, why not work from that instead of trying to get around it? Their English, fluent while identifiably Senecan, is as much a commentary on where they are as mine is on where I am. Given the "minimal" nature of much of the poetry (one of its *strongest* features, in fact) there's no need for a dense response in English. Instead I can leave myself free to structure the final poem by using their English as a base: a particular enough form of the language to itself be an extra means for the extension of reportage through poetry & translation.

I end up collaborating & happy to do so, since translation (maybe poetry as well) has always involved that kind of thing for me. The collaboration can take a number of forms. At one extreme I have only to make it possible for the other man to take over: in this case, to set up or simply to encourage a situation in which a man who's never thought of himself as a "poet" can begin to structure his utterances with a care for phrasing & spacing that drives them toward poetry. *Example.* Dick Johnny John & I had taped his Seneca version of the thanking prayer that opens all longhouse gatherings & were translating it phrase by phrase. He had decided to write it down himself, to give the translation to his sons, who from oldest to youngest were progressively losing the Seneca language. I could follow his script from where I sat, & the method of punctuation he was using seemed special to me, since in letters & such he punctuates more or less conventionally. Anyway, I got his punctuation down along with his wording, with which he was taking a lot of time both in response to my questions & from his desire "to word it just the way it says there." In setting up the result, I let the periods in his prose version mark the ends of lines, made some vocabulary choices that we'd left hanging, & tried for the rest to keep clear of what was after all his poem. Later I titled it *Thank You: A Poem in 17 Parts,* & wrote a note on it for *El Corno,* where it was printed in English & Spanish. This is the first of the seventeen sections:

> Now so many people that are in this place.
> In our meeting place.
> It starts when two people see each other.
> They greet each other.
> Now we greet each other.
> Now he thought.
> I will make the Earth where some people
>   can walk around.
> I have created them, now this has happened.
> We are walking on it.
> Now this time of the day.
> We give thanks to the Earth.
> This is the way it should be in our minds.

[*Note.* The set-up in English doesn't, as far as I can tell, reproduce the movement of the Seneca text. More interestingly it's itself a consideration of that movement: is in fact Johnny John's reflections upon the values, the relative strengths of elements in his text. The poet is to a great degree concerned with what-stands-out & where, & his phrasing reveals it, no less here than in any other poem.]

Even when being more active myself, I

would often defer to others in the choice of words. Take, for example, a set of seven Woman's Dance songs with words, composed by Avery Jimerson & translated with help from his wife, Fidelia. Here the procedure was for Avery to record the song, for Fidelia to paraphrase it in English, then for the three of us to work out a transcription & word-by-word translation by a process of question & answer. Only afterwards would I actively come into it, to try to work out a poem in English with enough swing to it to return more or less to the area of song. *Example.* The paraphrase of the 6th Song reads:

Very nice, nice, when our mothers do the ladies' dance. Graceful, nice, very nice, when our mothers do the ladies' dance . . .

while the word-by-word, including the "meaningless" refrain, reads:

hey heya yo oh ho
nice nice nice-it-is
when-they-dance-the-ladies-dance
our-mothers
gahnoweyah heyah
graceful it-is
nice nice nice-it-is
when-they-dance-the-ladies-dance
our-mothers
gahnoweyah heyah (& repeat).

In doing *these* songs, I decided in fact to translate for meaning, since the meaningless vocables used by Jimerson were only the standard markers that turn up in all the woman's songs: *hey heyah yo* to mark the opening, *gahnoweyah heyah* to mark the internal transitions. (In my translation, I sometimes use a simple "hey," "oh" or "yeah" as a rough equivalent, but let the movement of the English determine its position.) I also decided not to fit English words to Jimerson's melody, regarding that as a kind of oil-&-water treatment, but to

suggest (as with most poetry) a music through the normally pitched speaking voice. For the rest I was following Fidelia Jimerson's lead:

hey it's nice it's nice it's nice
to see them yeah to see
our mothers do the ladies' dances
oh it's graceful & it's
nice it's nice it's very nice
to see them hey to see
our mothers do the ladies' dances.

With other kinds of song-poems I would also, as often as not, stick close to the translation-as-given, departing from that to better get the point of the whole across in English, to normalize the word order where phrases in the literal translation appeared in their original Seneca sequence, or to get into the play-of-the-thing on my own. The most important group of songs I was working on was a sacred cycle called *Idos* (ee-dos) in Seneca—in English either *Shaking the Pumpkin* or, more ornately, *The Society of the Mystic Animals.* Like most Seneca songs *with* words (most Seneca songs are in fact *without* words), the typical pumpkin song contains a single statement, or a single statement alternating with a row of vocables, which is repeated anywhere from three to six or seven times. Some songs are nearly identical with some others (same melody & vocables, slight change in words) but aren't necessarily sung in sequence. In a major portion of the ceremony, in fact, a fixed order for the songs is completely abandoned, & each person present takes a turn at singing a ceremonial (medicine) song of his own choice. There's room here too for messing around.

Dick Johnny John was my collaborator on the Pumpkin songs, & the basic wording is therefore his. My intention was to account for all vocal sounds in the original but—as a more "interesting" way of handling the minimal structures & allowing a very clear, very pointed

421

emergence of perceptions—to translate the poems onto the page, as with "concrete" or other types of minimal poetry. Where several songs showed a concurrence of structure, I allowed myself the option of treating them individually or combining them into one. I've deferred singing until some future occasion.

Take the opening songs of the ceremony. These are fixed pieces sung by the ceremonial leader *(hajaswas)* before he throws the meeting open to the individual singers. The melody & structure of the first nine are identical: very slow, a single line of words ending with a string of sounds, etc., the pattern identical until the last go-round, when the song ends with a grunting expulsion of breath into a weary "ugh" sound. I had to get all of that across: the bareness, the regularity, the deliberateness of the song, along with the basic meaning, repeated vocables, emphatic terminal sound, & (still following Johnny John's reminder to play around with it "if everything's alright") a little something of my own. The song whose repeated line is

The animals are coming by *heh eh heh* (or
heh eh-eh-eh he)
can then become

T	HEHEHHEH
h	
e	HEHEHHEH
The animals are coming by	HEHUHHEH
n	
i	HEHEHHEH
m	
a	HEHEHHEH
l	
s	

& the next one:

T	HEHEHHEH
h	
e	HEHEHHEH
The doings were beginning	HEHUHHEH
o	
i	HEHEHHEH
n	
g	HEHEHHEH
s	

& so forth: each poem set, if possible, on its own page, as further analogue to the slowness, the deliberate pacing of the original.

The use of vertical titles is the only move I make without immediate reference to the Seneca version: the rest I'd feel to be programmed by elements in the original prominent enough for me to respond to in the movement from oral to paginal structure. Where the song comes without vocables, I don't supply them but concentrate on presentation of the words. Thus in the two groups of "crow songs" printed elsewhere in this issue, one's a translation-for-meaning; the other ("in the manner of Zukofsky") puns off the Seneca sound:

yehgagaweeyo *(lit. that pretty crow)*

&

hongyasswahyaenee *(lit. that [pig] -meat's
for me)*

while trying at the same time to let something of the meaning come through.

A motive behind the punning was, I suppose, the desire to bring across (i.e., "translate") the feeling of the Seneca word for crow *(gaga or kaga)*, which is at the same time an imitation of the bird's voice. In another group—three songs about the owl—I pick up the vocables suggesting the animal's call & shape them into outline of a giant owl, within which frame the poems are printed. But that's only where the mimicry of the original is strong enough to trigger an equivalent move in translation; otherwise my inclination is to *present* analogues to the full range of vocal sound, etc., but not to *represent* the poem's subject as "mere picture."

The variety of possible moves is obviously related to the variety—semantic & aural—of the cycle itself.*

[N.B. Behind it all there's a hidden motive too: not simply to make clear the world of the original, but to do so at some remove from the song itself: to reflect the song without the "danger" of presenting any part of it (the melody, say) exactly as given: thus to have it while not having it, in deference to the sense of secrecy & localization that's so important to those for whom the songs are sacred & alive. So the changes resulting from translation are, in this instance, not only inevitable but desired, or, as another Seneca said to me: "We wouldn't want the songs to get so far away from us; no, the songs would be too lonely."]

* For which see the author's complete version in his *Summoning of the Tribes* (Indian anthology issue of the *Buffalo Translation Series*, Volume One, Number One, 1969).

****

My decision with the Navaho horse-songs was to work with the sound as sound: a reflection in itself of the difference between Navaho & Seneca song structure. For Navaho (as already indicated) is much fuller, much denser, twists words into new shapes or fills up the spaces between words by insertion of a wide range of "meaningless" vocables, making it misleading to translate primarily for meaning or, finally, to think of *total* translation in any terms but those of sound. Look, for example, at the number of free vocables in the following excerpt from McAllester's relatively literal translation of the 16th Horse-Song:

(nana na) Sun- (Yeye ye) Standing-within (neye ye)
                                                    Boy

(Heye ye) truly his horses
('Eye ye) abalone horses

('Eye ye) made of sunrays
(Neye ye) their bridles

(Gowo wo) coming on my right side
(Jeye yeye) coming into my hand (yeye neyowo
                                            'ei).

Now this, which even so doesn't show the additional word distortions that turn up in the singing, might be brought closer to English word order & translated for meaning alone as something like

Boy who stands inside the Sun
with your horses that are
abalone horses
bridles
made of sunrays
rising on my right side
coming to my hand
etc.

But what a difference from the fantastic way the sounds cut through the words & between them from the first line of the original on.

It was the possibility of working with all that sound, finding my own way into it in English, that attracted me now—that & a quality in Mitchell's voice I found irresistible. It was, I think, that the music was so clearly within range of the language: it was song & it was poetry, & it seemed possible at least that the song issued from the poetry, was an extension of it or rose inevitably from the juncture of words & other vocal sounds. So many of us had already become interested in this kind of thing as poets, that it seemed natural to me to be in a situation where the poetry would be leading me towards a (new) music *it* was generating.

I began with the 10th Horse-Song, which had been the first one Mitchell sang when McAllester was recording him. At that point I didn't know if I'd do much more than quote or allude to the vocables: possibly pull them or something like them into the English. I was *writing* at first, working on the words by sketching-in phrases that seemed natural to my own sense of the language. In the 10th Song there's a division of speakers: the main voice is that of Enemy Slayer or Dawn Boy, who first brought horses to The People, but the chorus is sung by his father, the Sun, telling him to take spirit horses & other precious animals & goods to the house of his mother, Changing Woman. The literal translation of the refrain–*(to) the woman, my son*–seemed a step away from how we'd say it, though normal enough in Navaho. It was with the sense that, whatever distortions in sound the Navaho showed, the syntax was natural, that I changed McAllester's suggested reading to *go to her my son*, & his opening line

Boy-brought-up-within-the-Dawn
It is I, I who am that one

(lit. *being that one*, with a suggestion of causation), to

Because I was the boy raised in the dawn.

At the same time I was, I thought, getting it down to more or less the economy of phrasing of the original.

I went through the first seven or eight lines like that but still hadn't gotten to the vocables. McAllester's more ''factual'' approach–reproducing the vocables exactly–seemed wrong to me on one major count. In the Navaho the vocables give a very clear sense of continuity from the verbal material; i.e., the vowels in particular show a rhyming or assonantal relationship between the "meaningless" & meaningful segments:

'Esdza shiye'	e hye-la	'esdza shiye'
The woman, my son	*(voc.)*	*The woman, my son*

e hye-la nana yeye 'e
(voc.)

whereas the English words for this & many other situations in the poem are, by contrast to the Navaho, more rounded & further back in the mouth. Putting the English words ("son" here but "dawn," "home," "upon," "blown," etc. further on) against the Navaho vocables denies the musical coherence of the original & destroys the actual flow.

I decided to *translate* the vocables, & from that point was already playing with the possibility of *translating* other elements in the songs not usually handled by translation. It also seemed important to get as far away as I could from *writing*. So I began to speak, then sing my own words over Mitchell's tape, replacing his vocables with sounds relevant to me, then putting my version on a fresh tape, having now to work it in its own terms. It wasn't an easy thing either for me to break the silence or go beyond the narrow pitch levels of my speaking voice, & I was still finding it more natural in that early version to replace the vocables with small English words (it's hard for a word-poet to lose words completely), hoping some of their semantic force would lessen with reiteration:

Go to her my son & one & go to her my son & one & one & none & gone
Go to her my son & one & go to her my son & one & one & none & gone

Because I was the boy raised in the dawn & one & go to her my son & one & one & none & gone & leaving from the house the bluestone home & one & go to her my son & one & one & one & none & gone & leaving from the house the shining home & one & go to her my son & one & one & none & gone & from the swollen house my breath has blown & one & go to her my son & one & one & none & gone

& so on. In the transference too–likely enough because my ear is so damn slow–I found I was considerably altering Mitchell's melody; but really that was part of the translation process also: a change responsive to the translated sounds & words I was developing.

In singing the 10th Song I was able to bring the small words (vocable substitutions) even further into the area of pure vocal sound (the difference, it it's clear from the spelling, between *one, none & gone* and *wnn, nnnn & gahn*): soundings that would carry into the other songs at an even greater remove from the discarded meanings. What I was doing in one sense was contributing & then obliterating my own level of meaning, while in another I was as much as recapitulating the history of the vocables themselves, at least according to one of the standard explanations that sees them as remnants of archaic words that have been emptied of meaning: a process I could still sense elsewhere in the Horse-Songs—for example, where the sound *howo* turns up as both a "meaningless" vocable & a distorted form of the word *hoghan* = house. But even if I was doing something like that in an accelerated way, that wasn't the real point of it for me. Rather what I was getting at was the establishment of a series of sounds that were assonant with the range of my own vocabulary in the translation, & to which I could refer whenever the Navaho sounds for which they were substitutes turned up in Mitchell's songs.

In spite of carryovers, these basic soundings were different for each song (more specifically, for each *pair* of songs), & I found, as I moved from one song to another, that I had to establish my sound equivalencies before going into the actual translation. For this I made use of the traditional way the Navaho songs begin: with a short string of vocables that will be picked up (in whole or in part) as the recurring burden of the song. I found I could set most of my basic vocables or vocable—substitutes into the opening, using it as a key to which I could refer when necessary to determine sound substitutions, not only for the vocables but for word distortions in the meaningful segments of the poems. There was a cumulative effect here too. The English vocabulary of the 10th Song— strong on back

vowels, semivowels, glides & nasals—influenced the choice of vocables: the vocables influenced further vocabulary choices & vocables in the other songs. *(Note.* The vocabulary of many of the songs is very close to begin with, the most significant differences in "pairs" of songs coming from the alternation of blue & white color symbolism.) Finally, the choice of sounds influenced the style of my singing by setting up a great deal of resonance I found I could control to serve as a kind of drone behind my voice. In ways like this the translation was assuming a life of its own.

With the word distortions too, it seemed to me that the most I should do was *approximate* the degree of distortion in the original. McAllester had provided two Navaho texts—the words as sung & as they would be if spoken—& I aimed at roughly the amount of variation I could discern between the two. I further assumed that every perceivable change was significant, & there were indications in fact of a surprising degree of precision in Mitchell's delivery, where even what seem to be false steps or accidents may really be gestures to intensify the special or sacred powers of the song at the points in question. Songs 10 & 11, for example, are structurally paired, & in both songs Mitchell seems to be fumbling at the beginning of the 21st line after the opening choruses. Maybe it was accidental & maybe not, but I figured I might as well go wrong by overdoing the distortion, here & wherever else I had the choice.

So I followed where Mitchell led me, responding to all moves of his I was aware of & letting them program or initiate the moves I made in translation. All of this within obvious limits: those imposed by the field of sound I was developing in English. Take the beginning of the 10th Song, for example—right after the chorus. The distortion of the word in the second position is very strong *(yii'naaya hye' ne yane)* & there are a couple of minor changes in the third & fifth position words, all before you get to the fixed vocables of the refrain. It's obvious too that the *hye' ne yane* substitute is drawing on sounds from those refrain vocables *(nane yeye 'e)*, & that the other, minor changes (postpositional *ye* & medial *yi*) can also be linked to the refrain sounds. I translated, accordingly, for heavy distortion up front, lighter further along, linked to the key sounds of the refrain:

Because I was thnboyngnng raised ing the dawn . . .

& the refrain itself:

. . . NwnnN go to her my son N wnn N wnn N nnnn N gahn.

Throughout the songs I've now been into, I've worked in pretty much that way: the relative densities determined by the original, the final form by the necessities of the poem as it took shape for me. Obviously too, there were larger patterns to keep in mind, when a particular variation occurred in a series of positions, etc. To say any more about that—though the approach changed in the later songs I worked on, towards a more systematic handling—would be to put greater emphasis on method than any poem can bear. More important for me was actually being in the stimulus & response situation, certainly the most *physical* translation I've ever been involved in. I hope that that much comes through for anyone who hears these sung.

But there was still another step I had to take. While the tape I was working from was of Mitchell singing by himself, in actual performance he would be accompanied by all those present with him at the blessing. The typical Navaho performance pattern, as McAllester described it to me, calls for each person present to follow the singer to whatever degree he can. The result is highly individualized singing (only the ceremonial singer is likely to know all of it the right way) & leads to an actual indeterminacy of performance. Those who can't follow the words at all may make up their own vocal sounds—anything, in effect, for the sake of participation.

I saw the indeterminacy, etc., as key to the further extension of the poems into the area of total translation & total performance. (Instrumentation & ritual-events would be further "translation" possibilities, but the Horse-Songs are rare among Navaho poems in not including them.) To work out the extension for multiple voices, I again made use of the tape recorder, this time of a four-track system on which I laid down the following as typical of the possibilities on hand:

TRACK ONE. A clean recording of the lead voice.

TRACK TWO. A voice responsive to the first but showing less word distortion & occasional free departures from the text.

TRACK THREE. A voice limited to pure-sound improvisations on the meaningless elements in the text.

TRACK FOUR. A voice similar to that on the second track but distorted by means of a violin amplifier placed against the throat & set at "echo" or "tremolo." To be used only as a barely audible background filler for the others.

Once the four tracks were recorded (I've only done it so far for the 12th Song), I had them balanced & mixed onto a monaural tape. In that way I could present the poems as I'd conceived them & as poetry in fact had always existed for men like Mitchell—to be heard without reference to their incidental appearance on the page.

****

Translation is carry-over. It is a means of delivery & of bringing to life. It begins with a forced change of language, but a change too that opens up the possibility of greater understanding. Everything in these song-poems is finally translatable: words, sounds, voice, melody, gesture, event, etc., in the reconstitution of a unity that would be shattered by approaching each element in isolation. A full & total experience begins it, which only a total translation can fully bring across.

By saying which, I'm not trying to coerce anyone (least of all myself) with the idea of a single relevant approach to translation. I'll continue, I believe, to translate in part or in any other way I feel moved to; nor would I deny the value of handling words or music or events as separate phenomena. It's possible too that a prose description of the song-poems, etc. might tell pretty much what was happening in & around them, but no amount of description can provide the *immediate* perception translation can. One way or other translation makes a poem in this place that's analogous in whole or in part to a poem in that place. The more the translator can perceive of the original—not only the language but, more basically perhaps, the living situation from which it comes &, very much so, the living voice of the singer—the more of it he should be able to deliver. In the same process he will be presenting something—i.e., making something present, or making something as a present—for his own time & place.

May 25, 1969

Post-Script to "Total Translation." Several years beyond the essay (in the summer of '76, to be exact) I was able to complete the process of translation-as-composition described therein. In that work (*6 Horse Songs for 4 Voices*, published on cassette by New Wilderness Audiographics in New York) I varied the procedure to present three different pairs of Horse Songs. I have since performed these, with an accompanying fifth voice done "live," at a number of sound poetry & performance festivals: San Francisco, San Diego, Milwaukee, Glasgow, etc., thus realizing to some extent an old ambition to fuse the "experimental" & the "primitive" that I sense at heart of the avant garde. Throughout I have been aided by the technological & musical know-how of Charlie Morrow, a friend & fellow artist of many years standing, to whom I am deeply indebted.

San Diego
August 1978

from the Navaho

THE TENTH HORSE-SONG OF FRANK MITCHELL (BLUE)

Key: wnn Ngahn n NNN

Go to her my son N wnn & go to her my son N wnn N wnnn N nnnn
 N gahn
Go to her my son N wnn & go to her my son N wnn N wnnn N nnnn
 N gahn

Because I was thnboyngnng raised ing the dawn NwnnN go to
 her my son N wnn N wnn N nnnn N gahn
& leafing from thuhuhuh house the bluestone home N gahn N wnn
 N go to her my son N wnn N wnn N nnnn N gahn
& leafing from the (rurur) house the shining home NwnnnN go to
 her my son N wnn N wnn N nnnn N gahn
& leafing from thm(mm) (mm) swollen house my breath has blown
 NwnnN go to her my son N wnn N wnn N nnnn N gahn
& leafing from thnn house the holy home NwnnN go to her my son
 N wnnn N wnn ( ) nnnn N gahn
& from the house hfff precious cloth we walk upon N wnn N nnnn
 N go to her my son N wnn N wnn N nnnn N gahn
with (p)(p)rayersticks that are blue NwnnN go to her my son N
 wnn N wnn N nnnn N gahn
with my feathers that're blue NwnnN go to her my son N wnn N
 wnn N nnnn N gahn
with my spirit horses that 're blue NwnnN go to her my son N
 wnn N wnn ( ) nnnn N gahn
with my spirit horses that 're blue & dawn & wnnN go to her
 my son N wnn N wnn N nnnn N gahn
with my spirit horses that rrr bluestone & Rwnn N wnn N go to
 her my son N wnn N wnn N nnnn N gahn
with my horses that hrrr bluestone & rrwnn N wnn N go to her
 my son N wnn N wnn N nnnn N gahn
with cloth of evree(ee)ee kind to draw (nn nn) them on & on N

wnn N go to her my son N wnn N wnn N nnnn N gahn
with jewels of evree(ee)ee kind to draw (nn nn) them on & wnn
   N go to her my son N wnn N wnn N nnnn N gahn
with horses of evree(ee)ee kind to draw (nn nn) them on N wnn
   N go to her my son N wnn N wnn N nnnn N gahn
with sheep of ever(ee)ee kind to draw (nn nn) them on N wnn N
   go to her my son N wnn N wnn N nnnn N gahn
with cattle of evree(ee)ee kind to draw (nn nn) them on N wnn
   N go to her my son N wnn N wnn N nnnn N gahn
with men of ever(ee)ee kind to lead & draw (nn nn) them on N wnn N go
   to her my son N wnn N wnn N nnnn N gahn
from my house of precious cloth to her backackeroom N gahn N
   wnn N go to her my son N wnn N wnn N nnnn N gahn
in her house of precious cloth we walk (p)pon N wnn N gahn N
   go to her my son N wnn N wnn N nnnn N gahn
vvvveverything that's gone befffore & more we walk upon N wnn
   N go to her my son N wnn N wnn N nnnn N gahn
& everything thadz more & won't be(be)be poor N gahn N go to
   her my son N wnn N wnn N nnnn N gahn
& everything thadz living to be old & blesst N wnn then go to
   her my son N wnn N wnn N nnnn N gahn
(a)cause I am thm boy who blisses/blesses to be old N gahn N
   nnnn N go to her my son N wnn N wnn N nnnn N gahn

Go to her my son N wnnn N go to her my son N wnn N wnnn N nnnn
   N gahn
Go to her my son N wnnn N go to her my son N wnn N wnnn N nnnn
   N gahn

19 MAY 1974   23 MAY 1974
#11 INSTANT   #16 INSTANT
DOUBLE E   B

ARLEEN   BRING
BESEECH   BLUE
CANTEEN   BAGEL
DEEP   BECHON
EEK   BOVINE
FEEL   BROADEN
GENTEEL   BLACKEN
HEEL   BANTER
INDEED   BEAST
JEEP   BEIGE
KNEEL   BIBLE
LINSEED   BRITISH
MEETING   BRAINY
NEED   BROWSE
OVERSEE   BATTLE
PEER   BLOKE
QUEEN   BUTCHER
REDEEM   BRADFORD
SPLEEN   BITCH
TEEPEE   BELL
UMPTEEN   BANQUET
VENEER   BEQUEST
WHEEL   BARNYARD
XEE   BOTANICAL
YANKEE   BEDEVILED
ZEE   BEGUIDE

```
21 JUNE 1974      17 NOV.1974
#55   INSTANT     #130 INSTANT
3 LETTER          3 LET.DOUBLE

APT               ARP  AND
BUN               BAT  BEE
COT               CAD  CON
DUB               DUD  DIE
ERR               EAR  EAT
FIE               FIT  FOY
GIN               GOT  GUN
HIP               HOT  HAM
INK               IMP  ICK
JUG               JOT  JOB
KAT               KIN  KLU
LOB               LAD  LAM
MAT               MUD  MAP
NEW               NOD  NUT
ORB               OUT  OFF
PLY               PIT  PAT
QUH               QUE  QUO
RIB               RUB  ROT
SUR               SIP  SAC
TAP               TAR  TAD
URN               UTE  USE
VIE               VAL  VAN
WIT               WIN  WET
XEN               XOX  XAN.
YUP               YEN  YAN
ZOW               ZEN  ZUM
```

SOUND SONNET OF SAMANTHA & MICHAEL

Oh
AH

oh
aH

Ah
Oh

AH
OH

AH
OH

AH!
OH!

Umm !!!!
Umm !!!!

ELLEN ZWEIG

UNREQUITED LOVE SERIES: III THE MOVEMENT TOWARD...REPEATED

```
you who you who you        you who you who you        you who you who you
embrace me                 embrace me                 embrace me
who embrace me who you     who embrace me who you     who embrace me who you
moving                     moving                     moving
toward you to you who you  toward you to you who you  toward you to you who you
me you me you me you       me you me you me you       me you me you me you
who me moving to you       who me moving to you       who me moving to you
moving to you to you       moving to you to you       moving to you to you
      who who who   youwho      who   who whoyouwho    who   who   who
you     you you you        you   you   you          you    you you
   who who who   whoyou     who   who    whoyouwho  who   who   who
      you you you        you   you   you          you you
         who who   whoyou    who   who   whoyouwho  who
            you
                who     you              you
                   who  you        who      you  you
                        who              who  who

            you
               who     you                youwho
                   who
               you          who
                  who   you
                   youwho
```


Performance notes:

10 dancers, in five pairs, embrace and back off, repeating this motion. The same embrace and reverse embrace on video tape, several tv screens. I am surrounded by these embracing couples.

I read the first eight lines of the text, very seriously, getting faster as I repeat the eight lines seven times.

I shout "you who" with a greeting intonation (yoohoo) and wave to the dancers who reply "yoohoo" and wave back. We wave to the audience hoping they'll join in. The piece ends in a chorus of greetings "yoohoo".

The Movement Toward...Repeated was performed at the Guild House, Ann Arbor, Oct. 26, 1978.

Oct., 1978
Ann Arbor

CONTRIBUTORS

WALTER ABISH has published several books of fiction and is presently working on another tentatively titled "The Idea of Switzerland."

JONATHAN ALBERT, born in Queens, NY, in 1943, took his B.A. at the University of Rochester and his Ph.D. in sound composition at the University of Iowa. His poems and theater pieces have been performed around the U.S.

CHARLES AMIRKHANIAN, born in Fresno, CA, in 1945, has been the Sound Sensitivity Information Director of KPFA, the Pacifica Radio station in Berkeley, CA, for most of the past decade. He recently received an NEH grant to edit the letters of the American composer George Anthiel.

BETH ANDERSON, born in Lexington, KY, in 1950, has taught music theory, piano and voice on both the west coast and the east. Her compositions have been performed widely, and she has co-edited and co-published the periodical *Ear* since its inception in 1973.

ANONYMOUS wish to remain. . . .

DOUGLAS BARBOUR, born in Winnipeg in 1940, teaches Canadian literature at the University of Alberta, Edmonton, Canada. He has published *Songbook* (1975) and *Visions of My Grandfather* (1977). He and his departmental colleague STEPHEN SCOBIE form the basis of *Re:Sounding,* which they describe as "an experimental performance group of flexible membership."

EARLE BIRNEY, born in Calgary, Alberta, in 1904, taught for many years at the University of British Columbia. His publications include *Down the Long Table* (novel, 1955), *Rag and Bone Shop* (1971), *What's So Big about Green?* (1973), *Collected Poems* (1975), *Turvey* (novel, 1976), and *The Rugging and the Moving Times* (1976).

BILL BISSETT, born in 1939, writes from Vancouver that he is "from Nova Scotia & same as bfor is bfor as is bfor is same as bfor." He is a painter, poet, printer and publisher ("blewointment press"); his bibliography is mountainous.

WARREN BURT, born in Baltimore in 1949, studied at SUNY—Albany and UC—San Diego, before teaching at LaTrobe University in Australia from 1976 to 1978. He recently received a grant from the Australian Arts Council Music Board for further work in audio and video.

JOHN CAGE has been internationally published, performed, criticized and honored. His latest book is *Empty Words: Writings Since 1972* (1979). Born in 1912 in Los Angeles, he presently lives in New York, NY.

ALISSANDRU CALDIERO was born in Lucudia Eubea (Catania), Sicily, in 1949 and brought to the U.S. at the age of 9. He writes, "I stem from the folk tradition of the story teller (cuntastorii), who as a medium utilizes the body itself with all its resources for sound-word-gesture-image. This, coupled with searchings into the nature and origin of language, produces and shapes my work."

ROSEMARIE CASTORO, born in Brooklyn, NY, in 1939, has exhibited her sculpture around the world. Her poems and articles have appeared in several magazines.

GUY DE COINTET, born in Paris in 1940, has lived in Los Angeles since 1968. He has produced exhibitions, performances and books.

GEOFFREY COOK, born in 1946, writes poetry, criticisms and translations, as well as producing visual art. He presently lives in San Francisco.

MICHAEL COOPER, born in New York, NY, in 1952, is currently co-editor of *Ear* and vice-president of the Poetry Mailing List, Inc. In 1977, he received the Thomas Wolfe Memorial Poetry Award.

PHILIP CORNER composes with words and music in New York City and teaches as well at Livingston College in New Jersey. His music is published by Peters Editions, New York.

JEAN-JACQUES CORY, the author of *Lists* (1974), recently completed two book-length poems, "Particulars" and "Exhaustive Combinations." His work has appeared in *Beyond Baroque, Poetry Australia, Interstate, Kontexts* and several anthologies.

BRUCE CURLEY writes that he "is 23 and lives in Washington, DC. The woman he loves lives in Scottsdale, AZ. He will walk about as half a man until he sees her again."

CHARLES DODGE, born in Ames, IA, in 1942, is presently associate professor of music at Brooklyn College, CUNY. His record *Synthesized Speech Music* (1976) collects his text-sound works.

CHARLES DORIA, born in 1938, has taught classics at the University of Texas at Austin and both co-edited and co-translated the anthologies *Origins* (1976), *A Big Jewish Book* (1978) and *The Tenth Muse* (1978).

JON ERICKSON sent his contribution from 2575 N. Lake Drive, Milwaukee, WI 53211.

RAYMOND FEDERMAN, born in France in 1928, is a Professor of English at SUNY at Buffalo. His initial text-sound works were produced at WXXI-FM, Rochester, NY, as part of an award-winning series funded by the New York State Council for the Arts.

CAMILLE FOSS lives in New York City and works in theater and small visual pieces.

THE FOUR HORSEMEN are Rafael Barreto-River, Paul Dutton, Steve McCaffery, and bp Nichol. They first began to compose and perform together in May, 1970. Their collective works include a book, *Horse d'Oeuvres* (1975), and two records, *Canadada* (1973) and *Live in the West* (1977).

SHELDON FRANK is a writer living in New York City.

ELSE von FREYTAG-LORINGHOVEN (1894-1927) was a German woman who came to America after World War I, associating with the Dada movement and publishing regularly in *The Little Review.*

FERN FRIEDMAN, born in New York, NY, in 1949, has exhibited photo-narrative pieces which expose sociological performances. She writes that she is "interested in story-telling and movement as an element of performance."

KENNETH GABURO, born in Somerville, NJ, in 1926, is the director of the New Music Ensemble and the Lingua Press, a music publisher, both in San Diego, CA. He writes that he is currently working on three books, namely: "Compositional Linguistics," "Passing" (an autobiographical account of university life), and "Perform."

JON GIBSON, born in Los Angeles in 1940, has produced two records with himself as the composer and the principal performer, *Visitations* (1973) and *Two Solo Pieces* (1977). He also authored and designed *Melody III and Book II* (1977), which he describes as "a graphic realization of the structure of a musical composition."

ABRAHAM LINCOLN GILLESPIE (1898-1950) lived among the avant-garde in Paris in the 1920's, and published extraordinary writings that have recently been collected into a book.

ALLEN GINSBERG, born in 1926, has produced poetry that is read and remembered around the world. His recent books include *Journals* (1976) and *Mind Breaths* (1977).

JOHN GIORNO, born in 1936, has produced Dial-a-Poem Records for the past decade. The largest collection of his written work is *Cancer in My Left Ball* (1973).

PHILIP GLASS, born in Baltimore in 1937, is best known for the compositions Music in Changing Parts (1970), Music in Twelve Parts (1974) and *Einstein on the Beach* (1976). He says that his contribution here "encapsulates structural ideas since developed."

ANTHONY J. GNAZZO, born in Connecticut in 1936, has produced a book's worth of visual poetry, in addition to producing his own theatrical pieces and working as an audio engineer in Oakland, CA.

MALCOLM GOLDSTEIN's compositions include vocal and instrumental ensembles, electronic tape-collages, and choreographed theater pieces that have been performed throughout the U.S. and Europe. He presently teaches at Bowdoin College, Brunswick, ME.

MARK GOODMAN writes only that he lives at "526 Carpenter Lane, Philadelphia, PA 19119."

GLENN GOULD, internationally renowned as a pianist, has also produced audio documentaries, televised introductions to modern music, and many essays which ought to be collected into a book.

COURTENAY P. GRAHAM-GAZAWAY writes that she "arrived from Jupiter 1946, now traveling, living out of portable spaces, settling in the mind. First book *ime* (1969)." She has recently been self-publishing her journals.

BRION GYSIN, born in 1916, obtained American citizenship at the end of World War II. His books include *The Process* (1969) and *Let the Mice In* (1973). He presently lives mostly in Paris.

TERRI HANLON, born in San Francisco in 1953, writes that after initially using sound as an element of sculpture, she has "worked with sound as a direct document of material, mental and interpersonal processes."

LAFCADIO HEARN (1850-1904) born in the Ionian Islands, spent his twenties and thirties in America before settling permanently in Japan. The work reprinted here reproduces the street-spiel of New Orleans charcoal-sellers.

WILLIAM HELLERMAN is currently the director of Composers Forum, Inc., a New York organization that sponsors concerts, among other activities. Also a guitarist, he has performed widely.

SCOTT HELMS, a poet, architect, photographer and graphic designer, presently works for an architectural firm in St. Paul, MN. He lives with Kay Arndt and loves to sail.

DICK HIGGINS, born in 1938, founded and directed the Something Else Press (1964-74). He recently published a critical history of *George Herbert's Pattern Poems: In Their Tradition* (1977); a collection of theoretical essays, *A Dialect of Centuries* (1978); and *The Epickall Quest of the Brothers Dichtung and Other Outrages* (1978).

TOM JOHNSON, born in Greeley, CO, in 1939, has written operas, a book of drawings, chamber music, dance accompaniments, and a variety of theatrical works. He also writes music criticism and has contributed regularly to the *Village Voice* since 1970.

EUGENE JOLAS, born in New Jersey in 1894, grew up in France before returning to America at 17. As an adult, he settled in Paris and published *transition* from 1927 to 1938. He published five collections of poetry before his death in 1952.

KEVIN JONES, born in 1952, is the technical director and lighting designer of the Redbud Theater at Texas Womans University in Denton, TX. His text-sound pieces have been performed widely throughout the Southwest.

LIONEL KEARNS, born in Nelson, BC, in 1937, has produced poems and essays, in addition to collaborating in the production of two films. He also teaches English at Simon Fraser University, Burnaby, BC.

BLIEM KERN, born in Philadelphia in 1943, has worked in book design, exhibited his paintings and declaimed his sound poems over radio and television. His first collection, *Meditationsmeditationsmeditationsmeditations* (1973), appeared as both a book and a tape cassette.

JACK KEROUAC (1922-1969) was one of the major prose writers of his generation. His single most experimental piece, "Old Angel Midnight," appeared in part in *Big Table* (1959) and in another part in *Evergreen Review* (1964).

KENNETH KING has choreographed dance and performance pieces, and his prose has appeared in several periodicals and anthologies, including *The Young American Writers* (1967) and *Future's Fictions* (1971).

CHRISTOPHER KNOWLES, born in 1959, is a writer, performer and visual artist living in New York City.

RICHARD KOSTELANETZ has produced audiotapes that have been aired, both in concerts and over radio, around the world. He recently prepared *Wordsand,* a comprehensive traveling exhibition of his art with words, numbers and lines, in several media.

LAWRENCE KUCHARZ, born in Chicago in 1936, lives in lower Manhattan. He has published essays in *Ear* and done performance pieces both inside and outside of concert halls.

S.J. LEON is a native Philadelphian who has taught English literature in black southern colleges and more recently worked as a professional librarian in Philadelphia. *Between Silences* (1974) is a collection of his verbal work. He writes that he has "been interested in finding the linguistic equivalents for musical and cinematic structures and in enriching the expressive and evocative resources of language through atomization and pulverization."

CHARLES LEVENDOSKY, born in New York in 1936, has been poet-in-residence for the state of Wyoming for seven years. His books include *Perimeters* (1970) and *Aspects of the Vertical* (1978), both long poems, respectively about the U.S. and New York City.

ANNEA LOCKWOOD, born in New Zealand in 1939, studied in England, Germany and Holland before moving to the U.S. in 1973. She has co-edited the periodical *Women's Work,* and several of her audio pieces were recently published by the New Wilderness Foundation.

CINDY LUBAR is a writer/director living in New York City. She is the founder of the Cindy Lubar Theatre Company.

ALVIN LUCIER, born in 1931 in Nashua, NH, has taught at Wesleyan University since 1970. In 1966, he co-founded the Sonic Arts Union and from 1973 to 1977 he was the Music Director of the Viola Farber Dance Company. The book *Chambers* collects his writings.

TOBY LURIE, born in Seattle, WA, has authored three books—*Word Music* (1969), *New Forms, New Spaces* (1971), and *Mirror Images* (1974)—in addition to two long-playing records which have the titles of his first and third books.

JACKSON MAC LOW, born in 1922, has done text-sound works since 1954. He has also produced many volumes, both published and unpublished, of verbal art in other forms.

DAVID MAHLER, born in 1944, took his BA from Concordia Teachers College and his MFA from the California Institute of the Arts. He lives in Seattle, WA.

STEVE McCAFFERY, born in London in 1948, residing in Toronto, is a member of the Four Horsemen, a founding member of the Toronto Research Group, the editor of Anonbeyond Press and a contributing editor of both *Centerfold* and *Open Letter.*

AARON MILLER is Dean of Experimental & Interdisciplinary Programs at Northern Kentucky University. He is also the author of *Changes: Evocations of I Ching* (1972) and writer-producer-director of La Vida Flamenca, an educational film about Andallucian Gypsies.

CHARLES MORROW, born in New York in 1942, presently directs the New Wilderness Foundation and organizes most of its activities. His compositions have been performed around the world.

BP NICHOL, born in Vancouver in 1944, has authored numerous books of prose and poetry. He lives in Toronto and works with both the Toronto Research Group and the Four Horsemen.

CLAES OLDENBURG, born in Stockholm in 1929, grew up in Chicago and, after graduating from Yale University, worked as a newspaper reporter there for two years. He has since produced several visualverbal books, in addition to sculpture that has been exhibited around the world.

JOHN OSWALD lives in Toronto and Vancouver.

SPIROS PANTOS lives at 38101 Metro Villa Ct., Apt. 114H, Mt. Clemens, MI 48043.

MICHAEL JOSEPH PHILLIPS, born in 1937, took his doctorate in comparative literature at Indiana University in Bloomington. He has taught at several universities and writes that he "has published over 500 traditional and experimental poems."

PEDRO PIETRI, born in New York in 1944, has authored plays and poems. Two collections of the latter are *Puerto Rican Obituary* (1973) and *Up Town Train* (1975).

NORMAN HENRY PRITCHARD II, born in New York, NY, in 1939, has authored two collections of his poetry, *The Matrix* (1970) and *Eecchhooeess* (1971), in addition to doing performances of his work.

FAYE RAN, born in Havana, Cuba, is presently artistic director of Inroad Theatre/Film Production Company, Inc., which has produced her multimedia *Journey* in New York. She has also written books of poems and short stories.

HENRY RASOF took his M.F.A. in writing at Brooklyn College and presently teaches it at Hofstra University. His audio rendition of "Wichita Falls" appears in the anthology *Breathing Space* (1978).

ERNEST ROBSON, born in Chicago in 1902, describes himself as a "science poet and poetics scientist." His books include *The Orchestra of the Language* (1959), *Transwhistics* (1970), *Thomas Onetwo* (1971), and *I Only Work Here* (1975). He lives in Parker Ford, PA.

JEROME ROTHENBERG, born in the Bronx, NY, in 1931, has produced over a dozen volumes of his own poetry. He also edited and introduced a series of consequential anthologies: *Technicians of the Sacred* (1968), *Shaking the Pumpkin* (1972), *Revolution of the Word* (1974), and *A Big Jewish Book* (1978).

STEVE RUPPENTHAL, born in 1949, received his M.A. in music from San Jose State University in 1975 with a thesis on sound poetry. His own compositions include *Venomous Toads* (1974) and *The Same Language* (1977).

PATRICK SAARI, born in Pasadena, CA, in 1949, presently works, he writes,in Washington, D.C., "on a printing system for the Language Services of the International Monetary Fund and on freelance translations (*The Lost Civilization of the Etruscans*)."

R. MURRAY SCHAFER, born in Sarnia, Ontario, in 1933, has composed music, edited the musical texts of Ezra Pound, and written a remarkable book on sound in the environment, *The Tuning of the World* (1977). His other books include *Smoke* (a novel, 1976), *The Chaldean Inscription* (1978) and a third book whose visual title cannot be typeset (1977).

ARLEEN SCHLOSS, born in Brooklyn in 1943, says, "I present my work using my voice as an instrument. My performances also use audiotape, video, slides, fire and print."

ARMAND SCHWERNER, born in Antwerp, Belgium, in 1924, currently teaches at Staten Island College. The first eight *Tablets* were published in 1969; a more complete edition appeared in 1971. Subsequent *Tablets* have since appeared, in addition to a collection of new poetry, *The Work, The Joy and the Triumph of the Will* (1977).

JUDITH JOHNSON SHERWIN, born in New York, NY, in 1936, has authored poems, stories and audiotapes. She recently served as president of the Poetry Society of America.

MARY ELLEN SOLT, born in Gilmore City, IA, in 1920, teaches comparative literature at Indiana University. She authored *Flowers in Concrete* (1966) and edited *Concrete Poetry: A World View* (1970).

CHARLES STEIN, who lives on Phillies Bridge Rd., New Paltz, NY, sent no bio note.

GERTRUDE STEIN (1866-1946) was the great American person of avantgarde letters.

NED SUBLETTE, born in Lubbock, TX, in 1951, is now living in Brooklyn, NY. His text-sound text, *Embarbussaments* (1974), was published in 1977 by Lingua Press.

JOSE GARCIA VILLA, born in 1908 in Manila, has lived in New York since the thirties. His *Selected Poems and New* were published in 1958; his most recent collection is *Apassionata—Poems in Praise of Love* (1979).

LAWRENCE WEINER, born in New York, NY, in 1940, has exhibited his conceptual art internationally. His audiotapes have also been included in many exhibitions.

LARRY WENDT, born in Napa, CA, in 1946, studied at San Jose State University. In collaboration with Steve Ruppenthal, he is presently working on a book-length history of sound poetry.

JON WHYTE was born in Banff, Alberta, and presently lives there. His poems range in length from one word to 6,000 lines. An exhibition of his work, "Open Spaces," has been shown widely in Canada.

EMMETT WILLIAMS has recently been teaching at the Carpenter Center at Harvard University. *The Selected Shorter Poems* (1974) collects some of his verbal work; he has also made visual art.

REESE WILLIAMS is the initiator of Line Editions in New York. He also produced the record *Sonance Project* (1977).

ROBERT WILSON, born in Waco, TX, in 1941, has produced theatrical pieces that have been presented prominently in both the U.S. and Europe, including *Death, Destruction and Detroit* (1979), *Einstein on the Beach* (1976), *The Life and Times of Joseph Stalin* (1973) and others.

A.J. WRIGHT, born in 1952, has published nearly one hundred poems in magazines and anthologies. He works in the main library at Auburn University, Alabama.

NINA YANKOWITZ lives in New York City where she paints, writes and scripts. Her visual art is represented by the Stefanotti Gallery.

KARL YOUNG, born in Racine, WI, in 1946, has produced poems and essays, in addition to working in his own printing business in Milwaukee, WI.

HARRIET ZINNES, Professor of English at Queens College, CUNY, recently published a book of prose, *Entropisms* (1978), and a chapbook of poems, *Book of Ten* (1979).

ELLEN ZWEIG is completing her Ph.D. dissertation on Performance Poetry at the University of Michigan. She coedited *The Poetry Reading,* an anthology of texts and articles on poetry and performance.